D1570066

GUY DEBORD

REVOLUTION IN THE SERVICE OF POETRY

VINCENT KAUFMANN

Translated by Robert Bononno

University of Minnesota Press
Minneapolis • London

The publication of this book was assisted by a bequest from
Josiah H. Chase to honor his parents, Ellen Rankin Chase and
Josiah Hook Chase, Minnesota territorial pioneers.

The University of Minnesota Press gratefully acknowledges financial assistance
provided by the French Ministry of Culture for the translation of this book.

Originally published in French as *Guy Debord: La révolution au
service de la poésie.* Copyright 2001 Librairie Arthème Fayard.

English translation copyright 2006 by Robert Bononno

Published by the University of Minnesota Press
111 Third Avenue South, Suite 290
Minneapolis, MN 55401-2520
http://www.upress.umn.edu

Library of Congress Cataloging-in-Publication Data

Kaufmann, Vincent.
    [Guy Debord. English]
    Guy Debord : revolution in the service of poetry / Vincent Kaufmann ; trans-
lated by Robert Bononno.
       p.   cm.
    Includes bibliographical references and index.
    ISBN-13: 978-0-8166-4455-1 (hc/j : alk. paper)
    ISBN-10: 0-8166-4455-1 (hc/j : alk. paper)
    ISBN-13: 978-0-8166-4456-8 (pb : alk. paper)
    ISBN-10: 0-8166-4456-X (pb : alk. paper)
    1. Debord, Guy, 1931–1994   2. Radicals—France—Biography.   I. Title.
    HN440.R3K3813 2006
    303.48'4092—dc22

                                        2006008301

Printed in the United States of America on acid-free paper

The University of Minnesota is an equal-opportunity educator and employer.

12 11 10 09 08 07 06   10 9 8 7 6 5 4 3 2 1

for Alice Debord

CONTENTS

INTRODUCTION
A READER WITHOUT QUALITIES

Dogana di Mare: This photograph [see gallery in this book], attributed to one of Guy Debord's friends, was taken several months before his death in November 1994, during his last trip to Venice. Fifteen years earlier he had spoken of that same *Dogana* in the following terms: "In any case, one traverses an era like one passes the Dogana promontory—that is to say, rather quickly. At first, as it's approaching, you don't notice it. Then, you discover it as you come abreast of it, you cannot fail to recognize that it was designed to be seen in this particular way and no other. But we are already passing the cape and leaving it behind us, and heading into unknown waters."[1] Like many of the other images that appear in his films and books, especially the images of water he enjoyed, this one connects with Debord's interest in the ephemeral: the passage of time and his own passage through time. It reflects his sense of melancholy: beautiful like Venice disappearing in the fog, soft like Venice withdrawn from visibility, uncertain like Venice, a fragment of a past forever doomed to disappear.

Once, *la Dogana,* the Venetian version of Ellis Island, was the required entry point for foreigners arriving in Venice by sea, a statue of Fortune rising from its cupola. The image also reflects themes that became central to Debord's life: gambling, with its fortunes and misfortunes; adventure; unknown waters; the foreign; cities to explore and to lose oneself in, made poetic through their fragility and the absence of traffic. Perhaps it is only by boat that we can really lose ourselves. The picture suggests, discreetly, with that touch of fog and mystery appropriate to a life devoted to the repudiation of society's inquisitorial stare, the dismissal of its summons to appear.

Where, then, do we look for Debord? He is hidden within this image, as in so many others. For in spite of appearances, it is a picture of Debord; in any case it's an image that belongs to him. It was given to me along with many others and has been added to the books, films, documents, and stories in which I have struggled to see him and which I have tried to understand. And if this book has any meaning it is the desire to clarify the images Debord left behind, the images he wanted us to see, and the gestures he used in making his mark upon a world he spent his life fighting.[2]

Was this necessary, or even possible? I turned myself into a reader of the work of a man I did not know and who never sought anyone's approval. He never asked anything of anyone, never made the least effort to be understood (or not to be understood). He gave everything he had to those he loved and reserved his anger for those he despised. He admired the Austrian writer Robert Musil, author of *A Man without Qualities*, and he himself was a man without qualities, refusing honors as well as appearances. Many people felt he could not be classified. Yet, this is what drew me to him most, the fact that he was unclassifiable, difficult to approach, dismissive of those who tried to describe him, and always willing to challenge them. I admire his art of defiance, his belligerent and melancholy poetics. He forces you to keep your distance, he deprives you of the convenience and hypocrisy found in what Baudelaire referred to, in the beautiful language of his century, as *fraternal prostitution*. I am neither Debord's equal nor his brother, but these may be qualities no reader can claim to have. His work wasn't written so others could identify with him, become his well-intentioned or ill-intentioned equal. On the contrary, it bears witness, as does his life, to a passion for singularity, the fervent intention to escape all forms of identification as well as the procession of small and large appropriations they never fail to drag along with them. His work is in essence a rejection of all that. It is an attempt at absolute freedom, an obstinate attempt not to hide but to never swear allegiance to anyone. Just as struggle can be a kind of game, sometimes writing can be a form of defiance.

Was this possible, was it legitimate? Because I didn't know Guy Debord personally, I am not in a position to provide direct testimony about what he was like. Moreover, I doubt such evidence would be of much value, and the little interest and talent I have for investigative journalism warns me about seeking out such sources. I did not share in any of Debord's exploits or struggles, directly or indirectly. I haven't participated in political struggles of my own, which would enable me to speak to him as an equal, as a specialist of revolution posthumously discussing its good and bad points. I have always felt that I arrived too late for the revolution, but I have also been careful to avoid playing catch-up. I cannot even claim to be an impeccably credentialed researcher in the politics of the far left, with a long list of published titles behind me. And I am also incapable of pulling from my hat any long-standing fascination with Debord dating back to my youth, back to May 1968, for example. I also confess that the enthusiasm shown today by my contemporaries for Debord the theoretician often leaves me as skeptical as the anger and animosity he never failed to arouse. Everything leads to the conclusion, therefore, that given the numerous activities and commentaries recently devoted to his work, I can hardly claim any role other than that of an unqualified reader.

However, I do not consider this a disadvantage. In fact, I feel this is necessary if we intend to read and possibly understand Debord. I am unaware of having any ideological ax to grind, and that is the best reason I can put forth for the existence of this book, except for the following: no one else seems to have wanted to write it.

Everything about Debord's world was made to culminate in refusal: appearances to respect, identities to maintain, titles and honors, in short, all the mechanisms by which what he would soon refer to as the "spectacle" insinuates itself into our lives. Consequently, we must read everything, take everything into account if we wish to understand Debord or even avoid misjudging what he was. One of the most beautiful aspects of his work is its coherence, which is simultaneously obstinate, discreet, and luminous. It is this insistence on the same questions and the same principles over time, through what are apparently the most varied practices and forms (in the sense I am using the word, he was a great formal inventor). Nothing but Debord, but all of Debord is the principle on which this book rests.

Much has now been written about Debord, but his work has been dissected into pieces. Doctoral candidates on the theory of revolution only know him as the author of *The Society of the Spectacle*. They are uninterested in his more recent work. Others, connoisseurs of the classics of French literature, are exclusively interested in the "moralist" of his final years, whom they perceive this way solely because they have forgotten the early Debord, a man intensely involved in the avant-garde and contemporary political struggles. His early career with the lettrists is generally overlooked or viewed as some kind of vague prehistory. There is too much of a tendency to enter Debord's world by a single door. Those who pass through imagine it to be wide, although it is not, and it is rarely the only one through which it is possible to enter, forming, the majority of the time, no more than a single element in a complex arrangement. Some doors are miniscule, and—like the novels written by his first wife —we may doubt that they lead to Debord. Others, rather large, are systematically ignored or merely cracked open long enough to jot down a quick note before being slammed shut. It is easier to enter through those that have remained open for a long time. Consequently, many things in Debord's work have barely been read and are relegated to the rank of documentary curiosities. Who, for example, has ever seriously read a book like *Des contrats*, published posthumously in 1995, which constitutes one of his last acts, one of the last decisions made by Debord?

Because there was no reason not to do it, my focus here was to make use of every possible point of access and read everything, to treat every element of Debord's output as significant, to assume that all were subject to the same concerns, the same passion, the same challenge. I felt it was wiser to adopt such a perspective since Debord never tried to create an oeuvre in the traditional sense of the term. His approach to writing and cinema was parsimonious, and he participated in things only for as long as he felt was necessary. Thus the author of *The Society of the Spectacle* was as important to me as the author of *Mémoires*, relatively unknown in 1958, but already suffused with the wonderful sense of melancholy that appeared later in other books and films. I gave as much weight to texts like *"Cette mauvaise réputation..."* as I did to lettrist and situationist documents. I have examined his entire output. At a time when many feel it is not really necessary to read an author's work to have an opinion, we will now be able to judge Debord on his work, the entirety of his work.

Naturally, not all commentators choose to approach Debord through a single door. But it is one thing to show that there are several doors and another to show that they all open onto the same world. In that sense, one of the goals of this book is to put an end to spurious divisions that have given rise to endless polemics: between those who admire the artist and those who are outraged by the emergence of Debord the "writer," between partisans of a politically intransigent Debord and partisans of a theoretical

Debord who is now ripe enough for academia, between those who accuse him of theoretical error and those who see him as a failed writer, between those who paint him as a libertine and those who want to preserve him as a bitter libertarian, and so on. These miniscule, and often myopic, portraits suggest, somewhat surprisingly, a Debord who is versatile, protean, multi-talented, as well as a man continuously undergoing an identity crisis. But if there is one thing that characterizes Debord, it is the absence of problems and identity crises (in the most contemporary sense of the word), for reasons I will examine later. I am not saying that Debord never changed, that he was the same at twenty as he was at fifty. But there is great consistency in his life, just as there is in his work. He loved Mallarmé when affirming his belief in the written word: on several occasions Debord acknowledged his commitment not so much to the written word as to himself, his passions, his pleasures, and his refusals. It is worthwhile taking the trouble to understand this consistency, to see that Debord was not a personality with several more or less disjointed facets; he was always himself and, most important, only himself. The man who wrote prolifically (relatively speaking) throughout the last ten or fifteen years of his life is the same man who led the Situationist International—the theoretician and autobiographer, the revolutionary and the poet are one and the same.

I have suggested that Guy Debord's life was as consistent as his work, a claim difficult to refute once we realize the extent to which they overlap. His life and work are one, and rarely has the expression made more sense. Rarely have life and work coincided to this extent. This book could have been titled *Guy Debord, His Life and Work*, because they are one and the same thing, because they are part of the same *poetics*. Debord turned his life into a work of art, he never stopped inventing, constructing, following no other principle than an intransigent sense of freedom, and his books and films were made to bear witness to this, to make us aware. His writing style, which is said, wrongly in my opinion, to be classic, and his lifestyle are one and the same. Only Debord could have written what he wrote because only Debord lived what he lived. The "because" here is somewhat misleading. Although he obviously lived what he lived, he did so because he wrote what he wrote. The relationship between his life and his work is not one-way. The work bleeds into the life, it is as much a part of his affairs and his battles as it is his books and films. It is also present in the "avant-garde" groups he led—no doubt to prevent them from adopting the conventional paths they were accustomed to taking—and which I can't help but thinking are also part of his work, and possibly his work exclusively, in every sense of the word. Similarly, his life derives from his work, it is determined by its formal properties, through the creation of stories and legends. It merges into the singular elaboration of a style: writing, but more generally speech and life as well. It is embedded in the multiple ways he expressed his concern for authentic communication; it is inseparable from an art of speech and dialogue that was, in the sense Debord understood it, one of his great passions, and therefore one of the keys to both his life and his work. It is also worth remembering his taste for poetic adventure, which did not necessarily result in the production of obscure brochures.

In this amalgam of life and work, it is important to be selective about events in his life, as in the way in which they are presented. Throughout this book I have made a determined effort to avoid conventional biographical forms, which rarely illuminate the complex links between a life and a body of work. I have allowed myself to follow a fairly relaxed chronological approach, associated with moments or periods of his life that seemed to me particularly significant, moments of crystallization, when new configurations came into being: his lettrist youth, the beginnings of situationism, the insurrections of May 1968, and the long and very fruitful "final" years, which are often, and wrongly, seen as a period of failure and rancor.

In Debord's case everything leads us to believe that too strict a chronology must necessarily fail to account for the articulation between life and work, which is obviously regrettable since this articulation is an essential, if not the only, requirement in understanding Debord. Some of his first writings and films, as well as his initial activities with the lettrist avant-garde, will have repercussions throughout his entire life, and are present in his last works and final activities, and it is possible that only at the end of his life did the real significance of his so-called early work appear. Many of the positions and practices developed within the framework of the Situationist International intersect those invented ten years earlier as part of the Lettrist International.

How can we speak of his youth in Saint-Germain-des-Prés, the years of the "lost children," without evoking the films and books that, five, twenty, even thirty years later, bear witness to that exquisite loss? How can we discuss those years without referring to their later melancholic transformation into a golden age, one that is necessarily lost, or without relating them to other periods of Debord's life—his time in Florence during the seventies, for example, which made him feel as if he were reliving the upheaval of his youth, or, later on, his fascination with Spain? And is there anything more difficult than assigning, than localizing that melancholy through which his life merges with his own sense of mourning?

Debord's life was written without a chronology, it disqualifies it, resists its sense of order. The same is true for his thought, which is impossible to break down into a chronicle of supposedly formative influences. It is too forceful and too wound up with freedom and autonomy, too closely tied to experience to bend to such conventions. It cannot be constructed like a theory, with borrowings and debts itemized throughout the course of years. Naturally, Debord read and enjoyed books, and he never hesitated to use them, to put them to work for his projects and passions—it is this that he came to refer to as *détournement,* whose importance can be grasped when we look at his life in terms of the history of ideas. But I feel that he did so without debt or obligation (except possibly to Breton, whom he loved and hated), although there are those who see him as the (ungrateful) offspring of Henri Lefebvre, of the Socialisme ou Barbarie group, if not as a plagiarist of Marx's *Theses on Feuerbach.* The history of his ideas is inseparable from the singular adventure of his life, and the elements of that adventure that are insisted upon and repeated with obstinacy. The same holds true for the history of his "oeuvre," which oscillates deliberately and intricately between the poles of invention and repetition. It always says the same thing, but says them in new ways, adapted to new contexts. It certainly cannot be understood as a body of work that can be viewed as an end in itself, that develops over time, almost autonomously. Debord cannot be equated with the process of writing, he is not some statue yet-to-be-erected that is unceasingly retouched, nor a work in progress, even though he passes through writing and cinema in living his life.

Debord went on strike against the *Bildungsroman,* and against the novel in general. As an author, this is obvious, but it's also true for the fictional character he never was. He constructed his entire life so as to escape fiction, that which ties fiction to the visible, to representation, and increasingly today to autobiographical exhibitionism, explicit or not. In this sense too he rejected what he soon came to refer to as the spectacle. He never complied with the rules of visibility it imposes upon our lives. He invented his own life, along with the books and images that would extricate him from the tyranny of the contemporary biographical gaze, entirely conventional and always vaguely inquisitorial. His life and work are a challenge to that gaze, a challenge we are wrong to interpret as essentially a hatred of the image (there are many images Debord loved, ranging from classic cinema to his pictures of Venice). But he did everything he could to refute the gaze that attempts to identify, to assign, to conform. Against it he waged war, the intimate kernel of the war he intended to wage against a society he believed to be corrupt.

This book was written to describe that war: to detail the imagined and actual blows inflicted by Debord, to show how his writings and autobiographical films anticipate the "enemy's" gaze, enhancing our ability to contest it. It describes the inventory of tactics he put to work—his science of clandestinity and his use of the enemy's discourse, the art of the *dérive* and the reoccupation of the urban environment, and those revolutionary moments devoted to the service of poetry that have sometimes been qualified as "insurrectional" and whose effectiveness was tested primarily in May 1968. I wrote this book to describe that war and not to continue it, neither from Debord's point of view, for his war will do very well without my support, nor from the point of view of his antagonists, or those who have been attempting to assign him a life he never wanted, a certain kind of artificiality to which he did not attribute the least importance. The value of the Debordian biographeme, which is currently very high, and the time taken to read it are inversely proportional: it is the clumsy homage of the society of the spectacle to a man who wished to be its Other. Through a multitude of inquiries and excavations, we may end up knowing everything there is to know about him, though I have reasons to doubt this. But because we will also have less and less time to read him, we will fail to understand why we even wanted to know so much about him in the first place, and will have forgotten that he wrote books and made films, and especially why he did. I have decided to limit myself to what is necessary for understanding why Debord became Debord; to assess his poetic adventure and try to grasp how he wanted to bring to a close the history of the various avant-gardes, to illustrate the unstable and moving boundary between a singular body of work and a singular life. Because that is where things happen.

I hope this book will help to dispel some of the more tenacious myths about Debord's life. Debord refused to concede anything to the spectacle; he refused his own visibility and turned his life into what could be described as an art of clandestinity. Commentators attributed this to his desire to exercise power more effectively, which he could do because it remained hidden. Because society, or at least the so-called *intellectual* world, was incapable of even conceiving that one could shrug off the attractions of power and recognition, anyone who rejected them was suspected of being power hungry. And yet Debord did not seek power or recognition but clandestinity, and he did so to preserve his own sense of freedom, a distance he carefully maintained with those whom his sense of evasion fascinated or infuriated. Because he never actually went into hiding, there is little likelihood this was deliberate. He simply refused the many requests and directives to "appear." Debord was never interested in power, not during the course of the Situationist International, not before or after, and certainly not in his relationship with his friend Gérard Lebovici, whose assassination in 1984 led to outlandish and bitter speculation that made Debord out to be a kind of guru or prototerrorist hypnotist. Why not at least acknowledge that if he had wanted to, he would have had the means to obtain power, being of at least average intelligence and probably somewhat more inventive than others who have succeeded in such a quest? Similarly, and because the problem is the same, we should discount the idea of Debord's talent, and especially his penchant, for sudden, arbitrary, Stalinist exclusions organized by a leader who jealously monitored his hold on power. It is important that we reevaluate the sometimes irreconcilable breaks he engaged in, viewing them as marks of an ethics of the gift or an ethics of freedom, or as the signs of his desire to animate and maintain relationships. On this point, no one is required to believe my claims, but Debord's correspondence, which is now being published, discredits just this kind of cliché.

Another myth this book attempts to refute is that of a Debord who was, in the end, "co-opted," succumbing to the siren song of Gallimard or Canal Plus. The presumed reasons for this are varied: that it had always been his dream to do so, that he never worked at anything but his own more or less posthumous glory, that he was incapable of anticipating his own co-optation. Such claims supposedly serve as proof that his entire life's struggle was a failure. Some critics claim that Debord thought only of his literary fame, others that this was no way to make a revolution, and whether they expressed this with mockery or pity, they were all somewhat envious when Debord was published by Gallimard or appeared on television (more specifically, whenever a film he conceived for television was broadcast).

Obviously, neither group is capable of stating exactly what he should have done to avoid being co-opted (nothing, most likely, other than to keep quiet or remain in obscurity). They act as if being co-opted were mere child's play, a game their virtue alone protected them from (they, of course, had not been co-opted), whereas it is more likely their lack of talent that was the reason. The question of Debord's co-optation is a false debate in a world of real hostility, and has been used before in the case of other artists (Breton, for example). It is part of the chamber music of the avant-garde (illuminated by the standard figures) and returns as a Pavlovian reflex in the case of anyone whose singularity has left its mark on history. What exactly should Debord have done? What is being asked of him? And why him?

The question arises not only when mention is made of his co-optation, but in reference to a range of opinions and judgments about him. Some compare him to Bataille, although they by far prefer Bataille. Some see him as a tiresome avatar of Rousseau, although they equally dislike Rousseau. Some consider him to be the heir of surrealism, but are quick to mention that "Breton was not at all like him." Others explain that Debord was merely a pale imitation of the Cardinal de Retz, that his contemporary notoriety is overblown, and that in any case "the classics are something else entirely." And still others believe that "Foucault was not at all like him," and why not Henri Lefebvre? Moreover, they are all correct because Debord was indeed not like them, and we should begin by recognizing this. Did any of his critics ever ask if he tried to be the equal of Breton, or Bataille, or Foucault? How do any of them know that it was his ambition to become a writer, much less a classic writer, or a philosopher like Lefebvre, with his students and dissertations, or the leader of a revolutionary organization, monitoring its supervisory staff and security? What is it exactly that we are asking of Debord?

The improbable reader without qualities I imagine exists asks nothing of Debord. By asking nothing, we refuse to take our frustrations out on Debord by reproaching him for being one thing rather than another, accusing him of duplicity, or complaining because he was incapable of producing the theory for the next revolution, much less of becoming a part of it, with or without bombs. Such a reader asks nothing and may receive somewhat more in return, because he has the opportunity to see Debord as he is, as he was. To do so is to see Debord as the lost child he always wanted to be, an expert in loss and sensitive to the irreversible passage of time. It is to see in him the melancholy warrior who is also a game player, someone who turns war into a big game. It is to see him as a man in love with emotion and an expert in pleasure—the pleasure of love as well as that of drifting through cities—who creates international organizations to experience those emotions. And it is especially to see how those different aspects of the same personality are based on a body of work, on a style. Debord wrote as a strategist, he engaged in politics as a poet, he made war because he liked games, and he constructed avant-gardes out of a sense of melancholy, as if he foresaw their coming dissolution. And he did all this while remaining always the same, by remaining himself. When all is said and done, Debord as an author is not all that difficult to understand.

1. LOST CHILDREN

Origins

"Like lost children we live our unfinished lives." It was with these words that Guy Debord concluded his first film, *Howls for Sade,* made in 1952 when the author was only twenty years old.[1] Rather, it is with these words that he *fails* to conclude his film, for it is followed by the most famous blackout in the history of French avant-garde cinema: twenty-four minutes of silence and a black screen. No sooner are they mentioned than the lost children fall back into silence and darkness. They are bound to obscurity, elusive, made to be lost. Their adventures are not only unfinished but marked by invisibility and muteness.

Much of Debord's life, and certainly his early life, is characterized by silence and invisibility. The "lost children" are also the principal theme of his second film, *On the Passage of a Few Persons through a Rather Brief Unity of Time,* made in 1959, and they reappear explicitly in his third, *Critique of Separation,* filmed in 1961: "Everything involving the sphere of loss—that is, what I have lost of myself, the time that has gone; and disappearance, flight; and the general evanescence of things, and even what in the prevalent and therefore most vulgar social sense of time is called wasted time—all this finds in that strangely apt old military term, *lost children,* its intersection with the sphere of discovery, of the exploration of unknown terrains, and with all the forms of quest, adventure, avant-garde. This is the crossroads where we have found ourselves and lost our way."[2] The lines of force of Debord's early life can be found in this image, where they intersect.

The expression reflects his attraction for loss and disappearance—in every sense of the word—as well as his taste for adventure, for conflict, political struggle, and war. Before becoming a theoretician or the leader of the Situationist International, or even a writer, Debord saw himself as a lost child, recognized himself as one of them. To what extent, then, does everything he subsequently became follow from this? Here, it is still no more than a sign, but in his life it had an almost magical efficacy.

Who are the lost children? In the most literal sense of the term, they are soldiers chosen for impossible missions, the kind no one ever returns from. They are the ones who play no part in the economy of profit and loss, who are sacrificed in military operations that are certainly heroic but known to be hopeless. They are the children consigned to oblivion, never to be seen again. Debord insisted in representing himself this way, as paradoxical as this may seem, as one of many other lost children. The expression is always used in the plural in his work: one is never lost alone. This loss may even be essentially an act of sharing and community, as if the only thing we could really share with others was our own disappearance. He placed himself under this sign, lived and wrote under it. He spent a great deal of time exploring its potentialities, not only in his books and films, but in his life as well, which unfolds as an implementation—dramatization, narration, mythification—of everything suggested by this old military term.

How does one become a lost child? Most likely by losing one's childhood—by turning one's back on it, walking away from it, silencing it, not just for twenty-four minutes but for an entire lifetime. Lost children come into this world by disavowing the childhood they are given, and that is why they are born at least twice. It is remarkable that throughout his autobiographical work, which is at least as significant as the work of the theoretician he always refused to be, Debord blocks out the first nineteen or twenty years of his life, reveals nothing about them. Was he born in 1931 (December 28, in Paris) or 1951? The answer depends on which child we prefer: the one he began life as and about whom we know almost nothing, or the lost child he decided to become in 1951.

There are a number of explicitly, or implicitly, autobiographical texts by Debord that contain no reference to childhood, no allusion to the first years of his life, a time that many writers, good or bad, wouldn't give up for anything in the world, as if their status as writers depended on it. A period that blends literature and autobiography, childhood has become essential background material for practically every literary career. That Debord chose to remain silent about it is an indication of his lack of interest not only in Freudian stereotypes, but also in the need to become an author in sync with his contemporaries or to make concessions. In *In girum imus nocte et consumimur igni,* his last and certainly most beautiful film, the autobiographical narrative catches up with Debord, who has just turned nineteen: "I have passed my life in a few countries in Europe, and it was in the middle of the century, when I was nineteen, that I began to lead a fully independent life."[3] The lost child is born independent, is born into freedom or out of freedom. It as if he were free of his childhood, detached from it, and consequently without attachments, without bonds, without obligations. The only, and fleeting, exception to this law of silence, the only evocation of childhood, which is found in *Panegyric,* his most clearly auto-biographical book, confirms this sense of detachment: "It is reasonable to think that many things first appear in youth, to stay with you for a long while. I was born in 1931, in Paris. Just then, my family's fortune was shattered by the consequences of the world economic crisis that had first appeared in America a little earlier; and the remnants did not seem capable of lasting much beyond my majority, which in fact is what happened. So I was born virtually ruined. I was not, strictly speaking, unaware of the fact that I should not expect an inheritance, and in the end I did not receive one."[4] About his childhood, Debord remembered only his family's ruin, which made him the opposite of an heir and simultaneously detached him from his past and his family. He was like a man who had nothing and owed nothing to anyone. He was a man whose life, severed from the "family romance," was of interest to no one but himself. Having lost everything from the start, nothing was easier for him than losing those whose heir he might have become, or losing himself in their eyes. He made use of his own past to become, in 1951, a man without debts or responsibilities of any kind; a lost child and, somewhat later, also a revolutionary. He was a man with nothing to lose; he had made a clean sweep of his past. Having been born ruined, or nearly so, Debord's later life was characterized by a tenuous and carefree relationship to money—he spent lavishly and freely.[5]

However, one crash can hide another, sometimes several. The virtual ruin evoked in *Panegyric* is more than just a question of economics. The decline of the shoe-manufacturing business to which his family owed its prosperity did not begin with the Great Depression of 1929 but in 1927, when Vincenzo Rossi, Guy Debord's maternal grandfather and director of the firm, died suddenly. Yet, the remains of the family fortune were sufficient to ensure that until he reached adulthood, Debord lacked nothing, even during the war.

But there were other disasters during Debord's childhood. His father, Martial Debord, a pharmacist, contracted tuberculosis shortly after the birth of his son and died when he was only four years old. To avoid the risk of contagion, the child was not allowed to touch or even come near his father most of the time. What would it mean for a son to have a father who was untouchable and, eventually, invisible? His mother, Pauline, who was only twenty in 1931, was still young and attractive when her husband died and appears to have quickly grown indifferent toward her son, whose education was entrusted to Lydia Rossi, his maternal grandmother, known as "Manou." Later, Pauline had two children with Domenico Bignoli, an Italian who was already married (divorce was unthinkable at the time): Michèle Bignoli-Rossi in 1940 and Bernard Rossi in 1942. In 1944 she married the *notaire* Charles Labaste, with whom she settled in Cannes. Labaste's affairs prospered until the end of the war. Charles had two children from a first marriage (Bernard and Chantal) and decided to adopt Michèle and Bernard Rossi (although the adopted Bernard had to change his name to Patrick Labaste), but not Guy Debord. Under such conditions it would have been difficult for Debord to see himself as an heir. He was his grandmother's favorite, as several people who knew them claim, and kept his father's name, but that was the extent of his inheritance.[6] Is it any accident that the destiny of Guy Debord, who is today as little read, as little understood as he is well known, was tied up with the destiny of his name, his fame, or his reputation, no matter how bad? The counterpart of such an inheritance consisted—it's hard to imagine it being any different—in his exclusion, at least symbolically, from the new family created by his mother and Charles Labaste. This exclusion was not merely symbolic, however, because Guy and his grandmother did not live with the rest of the family. The home that Christophe Bourseiller describes as the "sprawling dwelling" in Cannes turns out, a few lines later, to be "quite simply too small for everyone."[7] "Too small"? In any case, Debord's anger toward his mother for having abandoned him—and how else could her actions be described?—was considerable.[8]

I do not raise this issue to suggest that Debord had an unhappy childhood or to reconstruct the kind of family romance favored by psychoanalysts, because such romances never explain anything other than psychoanalysis itself. But I would like to draw attention to the fact that in its military sense, even in its syntax, the expression "lost children" quite naturally leads to the question: lost by whom? Was it really their own decision? Who decided that they would lose themselves? I am less interested in answering the question than in pointing out the fact that it seems so natural, both in its military sense and in the case of Debord. And once asked, the answers we get are either too numerous or too beautiful to be true. It is possible to become lost to a father who is unapproachable because of disease, just as it is to a mother who is unapproachable because of her indifference. It is also possible that a child might not accept such alienation, that is to say, that he might very well accept it, bury it within himself, encrypt it melancholically by wrapping it in oblivion and silence, and in so doing bury the child he started out to be for those who ensured his loss. It's possible but, as eloquent as Debord's silence may be in this regard, it also renders such an assumption forever uncertain. The "favorite," the adored child of the grandmother he adored in turn, would have kept his most intimate wounds to himself, would have erased all traces of them. At most we can assume that this was how he learned to hide his tracks, to erase them, and to make use of writing only intermittently; that this was the origin of his art of *not being followed.* Disowned, the lost children have no issue, no heritage, no heirs; they bring with them only other lost children. Debord had no children because he never wanted them, because he never wanted the responsibility.

According to Jean-Michel Mension, one of Debord's companions from the "Saint-Germain-des-Prés years" (1951–53), the beginning of his "lost childhood," Debord once said that he had had no childhood.[9] This could be an acknowledgment of his suffering as a child, but others indicate that his revelation refers less to an unhappy childhood than to one obsessed with freedom. Entrusted to the care of his grandmother, Debord was a highly protected, even an overprotected child, who suffered in his sheltered environment because, from the beginning of the war, the Rossi-Debord family continued to move around, looking for security in a time of need and warfare. The family moved from Paris to Nice in the autumn of 1939, then to Pau in 1942, where Debord attended the Lycée Isidore-Ducasse, finally settling in Cannes in 1945. What Debord missed during his infancy and childhood was not just a mother and father, it was also freedom of movement, control over his time and his environment, the power to determine his own activities, his experiences, and his friendships, which tended to be ephemeral because his family was always on the move. It is worthwhile remembering this fascination with movement, with mobility, when considering the aesthetics of the *dérive* or whenever the situationist project for the collective appropriation of time and everyday life is mentioned.

Where do lost children come from? From those who have decided to lose them, certainly, but also from a thirst for freedom that is even more intransigent in that they know, or feel, they owe nothing to those who, having lost them, have at the same time walked away from their obligations. Lost children are destined for freedom, as they are for disappearance. They are born of the possibility—or the necessity—of answering the question "lost by whom" with "lost for whom," through which they are able to reclaim the initiative for their lives—their lost childhood only truly beginning when it is no longer endured but chosen. They grow up by freeing themselves of the rules imposed on them, imposed so that their childhood is as short as possible, so that they leave childhood behind as quickly as possible. In other words, they lose their childhood, the time of their childhood, only so that they can remain faithful to it and its passions. "I was born virtually ruined" is not a claim to an unhappy childhood. Ruin as form of luck: in *"Cette mauvaise réputation . . . ,"* Debord wrote that "money was not something I wanted as a child."[10] To prolong their childhood, the lost children escape those who want to make them model children, they free themselves from them. Getting lost is a way of finding themselves. It is important to remember this when speaking of Debord's fondness for games or when trying to evaluate the *infantile* aspects of the situationist project, which sometimes seems like a rereading of Marx by Peter Pan.

In any event, Debord soon developed a taste for freedom, something that was encouraged, during his adolescence in Cannes, by the relatively dissolute nature of a family environment he did not consider his own. He was content to appreciate the decadent side of their life, which helped solidify his distaste for work: "I have never seen the bourgeois work, with all the vulgarity their special kind of work inevitably entails."[11] He was born ruined, but he was also born decadent, and was therefore prepared for the art of perdition in which he intended to specialize, freed from all the obligations that stick to the skin of a bourgeoisie that still believes in its future, freed even from the type of revolt practiced by Bazin, which was so much in the air at the time. By 1945 Debord was living in the same house as his family but became increasingly estranged from them. He was a brilliant and lazy student who managed to win over a number of his friends at the lycée through his charm and his intellect, but spent as little time as possible at school. He had a relatively privileged childhood, increasingly removed from traditional family and middle-class values—values that were not upheld in his own family. His ideas turned instead to Rimbaud, Lautréamont, Arthur Cravan, and the surrealists. And although he obtained his baccalaureate (in 1951 in Cannes), it was as a minimalist proud of being last in his class and expecting nothing from his diploma other than his freedom: a visa for Paris, where, under the pretext of law studies that were never begun, the lost child was born and grew to maturity.

Childhood was a period of incubation. Debord soon learned to respect nothing, to free himself of all moral standards, to devote himself to transgression, but lightheartedly, almost good-naturedly. He disliked Proust but liked Robert Musil. Marcel versus Ulrich. The first is a child who refuses to lose himself, who will never give up his mother's affection, or his fascination with evil. The second is the man without any distinguishing features, without qualities, in love with his singularity, oblivious to gossip, incapable of playing the smallest social role, of living up to an image. And he is also the amnesiac child, beyond good and evil. He remembers his father when he receives a telegram announcing the man's death, which suddenly brings back memories of Agatha, the sister he discovered at the bedside of the now dead father, a woman who was dragged into one of the most notorious and incestuous love affairs of twentieth-century literature. It was a passion between two lost children and produced nothing, endlessly. From it neither Ulrich nor Agatha would recover—the impossible experience of pure freedom. Sisterly incest versus maternal incest, forbidden games in checked pajamas versus nights spent with Maman in her nightgown. Debord may have had other reasons for preferring Musil to Proust, but his preference underlines his need for the most absolute, the most transgressive freedom. It is certainly one of the most perfect images of what a lost child is or wants to become. Just as an attraction to the most satisfying disappearances in life does not preclude an attraction to their occurrence in literature as well.

Scratched Negatives and the Game of Appearances

Where do lost children come from? It's hard to say since no one is given access to their childhood, to the child they insist on remaining. They walk away from the family romance and their true birth doesn't take place until they are twenty years old. Lost children want nothing to do with a shared childhood, which is so brief and over before it begins.

They also reject death. In short, they want nothing that would deprive them of themselves, their presence, their melancholy neverneverland. Debord was horrified of death, avoided burials, including that of his adored grandmother. Like other melancholy individuals, he was not enthusiastic about mourning. It would, therefore, be extremely unwise to assume that Debord was suicidal or harbored an unhealthy interest in death, in spite of his suicide on November 30, 1994, from a bullet in the head, while he was suffering from polyneuropathy, a painful and incurable disease.[1] In the lettrist world he frequented after 1951, as later with the situationists, there was as little room for families and model children as there was for cadavers; generations were off limits. This is one of the most striking things about the "unitary urbanism" projects Debord and his friends were so enthusiastic about after 1953, first with the Lettrist International and then, after 1958, with the Situationist International. The "Formulaire pour un urbanisme nouveau" [Formulary for a New Urbanism] by his friend Ivan Chtcheglov, published in 1958 in *Internationale situationniste,* proposed a "Neighborhood of Death, not for dying but for living in peace."[2] And a "Projet d'embellissements rationnels de la ville de Paris," which appeared in 1955 in *Potlatch,* the international lettrist review, made the same point: "Elimination of cemeteries. Total destruction of corpses and similar reminders: no ashes, no traces (attention must be drawn to the reactionary propaganda represented, through the most automatic association of ideas, by this hideous survival of an alienated past. Can we look at a cemetery without thinking of Mauriac, Gide, Edgar Faure?)."[3]

No graves, no funerals. Only great writers who are enthusiastic about their childhood have a grave, as is appropriate for the spectacular corpses they always were. After all, that's why they're there—so we can remember them, so they can leave behind some trace of themselves, so we know they lived and how, so they can become national monuments. Their existence and their work blend together with the construction of their future biography or image as writers, as we are accustomed to saying. They are always at work at being embalmed, at making their remains comfortable (as Valéry said of publishing). This is the key difference with the lost child, who will at most become a lost writer, whose goal is to deprive his contemporaries not only of his physical presence but also of any possibility of observing his life, or even his corpse. After his death, Debord's ashes were dispersed by his friends over the Seine in Paris, from the point of the Vert-Galant, in conformity with what would have been his most insistent wish: to leave no trace of himself, or, more precisely, to leave no trace he himself did not arrange for. From beginning to end, Debord did everything he could to be seen head-on. His last "book," *Panegyric,* volume 2, is the exemplary and final witness of this concern.[4] It is a collection of images and quotes, a book made of images and quotes chosen by Debord. Incurably ill and on the point of death, it was Debord who, one last time, decided which images of himself he would leave behind, what he wanted to let others see and what he wanted to keep hidden.

Although Debord remained silent about his childhood, he was not necessarily more open about the rest of his life. His second birth (in 1951) is, at the very least, paradoxical. It occurred behind a veil of ambivalence, as if it too were always on the point of succumbing to the vertigo of his lost childhood. The silence and black screen with which *Howls for Sade* culminates is the emblematic proof. The exploits of the lost children are, like their childhood, also condemned to secrecy, which is logical because theirs is an extended and reappropriated childhood. This is apparent from the earliest pictures we have of Debord, those he used to bear witness to his "birth." The visual archive that appears in the second volume of *Panegyric* begins, after an introductory warning, with a portrait of the author. The date of this section of the book suggests that he was about twenty at the time. The photograph was taken in Paris, and it is no accident because his second birth coincides with his arrival in the city he remained an intimate part of for so long. In no other photograph does he look so young. Here, he is facing the camera, a slender young man without glasses. He looks into the lens, slightly uncertain, seemingly without any awareness of his later powers of seduction. He wears a dark shirt and jacket. The interplay of light and shadow that appears in other photos is not yet under control, and the scarf—which was later always dark against a light coat or light against a dark coat—is not present. The photo is slightly blurry and covered with dust. For someone who has suddenly appeared from nowhere, it is a rather hesitant introduction. But chosen some forty-five years later by an ailing Debord who was on the point of ending his life, the image of that initial hesitation confers upon the photograph a kind of retroactive deliberateness. Its presence at the beginning of *Panegyric* reveals its stubborn ambivalence regarding any form of manifestation or appearance, and perhaps, more radically, his rejection of appearances of any kind; an ambivalence that was as certain as his decision to disappear for good, made while he was completing the second volume of the book. His first appearance was blurry and dust-covered, just as Mallarmé's responses to journalists were obscure, and, like Mallarmé, he emphasized what was false about appearances and communication. And he added a layer of time, or, if we prefer, a layer of melancholy: the dust in this first picture is past time that has become visible. An appearance that is indeed very much like a disappearance. It has already taken place, it belongs to the past, possibly to legend: to a past that was never present, to the timeless "once upon a time" from which all legends start. Debord may have been born in 1951, but he did so as a self-effacing young man in a hurry to disappear again or to have already been there, as if he could only exist in the strange grammatical time of an absolute past.

Another picture, one that appeared in 1952 and has often been republished, most likely because of its emblematic value, confirms Debord's hesitation about appearing, as well as the deliberateness of such hesitation. This is the photograph that was printed in the single issue of the review *Ion,* which was published by the lettrists he had met a year earlier. In fact, Debord's birth is inseparable from his first meeting with the lettrists and Isidore Isou. During the early fifties, marked by the existentialism Debord had violently rejected, he recognized in Isou and his companions the heirs of the dadaist and surrealist attitude he had absorbed during adolescence. He was born in lettrism, that is, by joining a group that was supposed to embody the radical spirit of revolt that characterized the avant-garde of the interwar period. Along with several contributions, including the scripts for *L'Anticoncept* by Gil Wolman, Debord's closest friend throughout the years of the Lettrist International (1952–58), and *Howls for Sade* (milestones in the history of lettrist cinema), there are photos in *Ion* of the leaders of the movement. They include Isidore Isou (his real name was Jean-Isidore Goldstein), who had arrived in Paris from Romania in 1945 with the intention of at least equaling Tristan Tzara, his countryman and predecessor, in avant-garde provocation and radicalism. The young Romanian attempted, with some success, to resemble a young Elvis Presley on the point of launching his career. There was some irony in this, because Isou was one of the first to think of the young as an autonomous subversive force. Wolman presented himself as an intellectual Jewish dandy.[5] The others simply pose. Gabriel Pommerand, however, another noteworthy figure in the group (in 1945 he was the first friend or disciple of Isidore Isou), tried his hand at body art, although his efforts were somewhat timid, compared to subsequent developments in the field, in that he restricted himself to painting his face. Serge Berna, Michel Mourre's accomplice in the 1950 Notre-Dame scandal, which served retroactively as the foundational crime of the Lettrist International, tries to pose as little as possible.[6] He looks straight at the camera, making a visibly superhuman effort to express nothing, which makes him look like a psychopath. This was all more or less to be expected, part of the logic of the avant-garde manifesto; for what good is a manifesto if not to make manifest, to make visible, those who sign it, generally along with a good dash of provocation? The question arises, however, whether such a position was truly original, for the lettrist audience remained rather discreet and history has been relatively silent in recalling the exploits of men such as Isidore Isou, Michel Mourre, and Serge Berna.

Debord is also posing—leaning against a wall, his hands in his pockets, his head tilted to the side. To use a then-fashionable expression, he looks cool. He is by far the most seductive lettrist, probably because he is the one who least thinks of himself as a lettrist. The only problem is that the photograph was made with an intentionally damaged negative (based on a technique also used by Isidore Isou, especially in his 1951 film *Traité de bave et d'éternité* [Treatise on Slime and Eternity]). Debord's right leg and hand disappear behind a bright cloud of dust, his eyes look as if he had been blindfolded with a black stain, and the entire image is a little blurry and heavily scratched. It seems to belong to another time. It pushes the young Debord toward his own legend. For the moment, the man of action is interested in his image, or, more precisely, its disfigurement. He rises from the blur and dust, or returns there; almost as if he had never been there completely, as if the lettrist movement he had recently become a part of was already a memory. Greil Marcus sees him as a young man with his future before him, a man for whom lettrism is already part of the past.[7] But do lost children really have a future, or even a present? Even more than the first image in *Panegyric,* the photograph from *Ion* suggests that the future of lost children is tied to their disappearance. It signifies that Debord's life, destined for oblivion, will disappear from the Other's gaze; it shuns appearances, cannot be captured.

It is important to carefully distinguish among the various legends surrounding the life of Guy Debord, the various ill-intentioned or well-meaning rumors that created them, and his own penchant for legends, which affected his entire output, especially his autobiographical writings, one of whose principal characteristics is precisely its projection into a kind of absolute past. In a letter addressed to Asger Jorn at the time the Situationist International was founded in 1957, Debord reminds him of the necessity to forge a new legend around the movement, and everything leads to the conclusion that this necessity existed for him long before his first involvement with the lettrists: "We must immediately create a new legend of our own."[8] Debord's statement can be understood as an echo of another found in Gil Wolman's *L'Anticoncept,* from 1951: "We'll allow the legend to take shape in Saint-Germain-des-Prés for the tourists from other neighborhoods."[9] Debord always admired the work of the man who was his first accomplice during the lettrist period, and he certainly would have accepted Wolman's directive. Moreover, Wolman's formula emphasizes the ambiguity in the creation of a new legend: it seems to exist only for others (tourists, outsiders). Who experiences the legend? For whom is it made? Can we believe in a legend about Debord fabricated by Debord? Maybe our legendary heroes are never present in their own legends, never live them in the present. And it is the present that seems to escape these first two images, as it does in so many others. To create one's own legend is to consign oneself to the past, to a time that has passed, that has dissolved and is unchangeable. This was to become one of Debord's greatest temptations.

Debord often added to or helped maintain this ambiguity. The blurry portrait he chose for the back cover of the first edition of *The Society of the Spectacle* did as well.[10] Here as elsewhere he has decided to avoid our gaze or, at least, not to succumb to appearances, whose existence photography tries to get us to forget. This is not insignificant once we realize that rarely has an author been so closely identified—wrongly, in my opinion—with a single book. This is the book that made him famous, a book that is fundamentally a critique of the appearances put in place by modern capitalist society to maintain the principles of exploitation and oppression. The author of *The Society of the Spectacle* declared himself to be a lost child of the spectacle, which he remained for the rest of his life.

Using scratched images and books, Debord criticized appearances, made no effort to preserve them. This was true of physical appearance as well, since Debord's affection for lost childhoods had nothing to do with the fear of growing old. In 1980 Debord published a translation of *Stances sur la mort de son père* by Jorge Manrique, a fifteenth-century Spanish poet-warrior whose melancholy temperament captivated his translator, especially when Manrique discusses the process of aging: facial beauty, the freshness of the skin, its radiance and color are vain illusions in which we enclose the world.[11] Engraved on the body, aging is the irremediable mark of time, which will ensure its decomposition. Debord never tried to escape that process of aging. Lost children don't love death, but they know that time passes, that it can only pass, and that consequently it is already too late to become an adult, to become someone—with the attributes and appearances that entails. They have a sense of their transitoriness. Unlike so many others, who require their heroes to be forever young and handsome, the legend Debord constructed does not hide the marks of time on the body (for which reason it is not like other legends). It welcomes age and follows the progress of aging almost gleefully. The child devoted to perdition is not Dorian Gray. On the contrary, he seems attached to the possibility of his own disfiguration. This embodies the same tale of perdition, but is inscribed directly on the face, on the body: it is a process of becoming invisible, of returning to dust, to ashes scattered over the Seine.

Was this the same dust scattered across that first photograph? In 1978 Debord published his *Complete Cinematic Works* in book form. This contains texts and scripts for all his films together with a selection of stills. Remarkably, the very last page of the book contains two images from *In girum imus nocte* arranged one above the other: the very first, a portrait of Debord, already mentioned (which appears again at the beginning of volume 2 of *Panegyric*), and a photograph from 1977. Under the first portrait, that is, between the two pictures, we can read the following "legend" from *In girum imus nocte*: "I have always had a sensation of the passage of time." It is difficult, looking at these two portraits taken nearly thirty years apart, to avoid experiencing what the passage of time can be like. The images function as if intended to illustrate the work of disfiguration carried out by time on the author's face. The least we can say is that he "looks" his age, and with good reason since he seems to have deliberately aged for the occasion. Technically, the second picture is also "disfiguring." It is even less flattering than the first and seems to be older. It was taken with a flash in a tarnished mirror—the reflection of a reflection, the appearance of an appearance. It is both too contrasty and overexposed, invaded by so much light that the face that should be illuminated is partially obliterated. And when Debord uses it again in *Panegyric*, contrasting it again with the first photograph, now placed at the beginning of book 2, it is even worse. The enlargement emphasizes the overexposure. The contrast disappears and with it half of Debord's face, from which the right eye is almost completely erased: a lifeless mask instead of a pallid face. There is no sense of vanity, no complacency, no desire to arrange things to extend the illusion of youth and life. On the contrary, it is as if he had done everything he could to impress upon the viewer the passage of time, to eradicate whatever there may have been that was attractive in his face and precipitate his disfigurement. The only ones who preserve their good looks, at least in *Panegyric*, are those who have been loved, because they were loved. It was very beautiful.

The lost children were fond of ruin and disappearance. We should be cautious, however, about equating this with the oratorical disappearance found in Mallarmé or the pathos of the death of the author it justifies. There is nothing "impersonal" in Debord's disfigurement and obscurity. Nothing sepulchral either: the graves are less his doing than that of his biographers and commentators, who seem to prefer him dead. If he is careful to remain only partly visible in the images he published, he does so to affirm the precedence of his own image of himself. For those satisfied with appearances, he leaves only mutilated and scratched images, reflections of reflections. The only thing that counts is the way he sees himself, just as the only thing that counts—and his writing demonstrates this—is the way he sees the world. Death is in the gaze of the Other, it inhabits those who long for the spectacle. It is important to understand that Debord never made much of his own image, in every sense of the word, and consequently did not make much of its absence either, unlike those who refine their image as writers by withholding from the public any portrait, any photograph of themselves. The lost child prefers his own image of himself. He does not fear the Other's gaze, but he rejects it because it seems to him both deformed and deforming. He wants no part of it and anticipates the gaze he assumes to be deformed by its allegiance to the spectacle, which would degrade or disfigure his own appearance.

In this sense, Debord remained the lost child who was born around 1950. In any event, he remained lost in 1984 when the press, right and left, tracked him down and tried, unsuccessfully, to implicate him in the murder of his friend Gérard Lebovici. I will discuss Lebovici's death and the book Debord wrote about it, *Considerations on the Assassination of Gérard Lebovici*, in a later chapter.[12] Here, I would like to refer to a single episode, which is emblematic of Debord's relationship to the image, to challenge the unsupported claims of Debord's hatred of images of any kind. Following Lebovici's assassination, Debord, who obviously refused to have anything to do with the press, was assailed by journalists and photographers, who tried to photograph him surreptitiously from a distance. One of them, hiding in a nearby house (Debord was living in Arles), succeeded. The picture, taken with a telephoto lens, was of poor quality. It showed him at the window of his apartment and appeared in *Paris-Match*. Debord responded by having a photograph of himself taken, which he stipulated to be his "official" portrait, and had it published. He made a point to send a copy to the photographer who had photographed him in Arles.[13] This is about as clear an expression as we are likely to get that Debord did not care about how he was seen by others—or at least not enough to want to maintain that image at any price—and the precedence given to his own image of himself (or that of a complicit gaze). Is there any more explicit refutation of the derisive and paradigmatic prosthetics of the telephoto lens with which the spectacle attempts to construct an artificial reality? His response dismantled the myth of a man living in hiding, terrified of images, who was tracked down by a heroic press corps, which celebrated nothing but its own insignificant exploits. In *Considerations on the Assassination of Gérard Lebovici*, the episode was referred to as follows: "Paradoxically, in this clandestine period the press has published half a dozen photos of me, all of which were found in situationist publications. And I know that there exist many others. They insist upon the great age of these photographs, while they themselves are doing everything they can to make it all worse. The March 15 *VSD* featured a photo published in the 1967 edition of *The Society of the Spectacle* and described it the following way: 'Dating from 1959, one of the rare photos of Guy Debord, the situationist philosopher who inspired the anarchist ideas of Gérard Lebovici.' Only their lack of education and culture has prevented them from finding a rather recent photo of me, extracted with many others from my films and printed in my *Complete Cinematic Works,* published by Champ Libre. Described as 'Debord at forty-five,' it therefore dates from 1977. Because of the press's inability to find such things, we thus have their furious efforts (and their almost total failure) to capture a photo of me in 1984. In order to put an end to this insipid legend according to which I would like to hide myself from whomever, I am having a very recent photo of myself published in this book."[14]

From beginning to end, the lost child remained faithful to himself and to loss. From beginning to end, he refused to be the model child who poses and submits to the Other's gaze, becoming the person others want him to become. It is worth noting that in the "official" photograph sent to the press, Debord is careful not to smile. The whole affair must have put him in a bad mood.

Passing through Lettrism

But let's not get ahead of ourselves. The year is 1951–52, and Debord has just been "born." The photograph in *Ion* is the announcement of his birth. A young man with a bright future ahead of him, Greil Marcus says, as if the lost children had a future. But at the same time, he is obviously right. If Debord appears imprecisely—beneath the scratch marks, dust, and blur—as if he belonged to another time, it's because the period with *Ion,* the lettrist period, is not his moment, but Isidore Isou's. What the photo in *Ion* seems to say is that Debord had always been a lettrist, that from his point of view, lettrism is itself only a false appearance of the present, to be deformed, scratched out, erased with its own weapons. As Ponge said, you can't get out of the trees using trees, but maybe you can escape lettrism through lettrism. In any event, there was always something fuzzy about Debord the lettrist, something not quite in focus. After all, advances in photographic technique had nothing to do with the fact that later pictures of him were sharp, but rather with his decision to appear clearly, to reveal himself. For those who start out as lost children, it takes time to define oneself, to achieve clarity and focus.

In 1951 Debord had completed his baccalaureate degree with a passing grade. It was at this time that he met the lettrists in Cannes, where they had showed up to create a ruckus and make sure Isou's first film, *Traité de bave et d'éternité*, was screened. The film consisted of four hours of "discordant cinema," with its melodramatic images enhanced with scratches, shaky footage, blank frames, and a sound track that had no relation to the picture, consisting of monologues and "onomatopoeic" poetry (composed uniquely of sounds rather than words, onomatopoeic poetry being to lettrism what automatism was to surrealism, a kind of aesthetic matrix as well as quality label). As for casting, Isou's lettrist accomplices, who were unlikely to have been very demanding about payment, had the leading roles. The avant-garde, as we have seen, followed its course and decided to impose this decisive *destruction of cinema* (as Isou himself claimed at the time) on the assembled cinephiles, who were in principle convinced of the radiant future of their favorite art. The festival authorities ultimately agreed to show Isou's film (very possibly simply to get him out of their hair), but at the last minute presented only the film's sound track, which didn't really change things much as far as Isou's film was concerned. However, Debord and Wolman, who were present, took from this the underlying principle of their first cinematic projects: films without any images at all. As for Isou, his success was enormous and nearly unanimous, which is to say that he was booed by everyone in the audience. Even the young Godard was skeptical. (Was this the source of Debord's tenacious hatred for the man the situationists would later refer to affectionately as "the dumbest of the pro-Chinese Swiss"?) The only supporters were Maurice Schérer (later known as Eric Rohmer), who conscientiously praised the film in *Cahiers du Cinéma*, and Jean Cocteau (was he seduced by the Elvis Presley of postdadaism?), who arranged for Isou to be awarded a "Prix de l'avant-garde" that had been created specifically for the occasion.

Fascinated by the lettrists, Debord began spending a great deal of time with them when he returned to Paris a few weeks later. He became especially close to Marc'O (Marc Gilbert Guillaumin) and Gil Wolman. His birth as a lost child is indissolubly associated with his spontaneous attraction to Isou's lettrists, some of whom were also lost children of sorts. Debord singled them out as being the best that postdada or postsurrealist radicalism had to offer. More specifically, his birth took place between the time he met the lettrists and the moment he broke with Isou, in November 1952, a break that was in a way programmed by the picture that had appeared in *Ion*. Things happened so quickly that we can hardly speak of a true lettrist period for Debord, who passed through the movement led by Isou like a comet. Because his birth is associated as much with separation as it is with adherence, the situationist histories of situationism and its prehistory are generally both close-mouthed and critical when it comes to Isidore Isou and lettrism. The fact that Debord hesitated to reveal himself, that he managed his appearance—going so far as to scratch it out—is one thing, but it does not imply anything about the imminent disappearance of Isou. For example, Jean-François Martos, the most official historian of the movement, sweeps him aside in a short paragraph on lettrism: "In 1946 Isidore Isou founded the lettrist movement. But although lettrism became the successor of the artistic avant-garde of the past century, Isou's criticism of the arts gradually devolved into a mystical dead end and resulted in his rejection by younger lettrists, who, in 1952, formed the Lettrist International."[1] The issue was black and white—just like their future films. After 1952 Isou was considered over the hill, and his greatest crime was his failure to realize this soon enough (he may in fact never have realized this).

Debord came into his own through his association with lettrism, an association that was also a break, which the single issue of *Ion* preceded by seven months. There was nothing unusual about such a break, especially given the history of the artistic and literary avant-garde that had been in existence for nearly fifty years. And yet, it was Debord in all his singularity who began to emerge from this. To return to the images mentioned earlier, Debord's presence remains fundamentally ambiguous, as it would be so often in his life. This ambiguity is responsible for his effectiveness and, in strategic terms, his superiority over the more classically avant-garde position of the megalomaniacal Isou, who was unattracted to dust and obscurity. Debord was initially seduced by Isou, and, after 1952–53, the Lettrist International, founded at the time of the break with Isou, made use of some of the aesthetic techniques and provocative acts of early lettrism. Nonetheless, even from the beginning Debord was after bigger game. Into the almost parodic remake of dadaism developed by Isou and his friends, he introduced an awareness of his own image, a dialectic that he continued to perfect, and that centered around the representation of self, of appearance, of manifestation—and by extension the role of the subject in something like a revolutionary art, to the extent that it exists. In this image, where he looks like someone who once was a lettrist but is no longer, it is the Debord of the future who is struggling to appear, and to disappear, at a rate and in a configuration that are all his own. Far from being insignificant, this necessitated a break.

An opportunity presented itself with the arrival, in November 1952, of Charlie Chaplin in France, who had been forced to leave the United States by the McCarthy witchhunt. Although the Cold War was raging, the European left celebrated the event, with the exception of Debord and his closest friends, who greeted Chaplin's arrival with a tract that was giddily insulting: "Get lost, fascist worm, make a lot of money, be sophisticated (your hollow stomach was a big success with little Elizabeth), die quickly, we'll provide you with a first-class funeral. We hope your last film is really the last. The limelight has melted the makeup of the so-called brilliant mime and all we see is a sinister and uninteresting old man. *Go home Mister Chaplin.*"[2]

Debord and his colleagues had a precocious talent for invective, as well as effectiveness, not that Chaplin would have complied with the order to abandon the stage once and for all, assuming he was even aware of the insults in question. But obviously this was not their goal. As always, a nascent avant-garde directed its barbs at an existing avant-garde in a friendly attempt to shove it from the scene. Debord's gesture infuriated Isou and the lettrists and forced them to unmask themselves. Under pressure from his troops, the sub-Carpathian onomatopoeist was forced to publicly distance himself from his young protégés, who no longer had any desire to be his protégés and who immediately widened the divide between themselves and Isou, transforming it into irreversible hatred: "It's as if Isidore Isou had been nothing for us; as if his lies and denials had never existed."[3] Years later, Isou, who became increasingly unstable and no doubt jealous of Debord, maintained this hatred. Debord, whose sense of tolerance was not great, ended up by demonstrating toward Isou what might be called the indulgent generosity of the conqueror. Who today, outside the situationist movement and its followers, remembers the role played in the postwar period by the Elvis Presley of the French avant-garde?[4]

Sometimes one break can hide another, more important one. History does not tell us if Isidore Isou was pleased by the somewhat dubious honor of receiving a "Prix de l'avant-garde" from Cocteau in Cannes or by what would come to be his biggest success as a lettrist cinematographer: serving as the inspiration for two works that achieved far greater fame than his own film (at least for initiates of the situationist saga), namely, Gil Wolman's *L'Anticoncept* and Guy Debord's *Howls for Sade*. The screenplays for the two films appeared in the contents of the famous issue of *Ion* that contains the portraits of the lettrist family.[5] Things began to move quickly at this time. Gil Wolman and Debord had barely appeared on the lettrist scene when they began to overtake Isou, less spectacularly than they did at the time of Chaplin's arrival, but more systematically and artistically.

Wolman began with his *L'Anticoncept,* as if to show that, in terms of the destruction of cinema, there was still progress to be made. The image was now reduced to a long series of white spheres alternating with a black screen, while on the sound track, written and spoken by the author, could be heard a text that was not without force or beauty. Although still involved with the onomatopoeic rituals of the moment, Wolman appears to have discovered the charms of postsurrealist automatism, which places him within the tradition of Artaud and his *Pour en finir avec le jugement de Dieu* rather than Isou's lettrists. The last ten minutes of the "film" (there are still no images) are characteristic in this sense, for here the filmmaker mimics the sounds of a man vomiting. The technique, known as *"mégapneume,"* was intended to dearticulate language, to shift it toward pure sound, an interior breath—and to do so the director was prepared to turn his own stomach, or possibly the empty stomachs of his viewers, still hungry for images. Compared to this, the "divergent" cinema of Isou was academic. Initially projected onto a sounding balloon ("Everything round is Wolman," as the author himself once claimed) in February 1952 at the avant-garde film club of the Musée de l'Homme in Paris, *L'Anticoncept* was censored, although the reasons for the honor were never discovered since the censorship committee was not required to justify its decisions. Did the members believe the film was subversive (which might imply, although the assumption is somewhat risky, that they understood clearly what was involved, unlike Godard)? Or did they simply confuse Wolman's film with a Stalinist propaganda film? Such films were being imported in bulk from Poland and Bulgaria, and it was the committee's job to identify them.

Then it was Debord's turn. He left Cannes for Paris, where he frequented Isou and his followers, as well as the seedier cafés in Saint-Germain-des-Prés, places Sartre and his entourage avoided. He led the life of a kind of street punk, and this can be felt in his first film, *Howls for Sade,* which was also shown at the Musée de l'Homme, on June 30, 1952. The scandal was even greater, as far as any self-respecting (post)dadaist was concerned, with an uproar of boos and shouts. Michèle Bernstein, whom Debord met in 1952 and married in 1954, seems to have had considerable vocal, even guttural, talent, and led the display of avant-garde appreciation, screaming louder and longer than all the others in the audience. Rotten vegetables were thrown from the balcony onto the already indignant viewers below, and a fight broke out. It was later claimed in London that Debord's film had caused a riot in Paris, which was possibly just another way of creating a new scandal. But once again, the rebellion may mostly have been internal and the most significant aspect of the screening the split it introduced among the lettrists. Many members left the group—not to mention the theater—in protest, and Isou, confronted with the threat of mass defection, was forced to withdraw his initial support for Debord's film and to distance himself from him. Jealousy and the struggle for influence ensued. It was the beginning of the end for Isou, and a few months later, by the time of the Chaplin affair, it was all over. This was no accident. *Howls for Sade* was not really a lettrist film, in spite of the "ad" in *Ion.*

Having Boarded at Night the Lightest of Crafts

Why wasn't it a lettrist film? Along with the text of *Howls for Sade,* published in *Ion,* there appeared an imaginary script for the film (that is, a description of all the images that would be used). But it was never realized in this form. When it appeared, all the initially planned images had disappeared, to be replaced by a series of white and black screens, which concluded with the legendary sequence of twenty-four minutes of black screen and total silence. Was it laziness? Lack of money? What more could be expected of a delinquent filmmaker resolved to forge a career in the world of lost children? None of these factors, no matter how ironically prosaic, prevented "discordant" cinema, the worn film stock and onomatopoeic burps, from being consigned to the museum of avant-garde gadgets. The sound track in Debord's film was significantly redone, as is evident from the final version, published initially in 1964 in *Contre le cinéma,*[1] then much later in the *Complete Cinematic Works.*[2] Ultimately, all the onomatopoeic sequences were removed. Lettrism was deprived of its essence, its rationale; nothing was left of it but a handful of relics in Wolman's *L'Anticoncept.*

Between the film announced in *Ion* and the final film, more than just the images disappeared—all traces of lettrism did as well. Between the moment of its appearance in *Ion* and the famous film-club screening, Debord had abandoned everything he owed to lettrism. So what was left? A kind of imaginary or virtual film, at least if we acknowledge that cinema has to do with images. The filmmaker—ironically, this was the only professional activity that Debord ever acknowledged being involved in—appeared only for the duration of a hypothetical film. The images he projected would never be seen; he emerged only to disappear within the death of cinema he proclaimed, or, more exactly, that he would have proclaimed if the film had really taken place. In the final version of the film, a voice announces, "Just as the projection was about to begin, Guy-Ernest Debord was supposed to step onto the stage and make a few introductory remarks. Had he done so, he would simply have said: 'There is no film. Cinema is dead. No more films are possible. If you wish, we can move on to a discussion.'"[3] Guy-Ernest Debord should have appeared to announce the death of cinema, just as he should have made a film, and it would certainly have been beautiful. In any event, it is hard to imagine a more circumspect entrance into the history of film, which, through his circumspection, he intends to put an end to: "What a Spring! Notes for a History of Film: 1902—*Voyage to the Moon,* 1920—*The Cabinet of Dr. Caligari,* 1924—*Entr'acte,* 1926—*Battleship Potemkin,* 1928—*Un Chien Andalou,* 1931—*City Lights,* Birth of Guy-Ernest Debord, 1951—*Traité de bave et d'éternité,* 1952—*L'Anticoncept, Howls for Sade.*"[4]

"Cinema is dead. . . . If you wish, we can move on to a discussion." In its megalomaniacal parodic dimension, there is a strong element of post-dadaist juvenile provocation in this. Yet this sentence, one of the first published by Debord, constitutes a program that he adhered to, since he continued to attack the spectacle in all its forms, and film in particular, the art par excellence of advanced capitalism, which uses it as an effective technique of hypnosis. From the first, it was important to move away from one-way communication, from the passivity that characterizes modern forms of cultural consumption, to "discussion," to authentic dialogue, which is also conflict, of which scandal is the most extreme form. To move from film to discussion, to conflict, to make use of art as a means of division, in turn conferring on art that coefficient of reality and effectiveness that the avant-garde has so often attempted to give it. Ever since dadaism, such provocation and scandal have represented something like an irruption of the real into the world of art. In this sense, there is nothing gratuitous about provocation, or, more accurately, its meaning exists precisely in its gratuitousness, in the pure transition to action it aspires to and with which is reestablished, beyond the artistic artifact, a form of communication that is irrefutably authentic because of its adversarial nature. Debord entered the world of art through the exit door, situating himself at its extreme limit, bringing back what was most disruptive in dada. This was a far cry from the tedious platitudes about engagement proclaimed by many (crypto-)Stalinist writers living off their stipends.

A public deprived of images. *Howls for Sade* was like an initial draft of a position that would later come to be known as situationist. We can already catch glimpses of the complexity or subtlety that differentiates it from its dadaist origins. Deprived of a film, the audience was also deprived of Guy-Ernest Debord climbing onto the stage to begin the discussion, which means that the provocation would also remain virtual in a sense. The days of the Cabaret Voltaire, the clowning of Tzara and others on stages in Zurich and Paris, were over. In 1952 dadaist provocation was accepted, it was part of the spectacle, it signified the time-honored presence of a certain kind of avant-garde, and Isidore Isou was not the only one who failed to understand this. To give it back its intensity now involved the evasion or disappearance of the provocateur: "Guy-Ernest Debord was supposed to step onto the stage." He was absent not from the conflict but from the anticipated conflict, simultaneously heightening that conflict and demonstrating a precocious mastery of the art of not being where you are expected. *Howls for Sade* is a kind of provocation squared, playing off the presence and absence of the provocateur. If we examine the virtual version printed in *Ion*, the film's images consist, to a large extent, of a series of close-ups of the author (including, to be precise, a close medium shot of the same author drinking a glass of something, and a final shot where he leaves the Escapade to walk down Rue Dauphine), carefully framed by silent black screens.

Fort/da: Debord's first film was interspersed from start to finish by the appearance and disappearance of the author-provocateur. He extended over time the gesture of presentation and effacement visible in the intentionally worn photograph accompanying his "script." He extended that moment in time to twenty-four minutes—an eternity—as if, from the outset, Debord had always wanted only to make his disappearance last. It is

hard not to see Debord in *Howls for Sade* (given the rather limited number of planned scenes) and, at the same time, it's hard to see him. It's even
harder in that, when the film was made, when the time came to shift from
announcing a series of close-ups of the author to the close-ups themselves,
there was nothing there to see. There was no image and the filmmaker did
not even bother to show up in person to announce the death of cinema. The
scratched-film technique of the lettrists gave way to the scratched image,
now missing from the avant-garde's cinematic menu. Not enough has been
made of this distinction. There is something uniquely *unsituatable* in the
situationist position sketched out here. And that is why it is diametrically
opposed to the situation of the writer that Sartre had been trying to conceptualize for several years. An enthusiast of appearances, of taking positions, of supporting the proletarian comrades in Billancourt, enamored of
everything that was made manifest, Sartre was, from this point of view, the
one person Debord tirelessly criticized. Ultimately, this culminated in an
unshakable hatred for the man, something relatively rare in Debord.

So he howled for Sade, for someone who, two centuries earlier, also intended to disappear without leaving a trace; scattered ashes, howls for disappearance, for absence, for an unrepresentable that was not haphazard-
ly associated with Sade's name. And was Debord's film really a film about
Sade?[5] If the film is about anything, it is about this passion for disappearance. It all began (almost) with the legal definition of absence: "Article
115.—If a person has ceased to appear at his place of residence and nothing has been heard concerning him for four years, interested parties may
petition the civil court to officially recognize the absence of said person."[6]
Howls for Sade is a declaration of absence, a declaration of unsituatability,
like a customs declaration or a declaration of love, even though, in 1952,
Debord wasn't gone the requisite four years from his domicile to be declared legally absent (however, patience and legality had never been his
strong points; the lost child declares his own absence, he doesn't expect to
be acknowledged by the law). The break with his family became increasingly obvious and he had no permanent residence. He walked up and
down the streets of Paris, went from café to café, day and night, drifted, as
he would say, and visited the catacombs under the city for obscure games
of disorientation. Legend has it that he slept beneath the bridges with the
homeless. But that is legend; a hotel room on Rue Racine seems more likely.
What is certain, however, is that Debord seems to have decided, about the

time he made his first film, to disappear from the world he had been a part of for the first twenty years of his life. Which is why there exists no trace of that world, either in his life or in his work. Lost children and future situationists can't be placed under house arrest.

The sound track of the "virtual" version (the one in *Ion*) of *Howls for Sade* did not begin with Article 115 of the Civil Code but with this sentence, "At the beginning of this story, there were people made to forget it; and the good times that were more lost than in a labyrinth."[7] But is it really different? Here we begin with an evocation of a forgotten story, a story about people who forget the story that is supposed to be told, their own perhaps; people who are lost or who lose their time, in a story forgotten as if in a labyrinth—its first appearance in Debord's work (there were others; it is one of the most constant symbols of his desire for loss).

Starting with Debord's first film, the dialectic of appearance-disappearance became a dialectic of memory and forgetfulness in which memory was invoked only to recall what had disappeared without a trace. With Debord it was always a question not so much of bringing back what was lost as of acknowledging its irrefutable disappearance. *Howls for Sade* is a film made of forgotten moments, signs of disappearance. There is the emblematic trace of Arthur Cravan, who is evoked almost immediately after the opening sentence, "Arthur Cravan beneath the deep waters. He was lost track of shortly afterward in the Gulf of Mexico, where he took off one night in the lightest of crafts."[8] Cravan, the dandy who broke with his family (but a great admirer of Oscar Wilde, his wicked uncle), the protodadaist, the poet-boxer who was always playing, and played his boxing gloves off against his pen, the ring against the reviews, this "deserter from seventeen nations" who struggled to avoid the butchery of the First World War, is mentioned several times in Debord's writings and films.[9] He appears one last time in *Guy Debord, son art et son temps,* the film Debord made in 1994 with Brigitte Cornand for Canal Plus, and a few years earlier in the first pages of *Panegyric*: "The people I respected more than anyone in the world were Arthur Cravan and Lautréamont."[10] Did Debord admire Cravan not only because he preferred boxing to a career as a writer but, more important, because, after deserting several times, he ended up disappearing, shipwrecked? In 1920, Cravan's track was lost somewhere between the United States and Mexico, between the world of capitalism and the home of nearly permanent revolution (at least at the time). Lautréamont, as venerated as Cravan, does not contradict this assumption. For in leaving without giving an address, Isidore Ducasse showed signs of talent as well as precocity, and the speculations that associated his incessant changes of address in Paris with the obscure work of preparing for the Commune in no way detract from such a belief.[11]

Howls for Sade is a film made of forgotten stories, disappearances, a film about lost children, the way a film can be about war or love (which it is as well: some passages in the text read like declarations of love, and the first version includes several references to war and revolt). "Like lost children, we live our unfinished adventures" is the film's final sentence. It is the starting point for Debord's life as he tells it, the starting point of his struggle, his legend, and that of his companions. They were lost children, as Villon noted, the *poète-bandit* they so admired. And no one was more aware than Debord that this is where the legend begins, that this is where it happened, between 1951 and 1953, with this first film, which not only bore witness to it but helped create it. In *Panegyric*, he wrote, concerning the general hostility he aroused, "Some think it is because of the grave responsibility that has often been attributed to me for the origins, or even for the command, of the May 1968 revolt. I think rather it is what I did in 1952 that has been disliked for so long."[12] Debord did not become Debord, the man who was universally disliked, in 1968 but in 1952, and of that person no trace remains, other than the lost—lost from the beginning—traces in *Howls for Sade*. His birth certificate is a certificate of disappearance, of loss, covered by twenty-four minutes of black screen. There's nothing to see. That is what we dislike.

The adventures of the lost children were not yet over. They were missing an ending, in every sense of the word, without which there was no possibility of a narrative to tell their story. The legend that grew up around them is a broken one, made of adventures that are not only fragmentary but invisible as well. Doesn't the version of *Howls for Sade* appearing in *Ion* relate the "immeasurable unimportance of our lives"? Lives of "immeasurable unimportance" are made to escape notice. Instead of a narrative or film, only a few fragments of their adventures remain, the wreckage of a silent shipwreck, the debris from Cravan's and all the other lost children's nocturnal and flimsy craft. Even though it consists in part of quotes and appropriated texts, it is still possible to read a number of lines and "images" from this film autobiographically, as allusions to Debord's life in Paris in 1951:

the remnants of love affairs, faces known or loved, allusions to the lettrists, evocations of places, even schisms. But these are only fragments. No auto-biography is possible for someone determined to disappear. "I don't think we'll ever see one another again," says a voice in *Howls for Sade*.[13] Coming from nowhere and spoken to no one, the statement may just as well have been made to the reader or viewer. Debord's film is made in such a way that he will never be seen; it is made to dismiss him. We'll never see one another (again).

Howls for Sade, or the unwanted self-portrait. Conversely, it can also be said that by making the adventures of the lost children invisible, Debord is simply creating his paradoxical self-portrait. He gives the experience of loss the form that best suits him, makes his autobiography coincide with the narrative of the interruption of its possibility. In spite of the battle he intended to wage against the society of the spectacle, in spite of his refus-al to submit to the appearances and representations it attempted to im-pose, more specifically because of this refusal, Debord is indeed the au-thor of a fundamentally autobiographical work, one that is at least as autobiographical as "theoretical." Everything he did springs from a rich game of *fort/da* (I use this term because Debord liked games): an art that is at once the science of disappearance and of staging. He reveals himself wherever he disappears, wherever he is lost, wherever we cannot follow his tracks. He practices an art of evasion, of flight on fragile crafts, of groups and guilds that will never become a unified party. If he can be compared to anything—compared as a single thing, as *one* example that nothing pre-cedes or follows—it is a work stoppage, a wildcat strike, not so much by the image as by appearances, and *against* appearances, just as Mallarmé de-fended his right to go on strike against society. However, and this is where the autobiographical nature of his work is most relevant, he must make it known that he is on strike. He needs to stage and act out the strike, he has to show that he is a man who does not believe in his image, a man who rejects appearances. And from time to time he has to send his contemporaries his calling card to show them that they are not, that they do not exist, or at least won't see him again.

Debord's implicitly or explicitly autobiographical films and writings constitute an important part of his work. That this was already the case with his first film is even more significant because it is intimately associ-ated with the birth of Guy Debord as Guy-Ernest Debord: the twenty-four minutes of black in *Howls for Sade* serve, in this context, as a foundational myth. It is his first appearance, his first self-portrait, retroactively even more significant in that Debord was a man with a single project and a single battle. He always claimed to be faithful to himself, a man who would neither renege on a promise nor turn back. Even with his first film Debord concentrated on manipulating appearances, showering them with all the contempt they deserved. Because there is no user's manual of loss, Debord set the example—but one that was impossible to follow.

This is a point that deserves emphasis: Debord is one of the great autobiographers or self-portraitists of the second half of the twentieth century. And one wonders whether the notoriety that followed the publication of the first volume of *Panegyric* in 1989 was not tied, at least in part, to the negative character he gave to all of his appearances. He developed an unchallengeable form of autobiographical writing, through which a statement coincides with an act (and could coincide with an act only because it amounted to no more than "not showing himself"). In 1989 Debord was conscious of the singularity and exemplarity of his situation. He knew this, or at least presents himself as being as exemplary as Rousseau was in his own time, engaged in an undertaking that was in many ways unique and without imitators. This is why he again decided to tell his life story in a book such as *Panegyric*: "Much less do I wish to hide its traces, which I know to be exemplary. Because of the subject's many difficulties, it has always been rare for someone to set out to give a precise account of what the life he has known actually was. And this will be perhaps even more precious now, in an era when so many things have been changed at the astounding speed of catastrophes, in an era about which one can say that almost every point of reference and comparison has suddenly been swept away, along with the very ground on which the old society was built."[14]

In this light, it is clear that it is precisely because of their exemplarity that Debord's autobiographical writings must at the same time be "theoretical," or that, at the very least, there is continuity between these and his autobiographical writings in the strict sense of the word. From Saint Augustine to Rousseau and beyond, this has always been the case. Exemplarity always serves ideology (religious, political), at least when the opposite is not the case. With Debord this continuity is especially obvious in the most autobiographical of his films, which is also his last. *In girum imus nocte et consumimur igni* (1978) is, along with volume 1 of *Panegyric,* the most fully worked-out version of his autobiography, and undoubtedly the most beautiful.

The film does not start out autobiographical. It begins, like the film version of *The Society of the Spectacle* (1973), as a work of social criticism, with themes that will be familiar to anyone who has seen his previous films: the critique of passivity, of separation, of the vapidity of art in general and film in particular (I am not speaking here of the images, which are very different from one film to the next). But this tone is abandoned after some twenty pages (and a little more than twenty minutes), replaced by a long and explicitly autobiographical narrative, introduced in the following terms: "Thus, instead of adding one more film to the thousands of commonplace films, I prefer to explain why I shall do nothing of the sort. I am going to replace the frivolous adventures typically recounted by the cinema with the examination of an important subject: myself."[15] There is no film, let's move on to a discussion, to conflict, that is, to me. Such a change of register is indeed an echo of the declaration of 1952, and it is emblematic of Debord's oscillation between "theory" and "self-portraiture," or, if you will, of their continuity. Autobiography is here a form of social criticism by other means; exemplarity, in a way, constitutes the proof of the relevance of a theoretical discourse.

As I have already suggested, this exemplarity is negative. The period during which Debord was active, which he anticipated to a certain extent (if we imagine him beginning in 1952), is one in which autobiography, and more generally biography, triumphed. But it's just a short step from triumph to the most repulsive degradation. The death of the author foretold by Barthes and Foucault seems quite distant, and if there ever was a time when the author, modestly converted into an anonymous writer, signed his works only for the sake of form, he is now more alive than ever, and more desirous of proving this, of leaving traces of the life he so enjoys. Proof of this can be found in the recent success of intimate memoirs, correspondence, and biography, and more generally the autobiographical turn taken by contemporary fiction. Hasn't the right to create "personal fiction," as it is called, become as unquestioned as human rights once were? Everything would be for the best in the best of all possible worlds if contemporary authors still had the time, between book signings and television appearances, to lead a life that was unique enough not to depend on the clichés of sentimental personal fiction. It is one thing to have reestablished the author's rights, quite another to identify a life that is prestigious enough and, especially, unique enough to justify their use. The danger of the democratization of the right to self-expression is that when it is overused, the claim to authenticity and singularity that historically justified autobiography quickly fades into indifference and a lack of differentiation. It then becomes no more than a rhetoric of authenticity. Singularity is the condition of authenticity and authenticity is corrupted in the presence of the commonplace. From this point of view, the critical importance of Debord's actions lies in his ability to turn his epoch upside down, to make a break with it, to turn himself into its Other. Beginning with *Howls for Sade,* he anticipates and refutes, before and after the swan song of the pleasure of the text, the examination of the author our era demands with such avidity (refusing to fully recognize him unless he responds that he is present, unless he agrees to play the role of the author he claims to be, or, in Debord's words, unless he adheres to the spectacle). From his earliest to his last texts, he sticks to the image of the writer he decided not to be. He is someone who refused the situation of the writer, and of Sartre in particular. He wrote and filmed to scramble appearances, to scratch out the image of the writer, unlike many of his contemporaries, whose goal was often to coincide with, to unite with, such images.

Debord's challenge, his uniqueness, was recognized during his lifetime, for no one was *indifferent* to him, society seeing in him the authenticity it could only dream about. It was felt, although obscurely, that if Debord was a great inventor of autobiographical forms, it was because his life was unique and that he continued to reinvent himself. Great art, great style is based on an art of living—my apologies to those who strive to reduce it to a rhetorical device, whose classicism depends largely on the knowledge of the critic.[16] A sign of this is the dizzying rise over the past few years of the value of the Debordian biographeme on the literary stock exchange. No one is indifferent to Debord today, but apparently this is not reason enough to attempt to understand his singularity, or the passion for loss out of which his work was constructed. That is why there are now not just a number of biographies—which are just what they might be expected to be, that is to say, often somewhat myopic when it comes to Debord's own autobiographical project[17]—but several somewhat less contemporary texts by "situationist" participants, which manage to survive only because they promise some revelation about his life. There is a long line of people waiting in front of the offices of Allia publishers in Paris; they are former companions of Debord. They stand there patiently with their package of memoirs under their arm, which someone will transcribe for them if they don't know how to write or if they did not have the time to prepare something legible themselves.[18] For those who did not know him, there are always the novels by Michèle Bernstein, Debord's first wife, which have been recycled as "personal fiction."[19] Did Debord erase his tracks because he didn't want to be followed? What difference does it make? Bernstein's novels will suffice. You can uncover Debord's tracks beneath his first wife's attempts at appropriation, in spite of the contradictions.[20]

I Wanted to Speak the Beautiful Language of My Century

Howls for Sade was shown in June 1952, a few months prior to the final break with Isidore Isou and "right-leaning" lettrism. At the same time, there was formed what began almost as a secret movement within lettrism, then as an autonomous group—the Lettrist International (which was never very international or very lettrist). The new group consisted of Debord, Gil Wolman, Jean-Louis Brau, and Serge Berna. The film was shown exactly at the juncture—more specifically, the disjuncture—between the two lettrisms. With *Howls for Sade,* his act of birth, his first public demonstration, Debord shifted from Isou to himself: it was the first public manifestation of a life devoted to loss.

There would be others, later on, but they all had in common their focus on the early years in Saint-Germain-des-Prés, that is, 1951–53 (the period of "academic" lettrism and the beginnings of the Lettrist International). Some of Debord's work is exclusively associated with the period. The years 1951–53 were the golden age of the lost children. There is something unique about these years, and Debord returned to them repeatedly in his work. It was a period that became inseparable from its subsequent reexamination, from the texts and films that attest to its existence, all blending together with legend. Debord's revisitation of the past, his return, was always a movement toward loss, something that was to characterize his entire life.

It is important to examine Debord's life at the time through its later reexamination, because that life is inseparable from his attitude toward it in the books and films produced between 1952 and 1994 (with the second volume of *Panegyric*). The first reexamination takes place in 1958, shortly after the time when the Lettrist International, founded in 1952, becomes the Situationist International (SI). The SI was run primarily by Debord, but its international and artistic configuration was made possible through his meeting with the Danish painter Asger Jorn (1914–73), with whom he became close friends. The amateur filmmaker decided this time to make a book rather than a film, in collaboration with Jorn, which he called *Mémoires*. It is in this first book, one of his least known, that the dialectic between appearance and disappearance is systematized. After taking a closer look at the transition between the Lettrist International and the Situationist International, I want to examine the reasons for Debord's writing such a book at this time. The Saint-Germain-des-Prés period cast a shadow on the newly formed Situationist International, which, at least during the first years of its existence, did not harbor the enthusiasm for loss that was so important to the lettrist period. And one can only wonder what would have happened if, at the time it was founded in 1957, the most celebrated avant-garde group of the period had sloughed off its melancholy past and been less exclusively focused on the legendary passions of those bygone days in Saint-Germain-des-Prés.

Debord's *Mémoires,* his "antibook," wasn't put on sale until 1993, and, until its republication by Belles-Lettres, led an almost clandestine existence. Debord insists on this point in a preface ("Attestations") added to the 1993 edition: "I gave this antibook to my friends. No one else was aware of its existence. 'I wanted to speak the beautiful language of my century.' I wasn't terribly interested in being noticed. . . . In any case, I never said anything positive about the *Mémoires* when they came out. And I don't think there is any more to say about them now. I had, from the beginning, manifested my cool indifference to the public's opinion, since the public was not even allowed to see the book. Aren't such conventions a thing of the past? So, my *Mémoires,* in thirty-five years, has never gone on sale. The book's fame arises from the fact that it was only distributed as a form of potlatch: a sumptuary gift that challenges the recipient to give back something better in return. In doing so, smug individuals show that they are capable of anything, but in their own way."[1]

Mémoires was not made to be read, or was made not to be read, at least once we acknowledge that we can only read a book once it has been published, and purchased by a reader—no one, everyone, anyone. Debord radicalized the dismissal of the reader initiated by Baudelaire, who claimed to be writing only for the dead, or Mallarmé, for whom the book did not need to be made accessible to readers. So there was no publication, the public was not allowed to see the work: *Mémoires* could not be seen, did not concern them. The lost children are smug, they have no understanding or appreciation of publication. They have replaced it with secrecy, with anti-books. With the dark screen of *Howls for Sade*, Debord informed the public that he didn't care about it. The public had to wait until 1993 to retrospectively appreciate the indifference it had aroused thirty-five years earlier. At that time it was readmitted as a voyeur, a witness of what never concerned it, a witness to an intimate pact concluded between Debord and the friends to whom the book was offered. The potlatch, simultaneously gift and challenge, was to become one of the guiding principles of his life. Once again, it was the gaze of the Other that Debord attempted to short-circuit, to blind, and to impoverish. To an anonymous public (the figure par excellence of the gaze of the Other) he preferred readers he knew personally, readers he could see, who might receive the book the way they would a letter, and who were, as is the case with correspondence, obligated to respond with a "more lavish" gift, according to the logic of the potlatch. To be a reader of Debord is, from all appearances, something that must be deserved.

There is also an element of paradox in the title itself. Debord begins where others generally finish: by writing his memoirs, which made him one of the youngest memoirists in the history of French literature. Memoirs are often written by someone in public life. Unknowns don't write their memoirs. At most they may write an autobiography, which does not necessarily require any previous fame, although that doesn't hurt; in any case, it's generally recommended to at least wait until adulthood. Debord quite deliberately went about this in reverse. He led a life withdrawn from public view, sheltered from any official visibility, and he wrote his memoirs before living a life that might have justified such an undertaking. Moreover, he did not write them for the public at all; they were clandestine memoirs for clandestine characters. He took a position counter to the modern order of self-representation, and failed to appreciate the emerging dominance of autobiography, whose final and derisive advent he seems to have perceived. The interplay of appearance and disappearance established with *Howls for Sade* is here repeated and radicalized. In the "Attestations" of 1993 it is precisely the existence of the film that Debord chooses to refer to, as if to explain what led up to *Mémoires*: "I began with a film without images, the 1952 feature *Howls for Sade*. The screen was white when the voice was audible, black when there was silence, which grew longer; the final black sequence alone lasted twenty-four minutes. 'The specific conditions of cinema enabled me to interrupt the story with masses of empty silence.' The film clubs, horrified, were shouting too loud to hear what little there was in the dialogue that might have shocked them even more. In 1958, Asger Jorn provided me with an opportunity to go one step further. I published my *Mémoires*, which, frankly, were composed only of quotes from various sources, and did not include a single sentence, no matter how short, that was my own."

Mémoires is the story of a man without a biography, the story of a man whose life consisted in avoiding images and appearances. Debord, unlike many other writers, did not arrange his life as a function of a forthcoming (auto)biography but as a function of an autobiography he had intentionally short-circuited. "If you wish, we can move on to a discussion." There is nothing astonishing in the view that *Mémoires* is, strictly speaking, a book without an author, composed of quotes, as the cover indicates: "This book consists entirely of prefabricated elements." The negation of the autobiographical stance is thus complete: not only do Debord's memoirs fail to respect past narrative conventions, not only are they addressed solely to his friends, but they do not even have an author, or rather, through the use of anonymous quotes everyone has become their author. Debord's disappearance incorporates his rhetorical disappearance as a memoirist, multiple impersonalities, and the systematic use of quotes, which he theorizes as a form of *détournement* and which will become the pillar of the situationist aesthetic (or anti-aesthetic). Between the temptation of disappearance and the practice of appropriation there is a fundamental link. We have known this, or should have, from the time of Lautréamont, the "inventor" of appropriation, who was so gifted at avoiding detection. Appropriation is the art of word thieves who have nothing to lose, certainly not their reputation or their image as writers. Debord and the situationists later emphasized the "strategic" dimension of *détournement,* that is, its potential for appropriation and for turning the enemy's own weapons against it. However, appropriation has always also been a technique of disappearance, a technique for contesting the autobiographical order; *Mémoires* certainly did not invent this, but it may have been its first systematic application.

Interestingly, *Mémoires*—written for and by no one—is not only the work of Debord, but also of Asger Jorn, whom he met a few years earlier (late 1954) and who had become a coleader of the Situationist International. The words "Structures portantes d'Asger Jorn" are visible on the book's cover. Impersonality here goes hand in hand with friendship and, to a certain extent, *Mémoires* is the celebration of their meeting, was made to bear witness to it, while being "supported," made possible by it. The collaboration with Jorn also follows from the technique of disappearance, reinforces it. It is not common practice to write one's memoirs from appropriated statements, much less to rely on someone else's "supporting structures." So where is Debord in all this? He can be found among the quotes thrown or glued onto the paper, cut, truncated, rubbed out, reused, from literary texts, from potboilers, newspapers, and god knows where. They are mixed with images of all kinds, photographs, comic books, engravings, the whole mess bound, covered, and framed by lines and splashes of color. Debord is hidden among his memoirs, but finding him is another matter entirely.

Debord's meeting with Asger Jorn was one of the most important in his life and in the history of situationism. For one thing, it was one of the only friendships that lasted a lifetime, until Jorn's death in 1973, well beyond his withdrawal from the Situationist International in April 1961. The three photographs of Jorn that appear in volume 2 of *Panegyric* bear final witness to that friendship. And then, the creation of the Situationist International in 1957 was largely the result of their meeting, for it combined Debord's Lettrist International with the Mouvement pour un Bauhaus imaginiste led by Jorn.[2] More generally, the Situationist International of the early years took root in artistic circles in large part because of Asger Jorn's fame. The year chosen to introduce *Mémoires,* 1958, was therefore decisive. The Situationist International had recently been founded, and the transition from a relatively confidential group to one that was more public and international, and therefore better able to act, was about to be completed. Now, sheltered by the complicity of an important friendship, Debord returned to his own prehistory and the prehistory of the Lettrist International, that is, to the years 1952–53 (the book is divided into three parts, corresponding to three different moments in the Saint-Germain-des-Prés years: June 1952, December 1952, September 1953).

Was it simply a case of making an initial assessment while moving into high gear, and gaining access to additional resources to disturb the complacency of the contemporary avant-garde? Certainly this was part of Debord's plan, and many of his texts and films were later seen as assessments, as testaments to what had transpired. "Attestations" is the title of the 1993 preface: Debord's texts are not literature. More often they serve to bear witness to what has occurred, to relate what is or was. It remains to be seen, however—assuming it is an assessment—why it did not include the years of the Lettrist International, why, for example, the entire period during which the review *Potlatch* was published (1954–57) was passed over in silence. Why is it that, if only the years 1952–53 are considered relevant, they are treated so inconsistently? In other words, as with *Howls for Sade*, Debord remained silent about a number of things. If Debord, in 1958, looked back on his past, on his early years as a lost child, it certainly wasn't to clarify them and make them accessible. On the contrary, it was as if he wanted to distance himself further from them, to consign them to an absolute past, irrefutable and known only to those who had known him; everyone else would see nothing but ruins, fragments, broken pieces of some obscure disaster, worn traces of an adventurer's steps. There is nothing easier to forget than these *Mémoires*, which oscillate between evocation and revocation, and seem to bring back the storied years of Saint-Germain-des-Prés only to acknowledge their disappearance. Is this what we expect from an assessment? Or was it a way to provide the nascent SI with a legendary past, consistent with the promise Debord made in a letter to Asger Jorn?[3]

At the same time, there is little doubt that in what appear to be the most insignificant and incomplete quotes, in the most seriously cropped or worn photographs, the oldest sketches and maps of Paris, it is indeed the life of Debord and his friends that is revealed. For those who were part of his entourage or simply recognized themselves in the situationist movement, the autobiographical dimension of *Mémoires* has always been obvious, maybe too obvious, as if the techniques of distancing used by Debord meant nothing, at least not for them, as if it were an assessment they were also a part of. But has anyone every really investigated the style of Debord's *Mémoires*, its structure, the role played by the interruptions and intervals of silence? Has anyone ever asked what it is to write a memoir composed entirely of "prefabricated" elements, a series of appropriations? What is an autobiography without an author, written by no one and for no one? Why bury a life story or an era beneath the false surface of quotations, unless it's to make the autobiographical dimension indeterminate, to conceal it especially from those who have no business seeing it? It will always be possible to claim that *Mémoires* is an "antibook," made of whatever was at hand, a story designed to mislead the charmed slacker whom nothing seems to concern. Doesn't all avant-garde writing, on the outside, maintain the appearance of a collage pulled from the surrealist hat? The technique of appropriation serves to mislead the dull, to prevent them from looking too closely, from seeing that all those fragments thrown onto the paper are also, as the title suggests, the memories of an era that Debord took to be the cradle of his legend, his golden age. His writings are testaments, witnesses, reports of practices, acts, or even assessments, if you prefer, but they were not made to be read or understood by everyone, just like *Mémoires,* which was never sold until 1993. This point is worth repeating: Debord never chose to go into hiding, he never chose concealment for its own sake. He decided to write and show what he had done, but always chose the context and the audience in which it would be presented—such a choice being in principle the ultimate privilege of the spectacle. He struggled to impose upon this public his own point of view because he felt it worthwhile. But this was only possible because he began by sidestepping the dominant point of view. By being prepared therefore to lose this public, in every sense of the word: by blinding it, by leaving it nothing—or almost nothing—to see, by disorienting it and forcing it to keep its distance.

That is why it's impossible to interpret the complex question of *détournement* as simply as Jean-Marie Apostolidès has done in *Les tombeaux de Guy Debord.*[4] It's true that *détournement* is also based on a technique of dissimulation, if we insist on using the term, even though it would be more correct to speak of it as a ruse or feint. But it is at the very least problematic to attribute such a technique to the practice—considered shameful or inadmissible—of autobiography, a *larvatus prodeo* to which no more than a handful of self-proclaimed scholars hold the key. Reading Debord is not like a game of Trivial Pursuit, and I doubt that he was the least bit ashamed of his image or self-portraits. The concept of *détournement* entails the notion of detour, the intent to circumvent an obstacle, and contains elements of game playing and warfare. *Détournement* turns the reader or public into a warrior. It incorporates a strategy of blurring appearances, the rejection of comparative quotation demanded by the spectacle, which is currently so intrigued by the cliché of authenticity. Consequently, it also involves a rejection of an entire order of discourse, a logic of allocation, of pigeonholing, of signatures and responsibility through which everyone is in some way put back in his place or finds himself back there. But Debord, the lost child, did everything he could to avoid discovery, to not remain in his place. The spectacle has made authenticity a cliché we are assigned to, it continuously demands that we signal our presence. It is this imperative that *détournement* rebuffs; it is also, and perhaps especially, a technique of appropriation (which has never concealed its intentions), a technique for making the best use possible of words and texts. "Plagiarism implies progress," wrote Ducasse, its least improbable inventor, a man Debord deeply admired. With *détournement* the cliché is taken over for special purposes, as were the Sorbonne much later and, more ephemerally, the Odéon Theater, and a handful of factories. There was jubilation rather than dissimulation, none of the sorrow associated with hidden mastery. A challenge was launched against the cliché by a singularity whose self-rediscovery involved abandoning the cliché and reappropriating the *belle langue* of the century, as Baudelaire—here appropriated—had wanted to do. And Baudelaire, like Debord, was horrified by philanthropic journalists short on inspiration, who wanted to be considered equals or even friends. Charity leads to the spectacle, religiosity to the religious.

The Golden Age

Thus was introduced the first literary device conceived by Debord; its role was to "cover" an essential period in the life of its author, which extended from June 1952 to September 1953. *Mémoires* begins at the time of the first screening of *Howls for Sade* (an excerpt from the *Ion* script was quoted in the first part: the trace left behind by a birth, by a first appearance that culminated in silent obscurity). It was also the occasion, following the break with Isou, of the founding of the Lettrist International, in December 1952, with Jean-Louis Brau, Gil Wolman, and Serge Berna. Several others joined or simply associated with the founding members: Pierre-Joël Berlé, Mohamed Dahou, Françoise Lejare, Jean-Michel Mension, Éliane Papaï, Gaétan Langlais, and especially Ivan Chtcheglov, one of the few from that legendary period to be remembered by situationist historiography. The "golden age" corresponds more or less to the movement of this first Lettrist International (which should be distinguished from the second, founded in 1954 with an almost entirely different group, and associated with the review *Potlatch*).[1]

Nothing about the founding of the first Lettrist International is truly surprising given the fragmented history of the twentieth-century avant-garde, which, although not associated with any permanent revolution, was marked by the continuous hyperbole of self-proclaimed revolutionary radicalism. There was always a risk that behind the back of the most consciously extremist avant-garde movement another would arise, ready to consign it to the museums and schoolbooks, to compel it to undergo—simply because it claimed to be more radical and sometimes was—the torments and infamy of co-optation, or at least to accuse it of such infamy. In this sense, the emergence of the Lettrist International was not an exception. It was in the air, it was contemporaneous with the formation of many other small groups that sprouted up on the fringes of the more official avant-gardes (surrealism, which tranquilly moved toward its senility, the existentialist movement, which was still influential, and later, the groups that were really part of the American underground experience), all more or less ephemeral and informal. It was a period of respite, of a newly rediscovered freedom, following the ice age of the Occupation and the stranglehold of the Communist Party on the intellectual life of France after the Liberation.

Obviously, it would be wrong to think that Isidore Isou was a direct descendant of the surrealists and existentialists, and that Debord was a direct descendant of Isou. The histories of the avant-garde appear linear only in retrospect, with the subsequent success of those who participated. The emergence of the Lettrist International was, therefore, foreseeable. But this does not contradict the movement's specificity, does not mean it didn't serve as a unique event among the various possibilities of the avant-garde. It has been said that "international" lettrism to a large extent owes to Debord's ultimate fate the fact that it was not simply forgotten, like so many other contemporary movements. No doubt this is a defendable point of view, given lettrism's final assessment, but this does not really take into account what was to be one of the essential characteristics of the movement—the intent to leave behind no trace of itself and no works, the will to oblivion that is formally manifest in *Mémoires*, which constitutes if not the most explicit assessment, at least the most accurate, of what was at stake. It is one thing for an avant-garde movement to have been overlooked by history; it's quite another to have struggled to achieve this (Isou, whose presence among the French classics does not yet seem to be assured, was not the worst person Debord could have chosen as an ally).

In other words, if the founding of the Lettrist International was foresee-able, the same was not true of what might be called the day-to-day life of the new group. First of all, there was no group at this time, at least in the sense that avant-gardes have generally understood the term (and which was the same meaning Debord gave to the groups he would later form). Lost children are allergic to meetings at specific times, missed appoint-ments that must be explained, political headquarters, general secretaries, and membership fees, all of which were replaced by the rounds of drinks they offered one another in the cafés and bars of Paris when they had the money.

The first Lettrist International was not actually structured as a group; the bounds between inside and outside were relatively fluid. It was more like a tribe, to use the expression proposed by Jean-Michel Mension in the series of interviews in which he discussed his participation in the lettrist movement.[2] It was not as exclusionary as the later Lettrist International and Situationist International would become (people did break with the movement, however). Between those who were in and those who were out, there was often no more than an imperceptible difference—their partici-pation in *Internationale lettriste,* a mimeographed newsletter of three or four pages that appeared no more than four times in eighteen months. The first Lettrist International was the most indolent group in the history of the French avant-garde, the laziest, the most unproductive, the one that did the least to demonstrate its presence. For some, this was what made it so special; in any case, it was this that made it both legendary and un-equaled in Debord's eyes. In *Panegyric,* he gives the following description: "In the quartier of perdition where my youth went as if to complete its edu-cation, one might have said that the portents of an imminent collapse of the whole edifice of civilization had a rendezvous. Permanently ensconced there were people who could be defined only negatively, for the good rea-son that they had no trade, followed no course of study, and practiced no art. . . . This time, what was an absolutely new phenomenon, which natu-rally left few traces, was that the sole principle accepted by all was precisely that there could be no more poetry or art—and that something better had to be found."[3]

The first Lettrist International consisted of the lost children evoked in *Howls for Sade,* who had disappeared without leaving an address, having had no objective other than to leave no trace of themselves, no oeuvres.

What is interesting about *Mémoires* is its intent to bear witness to this desire for disappearance—an antibook for absent works of art. This was a group of good-for-nothings, who were proud of the fact, and who basically had one purpose in life: to lose themselves, to waste their time ("and in fact I don't believe that any of those who passed that way ever acquired the slightest honest reputation in the world").[4] They were experts when it came to going on strike against society, as Mallarmé would have said. None of them worked. Those who were broke got by thanks to those who, like Debord, managed to convince their families that they were students in order to obtain an allowance that was soon spent, and sometimes by theft and various scams. It was also at this time, 1953, that Debord became the anonymous author of the legendary "Never work!" graffito. In the "Attestations" added in 1993 to *Mémoires,* he reminds readers that this was one of his major works (although, or because, it had required a minimum of work): "Meanwhile, in 1953 I had myself written, but in chalk, on a wall along the Rue de Seine that the patina of years had blackened, the formidable slogan 'Never work!' At first it was thought I was joking (the passerby who is said to have preserved the document for posterity decided to photograph the inscription because he intended to use it for a series of humorous postcards)."[5]

Most members of the group spent their days, and often their nights, in the workers' cafés of Saint-Germain. There was one, a café on the Rue du Four ("Chez Moineau"), that served not only as a place to meet, but also, for many, a kind of home (one or two photographs taken in the café by the Dutch photographer Van der Elsken were published in volume 2 of *Panegyric*). Drunkenness took the place of permanent revolution, improbable cocktails were invented, and drugs were added for good measure (ether but also hashish, which they discovered through the Maghrebins in the group or their friends). Many spent a great deal of time there since they were living on the street (this was not the case with Debord, who stayed at a little hotel on Rue Racine). Chez Moineau—the international lettrists lived on the margins of the flower beds that served as the official avant-gardes, existentialist or postsurrealist. They mixed with those who in *Panegyric* were referred to as the "devotees of the dangerous life."[b] Villon and his companions in (mis)fortune, who five hundred years earlier hung around the same quarter, had been replaced by North African immigrants (this is what justified the label "international" among the dissident lettrists), petty thieves, deserters, mercenaries in wars past or to come, and, less danger-ously, drinkers and runaways, especially runaway girls, who soon became experts in dalliance. The "lost young hoodlum girls who kept us such good company in our dives must not have been so very different from the girls those others had known under the names of Marion l'Idole, or Catherine, Biétrix, and Bellet."[7] The dangerous classes are not necessarily dangerous, but when you mimic Villon it doesn't matter much: a legend is not a docu-mentary or a realist novel. The aristocratic Ghislain de Marbaix, a mythi-cal and seductive murderer, a brawler and pimp at times, whose principal lettrist activity seems to have been to serve as Debord's bodyguard, did an adequate job as Régnier de Montigny (one of Villon's accomplices), even though his only avowed murder was his own: "There was that 'noble man' among my friends who was the complete equal of Régnier de Montigny, as well as many other rebels destined for bad ends."[8]

Within the tribe, some were lettrists and some were not. As for their common interest in loss, it was of little importance since the main lettrist activity consisted in losing oneself rather than in demonstrating one's pres-ence. What could be more insignificant than Pierre-Joël Berlé's signature at the bottom of a lettrist manifesto compared to his brilliant career as a thief (hotels, cars) and legionnaire (possibly to escape prison).[9] Jean-Michel Mension was an artist of drunkenness and vagrancy. Jean-Louis Brau vol-unteered to fight in Indochina. Henri de Béarn later became an important player in the Gaullist movement. Éliane Papaï was the most famous re-form school escapee in the history of (pre)situationism.[10] What they pro-duced was idleness, and it was against this background that these lost chil-dren met others, somewhat less lost, more intellectual, but fascinated with those devoted to a form of systematic disappearance.

Debord spent a great deal of time in cafés; he liked to talk, he liked to drink, and he liked women, very young if possible, but he didn't take drugs—at least not very often—and was never a legionnaire, a thief, a runaway, or a vagabond, nor was he homeless. Most of the time he did not spend his nights at Chez Moineau. All the extant photos of Debord show that he dressed with care and had nothing of the vagrant about him. The bath-robe that Jean-Michel Mension saw when he visited Debord in his hotel is now part of the legend.[11] (However, it wasn't a very good idea to turn it into a sign of internal class struggle within the "tribe," between the "real" lost children and the "fake" lost children in bathrobes. Debord's struggles never interfered with his appreciation of form, or a certain sense of luxury that was inseparable from his understanding of gifts and gift giving.) Nevertheless, absolute idleness was the common ground for all the members of this first Lettrist International, for everyone who constituted the "tribe." It was only later, in 1954, that their paths diverged and the "intellectuals" of the group (Debord, Gil Wolman, Michèle Bernstein) sought new allies. The golden age of Saint-Germain-des-Prés lasted only a year, but it was a period of beauty, both unforgettable and irremediably lost. "Never again will we drink so young."

Mémoires served as the impossible assessment of that golden age. The book begins with the words "Do I remember you? Yes, I want to." It may be insignificant as a quote but it is obviously the memoirist who is speaking, as if to problematize his relationship to memory, to the past, to "you" (who, exactly?). In the pages that follow, other quotes about memory and the erasure of what memory attempts to preserve repeat the initial question: "the demands of a past that can only live again in memory or through 'repetition,' through which, no matter what we do, it will decay." Such comments reflect both a projected "book" and an era that is irrevocably over, that no book can bring back to life, weakened, destitute, disfigured and disfiguring, the exemplary witness of a life that cannot be shaped into a narrative, that shuns a very old order of representation through which lost children can be turned into child prodigies.

The golden age evoked in *Mémoires* was a world of reflections, something both present and intangible. To those who believe they have discovered Debord and his friends in this book, we can always respond that it is merely an exercise in appropriation, we can laugh at their lack of understanding. A sentence such as "the wine of life is drawn, and the mere lees is left this vault to brag of" is taken from Shakespeare rather than being an allusion to the social class of the customers of Chez Moineau. But how can we be sure? To those who are better read and who see in this only an example of *détournement,* we can respond that that's not really the issue, for this was part of lived experience and just as there is no smoke without a smoker, there is no appropriation without an appropriator. The appropriator is uncategorizable, mobile, as if he were comfortable *only* with diversion. We must accustom ourselves to understanding Debord in the sentences he diverted, in their appropriation, in allusions to his drinking ("it's a subject profoundly impregnated with alcohol," "under the influence of alcohol," "we drink all kinds of wine to excess"), in allusions to drugs, the pleasures of the flesh, and extreme youth ("Beneath that laughing face, that air of youthfulness that seemed to promise nothing but play," "you show considerable audacity for a girl your age," "she's quite lively"), or to the mythically scandalous projection of *Howls for Sade*, which was certainly almost as unbearable as Sade's work itself.

Debord goes on to evoke the tribe of lost children bound together by the rising tide of revolt ("a youth that benefited no one") and idleness, by time lost ("We lost the best years and soon the game would be over for good"), by the reform schools and prisons that some of Debord's companions had spent time in (and here he reproduces the blueprint of a prison). Scattered among the fragments of quotes and splashes of color are a number of photographs of those who were part of the tribe. The pictures are small, not very good, and almost always as cropped as the quotes: the lost children existed, the pictures prove this, but they are remote. In the third part (September 1953) there are allusions to the *"dérive,"* to "psychogeographic" experiments that were to dominate the second lettrist period. These assume the form of fragments of city maps, drawings for houses, and geographic maps—traces of what became the lettrists', and later the situationists', all-important "urban adventure." The last pages of the book are a veritable novel of chivalry, with pictures of castles to reinforce the impression. They confirm that the book was intended to mythologize a group. "Those who recognize themselves as companions in the Search." As if the tribe of Saint-Germain had been aware of the legend they were in the process of manufacturing.

Mémoires is neither a story nor a summary. I have quoted a handful of sentences to demonstrate that the book begins as the story of a bunch of drunks who hung out at Moineau's and ends with the Grail legend. In 1958 Debord was twenty-seven. Some of his friends from the lettrist years were still around or had recently left the area. But already the Saint-Germain-des-Prés of 1952–53 was part of a timeless past, of which *Mémoires* reflects the fragments that escaped the shipwreck. It took five years for the "tribe's" adventures to be transformed into a fragmentary novel of chivalry, a legend that would belong, like any self-respecting legend, to another, incommensurable time, which would constitute a record of sorts about the production of legends.

Saint-Germain was a legend that was *almost* experienced live. Almost, because I don't want to reduce what seems to have been a very intense experience to some retroactive reinterpretation, but to suggest, rather, that the interest in legend appears very early in Debord's work. The man of action he may not yet be first appears in the shadow of a legendary character, someone who projects himself into his own legend. And what is true of *Mémoires* is equally true, somewhat later, of the other books and films that refer back to the golden age of Saint-Germain-des-Prés: *On the Passage of a Few Persons through a Rather Brief Unity of Time, In girum imus nocte, Panegyric.* All these works say the same thing: it was very beautiful. But should we believe this because it was beautiful or because it is expressed so beautifully? The golden age of 1952–53 is impossible to disentangle from the texts and images that describe it, that constitute it after the fact by adding a necessary element of style.

Bernard, Bernard, This Bloom of Youth Will Not Last Forever

"Bernard, Bernard, this bloom of youth will not last forever" appears in *Mémoires.* Debord often quoted this phrase written by Bossuet for Bernard de Clairvaux, the founder and abbot of Clairvaux, a man of action as much as he was a polemicist and poet. Debord's first book is unquestionably melancholic. And the ironic rejection of an autobiographical order whose omnipresence he clearly anticipates reveals something else, and for some just the opposite of what I have described. One can write one's memoirs at twenty-seven so that the life to come escapes the limitations of biography or autobiography, but they can also be written because one has the profound feeling of having finished living, of having already experienced everything that it is possible to experience. The problem with the golden age is that it is golden, and will never return because it is golden. This is myth at the stage of melancholy, or more exactly at its most purely melancholic stage, for it is unclear that we moderns could conceive of myth in any terms other than as loss or as an absolute past (the myth, for us, is that the reality is unquestionably over, and for this reason it will never be anything but a myth).

Debord, the revolutionary, instead of affirming what had to be done or experienced at the moment he founded the SI, published a book that was almost secret, a confidential statement of lived experience, referring only to Saint-Germain-des-Prés in the years 1952–53. *Mémoires* deals only with the years 1952–53, as if nothing had happened between 1954 and 1958, as if nothing had been really experienced, as if life had stopped in 1953. And this is also true of the later cinematic and literary works, in which the Saint-Germain-des-Prés years always play an extremely important, if not exclusive, part. It's as if, when Debord decided to talk about his life, he was only able to talk about that golden age where he had expended so much energy in disappearing, in losing himself, in not being, as if he had never experienced anything other than those months of perdition; as if writing basically meant repeating the legend of his disappearance, as if he was unable to write—or film—other than by reiterating, or reinstating, his voluntary exclusion from the order of the spectacle. Saint-Germain-des-Prés served, for the writer Debord decided not to become, as a primal scene. Nothing, or nearly nothing, took place other than in Saint-Germain-des-Prés, that lost paradise in which it felt so good to lose oneself, where it felt so good to write nothing.

This was true as well of the films that Asger Jorn's financial support helped Debord make shortly after the appearance of *Mémoires,* during the first years of the Situationist International.[1] *On the Passage of a Few Persons through a Rather Brief Unity of Time,* made in 1959, begins with a series of images of building facades in Saint-Germain-des-Prés and was devoted entirely to evoking the memory of the people who had made it their refuge during the brief golden age of 1952–53. The 1959 film is also a history of oblivion and freedom, the same themes that appear in Debord's first two books. "They said that oblivion was their ruling passion. They wanted to reinvent everything each day; to become the masters of their own lives."[2] The lost children were passionate about oblivion; they became free by freeing themselves of their memory and their past. Memory is what makes you subject to the Other, to those who came before you. It forces you to gather to yourself phantoms and ghosts, parents and ancestors, who inhabit you without asking your advice. And they prevent you from belonging completely to yourself, which is why the lost children wanted no part of them: so they could live their own lives and make their time their own. "This group lived on the margins of the economy. It tended toward a role of pure consumption, particularly the free consumption of its own time."[3] The thirst for oblivion and the refusal to work are two sides of the same project for controlling time. Work is alienating, like memory, and it is better to replace both with exploration, or wandering and loss, which are most accurately represented by the figure of the labyrinth. "There was the fatigue and the cold of morning in this much-traversed labyrinth, like an enigma that we had to resolve. It was a trompe l'oeil reality through which we had to discover the potential richness of what was really there."[4]

Were this richness and this reality achieved? The Saint-Germain-des-Prés of the years 1952–53 shines like a golden age, an unforgettable experience, but when it came time to settle accounts, Debord cannot be criticized for gloating: "What should be abolished continues, and we continue to wear away with it. We are engulfed. Separated from each other. The years pass and we haven't changed anything."[5] Was the golden age a failure? Were the lost children magnificent losers, destined to be separated and disappear? There is no simple answer to these questions, which reflect the heart of the paradox of the lost children. It is not so much that they came together in failure or failed by coming together. Rather, their success, that is, their ability to fulfill their desire for absolute freedom, is inseparable from the absolutely ephemeral nature of the realization of such desire. Lost children are driven to oblivion, they have no past, but they also have no future, or, to be more precise, they know that they should expect nothing. "No one counted on the future. It would never be possible to be together later, or anywhere else. There would never be a greater freedom."[6] Perdition, the ability to lose (oneself in) time, is inseparable from the sense of urgency. Everything takes place in the here and now, with the awareness that soon, possibly right away if we delay, it will be too late, and separation and wear will occur. The lost children know what they owe to passage, to fleetingness. They know that their freedom occurs within the time of a suspended break, in which, having nothing to lose, having nothing to look forward to, they willingly take the plunge: "The extreme precariousness of their methods for getting by without working was at the root of this impatience which made excesses necessary and breaks irrevocable."[7]

The intensity of the experience was inseparable from the feeling of imminent disappearance. The truth of the golden age can be found in the shadow of its fleetingness. Once experienced, it was over, or at least destined for oblivion. That is why I spoke earlier of the legend experienced in real time. Experience does not stand on one side and on the other texts and films that would record it after the fact, works of art made to reclaim the lost time. The experience of loss comes unstuck, separates from itself; it can only be apprehended as something that has fallen immediately into the past, that has taken place, that can never recur, not in experience, not in a work of art. It is an experience that escapes repetition and representation, never having been present other than as an intuition of its immediate disappearance. The life lived in Saint-Germain-des-Prés in 1952–53 disqualifies any book, any film that would attempt to grasp it, and those of Debord in particular: "But even if such a film succeeded in being as fundamentally incoherent and unsatisfying as the reality it dealt with, it could never be more than a re-creation—as impoverished and false as this botched tracking shot."[8] More generally, the life disqualifies the art as such; it surpasses the art or at least allows only an art devoid of harboring any illusions about its redemptive capacity. *On the Passage of a Few Persons through a Rather Brief Unity of Time* on several occasions evokes the need to abandon literature, speaks of the "decay of art."[9] Literary or cinematic representations fail to account for absolute freedom, carried away with or by its own fleetingness, ultimately never having been present enough— or too present—to be seized or repeated. Art is short-circuited by the lost children, who do not want to be "repeated," who do all they can—which is to say, nothing ("Never work!")—not to return. On the other hand, this short-circuiting is their doing alone. For art to decay, for it to be really a thing of the past, you have to know how to lose yourself—a warning to the Scandinavian, Italian, and, later, German artists who subscribed to the ideas of the Situationist International. An assessment can also be a warning, especially when it denounces its own inability to correctly account for what has been experienced.

There is considerable melancholy in *On the Passage of a Few Persons through a Rather Brief Unity of Time*. The film's title refers, very specifically, to the feeling of fleetingness that is so integral to a sense of melancholy about the world. This same melancholy is palpable in Debord's next film, *Critique of Separation*, made in 1961, even though Debord's objective here is more theoretical. The entire film is a critique of "separation." From beginning to end, it says only and insistently that something has been lost, a separation has taken place. More concretely, it is now the social order that imposes the loss or lack of authentic communication upon us: "What communication have we desired, or experienced, or only simulated? What real project has been lost?"[10] Even though he didn't like Rousseau (too introspective, too exhibitionist, and too plaintive for his taste), there are Rousseauian accents in the Debord who regrets the disappearance of authentic communication. With this difference, however: that this disappearance is not situated, as it is in Rousseau, in some timeless and mythical past, but with precision. The golden age is once more the era of Saint-Germain-des-Prés, which is evoked as an exceptional moment in time during which another way of life may have been—briefly—possible: "And only a few encounters were like signals emanating from a more intense life, a life that has not really been found."[11]

It's possible that the "more intense life" the lost children sought was not found, or found only for a moment, before disappearing, before being lost to the world of oblivion. "How quickly we have lived," Debord added, as if his life were over, as if it had been extinguished along with the adventures of the lost children.[12] "Fair companions, adventure is dead," and the time of *Mémoires* began.[13] The children would not be back for further adventures or to play their role in the world of literary or cinematic appearances: "The sectors of a city are to some extent decipherable. But the personal meaning they have had for us is incommunicable, as is the secrecy of private life in general, regarding which we possess nothing but pitiful documents."[14] Fair companions, adventure is dead. It happened, once, between 1952 and 1953. It disappeared, is incommunicable, unrepresentable, definitively clandestine. Debord here provides one of the most explicit indications of the role played by the large number of images of places that "illustrate" some of his books and are found in all of his films: real places, deserted for the most part, as well as maps of cities, aerial views. These show the places where something had been experienced, but only to the extent that there is something visible or "legible" (a map is made to be read, not lived). They are images from which all sense of experience is missing, which allow us to glimpse the *incommunicability* of experience. Their function, like that of Debord's writing in general, is less to represent life, and even less to transmit it, than simply to evoke it, to make it more desirable and at the same time unreachable, absent, achievable only on condition of once and for all stepping outside art. My apologies to the "situationist" artists who joined Debord after 1958 and whose principal revolutionary vocation seems to have been to get thrown out of the group as quickly as possible: in 1958, the tribe was no longer what it had been and there were very few individuals who would continue to have time to lose—or the time to lose themselves in.[15]

It wasn't until 1978 and the appearance of *In girum imus nocte et consumimur igni* that the Situationist International became a part of legend. But the legend was created furtively, in a minor mode. It could be summarized in one or two pages: "In the years that followed, people from twenty countries entered into this obscure conspiracy of limitless demands. How many hurried journeys! How many long disputes! How many clandestine meetings in all the ports of Europe!"[16] Clearly, this is no match for the twenty or so pages the script devotes to the years of the "lost children." Like history, the golden age never repeats itself; it happened once and the impression remains that the further we get from it, the more substantial it becomes. In any event, Debord had never, until *In girum imus nocte et consumimur igni*, spoken of it as richly, in as much detail, or as lyrically, clearly assigning it a formative role.

Once again this new version of his autobiography opens, as it should, when he was twenty years old and, here as well, the following periods are evoked only in passing. Debord was born at twenty, and thirty years later it is still Debord in his twenties who appears on screen. This time he is accompanied by "the most ill-famed of companions"[17] in a Paris that never completely slept, where "a bacchanal might shift from one neighborhood to another, then to another and yet another," a city in which lived "a people who were not content to subsist on images." Rapid progress was made in melancholy urbanism. The Paris of the 1950s was viscerally allergic to the reign of the future spectacle, and no one would be surprised to learn that it has disappeared: "I shall limit myself to a few words to announce that, whatever others may say about it, Paris no longer exists." It is in this now lost Paris that "the negative held court," loss upon loss, lost places for specialists in loss, whose legendary exploits the remainder of the film once more evokes, the members of a secret society, the modern Knights of the Round Table: "Those who had gathered in this neighborhood seemed to have publicly and from the very beginning adopted as their sole principle of action the secret that the Old Man of the Mountain was said to divulge only on his deathbed to the most loyal lieutenant among his fanatical followers: 'Nothing is true, everything is permitted.'"

In 1978, the golden age was Saint-Germain-des-Prés. The version presented in *In girum imus nocte* became even more of a legend with the passage of time and as the situationist political project, whose films from 1959 to 1961 flow into one another, also disappeared, giving way to a lexicon of criminality, which was certainly more attractive as a legend than that of politics. "Although the select population of this momentary capital of disturbances included a certain number of thieves and occasionally a few murderers, our life was primarily characterized by a prodigious inactivity; and of all the crimes and offenses denounced there by the authorities, it was this that was sensed as the most threatening." The more time passed, the more the lost children retroactively drifted toward the criminal elements in society, and the purer the sense of loss, detached from any project, especially political. The same movement would continue later with *Panegyric* (1989) and it explains the role assumed in *In girum imus nocte* by the evocation of alcohol, drugs, suicide, madness (Ivan Chtcheglov), death, and delinquency (especially as represented by the emblematic figure of Éliane Papaï).

In girum imus nocte radicalizes, criminalizes, and mythifies, but the golden age remains the same. Debord again insists on the inaugural dimension of the Saint-Germain-des-Prés years, of their initiatory value, or, more literally, on the impossibility of return. Once we have begun to lose ourselves in the stony labyrinths of the old capital cities, we can never escape, we can only return to our loss. "It was the best possible labyrinth for ensnaring visitors. Those who lingered there for two or three days never left again, at least not until it had ceased to exist; but by then the majority had already seen the end of their none too numerous years. No one left those few streets and tables where the 'culmination of time' had been discovered."[18] Then Debord adds the following words: "The heat and chills of such a time never leave you. You have to discover how to live the days ahead in a manner worthy of such a fine beginning. You want to prolong that first experience of illegality."[19] How can you return to a place that has disappeared; how can you return to a place in which you disappeared? Saint-Germain-des-Prés is described here as a *point of no return,* and it is at this point that Debord has become what he is and what he will always be: "As for myself, I have never regretted anything I have done; and being as I am, I must confess that I remain completely incapable of imagining how I could have done anything differently."[20] The same idea occurs in the same terms in *Panegyric*: "Between Rue du Four and Rue de Buci, where our youth was so completely lost, as a few glasses were drunk, we could feel certain that we would never do anything better."[21]

All this took place between the years 1952 and 1953, the yardstick against which all future experiences were measured. At best these were no more than repetitions of that earlier period. This was especially true of the period Debord spent in Florence, in 1972. In *In girum imus nocte,* Debord wrote (or said) the following about the city, while on the screen there appears an image of Alice Becker-Ho (his second wife) and a young woman known as Céleste embracing, followed by a shot of Céleste naked:[22] "This is why I spent those years living in a country where I was little known. The spatial arrangement of one of the best cities that ever was, and the company of certain persons, and what we did with our time—all this formed a scene much like the happiest revels of my youth."[23] Florence 1972, where the golden age was repeated: free love, Debord and his companion fell in love with the same, beautiful women. Conversations were free-ranging and endless. The wine flowed in an endless stream, the clandestine authenticity of the Saint-Germain-des-Prés years of 1951–53 returned, a period when Paris was alive and not made of images. Their time was spent in talking, loving, and drinking, just like before, but the risks were different—the police and secret service were never very far away, the telephones were bugged. There were a number of people who, according to *Panegyric,* ended up dead or in jail because they "stayed too long at the revels of Florence."[24] In Italy, these were the dangerous years of terrorist attacks, something to which Debord never succumbed, and government repression, which he was always lucid enough and prudent enough to escape (although he was forced to leave Florence on a moment's notice). The only thing missing to complete the picture (or legend) was Villon, but Dante and Machiavelli served equally well as replacements. They had the advantage of knowledge of the terrain, they had already established their pedigree by being banished, and there was nothing like a good banishment to create a golden age, however lost: "I see again 'the banks of the Arno, full of farewells.' And I too, like so many others, have been banished from Florence."[25] Like Paris in 1952, Debord's Florentine adventure lasted only a short period of time and was filled with farewells, which only added to the charm. Sometimes, the golden age can be replayed, but only for those who have first lived through it.

The adventure was over. You can lose yourself only once, and never as completely as the first time (after Florence, there was Seville, and other places). From *Mémoires* to *Panegyric*, Debord's work is crisscrossed by a sense of mourning for Saint-Germain-des-Prés, by regret for an incandescent and incomparable experience. The unquestionable melancholy of those books and films treats the years 1952–53 as a kind of empty center to which one could return indefinitely, a gesture that is both evocation and revocation. It was as if everything that had been experienced had to be given a price by mirroring it, by revealing it, but also by stubbornly concealing it from indiscreet observers, by entombing it within a kind of crypt to which no one would have access. *Allusion, I know, suggestion*: my experience is my business, protects me from you; I am what I have concealed from you; I am (in) my crypt. The image of the crypt is used intentionally, to suggest more clearly the melancholic dimension of *Mémoires*—not only the book of that title, but all of Debord's autobiographical texts and films, the entire body of his work of *remembering*. To some extent, his work begins as an interminable act of mourning, one that is never over, never completed (Freud was careful to distinguish between mourning and melancholy). And what was experienced in Saint-Germain-des-Prés appears, from this perspective, inseparable from a more general feeling of loss, of the ephemeral, of the passage of time, which has also led some commentators to insist on the baroque dimension of Debord's work.[26]

The "Bernard, Bernard, this bloom of youth will not last forever," quoted in *Mémoires*, is, in this sense, a kind of slogan (which will reappear later in his other written works). It is worth noting that, when he was writing for the first time, Debord and Michèle Bernstein shared a small apartment in the Impasse de Clairvaux (named after Bernard de Clairvaux), at the end of Rue Saint-Martin. Thus, he made use of an act of *détournement* for his own funeral elegy, for the remembrance of the man he will no longer be, or, in any event, as an evocation of a *Vergänglichkeit* that is suggested at a number of points in his first book: "Time passes but does not yet flee," "the demands of a past that can only live again in memory, or in 'repetition,' where, no matter what we do, it will decay," "we have lost the best years, soon the game will be over forever," "as time passed," "we lived so quickly," and so on. We should also reconsider, from this point of view, the line "I don't think we will ever see one another again" in the script of *Howls for Sade*. The same phrase is repeated in *Mémoires* and adds, retrospectively, to this first film an equally melancholic dimension. *Howls for Sade* was already a way of mourning, for both the world and oneself: silence and a black screen.

The same melancholy accent is found in Debord's later films. It can be found in the lines "We continue to wear away with it. We are engulfed. Separated from each other. The years pass and we haven't changed anything," which appear in *On the Passage of a Few Persons through a Rather Brief Unity of Time*. The *Critique of Separation* explicitly ties the figure of the "lost children" to the experience of time flowing or escaping.[27] But it is in *In girum imus nocte* that the theme of melancholy is given its greatest amplitude, with its evocation of Paris before it capitulated to the spectacle and the ensuing falsification, a Paris not yet rotten with pollution, concrete, and asbestos, which concludes with "Paris no longer exists."[28] And Debord continues, this time with a reference to Heraclitus, pointing out that what was possible to experience in Paris before the fall is no more: "There was at that time on the Left Bank of the river—you cannot enter the same river twice, nor twice touch the same perishable substance—a neighborhood where the negative held court."[29] The relation to time passing is made here in the image of the river that can't be stepped in twice. That is why images of rivers (especially the Seine, where his ashes were scattered) and more generally water (the canals of Venice, which were filmed in long traveling shots) occur so often in *In girum imus nocte*. Bodies of water, movement over water, the passage of and in time, these are things to which we cannot return and constitute something like the fundamental rhythm of Debord's final film. Time is water: "The sensation of the passing of time has always been vivid for me, and I have been attracted by it just as others are allured by dizzying heights or by water."[30] Further on, the reference to melancholy is made explicit through the appropriation of the first two verses of the *Divine Comedy* and a quatrain from Omar Khayyám: "Midway on the journey of real life we found ourselves surrounded by a somber melancholy, reflected by so much sad banter in the cafés of lost youth. To speak more accurately and without allusions—'Tis all a checkerboard of nights and days, where Destiny with men for pieces plays: hither and thither moves and checks and slays, and one by one back in the closet lays.'"[31] In the wake of the chess board of Being and the box of Nothingness, we find Bernard of Clairvaux, invited by Bossuet to mourn the world: "Bernard, what do you want from the world? Do you see there anything that can satisfy you?"[32] The first two lines of *Panegyric* also evoke a baroque world, one that is unstable, rent by division and destruction, "All my life I have seen only troubled times, extreme divisions in society, and immense destruction."[33]

But was Debord only grieving for the years in Saint-Germain-des-Prés? We still need to explain, or at least try to understand, why it didn't pass, why the loss remained. Isn't it possible that Debord's melancholy has older and deeper roots? We have to assume this if we intend to take the complex notion of melancholy seriously, like Freud, who differentiates it from "normal" mourning in that the object of melancholy grief is unconscious. This is the reason for its longevity, its failure to dissipate. The loss associated with melancholy is impossible to accept, even if—or because—the real object has been forgotten. What was it, before the paradise of Saint-Germain-des-Prés, that Debord could not accept and would not reveal? What was the impossible loss for which he substituted the now lost paradise of the years 1952–53? Those years are the effect of an experience of loss and separation. What was it that made Debord decide to become, in a sense for his entire life, a lost child? For he responded to that initial impossible grief by methodically organizing his loss. Whatever the ultimate resolution of these questions may be, we can at least be more certain that this sense of loss was there from the outset in Debord's life and work. All else followed from that initial melancholia; the rest, especially Saint-Germain-des-Prés, would serve as the privileged figure, pampered and glorious, of loss, the shadow's visible face.

We will never be privy to the childhood or background of those lost children, for they have remained silent, have buried it deep within their selves. "What communication have we desired, or experienced, or only simulated? What real project has been lost?" a voice asks at the beginning of *Critique of Separation*.[34] Shortly after, the script continues with the following words, spoken against a background of scenes of Paris: "After all the empty time, all the lost movements, there remain these endlessly traversed postcard landscapes; this distance organized between each and everyone. Childhood? Why, it's right here—we have never emerged from it."[35] "We have never emerged from it"—the critique of separation as a regret for a lost childhood. The lost children are those who refuse to lose their childhood, who return to it, who have never left it. To my knowledge this is the only time that an avowal or regret of this nature occurs in Debord's work, the only time we see exposed a small strip of the wall of the crypt, ordinarily so lavishly covered with the excesses of the negative court of Saint-Germain-des-Prés.[36] Saint-Germain-des-Prés was not the source of the melancholy, though. On the contrary, the years 1952–53 emerge from that melancholy, they are the result.

Debord's life in general, like his desire for revolution, was always a *desire for oblivion*. Nothing made more sense than revolution, the abolition of the past, a tabula rasa. And nothing seemed easier or more natural than the alliance with a proletariat that was assumed to have nothing to lose, not even memory. This was explicitly formulated in the first issue of *Internationale situationniste*: "The situationists will put themselves at the service of oblivion. The only force they can expect something from is the proletariat, theoretically without a past, required to continuously reinvent everything, about whom Marx said that it is 'revolutionary or it is nothing.'"[37] Memory was not the strong point of the lost children: "They said that oblivion was their ruling passion."[38] Loss and adventure were made possible by mourning the world, which was also a way to forget the world, make a clean sweep of it all. The radicalization of the old avant-garde program to put an end to art found new forms of justification in this context. Attempted by lettrism in 1952, then by the Situationist International, the need for the abolition of memory became the new rallying cry. Debord emphasized this in a passage from *Critique of Separation*: "It is necessary to destroy memory in art. To undermine the conventions of its communication. To demoralize its fans. What a task! As in a blurry drunken vision, the memory and language of the film fade out simultaneously."[39]

Alcohol as an avant-garde technique, a way to dissolve memory and art. We drink to forget, and it is no accident that in *Panegyric* Debord spends considerable time describing his talent as a drinker, which he contrasts with his parsimony as a writer: "Among the small number of things that I have liked and known how to do well, what I have assuredly known how to do best is drink. Although I have read a lot, I have drunk even more. I have written much less than most people who write, but I have drunk much more than most people who drink. I can count myself among those of whom Baltasar Gracián, thinking about an elite discernible only among the Germans—but here he was quite unjust to the detriment of the French, as I think I have shown—could say, 'There are those who got drunk only once, but that once lasted them a lifetime.'"[40] While drunkenness promotes forgetfulness, it also reinforces the sensation of the passage of time: "At first, like everyone, I appreciated the effect of mild drunkenness; then very soon I grew to like what lies beyond violent drunkenness, once that stage is past: a terrible and magnificent peace, the true taste of the passage of time."[41] Memory is time that does not pass, it is time that has been held back or restrained.

Debord drank a great deal and wrote relatively little, and it is reasonable to claim that what he wrote or filmed reflects what might be called an alcoholic style. He struggled to forget, devoted himself to the passage of time. There was no search for lost time in Debord's work, no ghosts or specters. His work has silenced them, it swallowed them up and remained silent about them. That is why its "literary" dimension is not self-evident and why it was said that he was not a writer, even that he harbored a certain resistance to literature.[42] Of course, this doesn't mean very much, aside from the fact that he was in very good company (it is difficult, since Baudelaire, to find an important work of literature that does not participate in the desire to abolish literature). And yet, to view Debord purely and simply as a writer, even a great writer, can be problematic. To become a writer, to be recognized as a writer, does not seem to have been his intention, certainly not explicitly. Perhaps in his melancholy, in his passion for loss, there is something that distances him from writing, if it is true that writing is always, in one way or another, a space in which we can have our say. Debord represents the desire for oblivion and silence, for unending grief—words that cannot be spoken. And that is why we need to understand his writing as the archive of his disappearance, including the classicism that is sometimes said to characterize his work.

My Child, My Sister . . .

Among the manifold speculations concerning Debord's life, the recent spate of rumors concerning his love life should come as no surprise. Their lack of substance is generally proportional to their antipathy. The contradictory claims of Frédéric Schiffter and Jean-Marie Apostolidès play an important part in this debate. The first devoted the end of his *Guy Debord l'atrabilaire* to demonstrating that Debord's primary fault was to have been not a libertine but a remonstrative libertarian, and consequently incapable of appreciating the many charms of libertinage.[1] Apostolidès, in his *Portrait de Guy-Ernest en jeune libertin,* decided to interpret the remake of *Dangerous Liaisons* published in 1960 by Michèle Bernstein as *Tous les chevaux du roi* as autobiography.[2] The challenge was to show that Debord was never up to the libertarian morality espoused by the situationists and to portray him as the vulgar Valmont, who ends up coming to terms with Bernstein-Merteuil behind the back of Cécile, whom he loved along with Madame de Tourvel.[3] The subtlety of the arguments is perplexing. Since there is no sign of any enthusiasm for a libertarian morality in Debord's work (is it possible that Schiffter has managed to confuse Debord with Vaneigem?), isn't it possible that at least on an unconscious level, Debord must be a libertine? But since the signs of libertinage are hardly more numerous, it is just as reasonable to conclude that Debord was a libertarian—as if not being one was sufficient justification for being the other.

Neither author makes any reference to love; and with good reason, for it is not something one would associate with the atrabilious libertarian or the libertine. This is even more unfortunate because it seems to have been important to Debord, who fails as both libertine and libertarian, as even a cursory reading of his autobiographical work will show. He was said to be a calculating seducer or a choleric apostle of permissiveness, but this would be to ignore everything reflected in his actions, his words, and his films: that Debord loved a great deal, that he loved love, that from beginning to end he also chose love to "impassion his life" (as suggested by one of the first slogans of the Lettrist International). It was a particularly judicious choice. For of what use was love if not to add passion to life? And what better way to add passion to life than through love?

Is love possible when someone is dedicated to the passage of time, when the dominant sentiment is one of *Vergänglichkeit*? Is love possible when someone is surrounded by a "dark melancholy" that is generally associated with disaffection rather than passion? Certainly, at least to judge by Debord, who seems to have often used his melancholy to remain within the nexus of passion or at least along its cutting edge. If he was often in love, it was through intuition or out of awareness of the ephemeral nature of passion, his interest in its transience. He decided to add passion to his life and saw love as giving him the ability to turn his passion into an absolute—one that must inevitably dissipate—whose disappearance we sometimes anticipate so that it remains the absolute it once was. He was said to have been a man who had many quarrels and never sought reconciliation, as if a single mistake (a single act of "baseness," to use his words) were enough to condemn someone: the absolute of passion cannot be repaired, it is not compatible with compromise, it is blind to the reason of the other, to the relative, the relational, in which sense it is also more immoral and scandalous than the efforts of the most energetic libertine. The feeling of time's passage is the sentiment of the tragically transient nature of passion, whose intensity is the measure of its imminent demise. That is why Debord precipitated so many quarrels, for apparently futile reasons, reasons that were incomprehensible and even unfair: to avoid waiting too long, to avoid injury to himself, to avoid acknowledging his disappearance. It was this precipitation that resulted in his being accused of libertinage—quite independently of the novels by his first wife—whereas obviously there is nothing in his work or character that would lead to such a conclusion. "To conquer is our destiny," says the libertine. But this is certainly not the type of conquest Debord dreamed of, any more than the emotional emptiness it implies—not everyone is condemned to seduce only through deception. On the contrary, everything suggests that his desires served his passion and that it was passion he sought through his many affairs, and that in his own way he was extremely loyal, faithful to his passion, faithful to love.

Debord had numerous affairs. He was in love with love more than with his female conquests, and never experienced the need to discuss the physical dimension of love, dreaming of crimes other than those of the libertine. Eroticism is almost completely absent from his books (somewhat less so in his films). Sexuality doesn't seem to have presented any special problems for him, it aroused neither fascination nor guilt. He was faithful to love and to the women he loved, whom he often remained close to for years or, as he might have said, as long as was necessary. Michèle Bernstein was his wife for more than ten years, and for nearly the last thirty years of his life, he never lived far from Alice Becker-Ho, his second wife.[4] During both marriages he had several affairs, none of which resembled the traditional picture of clandestine adultery; not only was he open about his extramarital relationships, his spouses were often actively complicit in them. If it weren't for the certainty—which Schiffter's work quickly helped to establish—that he was a bilious scold, we would be tempted to believe that he was even happy in love. Or at least that it always represented for him, more than anything else, the possibility of discovering, or rediscovering, this most authentic form of communication, which was also current practice among those intent specifically on giving life a sense of emotional intensity. His published correspondence contains very few letters to the women he loved. But those that exist (most of them are addressed to Michèle Mochot-Bréhat) leave no room for doubt: their tone is radically different, they are the only letters in which Debord talks about himself, where he confides in someone else, discusses his uncertainties or even his pain (the result of heavy drinking). They are the only letters in which he asks for something from someone after a brief avowal: "I'm afraid of sleeping alone."[5]

In his own way, Debord was faithful to the women—at least some of them—who passed through his life, faithful to their memory. His books and films are filled with allusions to his most serious affairs, the women who counted in his life. A separation did not mean rejection. On the contrary, it helped precipitate the beauty of the absolute in the past so that it would never lose its luster. Imagine Don Juan recalling his first love. Debord certainly remembered Éliane Papaï, a young woman of Spanish-Hungarian background. She is beautiful in the photographs of her that still remain, and was part of the "tribe." She had a short, intense affair with Debord before marrying Jean-Michel Mension (who married her to avoid her having to return to reform school), then Jean-Louis Brau, one of Debord's former companions in the Lettrist International. Éliane Papaï's portrait, uncaptioned, is the first image of a woman in volume 2 of *Panegyric*, in the section devoted to Debord's years spent in Saint-Germain-des-Prés. The same picture appears, also untitled, ten years earlier in *In girum imus nocte*, with the following comment: "She who was the most beautiful that year," and in a voice-over he adds the following comment: "She vanishes, fleeing like a ghost which, while it remained with us, leaves nothing but disquietude in its wake."[6] Éliane Papaï was a disquieting presence. She jumped the wall of her reform school at night to join Debord. "Guy, is it that we enjoy nothing?—I don't think so." They could lose themselves in their love at night. It was as if their love vanished at dawn, fled daybreak, when Debord advised Éliane to return before her absence was noticed, and she reproached him for talking to her like her father. It was already over—a single shadow, a single dawn was all it took for the disquiet to return. And this may be the reason why Éliane Papaï always remained the symbol of his passion during the Saint-Germain-des-Prés years, something akin to the lost child's first love, or at least the first he chose to remember.

His last affair, some thirty years later, in which Alice Becker-Ho participated, involved a young Spanish woman, Tony Lopez Pintor, who appears in two photographs accompanied by a quote from Cervantes in *Panegyric*, volume 2. In volume 1 she is described as follows: "The young Musset drew attention to himself long ago for his thoughtless question: 'In Barcelona, did you see / an Andalusian with sun-bronzed breasts?' Well, yes! I've had to say ever since 1980. I had my share—and perhaps a very large share—in the extravagances of Spain. But it was in another country that that irremediable princess, with her wild beauty and that voice, appeared. 'Mira cómo vengo yo,' went the rather accurate words of the song she sang. That day we listened no more. I loved that Andalusian for a long time. How long? 'A time commensurate with our vain and paltry span,' as Pascal says."[7] Debord and Alice Becker-Ho met Tony Lopez Pintor at the end of 1978 in Geneva, and both of them fell in love with her. The three of them saw one another for several years, and lived together in Champot, in Auvergne, but also in Spain. And along with Tony, they fell in love with Spain, which became for Debord and Alice Becker-Ho an adopted homeland, a country of unrestrained passion, intransigent and destructive, where Tony grew sick and died a few years later. It was also a land where poetry was rediscovered. You couldn't have one without the other. Debord and Alice Becker-Ho began speaking Spanish, almost as if it were their native language. The circumstances give the Pascal quotation a very precise meaning, suggesting mourning, something irreversible. It may also be that Tony Lopez Pintor's death transformed her into the woman who is always approaching: *Mira cómo vengo yo*. In any event, there is no sense of sadness, no grief in these lines, which an extremely serene Debord devotes to the woman who seems to have been the last true love of his life.

Debord never lived alone. Throughout his life he always had long-term relationships and others in which he could experience the transience of passion. For years he experienced what might be called a differentiated form of polygamy—this differentiation being the condition needed to obtain the consent of his partners and spouses, who experienced this transparency as the condition of their own freedom, as if passion could only endure when shared in this way. What if Debord had never been a libertine or a libertarian, but had simply been free? Is this so difficult to accept? Would it be so unexpected in a man who, throughout his life, never wavered about his freedom, which had to be absolute, a man who knew how to live according to his desires, who was able to transform his life into a series of endless celebrations in Saint-Germain-des-Prés and Florence? These are evoked in *In girum imus nocte,* where they are said to resemble "the happiest revels of [his] youth."[8] Echoing this passage in the film is the voice of

Alice Becker-Ho, who in 1998 published a book of poems where she speaks of this, the sense of mourning as well as the evocation of a love that has vanished:[9]

> *It Was Childhood*
> One and the other
> As if it were self-evident
> Were certain of this
> Their lives would be short
> Disillusioned
> They were mistaken
>
> The women
> were willing
> Gave of themselves freely
> Seduced
> Submissive
> The men made them their mistresses
>
> It was childhood
>
> The game continued
> for a long time
> In conquered territory
> Then
> To celebrate the victory
> Of the two terrible Black pieces
> Handsome prince
> The king nodded
> And the party ended.

"It was childhood." The disillusioned, lost children indulged in their perverse games to remain children, to avoid growing old, knowing that life is short, as short as our passions. The poem seems to evoke the celebrations, the good times Debord and his companion experienced. Nearly all the women whose pictures appear in Debord's books and films are young, beautiful, androgynous, childlike. There is no question that Debord liked very young women, even girls, whom he called *"voyelles,"* androgynous women, and women who liked other women. Maybe the charms of "my child, my sister," the charms of sexual ambiguity, are the same. In any case, they reflect that youthful bloom that will not last forever, and they are all beautiful because they have become part of memory and legend.

No Turning Back

Of the passions Debord chose to recall, the majority of them are what might be termed "exotic." They are strongly associated with the foreign, a love of displacement and the displaced, which is not surprising for a man with his background. His life centered on discovery, transience, and travel, and travel brought with it a sense of excitement. This is certainly true of the years in Saint-Germain-des-Prés, described in *In girum imus nocte* as "the best possible labyrinth for ensnaring visitors."[1] It was true somewhat later during the situationist adventure, briefly mentioned in the same film. That Debord chose to remember in this context that the members of the Situationist International were indefatigable travelers is not without relevance: "How many clandestine meetings in all the ports of Europe"?[2] Meetings and adventures characterized by movement, by streets and ports, which is why they lasted only as long as they had to and no longer. The Situationist International was a travel agency. And travel was a mechanism for melancholy, it strengthened the feeling of transience.

Debord loved a great deal and traveled a great deal. But it was especially in the aftershock of May 1968 that his life became indistinguishable from that of a traveler and travel clearly became the vector of his melancholy and the sign of exile. He desired the foreign (and foreign women); he chose the foreign over the false appearance of identity; he sought recognition only in the foreign, and in the end became a foreigner himself, an exile.

Exile was what forced him to leave Paris. He had every reason to do so. There was government repression against those suspected of having "caused" May 1968. The situationists were under surveillance, as were most groups on the far left (but, unlike them, the SI was never banned, which proves that it must be distinguished, like water from fire, from the far left). Debord, whose lack of interest in playing the martyr had always made him lucid and cautious in politics, spent some time in Belgium, as well as in the French countryside, where an amnesty granted to the ringleaders of the May events saved him from arrest at the last moment. But that wasn't the only reason. Paris had undergone a series of transformations. "Paris no longer exists,"[3] or at least the Paris that Debord had loved: the Paris of small cafés open round the clock, the conversations lasting until dawn, the aimless walking.[4] The Paris of old had been replaced by the modern Paris we now know, emptied of its inhabitants, given over to cars, to merchandise, disfigured by concrete, systematically polluted, and awash in industrial food products that had been imposed on a helpless population ever since the destruction of Les Halles.

There were other reasons as well. The events of May 1968 were themselves affected—especially as portrayed in *In girum imus nocte*—by a sense of fatality that made it impossible to return to an idyllic past. The city had been the theater of war and had to be abandoned: "We would have to leave it, but not without having made an attempt to seize it by brute force."[5] They had to leave because the assault had failed, because the battle had been lost. Ten years after the events, May 1968 meant having to leave Paris. It meant exile, separations made irreparable because of the violence of the conflict, the war that forced everyone to choose sides: "Other eras had their own great conflicts, conflicts which they did not choose but which nevertheless forced people to choose which side they were on. Such conflicts dominate whole generations, founding or destroying empires and their cultures. The mission is to take Troy—or to defend it. There is a certain resemblance among these moments when people are on the verge of separating into opposing camps, never to see each other again. . . . It's a beautiful moment when an assault against the world order is set in motion. From its almost imperceptible beginning you already know that, whatever happens, very soon nothing will ever again be the same as it was."[6]

Nothing will be the same as before, nothing will return. May 1968, which had been described in the last issue of *Internationale situationniste* (September 1969) as a time of real dialogue and rediscovered sense of community, had evolved after ten years into May 1968 as the principle of separation.[7] May 1968 now meant "we will never see one another again"—to quote *Howls for Sade* (once again Debord's ideas are consistent with their expression). Later in *In girum imus nocte,* Debord refers to May 1968 as a moment of "splendid dispersion," after which there could be no reconciliation, no going back. And Debord effectively did nothing to return or to become visible. Instead, he chose to escape all forms of reintegration, co-optation, or recognition, and lived a more obscure existence. His life became more clandestine, he energetically cultivated his rejection of appearances in all their forms, appearances that were cherished at the time by other intellectuals, always ready to take off at the slightest rumble from the Renault plant in Billancourt: "After this splendid dispersal, I realized that I had to quickly conceal myself from a fame that threatened to become far too conspicuous. It is well known that this society signs a sort of peace treaty with its most outspoken enemies by granting them a place in its spectacle. I am, in fact, the only present-day individual with any negative or underground notoriety whom it has not managed to get to appear on that stage of renunciation."[8]

If we are to believe *In girum imus nocte,* the most complete version of Debord's autobiography, repression was not the reason he left. It seems that he left not to escape the police or even a Paris that no longer existed, but for his image, his newfound glory. Was he pursued by the police or by pro-situationists? Both probably, but the fact that he refers only to the second is not without significance. His exile appears to have been voluntary. It was based on his great need for clandestinity—it was almost a question of taste. Disappear is what Debord did best; it was a practice that in his case was raised to a fine art: "I have long striven to maintain an obscure and elusive existence."[9] The events of May 1968 would therefore have been only a step and at the same time the catalyst of what had always been an experience of disappearance, of separation, and this would continue to be at the center if not of everything Debord experienced, at least of everything he chose to make visible during the last years of his life.

To disappear, lose himself, go unrecognized, wander wherever space allowed, the way he did when he was young—this was the meaning of his exile in Florence, where Debord and Alice Becker-Ho rented an apartment from 1972 to 1975. In the Italy of the seventies, with its betrayals and confusions between revolutionaries and terrorists, the disappearances of Saint-Germain-des-Prés were replayed, practically for the last time. Florence— the charm of exile, meetings between strangers, good-byes spoken with the understanding that something was about to end: "I see her again, she who was like a stranger in her own town. ('Each of us is a citizen of the one true city; but in your meaning, I am one who passed my earthly exile in Italy.')"[10] It had been necessary to leave Paris, then Florence, then other cities and other countries; this was done to escape repression, of course, but also to escape visibility (for Debord there is a point where the two are identical).

After May 1968, after Belgium, the French countryside, and Italy, Debord continued to live abroad: Seville during the early eighties, where he also had an apartment and which was the last symbol of impassioned exile—one that was intimately associated with Tony Lopez Pintor—Arles, where he lived until 1987, attracted by the charm of its old city and because it was a kind of invitation to the voyage, equidistant from Paris, Spain, and Italy, where he continued to spend time (during his last years, Debord and Alice Becker-Ho spent a great deal of time in Venice, the sumptuous capital of melancholy, a city of the passage of time and water, which was already a central element in *In girum imus nocte*). He also lived in Champot, a village lost in the mountains of Auvergne, where Debord bought a house. In the early eighties there was a time when Debord had three homes (Seville, Arles, Champot), consistent with his refusal of an official residence, and also with his preference for mobility. Toward the end of his life he spent more and more time in Paris, but he did so because the reign of the "integrated" spectacular now dominated the entire planet. It rotted the surface of the world and there was no place where it would be possible to escape. Paris was no longer Paris, Florence no longer Florence, Seville no longer Seville, and Lisbon, disappointingly, had never been Lisbon. In any event, it was less a return to Paris than the transition from an exile in space to an exile in time. The Paris once loved was in ruins, and everything else as well. Once again it was time to think of Andromache: "Much later, when the flood of destruction, pollution, and falsification had conquered the whole surface of the planet, as well as pouring down nearly to its very depths, I could return to the ruins that remain of Paris, since by then nothing better was left elsewhere. No exile is possible in a unified world."[11]

The curse—or triumph—of the unified spectacle is that it wipes out any possibility of exile. It is the reign of generalized visibility, of the impossibility of disappearance. All cities are now equivalent because they have all been destroyed, emptied of the possibility of living an authentic existence, or, for that matter, a clandestine one. They have become shadowless sets without any secret passages; they deprive the melancholy lost children of the environment needed for their glorious perdition. Unable to find a place for himself, no longer able to lose himself, because everything now had its assigned place, including loss, there was nothing left for Debord to do but decree the disappearance of the world ("Paris no longer exists"). Rather, Debord acknowledged the disappearance of the urban world, the only one that ever really counted for him, the only one in which it was possible to wander and, on occasion, start a revolution.

Significantly, the chapter in *Panegyric* where Debord writes of the disappearance of Paris, his travels, and his exiles ends with a reference to Champot, where, until the end of his life, he would spend an increasing amount of time. Grief over the community, grief over the revolution: "I have even stayed in an inaccessible house surrounded by woods, far from any village, in an extremely barren, exhausted mountainous region, deep in a deserted Auvergne."[12] Even more inaccessible, even more clandestine: after the cities had become mere scenery, Debord chose a region of snow, wind, lightning, storms, and cool air. Parties took place under the stars and solitude could be found in the shadow of Alice Becker-Ho: "In regard to someone who was, as essentially and continually as I, a man of streets and cities—one will thus appreciate the degree to which my preferences do not overly distort my judgments—it should be pointed out that the charm and harmony of these few seasons of grandiose isolation did not escape me. It was a pleasing and impressive solitude. But to tell the truth, I was not alone: I was with Alice."[13]

Perhaps I should add, to better assess the symbolic nature of a story about exile that concludes in the snow of a barren mountainside, that the solitude in question was so serene because it was not only shared with his longtime companion, but the celebrations continued as they did before and there were many friends around. The laws of hospitality, which were so important to Debord and which are remembered by those who benefited from them, were observed to the end, everywhere. It is easy to see how a place like Champot could be considered a place of exile, but this exile was as impassioned and creative as it had been in other places, free of discouragement and bitterness. As it is evoked in *Panegyric*, it serves to represent what was already prefigured in the final sentences of *In girum imus nocte*: "for me there will be no turning back and no reconciliation. No wising up and no settling down."[14] The point of no return. From 1951, when he began his wanderings in the labyrinths and catacombs of Saint-Germain-des-Prés, until November 30, 1994, when he shot himself in Champot, Debord kept his word. He would never return from his exile, from his voyage of disappearance; he remained the lost child he had decided to become when he was twenty, when he decided never to become anything. To become is to return. But he will never wise up, the child will never be a prodigy. And where was the long-dead father to whom he could return? Since the beginning of time he had done nothing but separate from him, had done nothing but say good-bye—to him and to so many others.

It has been said that travel shapes our youth, suggesting also its simultaneous passage. In Debord's case, the effort does not seem to have been very successful. His various movements and travels allowed him to maintain his youthful vows of perdition, of elusiveness. Where do we look for Debord? In transition, in exile, in separation and mourning. That is where he can be found. A perfect example of this is his 1980 translation of *Coplas por la muerte de su padre—Stances sur la mort de son père*—by Jorge Manrique, which Tony Lopez Pintor had introduced him to. Manrique became the emblem of Debord's Spanish adventures, a kind of anticipatory funeral oration. Manrique was a Spanish poet and soldier (like other members of his family, especially his father), an adventurer like Dante or Retz, men whom Debord greatly admired. As expressed by Debord, who must have recognized himself in the knowledge he attributes to him, Manrique succeeded in "attributing to events in the world the results of [his] own historical operations."[15] His best-known work, *Couplets on the Death of His Father,* is filled with such profound melancholy that if Debord had been unable to translate it, he would have had to invent it. With the inconsolable Andalusian princess looking on in the background, Debord, as if grieving in advance, becomes a noble Spanish warrior without illusions, reflecting one last time on the *Vergänglichkeit* of pleasure and honor.

> Stanza II
> Beholding how each instant flies
> So swift, that, as we count, 'tis gone
> Beyond recover,
> Let us resolve to be more wise
> Than stake our future lot upon
> What soon is over.
>
> Stanza VII
> Behold what miserable prize—
> What futile task we set upon,
> Whilst greed awakes us!

And what a traitor world of lies
Is this, whose very gifts are gone
Ere Death o'ertakes us!

Stanza VIII
Yea, tell me shall the lovely blason,
The gentle freshness and contour
Of smiling faces,—
The blush and pallor's sweet occasion,—
Of all—shall one a truce secure
From Time's grim traces?

It would be easy to add passages from the *Couplets* (forty poems in all), which all share the same melancholy disdain for life's pleasures and the same mourning for the world that find frequent echoes in Debord's work. They all reflect the transience of the present and of beauty, the vanity of earthly pleasure, of the fame, power, and glory that Don Rodrigo Manrique, the poet's father, managed to obtain, but which he was more successful than others in renouncing:

Stanza XXXVIII
Unto my death I yield, contenting
My soul to put the body by
In peace and gladness;
The thought of man to live, preventing
God's loving will that he should die,
Is only madness.

It could be said that the thoughts expressed in the *Couplets* were commonplace at the time of their writing, when they were referred to as "vanities." But this is of little importance, especially for Debord, who had long been accustomed to the appropriation of commonplaces. We still need to explain why he chose precisely this poem rather than another, since the genre was well practiced throughout the fifteenth century. In his "Translator's Note," which follows his French translation, Debord indicates that not being a "Hispanophile," it was only the "circumstances of his errant life" that led to his understanding and appreciation of the true Spain, which qualified him to translate Manrique: "He [the translator] has for a long time been accustomed to behaving as if he were in his element whenever he truly enjoys something."[16]

Debord was at home in Spain and Manrique's Spanish because he had lived there and because he had loved there. His attachment to Spain gave him something akin to a right of appropriation: here, identification is clearly a question of social etiquette. Through the man he describes as the Spanish Villon, Spain becomes one of the figures of space-time characteristic of Debord. Manrique was one of the last legends used by Debord to comprehend a world devoted to adventure and transience (since one necessarily entails the other). Never again did Debord talk about himself so openly, reveal himself as much as he did in translating Manrique. And the condition that makes possible Manrique's melancholy outlook on the world—which Debord appropriates by becoming his translator—is the death of his father, the keystone of the *Couplets*. It is through the father's eyes that the world is seen as vanity and illusion (or spectacle, as Debord would write five hundred years later), and it is because the son adopted the perspective of the dead father that the world was doomed to its own future grief: "Than stake our future lot upon / What soon is over," wrote Manrique. Never did Debord come so close to a self-avowal as he did in this translation, which was one of his last acts and certainly one of his most literary—in spite of the mask of the translator, or perhaps because of it. It was as if the figure of Jorge Manrique enabled him to say something that was impossible to say in his own name: that his life was based on a melancholy identification with a father who had never been there. Jorge Manrique, in his funeral oration for his father, in which he assumes the role of the dead man so that his elegy would be credible, may have provided Debord with the ability to re-inscribe what had been unrepresentable and unspeakable in his own past, the possibility of a glorious reinscription of something he had promised to conceal. The father was gone, but the son's grief would mirror the father's heroism in life, as if that life were detached from itself and the pleasures of the world in advance. Debord, deprived of a past, oblivious of his own family romance, provided himself with a melancholy genealogy. It was as if he chose to translate Manrique, inhabit a legendary Spain rather than swallow a disappearance that stuck in his throat. "For me there will be neither return nor reconciliation." Mourning the world would never end. For the lost child, it was too late to go back, there was never anyone to return to.[17]

Whatever Was Directly Experienced Has Been Distanced through Representation

Debord was melancholic, there is little debate about this, but there is a problem in making melancholy the center of his universe (an empty or sealed center, as is always the case with melancholy). Certainly, Debord was partly a memoirist, who continued to return to his invisible past as a lost child, but there is also a political Debord, a theoretician, who is far more prominent. But can we be sure that we are talking about the same Debord? Can we be sure that in his radicality, Debord's political position does not also derive from melancholy? Can we be sure that a desire for complete change is so different from mourning the world? Do we know what revolution is, or even more simply, the desire for revolution?

Debord always contested any fragmentation of his life or his image; he wanted to be seen as a whole man and he decided to remain that way, rejecting compromise and informing those who approached him that it was *all or nothing*: "It is true that they were not ready to accept everything, and I have always clearly stated that it would be all or nothing, thus placing myself definitively out of the reach of their possible concessions."[1] The lost child would not return, much less cut up into recyclable portions. It was the same all-or-nothing logic that led Debord to reject the image of the theoretician who would become a public figure after the appearance of *The Society of the Spectacle* in 1967, and who is today certainly dominant, in spite of the biographical reassessments (or possibly because of them). It is important to understand—at least if we really want to understand Debord—that for him there was never a sharp dichotomy between experience and thought. On the contrary, everything he did, his entire life demonstrates a concern for not separating life from theory. Theory is not made to be taught in school or discussed in seminars by media experts, but to be lived at the right moment, and then forgotten. Theories are worthwhile only when they are based on life, and, like everything else, like life, they are subject to the principle of *Vergänglichkeit*. "I must first of all repudiate the most false of legends, according to which I am some sort of theoretician of revolutions. The petty people of the present age seem to believe that I have approached things by way of theory, that I am a builder of theory—a sort of intellectual architecture which they imagine they need only move into as soon as they know its address, and which, ten years later, they might even slightly remodel by rearranging a few sheets of paper, so as to attain the definitive theoretical perfection that will assure their salvation. But theories are only made to die in the war of time. Like military units, they must be sent into battle at the right moment; and whatever their merits or insufficiencies, they can only be used if they are on hand when they're needed. They have to be replaced because they are constantly being rendered obsolete—by their decisive victories even more than by their partial defeats. Moreover, no vital eras were ever engendered by a theory; they began with a game or a conflict, or a journey."[2]

Theory is a game, a conflict, a journey. Nothing distinguishes it from experience, whether in Saint-Germain-des-Prés or elsewhere. This is fundamental for understanding Debord, and will be useful when we examine the splits and expulsions that dotted the history of the Lettrist International and especially the Situationist International. But for now I want to point out that if this is the case, if the books in which theory takes shape are themselves the witness or archive of experience, among other possible witnesses, they must also be understood as the effect of this mourning for the world that we have been examining. Could *The Society of the Spectacle* also have been the result of an experience of loss?

The continuity between theoretical and autobiographical discourse is obvious in the majority of Debord's films, especially *Critique of Separation.* We have already seen this in the case of *In girum imus nocte,* which begins with social criticism before becoming autobiographical—serving as a kind of challenge issued to those who, in 1978, wanted to stick to theory and set aside questions of singularity and experience. "This is why those who impart to us their thoughts about revolutions usually refrain from letting us know how they actually lived."[3] In *Critique of Separation,* the first, implicit, subject of this film is the critique of the separation between theory and autobiographical discourse: because of its brevity, it is easier to see that these form two sides of the same activity.[4] *Critique of Separation* is exemplary, not only because it again evokes the exemplary adventure of the lost children, but because, in its brevity, in its concentration, it reveals, in a particularly obvious way, the melancholy dimension dominating the film's theoretical as well as autobiographical moments. The comment "What communication has been desired, or known, or simply simulated? What real project has been lost?" would, in this perspective, take on emblematic value. Because of the context in which it occurs, it evokes both a singular loss—the adventure of the lost children—and something much more general: the disappearance of communication as a historical phenomenon, as the heart of the structure of contemporary society.

Is it unreasonable to assume that through melancholy we can understand what many consider Debord's major work, and the one that is certainly his best known, namely, *The Society of the Spectacle*? Can we imagine *The Society of the Spectacle* being written by anyone other than the lost child Debord decided to become in 1951, and possibly before? Should we assume that in Debord's case his claim concerning the embodiment of theory in experience was not relevant? Do we make an exception for the author, in the sense that the author of *The Society of the Spectacle* would be exempt from experience, with the secondary advantage of also exempting all his readers? Not only would this be a paradox, it would imply that we were deaf to the true challenges of the book, to its enigma. For, if anything is true about *The Society of the Spectacle* it is that, thirty years after its publication, after having become one of the leading texts of far-left discourse, after literally falling into the public domain ten years ago, and having been quoted and commented on innumerable times, in many respects the book remains an enigma.

The commentary and quotes, of which there are many—often contradictory—reveal even more clearly the equivocal, or in any case complex, nature of certain passages (including some of the most famous). Do we know exactly what Debord means by "spectacle"? Can we know? Is it enough to refer to the young Marx, the author of *Theses on Feuerbach,* for example, rather than the theorist of scientific socialism? Can we simply retrace the genealogy of the concept of the spectacle by noting that it is present in Nietzsche or some derivative of alienation, fetishization, or reification? Have we understood *The Society of the Spectacle* once we realize that Debord read Hegel and the young Marx along with dissident Marxists such as Georg Lukács and, later, through his contacts with the theoreticians of Socialisme ou Barbarie, Karl Korsch, Anton Pannekoek, and Paul Mattick, or even typically French authors such as Lucien Goldmann and the inevitable Henri Lefebvre? We can ask, and it may even be useful to do so, which Marx Debord was inspired by and which other thinkers, Marxists or otherwise, had influenced him. However, in doing so it is important to avoid confusing influence, copying, and *détournement,* as Régis Debray and others do, or to claim for Debord an increasingly academic view of philosophy, one inversely proportional to the originality that is denied him. It is as if it were at best an accident, and at worst a form of cheating, that readers should take an interest in *The Society of the Spectacle* rather than the many books by Lefebvre or Lukács.

We can comment on *The Society of the Spectacle*, situate it within the history of ideas, within a philosophical tradition, and it is certainly important to do so.[5] But does this account for the singularity of the book, of what makes or has made this book an event? Does it account for its reputation? I'm not so sure. In many respects, the book's very existence remains inexplicable. Neither the intellectual and political context of the time nor that of the situationist adventure can fully account for this. *The Society of the Spectacle* remains a meteoric book, and, as I understand it, this is so specifically because it is only secondarily a work of theory. Its interest—its enigma—arises from the fact that it incorporates a way of life in a style, and succeeds because that life never lacked for style.

In other words, *The Society of the Spectacle* provides a "theoretical" form for a unique subjective position, for a life. Or rather, for a life that Debord never stopped mourning and which, in 1967, seemed more lost than ever. "The whole life of those societies in which modern conditions of production prevail presents itself as an immense accumulation of *spectacles*. All that was once directly lived has become mere representation." Thus begins the opening paragraph of *The Society of the Spectacle*, whose first section is titled "Separation Perfected." Six years after his film *Critique of Separation*, the last important work to appear before *The Society of the Spectacle*, it cannot be said that Debord was overcome with optimism. Separation was now "perfected" and, at the same time, life had entirely disappeared. Saint-Germain-des-Prés and the lost children were buried: from stories that connect the possibility of life to a process of disappearance or perdition, Debord, in *The Society of the Spectacle*, moves toward the recognition of the disappearance of life. Mourning for life and the world, which have been replaced by representations, by images. This concludes the book's second thesis: "The spectacle in its generality is a concrete inversion of life, and, as such, the autonomous movement of non-life."

The spectacle supplants life. It is only one door, of course, but it happens to be the first, the one through which we enter, the one through which the lost child that Debord began as entered theory. There is nothing more to experience; there is only submission to the order of the spectacle, the autonomous reign of merchandise, appearance, ideology, the reign of lies. Such a door unquestionably resembles those already open, or, more accurately, it explains that Debord had decided to cross over in the other direction many times. "Wherever the spectacle is found, I must be and I am, invisible." I am what escapes the spectacle, the false appearances of the present it imposes. It is certainly problematic to reduce *The Society of the Spectacle* to the melancholic threshold through which we enter the spectacle, but it would be equally wrong to forget that that is the way we came in, if only because it is through that door that we will return. This is especially true of the second part of the book (chapter 5), "Time and History," which presents, through an examination of humanity and its relation to time, a scenario where the first age is the golden age because it is followed by its manifold degradation. In the beginning was cyclical time, the effect of a direct experience of nature, and nomadism, a kind of primitive version of the *dérive*, which soon disappeared with the arrival of sedentary agriculture and humanity's submission to labor: "The shift from pastoralism to settled agriculture marked the end of an idle and contentless freedom, and the beginning of *labor*" (Thesis 127). It is an odd refrain. Paradise is what existed before labor and the division of labor, before exploitation, power, and the state, which inevitably followed. Paradise was the time when Debord, at twenty, wrote "Never work!" on a wall near the Seine. The time when he did nothing, when he was content to "drift" through Paris, an urban neo-nomad. It was when he didn't write, when writing didn't even exist yet and, as a result, didn't prevent anyone from living: "With writing came a consciousness no longer conveyed and transmitted solely within the immediate relationships of the living—an *impersonal memory* that was the memory of the administration of society. 'Writings are the thoughts of the State,' said Novalis, 'and archives its memory'" (Thesis 131).

In the beginning was idleness, immediacy; then came labor, the state, writing, mediation, separation, and division. The cyclical time that lent itself so well to laziness gradually disappeared with the historical consciousness of time. This was a scenario of decline, of degradation, with the inevitable moments of remission that exist under such circumstances. The emergence of the historical consciousness of time, during the Renaissance, had something joyful about it, but was replaced by the modern era's final confiscation of the use of time. Scenarios of degradation are never linear (at most, they may appear to be), and Debord's is no exception, especially when he evokes the Italian cities of the Renaissance as a golden age: "In the exuberant life of the Italian cities, in the arts of festival, life came to recognize itself as the enjoyment of the passing of time. But this enjoyment of transience would turn out to be transient itself. The song of Lorenzo de' Medici, which Burckhardt considered 'the very spirit of the Renaissance,' is the eulogy delivered upon itself by this fragile historical feast: *'Quant' è bella giovinezza / Che si fugge tuttavia'"* (Thesis 139). In the Italian cities of the time of Machiavelli and Dante, the time of degradation temporarily suspended its flight to enable those then living, and who were truly alive, to enjoy the passage of time, as much later those who made up the tribe of Saint-Germain-des-Prés would enjoy it; or as Debord did, one last time, when exiled in Florence, before being banished like Machiavelli. Not only is *The Society of the Spectacle,* an apparently impersonal book, hyperbiographical, but it even anticipates the life to come. It is autobiographical in a prescriptive sense (because Debord didn't live in Florence until the 1970s).

"Transient enjoyment." One step (one thesis) more and the Florentine paradise is over. Youth has vanished, the time of absolute monarchy and its monopoly over historical life has arrived, after the swan song of the Fronde: "The free play of the feudal lords' irreversible time had exhausted itself in their last, lost battles: in the Fronde, or in the Scots' uprising in support of Charles Edward. The world had a new foundation" (Thesis 140). Once we understand what the Fronde represented for Debord, whose admiration for one of its principal participants, the Cardinal de Retz (Gondi), never wavered,[6] we are forced to situate this passage in a perspective that is far more personal than theoretical, since the Fronde and Gondi are part of the "mental landscape" of the author of *The Society of the Spectacle.* The Fronde, the swan song of sovereign life, of lived life, with Gondi, its magnificent loser, its lost child: "Fair companions, adventure is dead." Can we be sure that *The Society of the Spectacle, On the Passage of a Few Persons,* and *In girum imus nocte* don't all tell the same story? It is always the same life that is lost, an immemorial time of idle freedom and the sovereign use of time that have yielded to the iron hand that governs labor, confiscates time, destroys community, and leaves us with nothing but survival: "Our epoch, which presents its time to itself as essentially made up of many frequently recurring festivities, is actually an epoch without festival. Those moments when, under the reign of cyclical time, the community would participate in a luxurious expenditure of life, are strictly unavailable to a society where neither community nor luxury exists. Mass pseudo-festivals, with their travesty of dialogue and their parody of the gift, may incite people to excessive spending, but they produce only disillusion—which is invariably in turn offset by further false promises. The self-approbation of the time of modern survival can only be reinforced, in the spectacle, by reduction in its use value. The reality of time has been replaced by its *publicity*" (Thesis 154).

I want to temporarily interrupt my commentary, however sketchy. A number of other claims could be made along the same lines. These need to be examined carefully, and *The Society of the Spectacle* approached cautiously. I am not suggesting that the book is also, if not essentially, based on a sense of melancholy for the world or life, and that this melancholy is Debord's, that it is what Debord *experienced*; and that if this is the case, then there is no reason to distinguish autobiographical discourse from theoretical discourse, since experience then coincides entirely with nonexperience, with the feeling of *Vergänglichkeit* or the loss of life. There is, between a book like *The Society of the Spectacle* and Debord's autobiographical works the same relation as exists between Rousseau's *Essay on the Origin of Inequality* or the *Essay on the Origin of Languages* and the *Confessions*. Social criticism is autobiography by other means. The comparison with Rousseau is also relevant, aside from the obvious differences between the two men, because both made use of a metaphysics of decline, a conceptualization of degradation and the disappearance of the living, which in both cases is suffused with a fundamental sense of melancholy. Where is Debord in *The Society of the Spectacle*? He is hidden among his theses and in the many appropriations they are based on, fragments of nonlife wrapped in their impersonal perfection, devoid of any unique subjective implication, of all life.[7] It is not accidental that *The Society of the Spectacle* absolutely avoids the pronoun "I." It is a book that imitates the absence of life and that presents itself as coming out of nowhere or from another world. Is it surprising, then, that, more than any of his other books, this is the one that earned its author the reputation of being a cold and distant theoretician? As if he had distanced himself from what had been experienced directly by the lost children of Saint-Germain-des-Prés, as if he had decided to grasp nonlife only by the means of nonlife. There is no place for lost children in *The Society of the Spectacle*.

2. AN ART WITHOUT WORKS

The End of Art

HOMAGE TO LETTRISM

The avant-garde is generally fairly critical when narrating its own history, replacing what is often a matter of ambience, cultural environment, and the interactions of several relatively active groups with narrow, linear genealogies. In a sense, these narratives resemble family histories, with their emotions, their upheavals, their skeletons in closets, the venerated or hated relatives, the ignored neighbors, lost children, and undesirable uncles, the kind you wouldn't want in your own family and who are best kept away from your daughters. In reading the histories of the situationists or situationism, Isidore Isou plays the role of such an uncle.

Jean-François Martos wrote him off in a short paragraph. In a slender book written during the flurry of events that took place during May 1968, Éliane Brau (Éliane Papaï) ignored Isou to promote Gil Wolman and Jean-Louis Brau (who became her husband). These men were not part of the early lettrist group but joined later, becoming, like Debord, "international" lettrists.[1] Anselm Jappe is somewhat more generous, pointing out some of the debts situationism owed to lettrism, but he is obviously not more convinced than many of the situationists of Isou's genius, although Isou is a far from insignificant character.[2] Only Greil Marcus shows genuine interest in the prehistory of "international" lettrism and gives credit to Isou.[3]

Born in 1925 in Romania into a Jewish family, his real name was Jean-Isidore Goldstein. He escaped Nazi persecution with the help of local Zionist groups and ended up in Paris in 1945 with nothing more than a suitcase full of manuscripts in French, a highly developed sense of megalomania, and a systematic theory of poetry and the meaning of life he had been developing since the age of seventeen. It didn't take long for Isou to surround himself with a handful of disciples (Gabriel Pomerand was the first) and become a talented cultural agitator, who made use of proven dadaist and surrealist techniques.[4] The first important demonstration by the new and still unknown lettrists took place in January 1946. They interrupted a talk by Michel Leiris, given on the occasion of the premiere of *La Fuite*, a play by Tristan Tzara, another Romanian Jew specializing in scandal, but one who had been tamed by communism. The disruption was referred to as a "lettrist" event. In the confusion of a successful media coup, Isou managed to get the attention of Gallimard, which was initially indifferent to the suitcase full of manuscripts deposited on its doorstep. His *Introduction à une nouvelle poésie et une nouvelle musique*, which can be considered as the manifesto or theory of lettrism, and a novel, *L'agrégation d'un nom et d'un messie*, were published in 1947. With respect to his theoretical work, it is at best difficult to read. If we had to classify him, he would be perfectly at home within one of the categories of *fous littéraires*, an inventory of which was provided by Raymond Queneau—unless we need a new category for those who combine avant-gardism and literary madness.[5] Such is the fate of theory whenever it is the product of a single individual, whenever it corresponds to a kind of absolute singularity, or cannot be shared other than as delusion.

Isou believed that the engine of all human evolution was not the survival instinct but the will to create. Mankind, he said, does not live by bread alone, but also by poetry. The idea is not fundamentally original, and it is not vastly different from the viewpoint adopted later by the situationists, who attempted to introduce poetry into everyday life understood as something beyond work or economy. The real revolution would take place beyond need, somewhere closer to desire. It would consist, according to Debord and his followers, in the invention of new games and new desires. Concerning everything else, there was no lack of disagreement. According to Isou, it was by devoting oneself to creativity, of which art remained the most essential form, that man truly became man, sovereign, that is, no more and no less equal to a god, instead of remaining a kind of subhuman. Because god established his existence only by creating the world, every creator—and Isidore Isou in particular—can, consequently, claim the same. It is easy to see that the messiah mentioned in his first novel was a substitute for Isou. In light of this, the relevance of the reproaches made to the founder of lettrism by radical (soon to be international) lettrists, some of whom had a hard time accepting his messianism,[6] becomes more comprehensible.

Consistent with what could be expected of a seventeen-year-old theoretician, Isou's philosophical point of departure was puerile, unexceptional (his entire theory of creation can be read as a kind of postromantic vulgate), and unquestionably megalomaniacal, based ultimately on the messianic arrival of "Isou." He combined all the conditions needed to cross the heavens of the Parisian postwar intelligentsia like a meteor, rather than to settle there, to crash rather than make a career for himself, a child possibly even more lost than so many others, leaving few traces of himself behind (how much do we know about lettrism today?).

So why the encounter with Debord? There is an element of contingency in all avant-garde encounters, but the one between Debord and Isou was not purely accidental. Should Isou be considered a kind of unsuccessful Debord or, on the contrary, one who succeeded only too well on the road to perdition? He was not without a certain seductive appeal (especially physical, with his "kid from Nashville" side). And he fascinated some of those he met, and seems to have enjoyed it (unlike Debord). He had a number of unquestioning disciples,[7] many in fact (in 1946 there were about twenty lettrists), and had a talent for dragging them along toward a kind of vanishing point, somewhere at the center of his megalomania, at the core of a madness into which he continued to burrow, long before he was finally put away.

Clearly, Isou deserves more recognition than he has received. He was adventurous and was responsible—directly or through the lettrist movement he led—for some of the most successful Parisian scandals of the postwar period. I referred to lettrism's official birth during the premiere of Tzara's *La Fuite*. In 1949, Isou added a new string to his bow, "pornography," by publishing *La mécanique des femmes,* with a preface in which he challenges the authorities to censor him or stop publication of a book that was essentially educational in purpose. The authorities, who obviously had different ideas about education, accepted the challenge, banned Isou's book, arrested him, and provided him with a psychiatric examination at no extra cost.

The first, but by no means the last. When we consider how much some people have done to get themselves arrested, frequently unsuccessfully, it is hard not to acknowledge Isou's position in the Republic of Letters of the avant-garde.[8] The lettrists are also credited (although Isou himself was not directly implicated) with the scandal at Notre-Dame-de-Paris, which took place during Easter Mass in 1950. Four people were involved, presumably part of the same group: Jean Rullier, Serge Berna, Ghislain de Marbaix, and one Michel Mourre, who played the leading role. Disguised as a Dominican monk, Mourre climbed the altar to proclaim that God was dead in a speech that was quickly interrupted by the Swiss guards. The reactions of the parishioners were extremely violent and the crowd tried to lynch the four "lettrists," who were saved only when the police showed up to arrest them. Mourre, then twenty-two, is a character whose development is difficult to follow, having undergone several identity crises. He was a teenage collaborator on the fringes of Maurras's Action française (he was arrested in 1944), a neofascist, and became a monk at one point in his life (at the time of the scandal, the habit, for once, made the monk) before embracing the lettrist cause. This was followed by another acute crisis of Catholicism. He was a lost child who didn't know which saint to turn to, but he devoted a great deal of energy to the process of discovery.[9] The Notre-Dame scandal earned him and his friends a spot on the front page of the newspapers and a retrospective homage by Debord in *In girum imus nocte.*[10] In the legendary prehistory of the Lettrist International, the scandal of Notre-Dame-de-Paris has the inaugural value of a proxy initiation.

There were other scandals involving Isou: the film festival in Cannes, and the arrival of Charlie Chaplin, who was criticized from the left by Debord and his followers. But his contribution to a nascent situationism was not limited to scandal. For example, Isou had been one of the first to conceive of the young as an autonomous "social" class and the distinct target of his calls to revolt. Lettrism lacked the fiber of proletarianism, but it had the stuff of youth. Isou saw the youth of his day as an amorphous mass on the margins of real society. It was characterized by its dependence (its alienation), and its exclusion from the labor market, while being on the point of creating for itself—this is the beginning of the fifties—an autonomous culture (an echo of American youth culture) and a semblance of purchasing power.[11] The situationists did not respond directly to Isou's gamble with youth. But it is interesting that for some of them, their apprenticeship at re-

volt took place in this "puerile" school of subversion, and they took something away with them, which they may have learned from this Carpathian
Peter Pan. For quite some time, Debord and his friends considered one another as children who refused to become adults and encouraged others to
lose themselves with them, to camp out under bridges and reject the same
things. This is a far cry from the political models and target public of traditional far-left movements, or the concerns of a man such as Breton for
the world of labor. But they are quite close to the "cultural" landscape—the
everyday life that needs to be reinvented—that Debord and the situationists would occupy somewhat later. Youth, which is not simply a question of
age, has little to do with need, but everything to do with desire. And if this
youth did not really exist yet in 1950 France, where the future "civilization
of leisure" was still embryonic and would have to wait until May 1968 for
its subversive potential to become a reality, nonetheless, by 1949 Isou intu-
ited that this was possible. Would he have been such a megalomaniac if he
had arrived twenty years later? Probably not.

His involvement in the field of poetry deserves some comment. Isou was
not content with vague pronouncements about creation as the salvation of
the human race. He had definite ideas and landed in Paris with a theory of
poetry or, if you prefer, a relatively personal version of the history of poetry
from which his new agenda flowed: lettrism. According to Isou, the history of poetry was characterized, until Victor Hugo, by an *"amplique"* phase
(that is, a period of development and growth), then, following Baudelaire, by a *"ciselante"* phase, which can be considered a critical phase of deconstruction, or the reduction of poetry to its simplest elements. Baudelaire
reduced it to poetic form, Verlaine to verse, Rimbaud to the word, Mallarmé
to a sound pattern, Tzara to nothing, to nonsense. Finally, Isou arrived to
take the final step, the reduction of poetry to the letter, the pure sign devoid
of meaning but also a condition of possibility for a new, as yet unknown,
meaning; a novel alphabet and a new language: the birth of onomatopoeic
poetry—although we are justified in wondering if this was really decisive or
even new. From dadaism to lettrism, progress was sometimes slow.[12] In any
case, the investment of the letter, the reduction of the poetic to the letter, is to
lettrism what automatic writing was to surrealism, that is, a founding ritual
as much as a technique of *sharing,* a technique of *communication.*[13] In this
sense, lettrism was the heir to the surrealist desire for absolute or immediate communication. It is also close to the nearly contemporary experience

of Artaud, who also struggled to reinvent an infra-language that preceded words, through the manipulation of letters (his famous "glossolalias"). It was the reduction of poetry to a pure principle of communication, a utopia of immediate communication that avoided the mediation of language (which is incapable, by definition, of immediacy), and rejected articulation, a condition necessary to language. It was no accident if the vehicle best suited to lettrist poetry was not the book but oral recitation, a commitment to immediate communication and efficiency. Lettrist poetry is even more tedious to read than automatic poetry. All its appeal, judging by the audiovisual documents we have today, lies in its enactment, in the oral performance of communication, which is its goal. Its meaning is acquired through the sharing it brings about (this too is analogous to surrealist automatic writing, which also starts from a desire to share, and which has meaning only as a collective phenomenon and encounter).

Like other avant-garde movements before it, lettrism wanted to destroy art in order to reinvent it, within a space supposedly located outside art, an authentic form of communication, and, by extension, a new way of living. Its weapon was the letter, the smallest element of language, but its scope was global, existential. In this sense, it wasn't fundamentally different from surrealism, or many of its variants, or the future situationist project, which made use of those earlier movements. Within this context, Isou's lettrism, with its desire to tear down art, had reached the end of the road, or just about. Behind Isou's back, there was not only Debord, who acknowledged its conclusion, but Gil Wolman and Jean-Louis Brau, who were close to Debord and who went even further in the direction of decomposition. They attacked the letter itself and the made-up words of onomatopoeic poetry by creating a poetry that was purely sound based, as if it preceded linguistic articulation and the production of phonemes, pure breath in search of articulation (Brau's *"Instrumentations verbales"* and Wolman's *"grands souffles"* and *"mégapneumes"*). They too expressed the loss of communication and, negatively, through provocation, the need to rediscover it. This was to become the task of situationism.

Isou's lettrism was not only ultimately an existential project but also, before the appearance of the "specialized" avant-gardes that acted locally (the Nouveau Roman, New Wave, and their equivalents in the plastic arts), a final effort to break down the entire field of art. There was onomatopoeic poetry, of course, but Isou also invented what he termed *"cinéma dis-*

crépant," typified by the *Traité de bave et d'éternité,* which was imposed on the Cannes Film Festival of 1951. There were also *"métagrammes,"* which can be described as an attempt to shift the letter not toward sound but toward the visual, toward the pictogram conceived as an analogue to pure sound as a vector of immediacy, as a means of going beyond articulated language, which was incapable of immediacy. Isou's lettrism was the Wagnerian *Gesamtkunstwerk* in the grip of decomposition, a project for the total destruction of art, that is, a project of total art, another avatar of what Mallarmé ironically referred to as the Book, and which is anything but.[14] This is important if only because the idea was passed on to situationism. Although situationism was characterized by the abandonment of the experiments with decomposition (the letter, the breath) and the positive search for new forms of communication, it was no less dependent on a totalizing conception of the poetic, because it aimed, specifically, to extend art to the totality of life. Present in every aspect of life, art would disappear as a separate practice, requiring readers and spectators on one side, and authors on the other. In this sense as well, situationism was dependent on lettrism. It inherited a conception of total art that is also, at the latest since Mallarmé, a conception of the end of art. There was nothing coincidental in the meeting between Debord and Isou.

A DISFIGURED LETTRISM

The Lettrist International, which was set up in 1952, at the time of the break with Isidore Isou, radically disfigured lettrism, which ended up being unrecognizable and soon even deprived of any distinctive characteristics. It was a parody of lettrism, as well as a parody of internationalism, and that may be why no other avant-garde group came so close to achieving its ends. All that was needed was to not take itself seriously and to do so with the dash of megalomania needed to fool the public. In any case, international lettrism—embodied in the Saint-Germain-des-Prés group between 1952 and 1954, then from 1954 to 1957 in a second group that abandoned the Rue du Four and Chez Moineau for the Rue de la Montagne-Sainte-Geneviève and that was united around *Potlatch*—was lettrism without the letter, reduced to pure negativity, to absolute idleness:[15] "We have fired Isou, who believed in the usefulness of leaving traces. Anything that maintains something helps the police in their work." The words appeared in the second *Bulletin de l'Internationale lettriste* (a two-page mimeographed sheet).[16] In that same issue, this time with Debord as the only signatory, occurred the first appearance of the formulation whose future was about to unfold: "Deliberately beyond the limited interplay of forms, beauty will be SITUATIONAL."

The break with Isou was in fact the creation of situationism, which was also an art without works, an art of the loss of self ("it's a question of losing oneself," wrote Debord in the same newsletter). It was also, from the outset, an art of disappearance and removal of the self from the gaze of the Other, and from the police in particular. It was pointless to leave traces; one should avoid being followed. The spectacle—the visible as well as the legible—was transformed into the principal enemy. It was the end of the *ciselante* period. After Isou and his letter games, Wolman and his *mégapneumes,* beauty would be situational or it wouldn't be at all, that is, it would become part of life and by the same token disappear, desirable because it was obscure. This was also the meaning of *Howls for Sade* and the twenty-four minutes of black screen and silence by which Debord terminated his association with Isou.

The break took place between the "written" version of *Howls for Sade* and the film version: disappearance, loss, nothing more to see. Aside from the projection of the film, there were no further scandals to speak of, or any of the sensationalism of which Isou was so fond, because these were mediatized, spectacular, and intrigued Gallimard. And there were almost no traces: *Potlatch* was, between 1954 and 1957, a mimeographed newsletter of no more than a few pages. The layout couldn't have been simplified any further, and it would have been impossible for the editors to do less to engage their public. Moreover, in conformity with its title, the bulletin was never sold, but given away. Initially printed in a run of about fifty copies, it grew regularly until it reached approximately five hundred. *Potlatch* was never available in retail stores, but was sent freely to addresses chosen by its staff "and to a few people who asked to receive it."[17] The confidentiality surrounding its existence (the same principle was followed at the time of the "publication" of *Mémoires*) was consistent with Debord's decision to promote a clandestine avant-garde whose clandestinity was a condition for the possibility of its authenticity. Only a relationship with a deliberately chosen reader, located beyond the margins of a simple contractual agreement, would allow for a genuine form of communication. Debord was not one for contracts; because a contract is always public, it acknowledges, implicitly or explicitly, submission to a third party. And from there to submission to the gaze of the spectacle, the pure gaze in general, was but a small step, a minor difference.

We must take Debord seriously when he rejected the label of "theoretician," which stuck to him after the publication of *The Society of the Spectacle*. For it is obvious that the book came about as a direct result of his experience—the search for a way of life constructed as poetic at the expense of creating a body of work—and with it the very concept of the spectacle. *The Society of the Spectacle* is the result of Debord's initial decision to withdraw from what he did not yet refer to as the spectacle, an initial decision to reject appearances and the effects of representation. The experience—for him necessarily clandestine—of authenticity precedes the spectacle, the same way existence precedes essence, and it is this experience that would culminate in the theory of its absolute reversal. Debord's "signature" is the concept of the spectacle, which today is found nearly everywhere, as "pro-situationists" never fail to remind us, accusing the enemy of appropriation and falsification. But this signature sanctions a way of life, from which it has obviously become detached by becoming a cliché. Debord's entrance on the avant-garde scene (which coincided with his break with Isou) was a rejection of the scene, it was a bet on obscurity. And if the Saint-Germain-des-Prés years would later achieve the prestige of a mythical golden age, it was because of this: because the clandestine nature of lived experience and the penchant not for the spectacular but for obscurity had become irrefutable and exemplary.

The first phase of the Lettrist International ran until the end of 1953. It was the period of pure, indolent negativity, later criticized (in 1957, at the time of the founding of the SI) for its nihilism. It was followed by a phase that could be called negative-critical or negative-terrorist; in any event, the lazy days of absolute indolence now seemed to belong to the past. Debord left the Rue du Four for the Rue de la Montagne-Sainte-Geneviève, taking advantage of the move to clean house, to completely change the personnel of the Lettrist International and structure it along much more rigorous lines. It saw the advent of *Potlatch,* during which time international lettrism underwent a period of increased discipline. Everything points to the fact that wine and young girls were still part of the picture, along with Debord's scathing sense of humor. But new habits were formed, especially the taste for expulsion, which Debord already began to conceive of as a weapon to advance his project.

From now on, lettrism would be militant, political, radical, and pure. It was no longer a question of tolerating fuzzy boundaries. Inside and outside were to be clearly defined; one would know who was in and who was out, or no longer in. With the second Lettrist International, Debord attempted to bring into being something that would ally the perdition of the "tribe" with the temptation to nihilism by adding an element of intransigence, by introducing a taste for "terror," that is, by providing lettrism with a style or appearance that was more political and more militant, in a word, by providing this international with a strategic imagination. "What these gentlemen lack is Terror," Debord stated, posing as Saint-Just in the first issue of *Potlatch*. He did the same in the third issue, where the name of Michèle Bernstein, his new bride, appeared for the first time, noting: "These people are referred to as 'lettrists,' the way people used to be called 'Jacobins,' or 'Cordeliers.'" The *Potlatch* period was also characterized by a politicization of speech, by the use of a radical form of social critique. The Spanish syndicalists and anarchists shot by Franco made their appearance in the very first issue, followed immediately by the rebels in Kenya, CIA activities in Guatemala, and the repression of student demonstrations in Bogotá. A few weeks later, the target was clearly French imperialism, and solidarity with North African immigrant workers and the first independence movements in North Africa was absolute.[18] Moreover, it was the presence among the ranks of the international lettrists of one or two North African immigrants (especially Mohamed Dahou) that justified the label "international" (there is no need to point out that the "French section" of the LI was the only one to have ever really existed).

The political positions of the LI were, from a revolutionary viewpoint, radical and staunchly anti-Stalinist. They were also the expression or result of a lifestyle that itself offered no concessions. They provided lettrist idleness with a kind of anchorage or revolutionary legitimacy: it's not the same thing to do nothing by doing nothing and to do nothing while proclaiming your support for revolutionary causes of all stripes. It's even feasible that, distributed quasi-clandestinely, with an initial printing of under a hundred copies, such political positions had as their goal to provide the lettrists' lifestyle with a kind of revolutionary collateral. Their intent was not so much to create pressure, to inflect the course of history, as it was to nourish a public label of radicality that would enable the lettrists to remain distinct from the rest of the avant-garde. Reasonably calm at the beginning of the fifties, comfortably divided among a large number of anarchist splinter groups and a more or less existentialist and fickle fellow-traveler status with the Communist Party, the "official" avant-garde was the primary target of the lettrists, judging by the number of gleefully insulting articles devoted to their contemporaries.

This point has been mostly overlooked by the (pre)historians of situationism: *Potlatch* was an irreverent review, almost sophomoric, filled with humor, agreeable to read, especially if you were appreciative of the art of invective it helped develop. Of all the avant-garde reviews, *Potlatch*'s format was the most minimal, with the result that there were no long articles. As a review, *Potlatch* was not long-winded, did not discuss or engage in dialogue—it assaulted the reader. It was the laziest avant-garde review ever to have existed and, as a result, the one most in a hurry to end with the avant-garde. Extreme radicalism was recommended to anyone who claimed the right to idleness, to anyone who refused the laborious side of moderate political-cultural militancy (from the distribution of brochures to the production of novels and dissertations on political philosophy). Having more important things to do (drink, wander, make love), the lettrists did things in a hurry. They argued and insulted, they assaulted the field of politics and culture with the most outrageous and mordant critiques. And they were often the funniest, the wittiest as well. Their commentary on the Nobel Prize refused by Sartre is unforgettable: "It means nothing to refuse the Nobel Prize. You still need to have been unworthy of it." There were other victims of *Potlatch*: the entire surrealist movement centered on Breton, Sagan, Le Corbusier, Chaplin, Aragon, Ionesco, Adamov, Isou, Malraux, Genet ("moral rot"), Camus, Artaud (his corpse was "overrated"), Caillois, Blavier, Ponge ("We despise you, you fraud"), Queneau, and so on.

In this milieu at least, the overt "terrorism" of the LI appears to have been somewhat effective. One such example is the "Rimbaud affair" of October 1954, the only encounter between lettrism and surrealism. Like similar encounters, this one was a complete failure, but it is hard not to conclude that the lettrists wanted it to fail, that their goal was to highlight their distance from the surrealists. The affair may seem banal in the context of the history of the avant-garde, where there has been no shortage of stillborn alliances, but it deserves closer examination. For the centenary of Rimbaud's birth, the surrealists and lettrists wanted to engage in a joint protest action against the planned official statue of Rimbaud in Charleville. Like so many other "joint actions," this one never took place because of early disagreements. The surrealists could not accept the publication in *Potlatch* 12 of a strange piece of self-criticism by André-Frank Conord, who had recently been expelled from the lettrists, or the misappropriation of a sentence by Lenin in the draft of a joint statement prepared by the LI. The verdict was clear: the lettrists were Stalinists—and on two counts—because they excluded their own members by forcing them to engage in self-criticism and because they falsified Lenin as Stalinists had done so often. The accusation makes little sense if we accept a fairly strict definition of Stalinism. In fact, the surrealists seemed to have been most worried by the LI's terrorist style. They preferred to conduct their expulsions more discreetly and had greater respect for Lenin (who was conveniently often forgotten). Given their history, we can only smile at the accusation of Stalinism that the LI's attitude inspired. Moreover, it succeeded—behind the back and at the expense of the surrealists—in establishing its own position on the avant-garde map, in the region of absolute radicalism. Once the author of a minimal but still revolutionary program, Breton now became the senile spokesman for the mediumistic sessions he supposedly conducted under the name of "Dédé-les-Amourettes" (the label stuck for as long as *Potlatch* was in print).

But the Rimbaud affair is interesting especially because questions of clandestinity and publicity played a key role. The surrealists chose to settle their scores with the lettrists by distributing a tract confidentially, presumably to prevent the lettrists from becoming aware of it. The lettrists eventually got hold of a copy and, faithful to their principle of publicizing every conflict, republished it in its entirety in *Potlatch* 14: "On November 29 some of our supporters, having finally obtained the names of the signers of the tract that Mr. André Breton devoted to us at the beginning of October, have taken possession of this tract. We provide our readers with the complete text of the Surrealist lampoon, whose principal claim to polemic originality is to have been distributed in secret. Mr. Breton and his friends have imprudently attempted to prevent us, come what may, from familiarizing ourselves with its content."

Clearly, there was little common ground between the surrealists and the lettrists in their understanding of clandestinity, or publicity for that matter. Their concept of what fell within the public domain obviously differed.

Whereas the aging surrealists were more interested in exhibitions and galleries than they ever were when they wanted to abolish art, the lettrists considered the public space as a site of conflict, a battleground, or at least a space amenable to declarations of war but not suitable for making agreements, even with Breton. It wasn't images that Debord rejected, as has sometimes been claimed, but the gaze of the Other, the right of inspection. To intervene "publicly" under the watchful eye of the Other would always entail some form of polemic. And with the Lettrist International it was this repudiation of the gaze of the Other that Debord meant to embody. He succeeded fairly well because with *Potlatch* he only *appeared* in his declarations of war. The problem for the Situationist International would be to *maintain* the sense of radical rejection that characterized the Lettrist International. Later, tired with the increasingly conformist and predictable maneuverings of the Situationist International, Debord regretted the loss of this rough-and-tumble aspect of the LI. What happened to the lumpen proletariat? What happened to Villon? The question reappears insistently in some of his last texts following the appearance of *In girum imus nocte,* as it does in Alice Becker-Ho's work on the "essence of jargon," in which she discusses the contributions of the Rom language to the jargon of the organized mob.[19] Never again will we drink so young, never again will we be so wild.

CO-OPTATION

At the time of the republication of the complete run of *Potlatch* in 1985, Debord wrote the following in the introduction to the new collection. Here, he addresses the question of the relationship between international lettrism and later, situationism, to art: "Considering the situation in 1954, *Potlatch*'s judgment concerning the end of modern art appeared rather extreme. We now know, through long experience—although having come forth with another explanation, we are sometimes led to question it—that since 1954 there has never again appeared, anywhere, a single artist of even the slightest value."[20] The proof of the end of art is our announcement of the event, which took place in 1954, followed by—as is plainly obvious—at least thirty years of an artistic wasteland.

In 1985, Debord hadn't the slightest doubt about the end of art predicted in the first issues of *Potlatch,* and even earlier. Once and for all he sticks to his initial position, or the initial position of his interaction with the avant-garde. He is less willing than ever to accept the slightest retrench-ment or revision of his position. From 1952 to 1985 and beyond, the "break-down of art" simply followed its natural course. Ionesco, Adamov, Godard, Robbe-Grillet, and many others were illusionists who indulged in hypo-critical attempts to reanimate the cadaver of art. This had once and for all become something derisive and insignificant; the cumulative attacks by Lautréamont, Mallarmé, Joyce, dadaism, and surrealism when it was still at the peak of its form signaled the decline. The old avant-garde was acknowl-edged, respected, even admired, but this was no reason to begin again, to repeat what had become, through constant repetition, its most charac-teristic boast—the announcement of the forthcoming death of art, whose obituary was indefinitely postponed. Avant-gardism was like alcohol. It was a poison that slowly killed (art), which is all to the good since most of those who demand its demise are generally not in a hurry.

Between alcohol and art, of the two we know that Debord and his friends preferred the first and that patience was not their strong point. Drink or de-stroy art, that was the choice. Everything that was put in place after 1952 with the Lettrist International was part of a project to precipitate the end of art, part of the desire to situate oneself beyond the traditional, individual prac-tices of art, including the avant-garde. How could art be done away with? Primarily by having nothing to do with it, by declaring it clinically dead, by pretending as if its funeral had taken place once and for all. The logic is tau-tological: art is alive because it is not yet (completely) dead, because I still believe in it; art is dead because I say it is dead, because I no longer believe in it. (There is nothing more salient, in explaining the fetishism of the mer-chandising so constantly criticized by Debord, than to use the example of Van Gogh's *Portrait of Doctor Gachet,* which recently sold for $82 million—the spectacle also comprises a heaping dose of belief *invested* in art.) In any event, the Lettrist International was based on a refusal to participate in any aesthetic endeavor, and with this, a desire to shift poetics toward life, in an attempt to reinvent it. A declaration of their intent, which plagiarized the "investigations" so favored by the surrealists and which can be found in the first issues of *Potlatch,* as well as in many other places, indicates this clearly:

What meaning does the word "poetry" have for you?

Poetry has exhausted whatever formal prestige was associated with it. Beyond aesthetics, it consists entirely in man's power to shape his life. Poetry can be read on men's faces. It is therefore imperative to create new faces. Poetry is embodied in the shape of cities. Therefore, we will construct amazing ones. The new beauty will be SITUATIONAL, that is, provisional and lived.

The latest artistic variants interest us only for the influence that can be invested in them or discovered in them. For us poetry doesn't signify anything other than the elaboration of absolutely new forms of behavior, and the means to nourish our enthusiasm in them.[21]

"The new beauty will be situational." Appropriated from both Sartre and Breton, the term is there from the outset (in fact, it was in use in 1952, in the second *Bulletin de l'Internationale lettriste*). And with it the future "aesthetic" of situationism was already programmed (especially the interest in architecture and urbanism), and, as shown by this passage, already manifested an interest in the ephemeral, or at least acquiesced to it. The new beauty, situational beauty, would be provisional, transient, destined to disappear without leaving a trace: an aesthetics paradoxically confused with its own disappearance, an aesthetics of disappearance. Its beauty is not for artists working toward their immortality or monuments to their glory, but for lost children. Leave no forms, no works. In terms of aesthetics, Debord and his lettrist accomplices stuck to these principles. In this sense, at least, international lettrism, not as well known as situationism, was more coherent and more radical, because no one who was part of the movement later developed a reputation in artistic or intellectual circles—with the notorious exception of Debord himself, of course.

The proof of international lettrism is that it renounced art and, conversely, the proof of art is its exclusion from the Lettrist International (and later the Situationist International). Lettrist art was based on a passion for idleness ("Never work!"), the firm intent to never arrive, to never succeed, which is why the most representative figures, the true heroes were—forty years and two panegyrics later—the ones who disappeared without a trace, the children who were most lost: the hooligans and hellcats, the drinkers, the drug addicts, and the mad (Ghislain de Marbaix, Éliane Papaï, Ivan Chtcheglov). It is an art that has merged with life, a life that is only authentic (that is, artistic or poetic) when it is clandestine, when it remains out of sight of the enemy, of representation, of spectacle. If a lettrist or situationist art exists, it functions as an invisible model: all representation is treason, including when it is the product of a real lettrist or a real situationist, who always risks interrogation, and therefore expulsion, when he emerges into the daylight. It is an art without monuments or museums. Later, in 1960, the situationists would welcome the creation in Silkeborg (Denmark, where, with the help of Asger Jorn, the SI was very active during the first years of its existence) of a situationist museum. But they were most enthusiastic about the "copy department" it contained, which had been set up to denounce those who were said to have copied the real situationists, who were determined to remain obscure: "Finally, and this is probably its most interesting aspect, this library has opened a *copy section* to preserve the artifacts imitating the work of our friends, whose unusual role in contemporary art is obviously not willingly recognized, precisely because they belong to the SI."[22] Unlike the Situationist International, whose size and more artistic configuration required a library of fakes, the lettrism of the *Potlatch* period never had a need for such an institution: it was too clandestine, too inimitable.

From 1952 to 1958, the lettrists made no concessions to their contemporaries in the avant-garde—who had little choice other than to be ignored or insulted—or, for that matter, to their own careers. They did not become artists or writers, and were prepared for the end of art they had announced in 1952. They kept their word, they had nothing further to do with art (recall that between the time he made *Howls for Sade* [1952] and the start of situationism [1957], Debord wrote no books and made no films). For this alone they deserve special mention as avant-garde radicals. They were to a large extent the most influential, indeed, the only group to have taken the final step, the only group who did not see the destruction of art as another aesthetic program, the only group who, by virtue of its systematic push toward perdition, remained unco-optable.

Co-optation was the avant-garde's nightmare. René Daumal predicted Breton's entrance into the museums, libraries, and literary histories. It is what happens to all avant-gardes, the thing they want most to avoid, and the thing they are regularly accused of by a newer, more radical, and shrewder avant-garde, until it too succumbs. How can co-optation be avoided, how can we prevent someone less co-optable from sneaking up on us unawares? That was the avant-garde's question in the twentieth century, its aporia. The only way an avant-garde writer could be sure of not being co-opted was—obviously—not to be read, and the only way he could be sure of this was not to write anything, or to destroy himself one way or another. From this perspective, the lettrists were the best of the avant-garde writers, the most unco-optable. They are even more difficult to read than the surrealist adepts of automatic writing or the proletarians of the "textual production" movement of the sixties and seventies, where the label of quality and political correctness meant unreadability.[23]

Contrary to what is sometimes imagined, it is relatively easy for an avantgarde to remain unco-opted, because not writing and not painting is accessible to everyone (and there were quite a number of such practitioners among the lettrists; they arrived as if by accident in Saint-Germain-des-Prés and never left). All it takes is to do nothing, to stop demonstrating, assuming that revolution was part of the agenda. This is the site of the avant-garde's aporia. The avant-garde is the herald of better times, it can avoid evangelism or messianism only with difficulty, and in any event must contemplate, sooner or later, its own practice in terms of transmission, no matter how paradoxical. It would like to remain unco-optable, but it must manifest itself, must be read, because it is generally acknowledged that the revolution concerns everyone, or at least the greatest number. In short, the avant-garde must make itself understood, possibly even liked, at least in the aesthetic sense, especially when it insists on maintaining its position. Love me not for what I do (art) but for what I would like to do (revolution); do not accept me, do not co-opt me. "Do not read me," they wrote. Every strategy developed by a twentieth-century avant-garde, the younger daughter of modernism, was part of this paradoxical admonition. But the lettrists never fell asleep over their art and thus escaped the nightmare of co-optation. They preferred not to sleep, not to dream, choosing instead to sleep on their feet, to drift in every sense of the word, to avoid bad dreams. They chose idleness, oblivion rather than co-optation.

Mission accomplished, or so legend has it. No one came to co-opt the lost children, no one found them, and no one was able to challenge lettrism's monopoly on the radicality to which its understanding of loss and idleness had entitled it. However, there is obviously a significant remainder to such a glorious destiny: Debord himself. His most resolute steps along the pathways to revolution ended by leading him to the Rue Sebastien-Bottin, like so many others who had sworn they would never have anything to do with Gallimard.[24] Much has been made of the change in publishers that took place in 1991. Some (among the somewhat anxious "prosituationist" movement) view this as a form of treason, others see it as the confirmation of what they had always suspected: that Debord was indeed a writer, or at least wanted to be, that he only worked for his own glory and recognition. At the time, he was said to be another fatality of co-optation, as if the history of Debord's life was the final performance of the history of the avant-garde as a whole. It has to be acknowledged, however, that it is difficult to avoid co-optation when you write so well. I know that someone will respond that if the bourgeoisie—that is, everyone's enemy—ended up by accepting Debord, it's his fault, actions speak louder than words, as Don Juan said. Even the extreme right got into the act.[25] But the obsession with co-optation should not let us overlook the fact that there is nothing obvious about writing well; that it is at least as difficult, even more difficult, to be co-opted (that is, simply read) than not to be co-opted (and not read). There has been a great deal of speculation recently to the effect that to be successful in one's work—or one's legend—the way Debord succeeded is not as simple as it seems. And many of those who formerly knew him and who are prepared to provide him with posthumous lessons in editorial correctness are at the same time struggling hard to latch onto his legend, with memoirs and interviews in tow. In any event, since an unco-optable writer is useful only when not being read, it is perhaps time to change the question and ask—more seriously than simply in terms of faithfulness or unfaithfulness to the spirit of revolution—how Debord's return (if there was one) to literature came about. Was it a return at all? Did he ever abandon the practice of writing, or, more accurately, did he ever renounce a poetic?

Before we put Debord on trial for co-optation or opportunism, it would be useful to assess the remarkable continuity of the poetic in his work and in his life, including the years of the Lettrist International and the Situationist International, whose supposed radicality is in no way incompatible with such continuity. We should also ask if these two groups made a difference, and in what such a difference would consist (what is it exactly that we expect our avant-gardes to do?). Are we so sure that they came into being—as the situationist histories of situationism claim—ex nihilo, the only embodiments of the spirit of revolt during the 1950s and 1960s?[26] Did the LI, then the SI, do better—or differently—than the other elements of the avant-garde, especially those that preceded them (Isou's lettrism or an aging surrealism), those they distanced themselves from and then dismissed? Notwithstanding the most spectacular breaks and conflicts, the same alliances and the same processes continue, and the upheavals remain for the most part internal to avant-garde discourse, and must be deciphered in that context.

Moreover, if the hostility of the Lettrist International toward Isidore Isou helped bring it into being, the same is not true of its relationship to surrealism. Breton was one of the most insulted personalities, especially by the lettrists, but he was also a man very much admired by Debord, who later praised him on several occasions.[27] Things were less clear than they seemed. And if Debord ended up by returning to literature, it may also have been because a platform such as surrealism—or Isou's lettrism—cannot be used as a starting point without suffering the effects of its dictates. No matter where one started, there was always the age-old question of poetics to be dealt with. And when one attempted to make it a part of experience, part of a "lived situation," which was, after all, the surrealist platform, it had even less tendency to vanish. It may be harder than one suspects to escape the end of art using end-of-art means.

ONE STEP BACK

In any event, the Saint-Germain-des-Prés years could not have lasted. That irremediably beautiful time, now long gone, later referred to by Debord in terms of pure negativity ("a neighborhood where the negative held court. . . ," negativity being the pure gold of the golden age), bears witness to an exemplary sense of idleness and clandestinity that the Situationist International would vainly chase after during its thirteen years of existence. Naturally, there was an incomparable whiff of illegality about these years, an irresistible aura of radicality. But marked by transience, by *Vergänglichkeit,* their ultimate destiny was disappearance, although Debord never explained exactly why, avoiding the question by referring simply to some dark, melancholy conscience, as if it had always been clear for those who lived through those years that they were too good to last. The underage runaways, the drug addicts, the prison terms, and the suicides no doubt perfectly suited the creation of a legend of lost children, but still someone had to survive to tell the tale, or make it up. By exclusively emphasizing idleness and loss, one ends up doing nothing and disappearing.

However, in a text titled "Un pas en arrière" [One Step Back], which appeared in *Potlatch* in May 1957, a time when the Situationist International (much less interested in idleness than its lettrist sibling) was being established, the pure negativity of the years 1952–53 seems to have lost its charm and gradually turned into nihilism—never a good sign within a revolutionary context: "We might, however, note that a certain satisfied nihilism, in the majority in the LI until the expulsions of 1953, objectively persisted under the guise of an extreme sectarianism that contributed to the distortion of many of our choices until 1956."[28]

This backward glance is interesting. It tells us that in 1953 the "tribe" and its art of the negative were now being questioned for the first time. Berna, Brau, Mension, Langlais, and others were expelled; they left Chez Moineau and never returned to the Rue de la Montagne-Sainte-Geneviève. In 1953, the Lettrist International purged itself for the first time of its nihilist tendencies, of those who confused the realization of the end of art with indolence. But the nihilist tendency lingered on and, to judge from the above quote, returned, strengthened by the same counterrevolutionary "sectarianism." Those who were unable to understand the reasons for the step backward necessary for founding the SI would have to leave as well. The avant-garde was unlucky. It seems to have been condemned to divide itself between those who didn't know how to move forward and those who didn't know how to go back.

In other words, was it necessary to be radical, can one be radical, and to what end? From 1952 to 1958, lettrism's radicality was exemplary; it was probably as radical as it is possible to be. That is why it became necessary, during the early years of situationism, to recall an existence that was now unquestionably over, with "works" whose only meaning seemed to have been to commemorate idleness: *Mémoires* (1958), *On the Passage of a Few Persons through a Rather Brief Unity of Time* (1959), and *Critique of Separation* (1961). Why did these three melancholy works appear during the transition between the Lettrist International and the Situationist International? Because with the internationalization of the activities of the radical lettrists, the massive arrival of artists from the North, and the decision to make use of larger structural models (primarily a real review, *Internationale situationniste*), the new group, to some extent at least, came out of hiding. It is difficult to change the world without making an appearance, without "going public" on the revolutionary exchange. And going public was not self-evident given Debord's relatively limited tolerance for the spotlight.

This is something that few histories of situationism emphasize: the extent to which Debord seems to have been ambivalent—especially during the SI's founding in 1957—about a Situationist International that could no longer cling to the obscurity he had been so intent on previously. Later, the signs of this ambivalence became more obvious. Members were expelled for whom Debord had, during the first years of the SI, made concessions, something he was unaccustomed to doing. Some years later, in 1971, he took obvious pleasure in the dissolution and disappearance of the SI: the charms of intransigence had been reaffirmed, along with those of a re-discovered obscurity. A good idea of this ambivalence can be found in the article "One Step Back" that appeared in *Potlatch* in 1957. It is the only re-treat that was, to my knowledge, ever acknowledged by Debord. He gave the following reasons for explaining the change in tactics represented by the transition from one international to another:

> The broadening of our forces and the possibility (and necessity) of genuinely international action must lead us to profoundly change our tactics. We must no longer lead an external opposition based only on the future development of is-sues close to us, but seize hold of modern culture in order to use it for our own ends. We must act immediately to elaborate a critique and the formulation of complementary theses. The faction around *Potlatch* must accept, if need be, a minority position within the new international organization, to permit its unifi-cation. But all concrete achievements of this movement will naturally lead to its alignment with the most advanced program. . . .
>
> To cite a specific case, friends worry about the sudden numerical predomi-nance of painters, whose work they inevitably judge insignificant and indissolu-bly linked with artistic commerce. However, we need to gather specialists from very varied fields, know the latest autonomous developments in those fields. . . . We thus need to run the risk of regression, but we must also offer, as soon as pos-sible, the means to supersede the contradictions of the present phase through a deepening of our general theory and through conducting experiments whose results are indisputable.
>
> Although certain artistic activities might be more notoriously mortally wound-ed than others, we feel that the hanging of a painting in a gallery is a relic as inevitably uninteresting as a book of poetry. Any use of the current framework of intellectual commerce surrenders ground to ideological confusionism, and this includes us; but on the other hand we can do nothing without taking into ac-count from the outset this ephemeral framework.[29]

This represented a transition from idleness to so-called experimen-tal art, a return to a strategy of "co-optation" or cultural appropriation. In 1957 this involved "taking over modern culture to use it for our purposes." Debord's correspondence for the period shows signs of this renewed ener-gy as well as his flexibility and astonishing patience with other members of the SI (from Pinot-Gallizio to Constant, and sometimes Jorn) who were not always able to appreciate the subtleties that distinguished real—that is, revolutionary—experimental art from false experimental art. Debord was rarely as conciliatory as he was at the time of the "one step back," represented by the founding of the Situationist International, and he went so far as to acknowledge that the *Potlatch* faction (already purged of its nihilistic-sectarian tendency) might temporarily hold a minority position within the SI. He not only justified the mass presence of artists within the SI but also mentioned, in the same text, the need for a "significant broadening of our economic base." Painting may have been a ridiculous holdover of earlier times but, as was true of the surrealist period, it was lucrative (especially in the case of Jorn's work). Is it possible to imagine the "tribe" of Saint-Germain-des-Prés making concessions to economic necessity or the unlikely presence of painters unable to give up the gallery circuit? To some extent, the founding of the SI was the indirect consequence of the radicalization that took place during the transition from lettrism to the Lettrist International, or at least it corresponds to the recognition of an impasse, an aporia. Within this context, the history of the SI during the next few years was that of a gradual *return* to the radicalism of the Lettrist International, a return to obscurity that was completed with its dissolution. But there was a long road yet to travel. History had only just begun and for several years was indistinguishable from the future of psychogeography.

Cartes du Tendre

Deeply marked by a sense of melancholy, Debord's initial experience was of something irrevocable. It was connected to the passage of time. Something had been lost, something—or someone—would never return. Return or reconciliation was impossible. Debord would remain where he always wanted to be.

But where exactly was that? The question has yet to receive an answer. It's not enough to know that the lost children had been part of the life of Saint-Germain-des-Prés or that Debord was a traveler, that he chose exile, and lived in Florence, Seville, Venice, and the Auvergne, rather than Paris. Not everyone is able not to return, to obscure their whereabouts. It requires not only a good deal of contempt for one's contemporaries and a well-established sense of defiance, but a genius for place, an art of occupying the terrain. The sense of time's passage was countered by a sense of the space in which it passed. The lost children hide in the cities they re-appropriate by becoming explorers and surveyors. They hide in the cities they have reinvented to conform to their desires: beautiful and necessarily lost. Perdition demands a science of place, it *is* a science of place as much as of transience, and to this science the lettrists would give the ironic name of *psychogeography.* Debord acquired this sense of loss during the mythic early years of international lettrism, but it resonated in his actions and in his writing for years. Did his work cling to an experience of time and space, seek only to provide a feeling of time and space, like the work of any true poet? All his writings and films confirm his involvement in a reinvented sense of time and space. Is it any accident that among the handful of "artistic" shots that appear in his films (the only images he made and did not reuse or appropriate) are the tracking shots of *In girum imus nocte,* filmed along the canals of Venice? Explorations of time and space, they are unquestionably emblematic of what was most important to him.

Psychogeography, as it took shape around 1952–53, served as a kind of initiation in the history of situationism and in Debord's life. The practice of the *dérive* was the founding myth of an art without works, an art that had slipped into life, been concretely reinvested in space. It embodied a refusal to make art, a will to initiate a radical break with the overly aesthetic practices of the avant-garde. It was for this reason that psychogeography underwent a resurgence after 1958, at the time of the founding of the Situationist International, somewhat similar to the way Breton reactivated automatic writing with each reconfiguration of the surrealists. For a number of years it was so important that many commentators decided it was the SI's most original contribution, its truly creative phase, unlike the sterile political-sectarian position it had drifted into in its last years. But it was not something original in 1958, nor as central as it is sometimes thought to be today, and, for that matter, no more central than its successor was sterile. If we remember it now it is because the contradictions of the SI coalesced around it. After 1958, psychogeography was the focus of some of the most important conflicts and disagreements among members of the still-young SI. And it was the deciding factor in determining the future of an art without works.

To evaluate the role of psychogeography in Debord's trajectory, I want to return to his first book, *Mémoires,* a key moment when the future situationist turned his back, not without regret, on the lettrist he had started out to be. We read, in the first pages of the book, "In this monstrous and derisive *carte du tendre* can be found the search for a character who is presented through his successive existences." It is hard to read such a sentence other than as an indication of a way to approach the book itself, assuming that what we are involved with here is reading. There are many other sentences like it, which seem to function in the same metalinguistic register. On the first page mention is made of a "curious narrative system," of the absence of "dramatic action," which Debord comments on in the following terms: "The purpose is not very clear, and the lovers of tidy stories will be disappointed: this story begins somewhat arbitrarily and ends the same way." Then we find the following clarification, intended for readers lacking the most basic avant-garde reflexes: "Contempt for method is pushed to the point of dismembering successive episodes: the major story lines are not taken up but are evoked indirectly through their secondary details." Debord's *Mémoires* is apparently the Mallarméan stage of the Nouveau Roman. Secondary details are mentioned instead of the major story lines, the effect rather than the thing is described, "allusion, I know, suggestion." At first glance, there was nothing very shocking in this for Debord's contemporaries, eager consumers, in the late fifties, of frustrating avant-garde tics (even less shocked in this case given the fact that *Mémoires* was never sold).

At first glance only, however, for Debord's "book" deserves a second. More accurately, it needs to be seen as much as read, for the text is also visual. The "prefabricated elements" of which it is made are difficult to read because they are not simply appropriated texts (and therefore already read, given as such), but also texts arranged in a space, texts that create space. They are held in position by Asger Jorn's "bearing structures," and can be read as well as seen, like a distant echo of Mallarmé's *Coup de dés*. And because the handful of sentences mentioned here are quotes, it is the mechanism as a whole that deviates from the imperturbable spirit of seriousness that characterizes most avant-garde montages of this type. Debord's labyrinths are not those of Robbe-Grillet.[1] These are only apparently textual; they were not made to lose oneself in, but to expel the reader, to enrage him, until he disappeared as a reader. Consisting of prefabricated elements arranged in a network across the pages of the book, *Mémoires* was the "anti-book" described by Debord in 1953. They break the book, desacralize it.

They play space against memory. It is not only the principle of authority that is short-circuited here, and the too conventional relationship to the reader (who is the author of *Mémoires* and who are the readers?), but the memorial or monumental function of the book, now made to serve an allusive and forgetful cartography. The book is disfigured in favor of the visual and, therefore, in favor of geography, a science of military origin,[2] an art of occupation and mobility rather than rootedness: *psychogeography* makes its entrance.

The *Mémoires* were made to escape the confines of the book; they are the remainders of a book that never really was. They are presented as a network, a map; they are the Baudelairean traces of the stony labyrinths of the capitals mentioned at the end of the book. "Search for a character throughout his successive existences." They relate to the life of a hidden character who must be found (and for whom this succession of existences helps turn into a legend—and where, other than in a legend, can we experience several successive lives?). They serve as a *carte du tendre*, a map for a large-scale game, an affective geography in which everything suggests that what is being described is Guy Debord, even if nothing ever confirms this explicitly. Debord is hidden among his *Mémoires*, but to find him is another story. This is a story that has not (yet) been written, that has been forgotten, that is the responsibility of the reader. It is up to the reader to restore the "major lines," to connect the dots on the map, to recognize and explore what is still described as "a network of memories, obsessions, vague thoughts, reflections, apprehensions." Echoing Mallarmé and Proust dreaming about the train schedule, Debord wrote his own schedule of desire; he drew the map and positioned himself, not in the space of the book but along the equivocal limit between the book and life. *Mémoires*, the trace of a work that has entered into life, might be a book, and might be a map for getting out. The book came out a few months after the inception of the Situationist International, almost as an overview of the efforts leading up to its creation, and possibly also to suggest that the suddenness of the new friendships with artists throughout Europe required an element of sophistication if it were to endure.

It is up to the reader to *retraverse* the map, in every sense of the word— to play Debord's game, to try to find him, the way others, in an earlier age, played the game of preciosity, out of a love of games or to turn life into a game, to give desire its chance. It is up to the reader to discover what kind of social behavior such a map points to, the life it traces in legend, to reconstruct the wanderings and driftings of Debord and his accomplices. But since the reader will only find fragments, since Debord has vanished into his map or his labyrinth, this same reader will have to pick up the trail, leave the book, which was only made for that one purpose—to expel the reader, to bid him adieu—and test his social skills rather than his reading skills.

Debord's first book is a map of the desire for verbal disappearance, a map whose reader is asked to make use of it to disappear in turn, to create his own labyrinths. A book as map, filled with geographic maps and layouts of cities and houses. Everything and anything is used not to create a handsome book but a map or a drawing that will help us get out, that will allow us to make the transition from book to life. In the fourth installment of *Internationale situationniste*, which appeared a few months later, a project for drifting through the old quarters of Amsterdam is illustrated by an aerial view of the city and a reproduction of the celebrated *carte du tendre* as it appeared in *Clélie* by Mademoiselle de Scudéry. The situationists didn't write texts, they proposed plans for an art of living, an art of loving, which is exactly what Debord did with his *Mémoires.*

Within this context, *Mémoires* is not only the first appropriated book but also a book adrift, a book that turns away from itself, the book as network, or map, the trace of one or more possible itineraries. The style of *Mémoires* is psychogeographic, which is why the allusions to the first systematic *dérives,* the experiments with exploring urban atmospheres conducted by the lettrists in 1952–53 with the arrival of Ivan Chtcheglov, are so abundant in the final section of the book. The book ends—or begins—with an invitation to drift: "the appearance of drifters," "cities for use by those who live there," "it is in the streets of Paris that a new power was formed, which didn't exist in the previous century," "the actual décor of the streets," "the systematic exploration of old maps," and so on. The *dérive,* which became, ever since the golden age of Saint-Germain-des-Prés, one of the most essential levers of future situationist poetics, is not only evoked in the last section of *Mémoires,* but constitutes its active principle, as if it were one of those stories that—as Maurice Blanchot has pointed out—returns to its own point of origin. *Détournement* and *dérive* are here two sides of the same technique of disappearance or indeterminacy. The *dérive* is an art of detour, as well as an art of appropriating the "actual décors of the streets," an appropriation that occurs through movement, mobility, and drift in the beautiful language of the century. Both were used to promote a project that, although gradually identified as belonging to the situationist group, would be led primarily by Debord—at least he was the only one to have fully understood its implications. Through appropriation and drift Debord established *his* labyrinth, as much to lose himself in as to lose those who tried to follow him without paying personally, without respecting the rules of potlatch.

The *Mémoires* are written in a psychogeographic style. This can be shown by comparing them with Debord's first two "works," which were also conceived in collaboration with Asger Jorn and which obviously share the same "aesthetic." In 1956, Debord created the *Guide psychogéographique de Paris*, which was subtitled *Discours sur les passions de l'amour*. It is another *carte du tendre* (more accurately, the first) and this time explicitly, for the *Discours sur les passions de l'amour* is a collage made from a magnificent bird's-eye view of Paris that results in a disjointed city that has been rearranged on the basis of "psychogeographic," that is, affective, or psychological criteria. It is a city into which a void has been introduced, intervals suitable to desire, a city made over for mobility, an experience made singular through dismemberment. Where is Debord in all this? He is hidden in the intervals, which are the difference between an objective aerial view of Paris and a *Discours sur les passions de l'amour*, the minimum of autobiographical information.

The same comparison can be made for *The Naked City: Illustration de l'hypothèse des plaques tournantes en psychogéographie* (the title *The Naked City* is an homage to the 1948 documentary film by Jules Dassin on the New York City police). Created in 1957 in collaboration with Asger Jorn, this other *carte du tendre*, which employs the same techniques of decomposition and recomposition of the urban landscape as the *Guide psychogéographique de Paris*, has become one of the most emblematic images of the history of situationism. The naked city, the city that is to be stripped and erotically invested, the dismembered urban body reduced to its erogenous zones. *The Naked City* can also be compared to the *Mémoires*, which appeared a year later, where the psychogeographic dimension appears more clearly in the content as well as the style or structure of the book.

By the end of the fifties, all of Debord's work was invested with a sense of the *dérive*, with a passion for the *mobility* that was the heart of lettrist

practices during the golden age of Saint-Germain-des-Prés and that remained so until the first years of the Situationist International. It was as if
the lettrists, then the situationists, sought to comply with the pure mobility
of impulse, never letting anything take shape, never allowing anything to
become immobilized in a form. The impulse originates in an art without
works, without objects. It is content to circumvent (or appropriate) them
without stopping, an impulse that favors idleness, "maps of the heart," the
pure passions of love, the love of love. It is an impulse that recoils from
whatever is stationary, monumental, one that is certainly not made to be
buried in books.

Who encouraged Debord to drift? Where did psychogeography originate? Everything points to the fact that the support of Ivan Chtcheglov, the
young Russian who was part of the "tribe" during the golden age and joined
the Lettrist International when it was founded, was critical. Brilliant, according to many who knew him, something of a visionary, but also unstable, Chtcheglov was arrested (along with Henri de Béarn) by the police
in 1950 for trying to blow up the Eiffel Tower, whose lights prevented him
from sleeping. According to Bourseiller, he was thrown out of the Lettrist
International in 1954 for belonging to a "Tibetan Lama movement" that
must not have had many members aside from Chtcheglov himself,[3] or, if
we are to believe a communiqué published in *Potlatch,* for "mythomania,
interpretative delusion, and lack of revolutionary consciousness."[4] There
is, in the reasons given for this expulsion, something tragically ironic. The
Potlatch memo suggests in fact that Chtcheglov had gone mad ("mythomania, interpretative delusion"). But if Debord and his followers had realized that Chtcheglov was really mad, or was becoming delusional, they
would have been careful not to criticize his madness or expel him. It took
Chtcheglov's internment (first intermittently, then chronically) shortly after
this break to open their eyes and bring them to criticize all forms of internment. Debord greatly regretted that some had thought it a good idea to ad-
vise Chtcheglov to isolate himself rather than seek help from his friends. He
contacted his Russian friend later, visited him when he was interned, saw
him when he was released, and tried to help him, at least until 1964. The
second volume of his *Correspondance* not only contains numerous allusions to Chtcheglov—demonstrating that his former companion's situation
continued to worry him—but also letters to his friend, which are among
the most touching, the most personal Debord has written. He shows him-

self to be extremely concerned with Chtcheglov's fragility and on several occasions mentions the dangers of disintegration associated with their former adventures in common.[5] But there are also letters in which he speaks of himself, of his alcoholism, his attempts at withdrawal, or his affairs (it is in a letter to Chtcheglov that Alice Becker-Ho is introduced for the first time).[6] There is also a very beautiful dedication included in the copy of *Mémoires* sent to Chtcheglov in 1963:

> For Ivan,
> Who not only has "his page" in this story (to be continued), but who is at home everywhere in it.
> —we will never again find them as we did that summer, with all its excitement—
> —drink and the devil have done away with the others—
> —this strange traveler WAS THEREFORE SUFFICIENTLY FAMILIAR WITH POISON.
> His friend,
> Guy[7]

The SI published, in the first issue of *Internationale situationniste* (1958), a very important text titled "Formulaire pour un urbanisme nouveau" [Formulary for a New Urbanism], written by Chtcheglov in 1953 (the text was published under the pseudonym Gilles Ivain), and in 1964 there appeared, again in *Internationale situationniste,* his "Lettres de loin" (which date from 1963).[8] Within the history of the situationist movement, Chtcheglov's expulsion is practically the only one that Debord publicly reversed, which makes him one of the only ghosts, one of the only phantoms in this story. Testimony is brilliantly provided in the moving tribute given him by Debord in *In girum imus nocte* when he recalled the golden age of Saint-Germain-des-Prés: "But can I ever forget the one whom I see everywhere in the greatest moment of our adventures—he who in those uncertain days opened up a new path and forged ahead so rapidly, choosing those who would accompany him? No one else was his equal that year. It might almost have been said that he transformed cities and life merely by looking at them. In a single year he discovered enough material for a century of demands; the depths and mysteries of urban space were his conquest. The powers that be, with their pitiful falsified information that misleads them almost as much as it bewilders those under their administration, have not yet realized just how much the rapid passage of this man has cost them. But what does it matter? The names of shipwreckers are only writ on water."[9] Ivan Chtcheglov, the tireless explorer of unborn cities, who disappeared without a trace, like Cravan on his fragile craft, was an artist of perdition. Unlike the others, he did not reemerge from the labyrinths that he created more than imagined, which he fabricated with space, with the city (I cite as proof the fact that he never left). It is this that, several years later, earned him a position as figurehead of this science of mobility, psychogeography, which Debord adopted as his own. It was Chtcheglov who pointed out the lay of the land to the lost children, the man who taught them about space and the art of occupying it. There was no one else in Debord's life whom he was so careful not to forget.

The Poetics of the Dérive

In public, the lettrists insulted Charlie Chaplin, celebrated the fall of Dien Bien Phu, and later made apologies for the Algerian partisans. In private, they cultivated their most secret gardens; they dreamed of labyrinths in which they could disappear and, when they couldn't build them, tried to transform the city itself into a giant maze. Such were the charms of the *dérive*, one of the major inventions of the lettrist and later the situationist movement, or at least one of its most characteristic practices. It would be wrong to conclude that the phenomenon was entirely new to the avantgarde, regardless of the originality of Ivan Chtcheglov's 1951 "Formulary for a New Urbanism" and the concrete experiences "programmed" by his essay.

What exactly did the "Formulary for a New Urbanism" and the psychogeographic experiments of the Lettrist and Situationist Internationals referred to in so many texts of the period entail? Primarily the desire to introduce poetry into a lived experience of the street, of the city. Psychogeography consisted in experimenting with the affective variants of the urban environment, an immediate aesthetic experience (this is obviously a paradox in terms of the Western philosophical tradition, which associates aesthetic possibility with distance and contemplation) brought about by walking around a city that is systematically explored. This is also the meaning of the *dérive*—literally, drift—which can be minimally defined as a controlled and, in principle, collective (in small groups) form of movement through several areas of the same city in order to distinguish, as objectively as possible, differences in ambience or atmosphere. Such practices were exercises in the recognition or interpretation of the urban fabric, or urban text, an anticipatory and ironic homage to all those who, ten or twenty years later, chose to drift more comfortably by means of the signifier. The lettrist or situationist artist was devoted to the interpretation of the city, the way others examined texts. He took pleasure in the city's streets, markets, and cafés rather than its libraries and books. And like any form of interpretation, this involved a certain number of rules. It required a structure. You couldn't wander the city in any old way. Debord was very specific about this, especially in an article titled "Théorie de la dérive" [Theory of the *dérive*]:

> Of the various situationist tools, the *dérive* is a technique for rapidly moving through various environments. The concept of the *dérive* is inextricably bound with the recognition of effects of a psychogeographic nature and the affirmation of a ludic-constructive form of behavior, which contradicts every conventional notion of an excursion or walk.
>
> When one or more individuals are involved in the *dérive*, they abandon, for a relatively lengthy period of time, the customary rationales for movement and action, their relationships, their work, and their own leisure time, to succumb to the enticements of the terrain and the encounters associated with it. The element of chance is less important here than one might suspect: from the point of view of the *dérive*, there is a psychogeographic contour map associated with cities, with their permanent currents, their fixed points, and whirlpools that make entering or leaving certain zones quite difficult.
>
> But the *dérive*, as a whole, comprises both this letting-go and its necessary contradiction: the domination of psychogeographic variants through an understanding and calculation of their possibilities. . . .
>
> One can drift alone, but everything points to the fact that the most fruitful numerical distribution consists of several small groups of two or three individuals with the same degree of awareness; cross-checking the impressions of these different groups enables us to arrive at objective conclusions.[1]

The *dérive* is a method of "rapid movement." It is impossible not to recall the title of Debord's second film, *On the Passage of a Few Persons through a Rather Brief Unity of Time* (1959), devoted entirely to the lost children of Saint-Germain-des-Prés. They moved from one environment to another, from one part of the city to another, and, most certainly, from one café to another, just as they passed through time. The *dérive* is the projection onto space of a temporal experience, and vice versa. It is the emblem of lost children, who drift, who abandon themselves to a principle of pure mobility, absent the customary reasons for going places—a directionless mobility, unproductive, serving no purpose, which is open to the "enticements of the terrain" and to encounters.

Yet those who drift are not passive, and we should not confuse the *dérive* with the contemplative charms of the conventional, or classically surrealist, promenade. From this point of view, we see that a not inconsiderable part of the "Theory of the *dérive*" is devoted to explaining that although the *dérive* is to some extent a bet against chance, chance is not the key element. On the contrary, the *dérive* entails a preliminary determination of environments, the possibility of calculating them, of establishing some form of objective understanding. It was important to avoid any confusion or similarity with other forms of urban experience, especially those of the surrealists, who were always suspected of subjectivity and passivity, of an allegiance to chance. From Debord's perspective, it would be highly unfortunate if the *dérive* were confused with the Parisian promenades of Breton and Aragon, which it resembles but with the addition of an "objective" understanding. The history of the avant-garde is inextricably linked to the notion of the promenade, a phenomenon it is difficult to escape even when it has been rechristened the *"dérive."*

Between the urban experiences described in books such as *Nadja* and *Le paysan de Paris* [Paris Peasant] and the way in which Debord presented the *dérive*, there were a certain number of points in common that trace the outlines of a relationship.[2] Although surrealism and situationism have other features in common, it is obvious that at this time Debord was uninterested in them, for rarely have avant-gardes maintained good relations with their predecessors, which they have always struggled to relegate to the past. Neither Breton nor the Aragon of the surrealist period would have disavowed the idea of being open to the enticements of the city or chance, or the rejection of ordinary activities and relationships, in short, everything that made the *dérive* an aimless wandering and the absence of goals the opportunity for an aesthetic or affective experience. Even the group nature of the *dérive*, which provided the objectivity of the psychogeographic experience, would easily have found favor with Breton. Wasn't his entire urban experience associated with encounters and sharing? The surrealist *"trouvaille,"* so often sought in flea markets or elsewhere, was never individual. It only had meaning and reality if it was the product of at least two individuals; it too was part of a project to *objectify* desire.[3] The surrealist promenades (at least those of Breton, for it was very different with Aragon) were no less productive of community or communication than those of the situationists, or at least this was their intent. Similarly, the question of objectify-

AN ART WITHOUT WORKS | 111

ing the aesthetic impression or sensation is already present and, as in the case of international lettrism or situationism, this objectification involved immersion in the urban milieu. (The only attempt at a surrealist *dérive* in the countryside turned out badly; Debord was quick to point this out in the same text, to highlight a difference that may not have been obvious.)

Psychogeography set in motion a surrealist experiment with the city. Many passages in Chtcheglov's "Formulary for a New Urbanism" also reflect this, in a way that is both conscious and constrained: "All cities are geological and you can't take three steps without encountering ghosts, armed with the prestige of their legends. We evolve in a *closed* landscape whose landmarks draw us incessantly toward the past. *Shifting* angles and *receding* perspectives enable us to perceive original conceptions of space, but this vision remains fragmentary. It must be sought in the magic lands of folklore and surrealist writings: castles, endless walls, small forgotten bars, prehistoric caves, casino mirrors."[4] This passage is not without ambiguity. It suggests, as was also the case with the surrealist experiment with the city, that psychogeography is fundamentally an experience of mobility, applied to space as much as to time. The objectification of urban environments entails a capacity for movement that is both spatial and temporal: the ability to recognize the city in its geological dimension and concentrate on the different temporal strata of which it is composed, as reflected in certain buildings, forgotten bars, and endless walls—one can also drift through a Paris that is in the process of disappearing. This mobility is essential. Chtcheglov confirmed the importance in the conclusion of his "formulary": "The principal activity of the inhabitants will be to DRIFT CONTINUOUSLY. The change of scenery on an hourly basis will be responsible for the complete sense of disorientation."[5] To drift from space to space, temporality to temporality, and, while drifting, to enter a logic of disorientation, the logic of the Paris peasant: even if the lettrist project was more systematic, more constructed, it duplicated that of the surrealists while attempting to distinguish itself from it. Moreover, Chtcheglov notes that the past also encloses us, which impedes mobility and blocks the vanishing lines of the *dérive*. And if the surrealists indicated which receding perspectives and shifting angles to follow, they looked too hard to find them in a past they were now a part of. Chtcheglov was interested in a "new urbanism," characteristic of the utopian strain among the early situationists. He introduced activism to the field of urbanism, something that was nowhere to be found among the surrealist dreamers, who were too passive, too ready to let themselves go, carried away by chance or the unconscious. To avoid this it was necessary to move beyond the past and passivity, drifting had to be more controlled, more systematic, and new cities and spaces had to be invented that would provide greater scope for the *dérive*.

I will return later to the utopian element in situationism, which was especially evident during the first years of its existence, but want to point out that Debord himself never showed much enthusiasm for it. He often seems much closer to the melancholic aspect of the surrealist urban experience (that of Aragon in this case, who was much more Baudelairean than Breton).[6] It was hardly arbitrary that the places he cared about, which served as landmarks for his *dérives,* are those that have since disappeared: the area around Les Halles, an emblematic crossroads, a meeting place teeming with life, or other areas that were still working-class in the fifties, any number of cafés, one more insalubrious than the next, no trace of which remains today or of their habitués: North African immigrants on Rue Xavier-Privas, Jews who spoke only Yiddish along Rue Vieille-du-Temple, Spanish Republicans in the "Taverne des Révoltés" in Aubervilliers.[7]

Debord's Paris of legend, the one he drifted through, is a Paris of the foreigner and the foreign, of disorientation, of travelers, of those who are away from home. It is also, on occasion, the subterranean Paris of truants and thieves. But it is especially a Paris marked by transience, condemned to a disappearance later identified in *In girum imus nocte* ("Paris no longer exists"). It is the city of "Andromache, I'm thinking of you," through which we can retrace our steps, possibly through Benjamin, to the sources of a perception of the city as both modern and melancholic, that is, to Baudelaire once more. The old Paris is no longer, the shape of a city changes more quickly than the heart of a mortal, and this is why, since Baudelaire, the city has served as a source for poetry. It does so in its temporal-geographic dimension, precisely because of everything that has disappeared, the remains of another time. We can say—appropriating the title of a book that meant a great deal to Debord, one he quoted often—that the psychogeographic investigation of the city was necessary because of what was assassinated by the boulevards of Haussmann's time, and the expressways and ring roads of Debord's:[8] rupture, the abolition of the past and its symbolic efficacy, the interruption of space and communication, through which the society of the spectacle robbed the city without leaving any possibility for the *dérive*.

In the fifties Debord was a master of the *dérive*. He was during the sixties as well, according to several reports of the situationist movement (especially in London, but in Brussels and Amsterdam as well). He was a tireless drifter, he could walk across Paris, with friends or lovers, for days and nights at a time (wandering not only through urban space but through time, never as palpable as when life no longer conforms to a regular succession of days and nights). He initiated a number of his companions into the psychogeographic experience, taught them how to see a city. He participated in the riskiest *dérive*s, including, at least since the period of Saint-Germain-des-Prés, a fondness for exploring the catacombs of Paris (preferably the sections off limits to the public), at least one of which came close to ending badly when the lights failed. Obviously, there is considerable risk, when playing with lost children, of losing oneself for good. And even if no one ever really got lost in the catacombs, it would have been a fitting ending for such authentic *amateurs*.

In later years, Debord and his associates would imagine other labyrinths. The catacombs were replaced by the subway tunnels, which they explored after closing, or by homes in the process of demolition. Gradually, the cities as we know them today got the better of the *dérive*, which was unable to resist the relative uniformization of environments or the homogenization of life or the functionalization of urban space, its systematic exploitation. Les Halles disappeared, and with it the possibility of deciding what to eat in Paris, food now being shipped in, after being sterilized and packaged. During the sixties, Paris, like the rest of the world, was gradually deprived of the right to taste. Today, who would want to "drift" down the Rue Saint-André-des-Arts or the Rue Mouffetard, surrounded by tourists from around the world? Certainly not Debord, whose exploration always led him to places and persons on the margins of society, toward those who struggled to resist the spectacle and the forms of appearance it imposed. Like Baudelaire, he had his little old women, the blind men, the passersby, and his swan. And, like Baudelaire, he loved them, spoke with them, spoke—and drank—a great deal in fact with the people he met during his *dérives*. Even hasty walks through changing environments do not stand in the way of authentic contact and dialogue. In fact, the opposite is true, and this is an essential difference with walks and travel in general. The *dérive* bears no resemblance to a tourist activity, spectacular, or even voyeuristic (old Aragon, I salute you) activity. It is not, strictly speaking, an aesthetic experience, recycled, almost before it begins, into a book. On the contrary, it implies an experience "from within." Its authenticity requires this. The apparently serious term "psychogeography" comprises an art of conversation and drunkenness, and everything leads us to believe that Debord excelled in both.[9]

The *dérive* is a "technique for moving quickly through varied environments." It is a technique of transience, devoted to places themselves transient, like the passages that Aragon and Benjamin were once so fond of (and they also provide a clear illustration of what the lettrists called a "situational" art, which was both temporary and lived). The city entered modern artistic consciousness because of its transformations and disfigurements, the mirror of a vanished fullness or unity that had to be reconstructed. There is nothing surprising, therefore, in the fact that, having been lost from sight after Breton and Aragon, it returned with the lettrists and was well positioned on their poetic agenda, because a new phase of modern urbanism had been established in the fifties, following the years of glaciation resulting from the Occupation and the war. Rarely have cities been transformed as they were during the 1950s and 1960s. They were reconfigured according to the needs of the automobile, and emptied of their inhabitants, who were forced to make room for stores and offices; they became places of separation and solitude. They were bathed in hygiene and light, the last empty and clandestine lots disappeared, and with them the dangerous classes. *Fast cars, clean bodies.* Everything is functionalized, identified, monitored, culminating in a process that had begun a century earlier under the auspices of Baron Haussmann's "scientific" urbanism. From this perspective, the practice of the *dérive* appears as a military, erotic and (therefore) poetic attempt to conquer or reconquer the terrain lost to the enemy, a technique of subjective reappropriation of functionalized social space.[10] Which again reveals the similarities with *détournement*: not only is the *dérive* an art of the detour, but, like *détournement,* it also implies an attempt to reappropriate the urban space, it assumes a contested relation to a space considered to have been occupied by the enemy. As Debord suggests in his *Mémoires,* the drifters were modern Knights of the Round Table who had gone off in search of the Holy Grail. They had waged war on modern urbanism using their passion, their discipline, their virtue, their courage, and their skill. And, like their legendary ancestors, almost to a man they ended up vanishing.[11]

It was wonderful while it lasted, however. The lettrist knights had their letters of nobility, as would be appropriate for any knight. In this respect, they were not without predecessors—the surrealists, to begin with, but Baudelaire as well, who was to a large extent the originator of the modern aesthetic of mobility.

This was not an art of walking, but of displacement: a rejection of the fixed, the static, the monumental, as well as a refusal to be identified. Baudelaire, that other lost child (his correspondence provides ample support for this), was the first to emphasize the virtues of *movement* and *escape* that were discussed in the "Formulary for a New Urbanism." In both his art and his life, he escaped the injunctions of polite society and, with what could be described as unshakable determination and in spite of all appearances, struggled to avoid recognition. In terms of order, the role of art is to reveal, to fix, to identify, to produce monuments. From the point of view of someone like Baudelaire, or, to a greater extent, Rimbaud, art was the vanishing point or line that tears into the panoptic structures of the society of the spectacle. It became—and this may also be another sign of modernity—a science of mobility and clandestinity. And from this viewpoint, the lettrist *dérive* would be a form of pure and radicalized modernism, art reduced to a pure principle of mobility that would allow us to escape the gaze of the Other, an art that ran counter to monumentality (monuments, by definition, are never mobile). It is an art without works. And it helped to bring about one of the oldest dreams of the avant-garde, namely, to introduce art to the streets, to the city, to life. Writing has been dismissed, to be embodied in life, in the body in movement, for which no better characterization can be found than Rimbaud, who began by giving us shocking descriptions of modern urban mobility in *Illuminations* and ended up involved in obscure business deals in Abyssinia. Rimbaud, the tireless walker, was as much the inventor of the *dérive* as Baudelaire. He is the lost child, the lost boy, par excellence, a blend of seduction and debauchery. He dabbled in clandestine and hardly admissible pleasures, he moved around continuously, between Charleville, Paris, and other points, and had no fixed domicile. He was lazy and proud of it, and may even have had a hand in the Paris Commune. He was the goldsmith of vagrancy, he escaped identity and identification—his "I" is an Other, not the person you think it is. And he left for Africa to become less visible, more inexplicable, more evasive, to lose himself, returning only to disappear for good, a dying leopard with his spots and his gangrene.

In this sense, psychogeography resembled something like the final chapter of what Roger Caillois tried to describe in 1938 in "Paris, mythe moderne."[12] The lettrists embodied, possibly for the last time, a clandestine and marvelous Paris, the reverse or lining of official, functional Paris, shaped by the architects and urban planners of the Empire and the French Republic; a Paris made of passages and secret detours, a Paris laid out for the specialists of labyrinths and catacombs described by Balzac, Féval, Sue, and so many of the crime novels of the nineteenth and twentieth centuries (which Debord was very familiar with and appropriated on occasion). Because it no longer exists and was, in any case, never visible, that Paris must be mythical. The flaneurs are the descendants of the Treize, of Vautrin, of Rouletabille, and many others. They reactivate not only the myth of Paris but also that of a hidden power that drives it, tireless bandits working in the wings at destroying the scene and the spectacle, phantoms of a large-scale opera. They are also the descendants of Baudelaire, of Rimbaud, of Breton, and of Aragon—although they dismissed Breton and Aragon, who were in too much of a hurry to transform their *dérives* into books, too fascinated with representation. The *dérive*, however, was devised to cause the *dériveur* to disappear, or at least it was not designed to bring him into view. It was an immediate experience, an experience of immediacy, which distanced the subject from the possibility of representing himself, of (re)appearing, of becoming manifest. There is something ascetic in this, for it requires the subject to disappear, entails a release from the self. Necessarily clandestine, it is intended not just to disorient the subject but to turn him away from himself, to prevent him from grasping who or what he is. It adamantly rejects the introductory "Who am I?" of *Nadja*, substituting in its place "Who am I losing?" This becomes more obvious with the technique of the "possible rendezvous," which Debord describes as follows:

> Compared to disorienting behavior, the element of exploration is minimal in the "possible rendezvous." The subject is asked to go alone at a specific time to a predetermined location. He is freed from the painful obligations of the ordinary rendezvous since there is no one waiting for him. However, having been led, unexpectedly, by this "possible rendezvous," to a place he may or may not

know, he is free to observe his surroundings. At the same time, this same location may be used for another possible "rendezvous" by someone whose identity he does not know in advance. He may never even have seen this person before, which will encourage him to strike up conversations with various passersby. He may meet no one, or accidentally meet the person who has established the "possible rendezvous." In any case, especially if the place and the surroundings have been carefully chosen, the subject's use of time will take an unexpected turn. He may even telephone someone who does not know where the first rendezvous has taken place, and ask for another "possible rendezvous." The variations on this pastime are nearly infinite.[13]

The *dérive* can be compared to the technique of disorientation. It is not designed to help us understand a comprehensible and eventually presentable ego. Debord goes on to note that "What can be written down serves only as a password in this great game." In place of surrealist writing, the *dérive* stepped in, descriptions of which—and they are rare—served as simple passwords for an initiation that took place on another terrain.[14] The adventures of the participants remain clandestine, the players invisible. They literally melt into the landscape, disappear behind the drawings, maps, aerial photographs of cities, and images of buildings, which adorn the early issues of *Internationale situationniste* as they do Debord's works, from *Mémoires* to *In girum imus nocte* and beyond. Maps of the heart on which to dream, on which to imagine desires as yet unknown, but which exist in the absence of any dreamer or any image, drawings and stones for experiences that cannot be transmitted. "The sectors of a city are to some extent decipherable. But the personal meaning they have had for us is incommunicable, as is the secrecy of private life in general, regarding which we possess nothing but pitiful documents."[15]

Where were these *dériveurs*? They hid themselves in the sinuous folds of large cities. What they experienced is incommunicable, unrepresentable. It happened and will never return other than as allusions and suggestions, maps and drawings, photos of cities in which to wander. It will also return, but as if in relief, in the form of social criticism, that is, a description and denunciation of the way in which spectacular power dissects the urban landscape for its own profit, a form of criticism found in the pages of *The Society of the Spectacle* devoted to city and regional planning. In its mourning for the world, this book, one of Debord's most important, was not unrelated to his experience of loss, and in this sense it is much less theoretical than has been acknowledged. The pages on regional planning, beneath the veneer of theory, are also based on Debord's and his friends' psychogeographic experience. The theory of "unitary urbanism," which the situationists contrasted with the urbanism of power, was developed by drifting, by walking, by evaluating the ambience of the oldest parts of Paris and other European capitals. Debord found theory through the soles of his feet. While he could write in *The Society of the Spectacle* that "the effort of all established powers, since the experience of the French Revolution, to augment their means of keeping order in the street has eventually culminated in the suppression of the street itself,"[16] it was because he worked to delay this suppression, because the *dérive* consisted, if not in re-creating streets, at least in occupying them for as long as possible. *The Society of the Spectacle* imitated the absence of life, the raw material of the spectacle; it abolished any reference to the authorial "I," to a lived singularity. Similarly, Debord's theses on urbanism and regional planning can be read as the exact opposite of the psychogeographic experience of the lettrists and situationists. Psychogeography was a conquest, or reconquest, of the *reality* of space. And the spectacle is what removed reality from space (as from life in general). Debord is quite specific about this: "The economic management of travel to different places suffices in itself to ensure those places' *interchangeability.* The same modernization that has deprived travel of its temporal aspect has likewise deprived it of the reality of space."[17] At the same time, we can understand that the reality of space depends essentially on the subject's ability to occupy it. It is a matter of subjectivity or subjectivization, that is, of singularity, of differentiation, to which is opposed the generalized interchangeability brought about by the economic management of space.

Psychogeography and Psychoanalysis

The *dérive* was an experiment in divestiture, whereas psychogeography is the culmination rather than a break with the urban adventures of the surrealists. For it was often their intent to disorient, to confront the subject with a sense of alienation that was as disturbing as possible. It is no accident that de Chirico, a master at the representation of unsettling spaces, was a tutelary figure for both the surrealists and the lettrists. In any event, it is difficult to imagine Breton, so sensitive to the discovery of absent objects, finding fault with Chtcheglov's comments about de Chirico:

> We know that an object, if not consciously noticed during an initial visit, can, because of its absence during subsequent visits, create an indefinable impression: through a correction of time, *the object's absence becomes a sensible presence*. Better yet, although it remains generally indefinite, the quality of the true impression, though it depends on the nature of the missing object and the importance given to it by the visitor, can range from serene joy to terror. (It matters little if in this precise case the vehicle of the emotion is memory. I have chosen this example simply for its convenience.) In de Chirico's painting (the Arcades period) an *empty space* creates *fully saturated time*. It is easy to represent the future that similar architectures have in store for us, and what their influence will be on crowds. Today we can only feel contempt for a century that relegates similar *models* to so-called museums.[1]

De Chirico, who was able to embody the disquiet, the insistent absence of the obscure object of desire, was not made for the museums but for the street. He is not a painter but an architect—this is the principal difference between the surrealist de Chirico and the lettrist de Chirico. He proposed models for cities of the future and new spaces in which to wander or experience unknown desires. This difference should not mask the fact that the psychogeography described here by Chtcheglov is, like any surrealist automatism, a technique for objectifying desire. In other words, the *dérive* also possesses a (psycho)therapeutic value—as did many surrealist creations.[2] By disorienting us, by thrusting us into a sometimes disquieting estrangement, it brings unknown or forgotten desires to the surface: "A complete reversal of the intellect has become essential, [to be enacted] through the revelation of forgotten desires and the creation of entirely new desires. And through an *intensive propaganda* promoting those desires."[3] The uncanny *(das Unheimlich)* is a psychoanalytic term; in any event, it was coined by Freud. It relates to the unconscious, but without the comfort of therapy, whose role would be to prevent estrangement from becoming too disquieting. If we turn again to the disquieting de Chirico, we encounter psychoanalysis, as did Chtcheglov dreaming of new cities that could accommodate experiments with new forms of behavior: "A rational broadening of ancient religious systems, old folktales, and especially psychoanalysis to promote architecture becomes more urgent with every passing day as the reasons for our excitement disappear."[4] A decade later, and after having spent considerable time in psychiatric institutions, Chtcheglov described the *dérive* similarly in his "Lettres de loin," published in 1964 in *Internationale situationniste*. The principal difference with the 1953 text lies in an awareness of the dangers of mental disintegration associated with the *dérive*. It is possible that the inventor of the *dérive* was also its first and principal victim:

> The *dérive* (through actions, gestures, walking, encounters) was exactly *to the totality* what (good) psychoanalysis is to language. The analyst tells you to say whatever comes into your head. He listens, until the moment when he highlights or changes (you might say appropriates) a word, an expression, or a definition. The *dérive* is indeed a technique, almost a form of therapy. But just as analysis alone is almost always contraindicated, the continual *dérive* is dangerous to the extent that the individual who has gone too far (not without a base, but . . .) without protection is threatened by breakdown, dissolution, dissociation, disintegration. And this is followed by a return to what is known as "everyday life," which is to say "petrified life."[5]

Chtcheglov's lucidity concerning the risks entailed in experiments in self-exposure like the *dérive* (as well as psychoanalysis) is impressive given his fate. It suggests that the lettrists' pyschogeographic adventures had, at least for some of them, the value of a borderline experience, located somewhere on the same plane as the surrealist experiments in hypnosis interrupted by Breton or other experiments in "dissolution"—Bataille's erotic experiments, the experiments by members of the Grand Jeu, who insisted on the virtues of hard drugs (René Daumal, Roger Gilbert-Lecomte). Experimentation on the self to the point of dissolution has often been a pastime of avant-gardes, and those who have been imprudent enough to go down this road have often found little but the unfortunately posthumous compensation of a mythical prestige in exchange for what they lost in life. More generally, psychogeography is not only art, but also the street as a form of analysis. Free association is replaced with aimless wandering, and based on Debord's descriptions, this is just as restricted as the "free" association practiced on the psychoanalyst's couch. Like the patient, the *dériveur* must temporarily cut himself off from his day-to-day experiences (friends, work); he must wander without any specific goal, just as the patient speaks without any specific intent. Marx claimed to have set the Hegelian dialectic back on its feet. The lettrists could say that they did the same thing with Freud. The *dérive* was therapy back on its feet, it was Freud alienated from his couch, thrust into the street and simultaneously put out of work. You cannot drift on all fours, or lying down on a couch, or while dreaming. Moving from language to what Chtcheglov called totality, psychoanalysis remains a separate practice, incomplete, which has to be replaced by a therapeutic practice whose object is life in its totality. We can see this in another text devoted to situationist experiment in general, the "construction of situations" (the *dérive*, however, is the most convincing example, the best developed, and the most concrete):

> The experimental direction of situationist activity is the creation, based on more or less clearly recognized desires, of a temporary field of activity favorable to those desires. Its creation alone may bring about the clarification of primitive desires and the confused appearance of new desires whose material roots will lie precisely in the *new reality* formed by situationist constructions. We must therefore envisage a kind of situationist psychoanalysis, in which, in contrast to the goals pursued by the followers of Freudianism, everyone who participates in the adventure must find desires for specific environments and *fulfill them*. Everyone must search for what he loves, what attracts him (and here too, unlike certain trends in modern literature—Leiris, for example—what is important to us is not the individual structure of our intellect, or an explanation of its formation, but its possible application in constructed situations).[6]

Clearly, there is an element of psychic behavior, even psychotherapy, in psychogeography.[7] Once again, the lettrists acknowledged the therapeutic dimension of the avant-garde project in general, as indicated by the reference to Leiris immediately following the reference to Freud.[8] They acknowledged it, but only to try to improve upon it. They had no time to lose, they were the avant-garde and they were impatient; therapy and interminable analysis were not their cup of tea. Desires were made to be satisfied, and what is known of the day-to-day existence of Debord and his friends suggests that many were. Neurosis does not appear to have been very important to the tribe of Saint-Germain-des-Prés, who not only had no interest in it but would not have had the means to treat it if they did. In their eyes, psychoanalysis suffered from the critical defect of requiring patience, of being at best a promise of happiness rather than happiness itself. It was an art of compromise, and compromise was as inexcusable as neurosis (in any case, they amount to the same thing, neurosis being the art of compromise, a renunciation of life, channeled into personal survival, the precociously senile disease of the society of the spectacle).

The individual or subjective dimension of the therapeutic heritage of the avant-garde also had to be overcome. From this viewpoint, the *dérive* was psychoanalysis upside down, used for the abolition of individual subjectivity, or, more exactly, as a way to overcome it by incorporating it into "constructed situations" that were necessarily collective. Consequently, psychoanalysis was placed at the service of the revolution, which never really knew what to do with the subject or his most obscure, and least admissible, thoughts. Where it was, I must disappear. And I will disappear not according to the logic of sacrifice (at least apparently) but according to the logic of the presence of an authentic subjectivity, free, sovereign, unfettered by the miasma of individual unconscious. The true subject comes into being to satisfy his desires and apply them within a collective situation. At the same time, he will disappear as an individual. The individual he started out as now exists as a kind of resistance to the fulfillment of desires that are no longer only his own, that arise by being shared. In focusing on the "individual structure," the subject remains fundamentally reactionary. He remains a subject deprived of true subjectivity, a null and void subject. If he chooses therapy or writing, if he decides to remain supine instead of drifting on his own two feet, he will prevent the revolution from taking place. Individual subjectivity presents itself lying down or seated. When it stands upright, when it drifts, it is no longer the same subjectivity, the revolution is already under way. Its enactment on the streets of the worst neighborhoods of Paris strongly contradicts what is presented to it on the psychoanalytic couch and other pathways of the signifier.

The *dérive* is collective, its goal a community of desire. There can be no revolution without a collectivization of the means of production, but no revolution either without a collectivization of desire, without shareable and shared desires. In later years this became the starting point for the utopian element in situationism, as it was for so many other utopias. But it is also essential for understanding the nature of Debord's revolutionary project as well as his originality. We can characterize this as the desire to relate the question of subjectivity to that of revolution, a desire to free the subject from the status of obscurity or superfluity to which Leninist revolutionary models consigned it, with terrifying consequences. The revolution according to Debord was also, perhaps primarily, one of subjectivization, in fact, it is the only principle of subjectivization possible.[9] Aside from the first issues of *Internationale situationniste,* the notion of "situationist psychoanalysis" was not picked up again. But Freud was not forgotten because his appropriation, both textual and conceptual, was evident in some of the most significant passages of *The Society of the Spectacle*:

> The economy's triumph as an independent power inevitably also spells its doom, for it has unleashed forces that must eventually destroy the *economic necessity* that was the unchanging basis of earlier societies. Replacing that necessity by the necessity of boundless economic development can only mean replacing the satisfaction of primary human needs, now met in the most summary manner, by a ceaseless manufacture of pseudo-needs, all of which come down in the end to just one—namely the pseudo-need for the reign of an autonomous economy to continue. Such an economy irrevocably breaks all ties with authentic needs to the precise degree that it emerges from a *social unconscious* that was dependent on it without knowing it. "Whatever is conscious wears out. Whatever is unconscious remains unalterable. Once freed, however, surely this too must fall into ruins?" (Freud) (Thesis 51).

When the economy becomes autonomous, that is, tyrannical, imposing its own law, when it no longer serves the society's most fundamental needs, when it creates pseudo-needs to ensure its own dominance, it loses its position in the social unconscious. The more factitious is the dominance of commodities, the more it operates within its own spectacle and the less it will go unnoticed, ultimately working to ensure its own loss (the effectiveness of the unconscious being associated precisely with its ability to remain unconscious). From this viewpoint the fall of the society of the spectacle will entail the removal of a repression concerning the role played by the economy, by a conscious awareness of the role it plays. Is such an appropriation or cathexis of the Freudian problematic within the political-economic domain relevant? The question remains open, since it is true that there is nothing today that seems capable of arresting the domination of the commodity: awareness of this domination appears to be powerless to do anything about it. The dominance of the commodity may be no more unconscious than the difference between use-value and exchange value, no more unconscious than the unconscious, which may not be at all. Such a comparison serves to underline that the position the author of *The Society of the Spectacle* intends to occupy is that of an *analyst* of society, as Freud was an analyst of the individual unconscious, since he obviously struggled to contribute to making the "social unconscious" conscious. As an analyst, he stood in marked contrast to politicians in the conventional sense of the term (and sometimes to sociologists and philosophers as well), who are adept at more or less localized therapeutic interventions. Debord did not intervene, he wanted no part of any of the many therapeutic avant-gardes, with their various messiahs. He was content to listen and, like an analyst, he merely gave a voice to—a kind of radical "a word to the wise is sufficient"—the conditions of possibility for the advent of the subject *in* society and not only in the asocial alcoves populated by Freudian couches:

> By the time society discovers that it is contingent on the economy, the economy has in point of fact become contingent on society. Having grown as a subterranean force until it could emerge sovereign, the economy proceeds to lose its power. Where economic id was, there ego shall be. The *subject* can only arise out of society—that is, out of the struggle that the society embodies. The possibility of a subject's existing depends on the outcome of the class struggle which turns out to be the product and the producer of history's economic foundation (Thesis 52).

> Consciousness of desire and the desire for consciousness together and indissolubly constitute that project which in its negative form has as its goal the abolition of classes and the direct possession by the workers of every aspect of their activity. The opposite of this project is the society of the spectacle, where the commodity contemplates itself in a world of its own making (Thesis 53).

What is situationist desire? It is a politicized desire, the desire of consciousness as much as the consciousness of desire. Its realization is dependent on the "results of the class struggle," that is, it depends on the triumph of the revolution. The sovereign and free subject imagined by Debord—who, to a large extent, he struggled to be and whose possibility he tried to prove *by example*—will come into being by tearing him from the society of the spectacle, the source of all alienation. And during this process, he will also lose "his" unconscious. The revolution according to Debord frees us not only from the exploitation of man by man, but also from the mirror stage and the various obstacles thrown up by the domain of the symbolic. It brings into being a subject who will identify only with himself and will focus his efforts on the immediate realization of his desires, without delay. No sooner desired than realized is the slogan of the day. There is nothing more neurotic than having to wait for the big evening to arrive, to put off living until a later date. Desire must not be given the chance to become stuck in an image or fantasy, the open doorways to the society of the spectacle. Situationist desire is itself avant-garde and, consequently, is beyond any possible representation, immediately coincident with its realization:

dérives and maps of the heart replace the couches and interminable stories concocted on them.

True subjectivity, the kind that results in the fulfillment of desire, is possibly the unique object—though reversed—of *The Society of the Spectacle*. Debord struggles to describe as objectively as possible the conditions of possibility; its advent is linked to the exposure—and ultimate destruction—of the spectacle: *The Society of the Spectacle* as a theory of an unknown or future subjectivity. This is no doubt why—at least one of the reasons why—this apparently theoretical work had such considerable success and achieved the status of an essential reference in libertarian and far-left circles. Debord spoke to his readers of the life they weren't living, and the conditions they needed to fulfill to do so. But *The Society of the Spectacle* is also a map, more warlike than tender, of a territory to be subjectively conquered, appropriated, invested, and can be related to those aerial views of cities, those maps and photos in which no one ever appears.

More generally, we find that situationism, which some have attempted to reduce to being a footnote to the history of the austere and often unpalatable work of Socialisme ou Barbarie, has always entailed the idea of desire (and its realization), the idea of what lies beyond need. It struggled to conceive of something beyond the world of labor or even any form of social contract. It did not spring from the postsurrealist movement for nothing, nor is it irrelevant that it was contemporary with the development of the "civilization of leisure," that is, in Debord's terms, the increasingly total subjugation of free time to the grip of the spectacle, whose most visible traces were, during the fifties, the growth of youth culture, tourism, the emergence of television, even the "cultural state" proposed by Malraux (who was copiously insulted by the lettrists even before he became France's first minister of culture).

Situationism wanted to be international but over time became increasingly French. It was inseparable from the Gaullist cultural state, which for decades co-opted a great deal of revolutionary goodwill, that is to say (in more situationist terms), leftist conformism. It constituted a response to the development of such a civilization. It began with the desire to liberate free time from the grip of the spectacle and, since one is the condition of the other's possibility, to liberate labor time as well. In the political and literary history of France, it was almost a first. For the far left and the avant-garde, there were few aside from Bataille who could provide such a radical challenge to Marxist assumptions about the future revolution, or conceptualize excess or expense, and it's far from clear that Bataille really was part of the far left (was Debord, for that matter?).

The name "potlatch," which had considerable importance in the work of Georges Bataille, was enough to suggest a proximity or, more accurately, a point of contact between Bataille and Debord. Both struggled to conceptualize something beyond need, which led both men to incorporate the concepts of the gift and the potlatch in their thinking and to reject out of hand the Stalinist-Leninist model and its praise for work and productivity. In the history of French twentieth-century avant-gardes, Bataille and Debord went farthest in their search for an alternative to Marxist-Leninist loyalty by trying to conceptualize something that transcended the economy. In Bataille, this led to an examination of religion, the question of sacrifice, expense, and eroticism; in Debord, by what he sometimes called the "potlatch of self-destruction," which can be thought of as the emblem of a kind of revolutionary absolute. This does not mean that their ideas were identical or that they had more than this in common. Debord had read Bataille (especially his theoretical works such as *The Cursed Share* and *Eroticism*) and, although he could not have been unaware of his debt to Bataille, he never quoted or appropriated him, most likely because there were just as many points of disagreement between the two men. It is hard to imagine Debord being sympathetic to the Bataille who wrote *Inner Experience*. Debord's thought was characterized by a rejection of any idea of transcendence. Given his lifestyle, it is hard to see him succumbing to the charms of the dialectic of law and transgression, since everything points to the fact that for Debord this was nothing but a trumped-up form of modernism—as was the work of Lacan, which is so dependent on Bataille.[10] More generally—and this concerns not only Bataille but also his ambivalent relation to Freud—Debord's thought left no room for eroticism or fantasy. This is not to say his thought or life were austere. More than others, he made ample room for pleasure in his life, especially since pleasure was never problematic for him, and precisely because it concerned him and him alone. But situationism was made for the *dérive*, that is, for dreaming or sleeping on your feet. It consisted in constructing situations, fulfilling desires rather than dreaming about them while lying alone in bed. It was designed to purge life of fantasies. These prevented life from being shared and blurred the boundary between the lived and the not-lived, they contaminated life with an imaginary component, allowing it to be tempted by the spectacle, to succumb to passivity. "The adventurer is one who encourages adventure, rather than someone to whom adventures happen," Debord wrote.[11] In such a context, it is difficult to imagine Debord being enthusiastic about psychoanalysis or feeling anything more than esteem for Bataille, the theoretician of expenditure. Bataille was also the man who incorporated in his fiction a number of fantasized self-portraits through the use of pseudonyms and dissimulation, blurring the boundary between his real life and his imaginary life. He systematically assumed a position contrary to Breton's desire for transparency, which, from this viewpoint, Debord inherited: fantasy can never be exemplary and, therefore, never revolutionary.

Unitary Urbanism: Between Utopia and Architecture

Psychogeography was a central element of early lettrism and an integral part of situationism until 1962, at which time Debord and his companions decided that the "one step back" represented by the transition from the Lettrist International to the Situationist International had lasted long enough and it was again time to make a final break with art (thereby repeating the initial break that characterized the transition from Isou's lettrism to international lettrism).

From 1953 to 1962, the *dérive* was very much in evidence; it was the essential element in an art of "experience," assumed to coincide with life and free of any form of representation. However, psychogeography was more than the *dérive,* which was a practical matter or, more literally, an exercise in reconnaissance. When it was reactivated at the time of the founding of the SI, psychogeography was also an architectural project. The "Formulary for a New Urbanism" by Chtcheglov-Ivain, (re)published—probably for this very reason—in the first issue of *Internationale situationniste,* made it very clear that architecture was the condition of possibility for the *dérive.* This, wrote Chtcheglov, would only achieve its full potential or plenitude when completely new cities had been constructed for that purpose, and those new cities would be the result of experience with past *dérives.* If de Chirico made them dream, if he encouraged them to drift, it was because he was above all an architect. The *Unheimlich* of the Arcades period had to be actually embodied in a space-time. The lettrist appropriation of psychoanalysis diverted it toward an architectural utopia. It is worth quoting Chtcheglov at length:

> This new vision of time and space, which will be the theoretical basis of future constructions, is not ready and will never be completely ready until experiments with behavior are conducted in cities intended for that purpose, where buildings endowed with great evocative and influential power, symbolic edifices representing desires, forces, and past, present, and future events, will be systematically combined, along with essential structures possessing a minimum of comfort and security. A rational expansion of ancient religious systems, old folktales, and especially psychoanalysis for architectural purposes becomes more urgent with each passing day, as the reasons for our enthusiasm disappear.
>
> In a sense, everyone will inhabit his personal "cathedral." There will be rooms that will do a better job than drugs at making us dream, and houses where one can only make love. Others will powerfully attract travelers. . . .
>
> This project can be compared to the Chinese and Japanese gardens of trompe l'oeil—the difference being that those gardens were not made to be fully lived in—or the ridiculous labyrinth of the Jardin des Plantes, where we can read, the height of stupidity, Ariadne out of work: *No game playing inside the labyrinth.*
>
> This city could be envisaged as an arbitrary combination of castles, grottos, lakes, and so on. This would be the baroque stage of urbanism considered as a means of understanding. . . .
>
> The neighborhoods in this city could correspond to the various feelings cataloged, which are found *by accident* in everyday life.
>
> Strange Quarter—Happy Quarter, especially designed for residences—Noble and Tragic Quarter (for well-behaved children)—Historical Quarter (museums, schools)—Utilitarian Quarter (hospitals, hardware stores)—Sinister Quarter, and so on. . . .[1]

There was a transition from religion, fables, and psychoanalysis to architecture, to the construction of new desires. In 1953 this was the "program" of lettrist, then situationist, urbanism, which was qualified as utopian for several reasons. First, and most trivially, because the program was never realized—not in 1953 and not later. The lettrist city remained an imaginary one, as did the situationist city after it (although a number of situationist ideas ended up as elements of concrete architectural projects).[2] Reading Chtcheglov, it would likely have been part Japanese garden or part botanical garden and its labyrinths made a part of everyday life. The ludic function of space would have been emphasized; it would have been a Louis II Bavarian castle, with its lakes and grottoes: the image of a city that could only be re-alized in dream.[3]

The "Formulary for a New Urbanism" can be considered utopian to the extent that it was presented as a program intended for the collective ful-fillment of all desires, including those new and as yet unknown. Like all utopian projects, it set forth the conditions for the realization of desire. It was created to provide desire with its own space, through the presence of "buildings symbolizing desire," transcending those "establishments neces-sary to ensure a minimum of comfort and security." It transcended need. It symbolized desire, gave it a place in the social space. Psychogeography was Fourier and the Saint-Simonians reborn as architects, the architects they had always been.

Any reader of Fourier is familiar with the role played by architecture in his utopia. The "new world of love" and the "phalanstery" are unthinkable without the presence of places set aside for the countless pleasures and de-sires that are supposed to take place there. The phalanstery is architectural in nature. For Victor Considérant, the "architect" of Fourierism, the term "phalanstery" was equivalent to "a palace for social activities." We could even say that the new world of love was no more than that: a project for dif-ferentiating space, a totalizing project for spatializing or implementing the figures of desire, with underground or aboveground passages to move from one place to another, to drift from one desire to another, as the lettrists had planned. One of the first things the Saint-Simonians did when Barthélemy-Prosper Enfantin withdrew in 1832 to Ménilmontant and communal life was to imagine, primarily with the encouragement of Michel Chevalier and Charles Duveyrier, a new city, a city that had become completely organic, whose model was the human body. The Saint-Simonians (although they were far from being alone in this) dreamed of a harmonious city, all of whose parts were to be created together, as if by a stroke of a magic wand. They imagined a city that eliminated the chaos of the historical city, made of heterogeneous deposits and sediments that engendered separation and hindered communication. The organic city was the city given over to the desire for communication and community—simply speaking, to desire.[4] In this sense, they also prefigured what the situationists tried to conceptual-ize under the heading "unitary urbanism," that is, a defunctionalized city, freed of the multiplicity of separations (between work and leisure, private and public) that structured it. From this point of view as well, the situation-ists shared with the Saint-Simonians their interest in mobility. Just as they emphasized iron structures to realize an infinitely transformable city (Paris replaced by a kind of giant erector set), the situationists hoped to create places and cities that were infinitely changeable. Mobility was already on the agenda in the "Formulary for a New Urbanism":

> We propose the invention of new movable sets. . . .
>   The architectural complex will be modifiable. Its appearance will change par-tially or completely depending on the will of its inhabitants. . . .
>   Previous communities offered the masses an absolute truth and unquestion-able examples from myth. The appearance of the concept of *relativity* in the modern lexicon leads us to anticipate the EXPERIMENTAL side of the next civili-zation, even though I find the word unsatisfactory. Let's say more flexible, more "amused." On the basis of this mobile civilization, architecture will be—at least initially—a means for experimenting with the thousand ways of modifying life, looking forward to a synthesis that can only be legendary.[5]

Psychogeography may be the very essence of utopia, if only because the entire Western utopian tradition was born in the sixteenth century with the discovery of the New World, with the possibility of an entirely new under-standing of the "psychological" (and by extension the social) and the geo-graphic. The utopian tradition has always wanted to reorganize space in a way that would take into account human desires, as well as to order the world, to create a hierarchy. According to its etymology, architecture is ul-timately a science of foundation, of beginning, and of ordering. Is that why it is beautiful only when utopian, when it has not embodied itself in some concrete form of organization or structure, social or architectural, when it does not appear in any codes of law or engraved in stone or iron; only when it has remained *literature*? In any event, it was perfectly clear to the lettrists that when Chtcheglov called for the introduction of movable sets, he could only be referring to a horizon or vanishing point, a reversed image of that other form of mobility and flight embodied in the *dérive*: to my knowledge, none of them ever drafted any architectural plans. To imagine a new city made of movable sets, to move around in a real city in order to reappro-priate it—everything leads us to believe that there is a point where the two terms amount to the same thing. That is why the lettrists were as critical of "avant-garde" architecture as they were of art. No project was spared, espe-cially if it had been realized.

Le Corbusier was the most obvious target, but everything associated with functionalist architecture, at its height during the fifties and sixties, served as a foil for lettrist psychogeography. The "Protestant Modulor, Corbusier-Sing-Sing" was accused of building churches (which were diametrically opposed in every sense to the invisible and mobile "personal cathedrals" imagined by Chtcheglov), or worse, of constructing habitable cells modeled after prisons and, a worthy heir of Haussmann, of wanting to eliminate street life: "This, then is the program: life finally will be divided into closed islands, monitored societies; the end of any opportunities for insurrection and encounter; automatic resignation."[6] If he hadn't been preceded in this by nearly a half-century, Le Corbusier could just as well have been the inventor of the panopticon whose irresistible appeal to those in power was described by Michel Foucault.[7]

ASGER JORN

The lettrists again attacked Le Corbusier when, in November 1956, they called for a boycott of the "Festival de l'art d'avant-garde," which was to be held in Marseilles at the newly completed "Cité Radieuse."[8] This is not without relevance when we consider that the possibility for enlarging the group (which would later become the Situationist International) was in the process of being concretized and that the "one step back" taken with the founding of the SI soon introduced the problem of the status of situationist "architecture," which some were not yet ready to acknowledge as being no more than literature. More generally, the antifunctionalist theme was critical to the founding of the Situationist International or, to put it another way, the meeting between Guy Debord and Asger Jorn.

In the fall of 1954 Jorn became aware of the existence of the Lettrist International, primarily through *Potlatch*. What did he find so interesting in the lettrist review, most of whose contributors were fifteen years younger than he? The radicality of their statements most likely, their hostility to contemporary avant-gardes, to abstract painting as well as to the socialist-realist movement that dominated the artistic landscape, but especially their mutual interest in the idea of psychogeography, which reflected Jorn's own concerns, his debate with functionalism.

Born in 1917 in Silkeborg, Denmark, Asger Jorn (his real name was Asger Jørgensen) was no longer unknown when he discovered lettrism. In 1937, having arrived in Paris, he painted a fresco for Fernand Léger (who had no hesitation in signing it). He also worked for Le Corbusier, enlarging the children's drawings for the Temps Nouveaux pavilion at the Paris World's Fair. He then worked for the Spanish Republican government, traveled and painted throughout Europe and Tunisia. He met Christian Dotremont in 1947 during the International Conference of Revolutionary Surrealism[9] and made the first "word paintings" with him.

In 1948, he participated in the foundation of Cobra, which until 1951 brought together a number of artists from the Danish group Host, the Belgian Revolutionary Surrealist group, and the Dutch Reflex group (Cobra was an acronym formed from the first letters of Copenhagen, Brussels, and Amsterdam). Together with Jorn, one of the most active members, and Christian Dotremont, some of the best-known members were Karel Appel, Pierre Alechinsky, Raoul Ubac, and Constant Nieuwenhuys, known as Constant (born in 1920, Constant was the only member of Cobra to also participate in the situationist movement). Cobra has often been described as a kind of synthesis of expressionism and surrealism, a gamble on the spontaneity of expression rather than on the formalism, abstraction, and rationalism that were then dominant (embodied by Le Corbusier and Mondrian in painting). The group revolved around the attempt to provide expression itself with the element of freedom and revolt it was assumed to possess during the height of surrealism. Once again it was a question of reintroducing revolution and its long-standing accomplice, freedom, into art itself, or to imbue revolution once more with the notion of subjectivity. Cobra intended to give priority to morality (obviously understood as revolutionary morality) over aesthetics. It also took the side of a "collective popular culture" that would need to be reinvented and stand in opposition to artistic individualism.[10] The war between imagination and reason, between spontaneous community art and formalized or stylized individualism, was an old one and Cobra placed itself squarely in the first camp. Jorn was equally clear when he argued, in 1953, with Max Bill, who offered him a position in his new "Bauhaus" in Ulm. The Hochschule für Gestaltung in Ulm embraced the idea of industrial art (a project involving close collaboration between the artist and the artisan), which had already been promulgated by the first Bauhaus in Weimar, directed between the two wars by Gropius. Consequently, it adopted a program Jorn considered to be rationalist and technocratic. So he turned down Bill's offer and founded (also in 1953) the resolutely antifunctionalist International Movement for an Imaginist

Bauhaus with the help of the Italian painter Giuseppe Pinot-Gallizio, who gave Jorn access to his studio in Alba (near Genoa) in 1955. This was art not in the service of social integration or industry but, as with Cobra, art serving the combat against social norms, the rational order, and the conformity of functionalist artists and architects. In a text republished by the situationists in 1958, Jorn stated, and rightly so, since the principal themes of psychogeography (mobility, the construction of environments) had already been established:

> Obviously, we are not opposed to modern technology, but we are against any idea of the absolute necessity of objects, to the point of also doubting their effective utility.
>
> The functionalists also ignore the psychological function of the environment. Just as the café has no value insofar as our health is concerned but is of psychological and sensory importance, similarly the exterior view of the buildings and objects that surround us and which we use has a function independent of their practical use. The exterior of a house should not reflect the interior, but should serve as a source of poetic sensation for the observer.
>
> Instead of relying on the free play of imagination to renovate today's architecture, we have enthusiastically moved in the opposite direction. We attempt, through the scientific analysis of biological life, to discover plant and animal constructions that might serve as the basis for architectural constructions. But there are more reasons why these attempts to make architecture a pseudoscience are still of secondary importance. . . .
>
> The functionalist rationalists, because of their ideas about standardization, have imagined that we could arrive at final, ideal forms for different objects of interest to mankind. Evolution today shows that this static conception is incorrect. We must arrive at a dynamic conception of forms, must confront the truth that every human form exists in a state of continuous transformation. We must not, like the rationalists, avoid this transformation. The failure of the rationalists is to have misunderstood that the only way of avoiding the anarchy of change consists in becoming aware of the laws by which the transformation takes place, and making use of them.[11]

Jorn's Imaginist Bauhaus was art refusing to ally itself with scientific and industrial rationality; it was art in the service of the free play of subjectivity, and consequently devoid of any instrumentalization (political, economic, social). It was also an experimental art used for mobility and change. It was as useless as the café (or alcohol, as Debord would no doubt have added). Clearly, there are a number of points common to both Jorn's imaginist art and the experiments of the lettrists. As such, Jorn's program implies the practice of appropriation, which here seems inseparable from a critical attitude toward functionalism and industrial art. In this context, appropriation consists in *not using* objects and discourses.[12] Interestingly, Jorn frequently succumbed to the charms of appropriation in the field he knew best, painting, by repainting other paintings, often painting directly over their surfaces and thereby changing or caricaturing them.

The establishment of an International Movement for an Imaginist Bauhaus was contemporary with the first contacts between Debord and Jorn. Ideas circulated freely between the two groups. The lettrists followed with interest and sympathy the first (and last) steps of the Imaginist Bauhaus, and with their customary charity they applauded the resignation of Max Bill from the Ulm Bauhaus in 1956. Although it was clear that psychogeography formed the core of their ideas by 1952–53 (that is, before the meeting with Jorn), it was Jorn who was largely responsible for the systematization and concretization of their critical discourse on architecture. The psychogeographic period of the first years of situationism also has its origins in the contacts that took place from 1954 to 1957 between the lettrists and the "imaginist" movement.[13] It was beautiful, like the confluence, on the metallized covers of the later *Internationale situationniste* review, of a group of drinkers and drifters in love with big cities threatened with disappearance and artists who were steeped in rural life and the search for a revolutionary radicalism that seemed to escape their brushes. Beautiful, because given the differences in what they did, where they came from, where they were going, and their age (the "imaginists" were on average fifteen years older than the lettrists), there was something infinitely random about the undertaking.[14] It could easily not have taken place. The only real necessity was the friendship between Debord and Jorn. Given the many tentative avant-garde movements at the time, the lettrists, like the "imaginists," could have made other alliances, formed other internationals. As chance—or the necessity of a friendship—would have it, things turned out differently. It also led Debord, Jorn, and their friends to develop the psychogeographic utopia, which was the only common denominator among those who participated in getting the situationist adventure off the ground. Debord's "one step back" in 1958 was the step the radical lettrists had to take to meet the "imaginist" artists. It was what led them to the point where Chtcheglov found himself in 1953: on the side of the architectural utopia the SI would systematically develop during the first years of its existence; as a way to avoid abandoning art once and for all.

UNITARY URBANISM

Written in 1953, the "Formulaire pour un urbanisme nouveau" re-appeared in the first issue of *Internationale situationniste*. The second issue contained Debord's "Théorie de la dérive," first published in *Les Lèvres nues* in 1956, along with the "Essai de description psychogéographique des Halles," signed by Abdelhafid Khatib. This article ends with a call for a ludic recycling of Les Halles in Paris. The situationist man did not live on bread alone, rather, he only began to live when need had been transcended, in this case nutritional need:

> It is important to take advantage of the slowdown in practical-nutritional activity to encourage the large-scale development of interest in the play of construction and mobile urbanism that appeared spontaneously "in the frigid waters of egotistical calculation." Obviously, the first architectural step would be the replacement of the current pavilions with autonomous series of small situationist architectural complexes. Among these new architectures and along their outskirts, corresponding to the four zones we have planned for the site, should be constructed labyrinths that change continuously, with more appropriate objects than crates of fruits and vegetables, the materials of the only barricades in existence today.[15]

Khatib's article is entirely consistent with the "Formulary for a New Urbanism" in its combination of the *dérive* with clearly utopian projects, especially in light of what has since become of Les Halles. There was nothing really new in the earliest psychogeographic tracts published by *Internationale situationniste*, and it's rather their lack of novelty that needs to be questioned. Why, for example, republish articles from 1953 or 1956 in 1958? Obviously, because they were felt to be as good and as relevant as before. In any event, the situationists considered writing to be not literary but strategic. It was not a matter of creating an original body of work simply for the pleasure of doing so, but of making the best use of existing texts, as was also shown by the practice of appropriation. Debord never wrote a text unless he felt it was absolutely necessary. We also need to examine the configuration of the newly created Situationist International, which now included a number of artists. As extreme as their avant-garde radicality might seem, these members had solid careers behind them (some of them, especially Jorn,

Pinot-Gallizio, and Constant, had become familiar with avant-garde move-ments and art galleries long before they joined the SI).

They wanted to take stock of the situation, make sure that after their "one step back" they took off in the right direction. I won't discuss the dis-cussions and conflicts that constituted the day-to-day workings of the early SI. Most of them revolve around the question of the role of artists, acceptable and unacceptable compromises. There were numerous polem-ics, not always essential, and often predictable. Confirmation can be found in Debord's *Correspondance*. The first volume (1957–60) provides impor-tant information about the period when the SI was founded, especially the association with Pinot-Gallizio, one of Debord's principal correspondents until their split. This was also the period of the debate with Constant, who quit the SI in 1960. The second volume contains details of the events that led to the break with the Belgian situationist Maurice Wyckaert (whom the SI reproached for his lack of clarity concerning the maneuvering of the art dealer Van de Loo). Debord also discusses the break with the German group Spur, with whom the SI continued to maintain—at least initially—cordial relations (primarily by supporting its former German associates when they were charged in Munich with blasphemy and public indecency). However, there are also a number of letters in this second volume suggesting that the break with Jörgen Nash and the Scandinavian group was much more high-ly charged, to the point that "Nashism" would become the official name for any attempt at artistic co-optation of the situationist experiment (espe-cially by former situationists).

Reading Debord's *Correspondance* helps clarify a number of points. In general, one finds that as radical as the SI considered itself—or would have liked to be considered retroactively—its practices and interests did not dif-fer greatly from those of many other avant-garde groups of the same pe-riod: there were negotiations with galleries, artworks to exhibit, texts to be printed, territory to conquer, rivals and enemies to combat. And what is most astonishing in Debord's letters is that he took great pains to *promote* the work of his friends. He spent considerable time and effort arranging ex-hibitions for Pinot-Gallizio in Paris and almost everywhere in Europe, and trying to find common ground with Constant, who was apparently moving quickly toward initially subtle but then explicit forms of resistance. What is striking in these letters—especially concerning the portrait of Debord as a Stalinist-sectarian elitist that has been so complacently bandied about—is not only the kindness expressed in his discussions with others (which did not rule out frankness or firmness), his patience when arguing, and a "political" flexibility that contrasts with certain forms of behavior objectively incompatible with the SI's platform, but the friendship, or at least cordiality, that remained after the breakups, and Debord's generosity in supporting the work of his friends, his sense of value, his sense of gift giving.

Reading between the lines of his correspondence, it is relatively easy to understand why Debord often broke with his friends—the potlatch often seemed to be unilateral and one wonders what he received in return for his efforts. Obviously, we would need access to additional information to confirm this supposition, but Debord's letters sometimes give the impression of an *asymmetry* between giver and receiver. Couldn't this also be the reason why so many who were excluded from the SI simply left and remained silent? Couldn't we assume that they had received, and for quite some time, more than their due? From this and the correspondence concerning the early years of the SI, it is clear that the only relationship that was not asymmetrical was the one between Debord and Jorn, whose generosity also seems to have been genuine. Is it so surprising, then, that this was the most lasting friendship of Debord's life (together with his later friendship with Gérard Lebovici)?

During the early years of the SI, the most interesting debate, in terms of substance, was the one between Debord (as well as Jorn) and Constant. To some extent, this also served as the model for a number of other future debates and conflicts. The Dutch artist was the only truly discordant voice to make himself heard and it is remarkable that he did so right from the beginning of their relationship. Constant wanted to initiate a dialogue about techniques for creating sets and environments imagined by the newly minted situationists. In other words, he introduced the question of the transition from Chtcheglov's utopian program to an *artistic* one: how to transform a utopian formula into a set of specifications for revolutionary artists? "The artists' job is to invent new techniques and use light, sound, movement, and in general anything that can influence environments. Without this the integration of art in the construction of the human habitat will remain as chimerical as the proposals of Gilles Ivain."[16] From the outset, the SI was divided by a debate between artist-technicians on the one hand (in several letters to Debord, Constant attacked those on his right whom he suspected of being more invested in art than he was, especially Pinot-Gallizio), and unitary utopians on the other, notably Jorn and Debord. These wanted no part of technique except within the framework of a project for *unitary* urbanism, that is, a project for changing *every* aspect of life, for transforming society—in other words, a project for revolution. In response to Constant's questions, Debord and Jorn answered by defending Chtcheglov's (Ivain's) position: "Gilles Ivain's proposals in no way contradict these considerations regarding modern industrial production. They are, on the contrary, constructed on that historical basis. If they are chimerical, they are to the extent that we do not have concrete access today to the technical means . . . ; not because those means do not exist or because we are unaware of them. In this sense, we believe in the revolutionary value of such momentarily utopian claims."[17] The "momentarily utopian" position (Ivain's) is revolutionary not only because it implies a unitary urbanism, a project for the complete transformation of the city that can only occur within a revolutionary context, but even, perhaps especially, because it disqualifies the artist-technician position espoused by Constant and others. During situationism's early years, Debord never showed much enthusiasm for utopias of any kind. He would later take the part of political struggle against that of utopia, choosing unitary urbanism over art, as if he wanted to put pressure on the artists in the group and force them to give up their special identity as artists.

This is why there was renewed interest in the *dérive*, the subjective implementation of unitary urbanism, in the second issue of *Internationale situationniste*: instead of architects' models and studios, the situationists offered a psychogeographic experience of the street itself—mobility and idleness against monuments and models. And in the third issue, Pinot-Gallizio, known for his work with "industrial painting" and a specialist in the discrepancy between situationist radicalism and artistic opportunism, took a turn at utopia with his "Discours sur la peinture industrielle et sur un art unitaire applicable," an essay that showed definite traces of futurism. The article is interesting because it was written by the SI member who seemed the most interested in exhibitions and galleries. Moreover, in the context of the debate that pitted Constant against Debord and Jorn, it suggests a kind of utopian initiative, an attempt to escape the question of technique introduced by Constant—unless it is a case of Pinot-Gallizio trying to detach himself from a personal strategy that was too obviously "artistic."[18] Yet we also learn that "the world will be the stage and parterre of a continuous play. The planet will transform itself into a Luna Park without boundaries, producing new emotions and passions."[19] Obviously, those new emotions and passions would involve techniques that were also entirely new, so new that no one claims to know what they are (not even Constant). Even when they are known, it will still be impossible to repeat them. For they are singular techniques used to create singular sets, unprecedented, never seen before; and ultimately, they are not really even techniques because they cannot be used to reproduce anything. Rather, they should be considered techniques of nonproduction, possibly as techniques of destruction or self-destruction of whatever it is they allow to be produced. They will last only long enough to inspire passions and emotions that are as ephemeral and new as they are, associated with a sixth or seventh sense that has yet to be discovered, resolutely situated beyond the visible and the audible:

> The new sets—which range from the fabric of the habitat and means of transport to ways of drinking, to food, lighting, experimental cities—will be unique, artistic, impossible to repeat. They will no longer be called buildings, but furniture, and merely functional, since they will be momentary instruments of pleasure and play. In a word, we will become poor again, very poor and also very rich, in the sprit of new forms of behavior.
>
> All our goods will be collective and rapidly self-destruct. Poetic quality will no longer act on the senses we know but on those we do not yet know. There will be no more architecture, no more painting, no more words or images. In the future our works will be without surface or volume. We are near the fourth dimension of pure poetry; near a magic that has no master, but which can only be realized by everyone.[20]

Situationist man feeds on the invisible, evanescent, and ephemeral objects of desires yet to come. He aspires to a wealth made of mobile and self-destructive potlatch-objects. He comes into being in and with the emergence of a space governed by a "fourth dimension of pure poetry," the nearly mystical or divine keystone of the utopia of Pinot-Gallizio. This fourth dimension, a dream transmitted by the Saint-Simonians to the avant-gardes and before them to Wagner, is necessary to escape art and its techniques (its images, its texts, its words). Do anything to avoid becoming an artist. Pinot-Gallizio took up the challenge, but although he failed to find the modern Grail of pure poetry,[21] he seems to have resigned himself fairly quickly to collaborating on new art projects with "ideologically unacceptable milieus," according to the expression found in issue 5 of *International situationniste* announcing his exclusion.[22] The utopian is an idle artist dreaming not only of new techniques but of new meanings, which call forth a new *Gesamtkunstwerk*. The end of art is replaced by a principle of immediacy and totality: progress has been slow since the Saint-Simonians.

In the same issue of *Internationale situationniste* where Pinot-Gallizio dreamed of situationist Luna Parks, there appeared, as a response to the questions posed by Constant about technique, a very complete program of "unitary urbanism." This opened with a critique of real urbanism and the reconfiguration of modern cities by those in power, who emptied them of their inhabitants and invested them with separation rather than communication and community. It was a global critique and, therefore, on its positive and creative side, its means had to be global as well. In other words, unitary urbanism was opposed, by definition, to urbanism as a separate discipline, just as invisible situationist art was opposed to conventional forms of art: "No isolated discipline whatsoever can be tolerated in itself; we are moving toward a global creation of existence."[23] Covering all aspects of life, it ultimately coincided with revolution, as did situationist art in general. These could only come about together: "Unitary urbanism merges objectively with the interests of a comprehensive subversion."[24] Here as well, the theme of utopia is what enabled them to anticipate, during the late fifties, a rather uncertain revolution without falling into the trap of art in which so many avant-gardes perished, without capitulating to architecture, to order, to the fixed and the monumental. The program for unitary urbanism especially emphasized *mobility*, which should be understood as subversion in the virtual state. It was one thing to plan the transformation of the urban environment into a site for "participatory" play, quite another, more revolutionary, to imbue the city thus transformed with perpetual mobility: "Unitary urbanism is opposed to the temporal fixation of cities. It leads instead to the advocacy of a permanent transformation, an accelerated movement of the abandonment and reconstruction of the city in temporal and at times spatial terms. . . . Unitary urbanism is opposed to the fixation of people at certain points of a city. It is the foundation for a civilization of leisure and of play."[25]

From the necessity of overall subversion, the urbanist program drifted toward the utopia of a city-in-motion, whose residents were not identified or assigned to any fixed domicile. It targeted the utopia of the city-as-desire, which would be cathected and decathected according to the free flow of

La Pointe du Vert-Galant (*In girum imus nocte et consumimur igni,* 1978)

1951

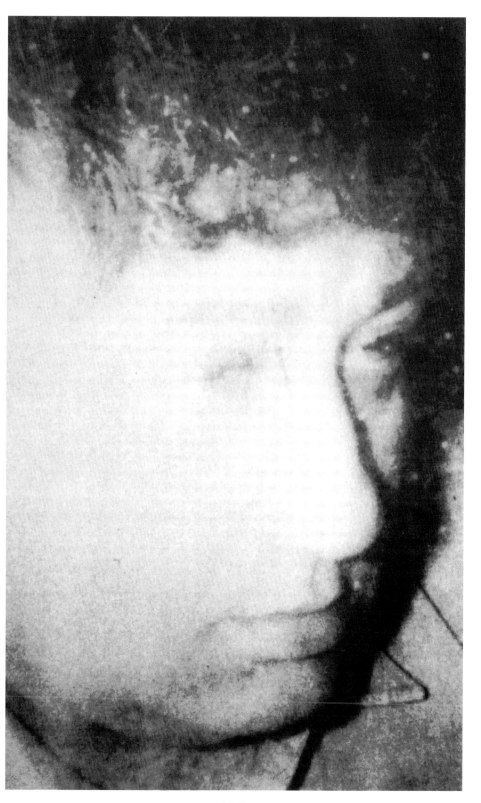

1977

GUIDE PSYCHOGEOGRAPHIQUE DE PARIS

ÉDITÉ PAR LE BAUHAUS IMAGINISTE

PRINTED IN DENMARK BY

PERMILD & ROSENGREEN

DISCOURS SUR LES PASSIONS DE L'AMOUR

pentes psychogeographiques de la dérive et localisation d'unites d'ambriance

par G.-E. DEBORD

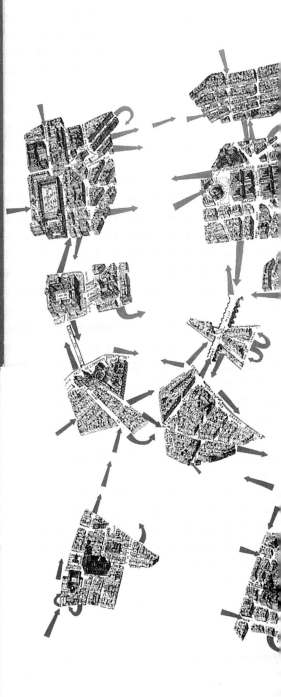

Page from *Guide Psychogéographique de Paris*

1952 (from *Ion*)

Paris, Rue du Bac
(Hôtel de Clermont-Tonnerre), 1990

Paris, 139, Rue Saint-Martin, 1969–79

Venice, January 1994. Photograph by M.-L. Labrosse.

Arles, 33, Rue de le l'Hôtel-de-Ville, 1984

Champot

With Alice Becker-Ho, Paris, 1965

Photograph for the dedication of the film *The Society of the Spectacle*:
with Alice Becker-Ho, summer 1968, in the Vosges.

Cannes Film Festival, April 20, 1951, after the screening of Isidore Isou's film *Traité de bave et d'éternité* (Treatise on Slime and Eternity). Guy Debord is third from left; Isidore Isou is third from right.

On the set of *Critique of Separation,* 1960

The Charge of the Light Brigade
(*In girum imus nocte et consumimur igni,* 1978)

On the set of *Critique of Separation*, 1960

On the set of *Critique of Separation*, 1960

passion and impulse, that is to say, rather quickly. And from utopia it drifted ... toward the *dérive,* whose necessity was thus confirmed. If the mobile
city would not come to the situationists, they would go to it, into it, so it
might become subjectively mobile. The *dérive* was the only possible implementation of this science of mobility that unitary urbanism wanted to be,
the only form of experimentation possible.

THE NEW BABYLON

It was in this context that Constant presented the drawings and models of his New Babylon in issues 3 and 4 of *Internationale situationniste.* In
actuality, there were no more than a handful of drawings, which leads us
directly to the heart of Constant's ambivalent relationship with the radicality of the situationist project; for although he supported it, he intended to
remain an artist and continued to exhibit his work (in 1959 he exhibited
fragments of New Babylon at the Stedelijk Museum in Amsterdam).

The New Babylon was Constant's major work, his version of a utopian
Gesamkunstwerk, to which he continued to add drawings and models, long
after his break with Debord in 1960. In fact, he continued to work on it until
1969, after which he devoted himself entirely to painting. There were several large exhibits of his New Babylon, including at the Kunsthalle in Bern
in 1966 and the Gemeente Museum in the Hague in 1974. In the interim,
the work went on to become one of the most important references for urbanist architecture during the sixties. In the mid-sixties, Constant became
one of the icons of the "Provos" movement in Amsterdam (inspired by psy-
chedelic libertarianism) and his project was often quoted, discussed, used,
even appropriated by "real" architects. Between the man who was fundamentally the author of a single work, total and monumental, and Debord,
so attached to idleness, one suspects that it would have required all the
benevolence and optimism of Asger Jorn simply to make such a meeting
possible.

The New Babylon is indeed Constant's work. It is relevant here, in a book
about Debord, because it represents a turning point in the history of situationism and falls on the boundary over which that history flowed. It was
the tipping point around which the SI was capable of taking a step back as
well as a step forward. When Constant first presented the New Babylon in
Internationale situationniste, he began, significantly, by reaffirming his interest in techniques for carrying out the projects of unitary urbanism, but

he was also careful to support the situationist utopia of mobility: "We are in the process of inventing new techniques; we are examining the possibilities offered by existing cities, and making models and plans for future ones. We are aware of the need to take advantage of all the new technologies, and we know that the future constructions we envisage will have to be flexible enough to respond to the dynamic conception of life, creating our surroundings in direct relation to constantly changing modes of behavior."[26]

He then turns to the crux of the matter, the New Babylon. This consists of a project for a suspended city and owes its name to the celebrated hanging gardens of ancient Babylon, with its suggestion of pleasure and debauchery. (It is noteworthy that the Paris of the Commune [1870–71], the legendary ancestor of unitary urbanism, was described in contemporary newspapers—most notably in Germany—as a new Babylon, a place of debauchery and anarchy.) Changing life meant, for Constant, elevating the level of life. Rejecting the functionalist urbanism that destroyed the city as a community and the "green city" whose hated emblem was the newly constructed city of Brasília,[27] Constant intended to return the city to its communitarian essence by elevating it, by building a city on columns.[28] Unlike official urbanism, which made use of the needs of circulation to interrupt communication, Constant's suspended city simply abandoned the ground level to functional transport. Circulation occurred below the space of daily life, which was now given over to its communicative essence. Real life rose a level, spreading out over an infinity of communicating spaces and labyrinths, which no Baron Haussmann would ever truncate or pollute. The street, the object of so many avant-garde desires, especially when the street included crowds and revolution, was thus freed of its sickening functionality, given over to desire through the act of elevating it. It was divided into a ground floor of need, abandoned to individualizing automobiles and "shared" transportation for disconnected groups, and a first level reserved for passion, that is, genuine transport and mobility—groups fusing with one another. There were terraces on the second level. From unscheduled meetings to shocking encounters, people could even drift over the city by helicopter (the advantages of such a solution over automobile transportation are obvious):

> The terraces form an outdoor terrain that extends over the whole surface of the city and can be used for sports, as landing pads for planes and helicopters, and

for vegetation. They will be accessible everywhere by stairways and elevators. The different levels will be divided into neighboring and communicating spaces, climate-controlled, which will make it possible to create an infinite variety of environments, facilitating the casual movements of the inhabitants and their frequent encounters. The environments will be regularly and consciously changed, with the help of all technological means, by teams of specialized creators, who will thus be professional situationists.[29]

Constant concluded this first description of the New Babylon by insisting on its technical feasibility. This was discussed again in issue 4 of *Internationale situationniste* in an article titled "Description de la zone jaune," which was accompanied by photographs of models and drawings that were much more precise than those that had appeared previously. This second description also emphasized the communicative nature of the project ("The remainder communicates from within and forms a large common space") and was accompanied by horizontal and vertical scale drawings.[30] This was a kind of homage to Victor Considérant's Palais Social and the communards, who, in 1871, were able to defend the streets so well because they were reinforced by a parallel system of communication connecting the houses of Paris with one another. Constant's project was intended to foster the *dérive*. The "yellow zone" consisted of labyrinth-houses that promoted adventure; inhabitants could move among rooms given over to quiet (covered with soundproofing material), to noise, echoes (filled with radio transmitters), images, meditation, relaxation, or eroticism. With the exception of the burial area imagined by Ivain, "not for dying but for living in peace," the city enacted the utopia of the "Formulary for a New Urbanism," at least in the form of an architectural project, with its drawings and models. The châteaux of Louis II of Bavaria faded away before the hanging gardens of the New Babylon, and the botanical garden before the labyrinths of the "yellow zone."

The distinction may seem insignificant; however, it encompasses the question of the realization of utopia. Are Chtcheglov's chimeras intended to be embodied in Constant's (Constant, the artist-architect) drawings? Does the "utopian instantaneity" of the chimeras retain its revolutionary value when concretized in models, when it is provided with the concrete technical means through which it can detach itself—like a figure that stands out from its surroundings—from the project of generalized subversion that constituted the overall situationist framework? Can models of perpetual change be built, and signed? Can houses be constructed that do not uniquely associate their inhabitants with a residence? In other words, can we build models of revolution, or of what is only possible through revolution? Can we build the city and the "neighborhoods" the city occupies, even when they are experimental? The impossible temporality of this last question leads one to suspect the strongly negative answer that situationism would soon provide. Constant recognized this when he left the SI, at just about the same time that *Internationale situationniste* published his "Description de la zone jaune"—the summer of 1960. This is the most likely reason for Constant's being referred to as a "technocrat" in the following issue.

It seems to me that these are the real reasons for the break between Constant and the situationists. They are visible in the texts and projects introduced in the first issues of *Internationale situationniste*. There were other reasons given for the break, but they were primarily pretexts, only in this case the pretext was far from insignificant. In the spring of 1960, the SI (that is, Debord and Jorn) decided to exclude Anton Alberts and Har Oudejans, two promising Dutch architects who had recently joined the SI after being recruited by Constant. Unfortunately, they were discovered to be in the process of designing a church, which they must have confused with the "personal cathedrals" referred to by Ivan Chtcheglov. And yet, wasn't building a church the best, if not the only, way to realize what Pinot-Gallizio called the "fourth dimension of pure poetry"? For it was a construction of pure spirit, an object of pure belief, which in principle required a place—a church—for its embodiment, and possibly a messiah, as Isidore Isou would say, to ensure its longevity. Between architecture, utopia, and the religious, the boundaries have always been permeable and the misunderstandings numerous. Debord had never been very enthusiastic about the "fourth dimension of pure poetry" or churches, which he felt, even as a lettrist, should be destroyed, unlike some of his colleagues, who dreamed of transforming them into haunted houses. For Constant, the exclusion of his architect friends was an opportunity for a final evasive maneuver. He did not protest their exclusion and decided to quit the SI (the real settling of scores didn't take place until later). His position seems to involve a kind of two-sided strategy (which should not be understood pejoratively): one foot in architecture, one foot in utopia and unitary urbanism. He never seems to have been able to decide between these two positions, at least until the comple-

AN ART WITHOUT WORKS | 145

tion of his New Babylon. What is certain, however, is that with one foot stuck in art, it was unlikely he would side with the *dérive*.

Constant's situationist adventures are not an isolated case. They greatly resemble the position of a number of artists who were part of the SI between 1958 and 1962. However, the stature and importance of the New Babylon made it somewhat special, since it was the largest and most important art project developed within the situationist movement. Other situationist art projects deserve further comment, at least within the context of a detailed study of the history of the SI. Here, I will focus on only one of them, also Dutch and as exemplary as Constant's. This was the project for a situationist exhibition at the Stedelijk Museum in Amsterdam in 1959.

The exhibit was to consist of a labyrinth approximately two hundred meters in length, along with a *Cave of Antimatter* by Pinot-Gallizio (an "ambiance" created from mirrors, perfume, and music, along with a number of leading fashion models who had been "diverted" from their original function) and works by Maurice Wyckaert, who represented the Belgian section of the SI at the time. The show was supposed to be a kind of total immersion in the uncanny for the viewer/flaneur, much as the surrealists had imagined. Although the SI was still in its early stages of development, the Amsterdam project, as experienced, represented more than just a step back. The very originality of the situationist project consisted in conflating the space provided for the labyrinth in the museum with the real urban space that surrounded it, that is, all of central Amsterdam. The exhibit was to serve as a small-scale duplication of what would have in fact been experienced in the streets of the city. In other words, it had no meaning other than to the extent it reflected the practice of the *dérive*. Under these conditions, is it so surprising that such a project was never realized, because its authors failed to come to an agreement with the director of the Stedelijk Museum, Willem Sandberg, who had asked for accurate drawings for the labyrinth? Obviously, Sandberg had failed to understand that the real labyrinth was the city itself and that the *dérive* that was supposed to embody it was a de facto rejection of the drawings he—as someone who had co-opted desire and mobility—insisted on. The drawings were never supplied. Given the obvious bad faith of the SI in the adventure—and we can imagine the extent to which it divided the group—nothing prevents us from assuming that, from Debord's point of view at least, what was at stake in the exhibit was not so much to provide a small turnkey situationist labyrinth that would be admired, much as the palace of the Postman Cheval or the grottos of Louis II of Bavaria, as to turn the monumental logic of the museum against itself, to infuriate, if not the Stedelijk Museum, at least its director. The only possible situationist exhibit was the *dérive* in an urban environment, at least until the open-air festival of May 1968.

Constant's resignation, which Raspaud and Voyer categorized as an "ignominious avowal," was followed by the exclusion of other Dutch artists in the spring of 1960—Alberts, Armando, Oudejans—along with the Italians Melanotte, Pinot-Gallizio, and Wuerich.[31] They were all convicted of not having renounced their artistic activities, condemned for holding exhibits in broad daylight, or worse, in the case of Alberts and Oudejans, for collaborating with God. For artists and architects, the SI of 1958 to 1962 was a bit like a train station. The Dutch and Italians of the early SI were gone by 1960 at the latest. These were replaced by a carload of Germans who arrived in 1959 (this was the Spur group from Munich) and a handful of Scandinavians brought in by Jörgen Nash, Asger Jorn's brother. They were all asked, more or less politely, to leave—the Germans in 1962, followed by the Scandinavians (who had helped push the Germans out) a few weeks later, accused of having become vulgar "Nashists." They all defended a position close to that of Constant; they all wanted to give experimental art a chance, that is, to provide drawings, models, and concrete techniques for the utopia of unitary urbanism. They all repudiated their situationist vow to renounce art once they were thrown out of the SI, and resumed their careers where they had left off (for example, Nash created, not without a sense of provocation, a Situationist Bauhaus in Sweden, which the SI naturally denounced with particular spite). In 1962, Debord and his closest allies (Michèle Bernstein, Raoul Vaneigem, Attila Kotanyi, Mustapha Khayati) decided once and for all that situationist art did not exist, thereby putting an end to the "first period" of the Situationist International. Raoul Vaneigem made his well-known statement during the fifth SI conference in Göteborg, which neither the Germans nor the regional members could accept: "It is not a question of developing the spectacle of rejection but of rejecting the spectacle. In order for their development to be *artistic*, in the new and authentic sense defined by the SI, works of art can no longer serve as elements for the destruction of the spectacle. There is no situationism, no situationist work of art, and certainly no situationist spectacle. Once and for all."[32]

The utopia of unitary urbanism was sharp as a razor. Either it cut the artist off from the revolutionary he pretended to be, or it cut the revolutionary off from his artistic base and consigned him to the absolutism of some reckless initiative, which culminated, in every sense of the word, in May 1968. It was the limit of art, its mirror or forbidden image, both the shadow cast over art by the future revolution and the shadow cast over the revolution by an art that refused to disappear. Situationism may have produced nothing as beautiful as Constant's New Babylon, and it was never so beautiful as when the utopia of unitary urbanism was dominant or when Debord collaborated with Jorn, who quit the SI in April 1961 to regain his artistic freedom.[33] But was it made for such beauty? As time passed, Debord tended to answer in the negative. Architectural models were never of much interest to him; he saw them as open doors to technocratic reformism. He preferred urban maps that had been redrawn according to his interests and the potlatch of self-destruction to which he consigned the situationist project, all situationist projects. With Jorn gone, situationism gradually became an art without works, an art of idleness, an art of pure critique, an art of destruction and self-destruction. And in that sense it was, more than ever, Debord's art.

3. THE LIGHT BRIGADE

Means of Communication

From 1958 to 1962, the Situationist International regenerated itself several times, breaking with its artists and architects, who generally had little remorse about leaving the group. With their departure, the question of unitary urbanism moved into the background. There was little mention of the *dérive* in subsequent issues of *Internationale situationniste*. The pyschogeographic references and the projects for utopian cities disappeared, along with their models, through which they were embodied in the—inevitably technocratic or even reformist—architectural order.

However, there is nothing to indicate that the exclusion of the latest batch of artists from the SI (the Scandinavian "Nashists," who were shown the door in 1962) constituted a breakup or a significant change of direction for the SI. It was, at most, a temporary diversion, inevitably conflict-laden, from the step back taken by an SI in the process of circling the wagons. It was a clarification, a return to a stance that was more coherent, more radical, and certainly closer to that of the now defunct Lettrist International.

Debord has often been accused of a nearly pathological inclination toward expulsion. But the fact that there were so many expulsions in so short a time, often concerning individuals who had only recently joined the SI (thirty-two departures in the course of the first four years), indicates that they were, to a large extent, the precursors of a more genuine form of joint activity. They were the result of endless discussions and misunderstandings about the real nature of the program. In the majority of cases, they were characterized by none of the drama associated with those lengthy friendships that culminate in bloodshed or violence. Reading Debord's *Correspondance* shows that there was nothing pathological in them and that they sometimes occurred within a context that remained relatively cordial. The SI did not really change direction, especially since unitary urbanism remained one of Debord's preoccupations. *Internationale situationniste* devoted several articles to the subject in the forthcoming years, and *The Society of the Spectacle* an entire chapter. Unitary urbanism survived, but in politicized form, and developed its critical side, freed of the chimeras, utopias, and models that had characterized it until then.

With the systematic emphasis on a comprehensive critique of society and the insistence on the need for generalized subversion, of which *The Society of the Spectacle* was the most visible theoretic effect, unitary urbanism became one aspect of what I would call a politics of communication, which became central during the second phase of the history of the SI, which ran from 1962 to 1968. This politics would, over the years, coincide to an ever greater extent with a poetics of revolution, often neglected by Debord's commentators, who have reduced it to a problematic form of extreme-left politics. Was this the result of the 1962 "decree" concerning the non-existence of situationist art? It has been too readily acknowledged that with this the question of art had been settled once and for all, that the SI had finally evolved from its artistic to its purely political phase, exchanging its avant-garde status for allegiance—all in all, hardly original—to some ambient proletarian messianism. I stress this point because art (in the broadest sense of the term, one that entails the production of works of art) and poetics, in the broadest sense, are often confused. By the same token, we thereby limit not only our ability to understand the continuity and specificity of the SI's activities (for example, during the events of May 1968), the poetic dimension of events, but the overall consistency of Debord's life.

I realize that everyone changes (Brecht believed that the ability to change was one of our principal qualities) and I don't doubt that Debord also changed. Nonetheless, he remained impressively faithful to himself. He insisted on this in 1978 and again in 1989. Looking back on his activities, friends, and lovers of 1951, Debord never denied what he had been. He decided once and for all that he would explain himself to no one, and from that time on it's difficult to see what might have led him to betray that fidelity to self. In any case, it is wrong to claim that there was an artistic period of the SI, followed by a political period, and that Debord wrote his last books (his finest, in my opinion) out of rancor or bitterness, carried away by the passing of the seventies or eighties. He did not become an artist or writer belatedly, for the simple reason that he never stopped being one and that it was as an artist, more exactly a poet, that he conceived of revolution and experienced the events of May 1968.

FROM THE ABEYANCE OF MEANING TO TRANSPARENCY

Debord responded to his era as a poet, as someone who was always concerned with the question of communication and its forms. Historians of situationism rarely insist on the decisive and often melancholic search for authentic forms of communication that characterized not only the history of the SI but Debord's work and life as well, if we are to believe those who knew him. He spent a great deal of his time drinking, womanizing, reading, somewhat less time writing, and said little about his childhood. And although he refused to speak to certain people, he was on good terms with many more. Dialogue was one of the things he cared deeply about, providing it met certain formal criteria. Because he never had a job, he had a great deal of time to focus on such issues. The laws of hospitality and the art of conversation were of paramount importance to him, and these were made more intense and purer by drinking—with his close friends, with colleagues, sometimes with the first person who happened by. He spent a great deal of time in cafés. Some of Debord's interlocutors did not know "who" they were speaking to, or learned only later. Debord enjoyed anonymity, took pleasure in being himself, in escaping his image, appearances, even his name. His attachment to speech and communication is one of the keys to his life and work (they are almost always the same thing). His example is so luminous that it is blinding and casts an aura of mystery onto an otherwise simple existence. His biographers have preferred a life interspersed with adventures, plots, mistresses, crimes, and spectacular exploits to one defined by an art of conversation—something obviously much harder to account for.

Debord was engaged in a need to communicate and a search for authenticity that are present in his earliest writings, for example, when he decided not to sell his *Mémoires* commercially but to give copies to his friends. We find these same concerns, but reversed, in the techniques employed in his later writings for keeping the reader at a distance, as if the reader were no longer worthy of being addressed, as if he were there only to be deprived of this authentic communication, since he was responsible for having allowed it to dissipate in his complacent acceptance of the society of the spectacle. From beginning to end, the desire for communication and transparency was present; the theoretical existence of a transparent form of communication mattered little. The only thing that mattered was Debord's point of view, the point of view of his desire, and the weighty burden of melancholy associated with it. At the time of the SI, his statements were clear and positive; he had not yet experienced the reversal of his later years, and he was at the center of the ongoing discussion about the necessity for superseding art. A passage in *The Society of the Spectacle* demonstrates this. In it he compares a politics of communication to the failure of communication characteristic of avant-gardes:

> The fact that the language of real communication has been lost is what the modern movement of art's decay, and ultimately of its formal annihilation, expresses *positively*. What it expresses *negatively* is that a new common language has yet to be found—not, this time in the form of unilaterally arrived-at conclusions like those which, from the viewpoint of historical art, *always came on the scene too late*, speaking *to others* of what had been experienced without any real dialogue, and accepting this shortfall of life as inevitable—but rather in a praxis embodying both an unmediated activity and a language commensurate with it. The point is to take effective possession of the community of dialogue, and the playful relationship to time, which the works of the poets and artists have heretofore merely *represented*.[1]

Welcome to modernism. The merit of modern artists, specialists in decomposition such as Mallarmé and Joyce, was to have exposed artistic communication to the incommunicable, or to expose it as incommunicable. Thus they are the critical reflection of the society of the spectacle, which is characterized by the absence of any authentic form of communication. The *Sonnet en Yx* is a revolutionary pamphlet. They denounce the true nature of the spectacle by going on strike against it, or against society, as Mallarmé wanted. To escape the false appearances of the present and of communication, they distorted it, they introduced the incommunicable. It was unreadability raised to the level of a revolutionary value, a move later actively promoted by the Tel Quel group. Unreadability, as something incapable of exchange, escapes the law of exchange.

Yet modern art's passion for decomposition, which Debord understood better than many others and much earlier, is what constitutes its final aporia and demands its transcendence. Communication must be sought beyond the established and individualist forms of art, including avant-garde art. Here too, situationism was clear about the avant-garde of the interwar period, especially dadaism, which initially gambled on provocation as an immediate and authentic form of communication—a successful scandal being the best form of dialogue—and later, during its Berlin period, on a commitment to the aborted Spartacist uprising. Its assessment of surrealism was equally lucid. We tend to forget that surrealism, through the automatism that expressed itself in what were often collective forms of writing, and through meetings and games, was an antiart project whose goal was the reinvention of communication. From this perspective, the avant-garde has always, in its most collective moments, helped carry the torch for a modernist politics of negativity. The situationists were highly conscious of the avant-garde's position and affiliations. The dadaist and surrealist excesses were what situationism had to transcend in order to succeed: "For dadaism sought to *abolish art without realizing it,* and surrealism sought to *realize art without abolishing it.* The critical position since worked out by the *situationists* demonstrates that the abolition and the realization of art are inseparable aspects of a single *transcendence of art.*"[2]

The transcendence of art, the goal of so many avant-gardes, is the rediscovery of authentic communication. It is the transition from "speaking to," which assumes the representation of experience by an individual, to "speaking with," which implies the simultaneity of experience and dialogue. It is the transition from artistic representation—in all fields of art—to its transcendence, to communication as act or event, which logically entails the disappearance of the "author"—who by definition always precedes the moment of communication—as well as his idleness. This transition, which is to the avant-garde what the Northwest Passage was to the explorers of North America, haunts dadaism, surrealism, and other avant-gardes as well, which have all tried to achieve it by different means.[3] Artaud, Bataille, and Sartre were preoccupied with this search, which typified the "situation of the writer," so diametrically opposed to situationist commitment.[4] Everyone will work toward restoring an authentic form of communication, everyone will work toward eliminating the separation between individuals, and possibly their division into social classes. There were, as well, a number of experiments in "community" art that were contemporary with the situationists, who had nothing but contempt for them. They can be found primarily in theater, more specifically at the borderline between theater and "happenings," a term used to emphasize the actuality of the poetic at the expense of representation. Typical was a movement such as Fluxus or, in the French context, Jean-Jacques Lebel, the author of a number of events of this type. The best-known example is that of the Living Theater, which was explicitly inspired by Artaud and was very active in France in May 1968, but there have been countless examples of theatrical events based on direct audience participation. Retrospectively, and from a situationist point of view, many of these could be considered a parody of the central element of Debord and his colleagues' project; a parody, a version captured by the spectacular through a lack of awareness of the necessity for a comprehensive subversion of the dominant order.

Situationism was, if not the most radical version of the very old project to rediscover a community that transcends art (what measuring stick do we use to measure the radicality of the avant-garde?), at least the purest and certainly the most political. Following the period of unitary urbanism, it emerged as the avant-garde movement that made the least use of artistic means for its realization, presenting itself not only as the last possible avant-garde (and possibly in fact being the last), but also as a kind of synthesis or sketch of the ancient project to make the transition from art to a communitarian transcendence of art.[5] Situationism was the avant-garde reduced to the desire for immediate and authentic communication. Intersected by a Rousseauian-utopian belief in lost transparency on the one hand, and the melancholy typical of Debord on the other, everything seemed to lead to an embrace of this tradition, even some of its most metaphysical claims.[6] And his principal ideas and experiences, between 1962 and 1968, were organized around this "theme."

FROM URBANISM TO TOTALITY

Just as unitary urbanism was not completely abandoned after 1962, the question of communication did not become an issue only at that point in time. In fact, it intersected a number of projects associated with unitary urbanism, including Constant's descriptions and models (as early as 1948 he came out in favor of the reinvention of a "collective art"). The impossible situationist architecture not only constructed mobility but also produced communication. One requires the other, one *is* the other. Constant's New Babylon was fundamentally an arrangement of *communicating spaces*— the term recurs several times in the descriptions and models. Inhabitants constantly move from room to room, from floor to floor, through passages, hallways, and stairways arranged in all directions that resemble some of the architectural models imagined by the Fourier of the *Nouveau monde amoureux*. Breton used to leave the door to his hotel room ajar so he might be surprised by some beautiful stranger. Situationist architecture takes a step beyond this, beyond doors and doorways. It does away with these entirely, and has little concern for interiors, or the interiority that is always difficult to communicate. It assigns the individual to the exterior of a collective subjectivity. It forbids individualism and—to a large extent—private life.

Constant's New Babylon saw the city as a communications network, "the natural expression of collective creativity."[7] Cities are the natural environment for socialized man, organically connected to the community, providing they are able to function as a network. They must abandon the promotion of isolation, separation, and individualism imposed by official urbanism, which attempts to subject them to the bronze (more accurately, steel) law of the automobile. Automobile traffic is the bête noire of situationists, who are the witnesses and contemporaries of its massive growth. The city is the emblem of the techniques of separation and individualization used by the power structure. An individual means of transport is the opposite of a means of communication: we speak to no one, we meet no one, we remain alone. Emblematically, transports for situationist man do not make use of automobiles but of foot power, through the *dérive*—whether fueled by love or alcohol—the quintessential figure of authentic traffic and communication. "Anything but the automobile" could have been the situationists' slogan. In a wonderful burst of utopian élan, generally not his strong point, Debord even looked to an aerial replacement for automobiles—the helicopter.[8]

The young followers of Saint-Simon dreamed of a new universal language, constructed with mathematical rigor (and they decided that while waiting to discover it and given their limited talents for foreign languages, French would have to serve for universal communication). The organic city they imagined was part of the same order of ideas: chaos would be replaced by harmony and communication. Is it so surprising that the same

Saint-Simonians, having left for Egypt after their communitarian reversal in Ménilmontant, were the first to float the idea of digging a canal between the Mediterranean and the Red Sea? Or, if they were counting, that twenty years later they would be among the principal engineers on the construction of the French railway network? Once a specialist in a means of communication, always a specialist. And following the period of unitary urbanism, the situationists also remained specialists, not by offering their services to the government, as the Saint-Simonians did, to develop, for example, helicopter transportation, but by radicalizing their politics and their utopia of authentic communication. Against a backdrop of proletarian revolution, this would serve as a principle for subverting all the methods of pseudocommunication imposed by government (the automobile, modern cities, television, Club Med vacations, cultural activities in general, and, naturally, all art) and a project for reinventing communication and community. Situationism is fundamentally the idea of sharing, of generalized participation, of a generalized collectivity that invades all aspects of life, eventually replacing it:

> The constructed situation is necessarily collective in its preparation and development. However, it appears, at least during the period of primitive experimentation, that an individual must exercise a certain control in a given situation: by being the director. Starting with a projected situation—studied by a team of researchers—that would combine, for example, an *emotional meeting* of several persons for an evening, it is essential that we distinguish between a director, direct agents living in the situation—having participated in the creation of the group project, having worked on the practical composition of the environment—and passive spectators—strangers to the work of construction—who should be *brought into the action.*[9]

This description, which appeared in the first issue of *Internationale situationniste,* is interesting because of its ambiguity. The collective dimension of the "constructed situation" is clearly stated. This consists fundamentally in the event or in the advent of communication, but the transcendence of art that is supposed to occur along with it is not much clearer than it is with Constant's models, roughly contemporary with this text. Situationism not only has one toe in architecture, it has another in theater as well. The constructed situation requires a builder, a "director," an open door to the return of the author. Passive spectators have not completely disappeared either, even though the goal is to engage them in action (which is, after all, the intent of all the experiments in participatory theater that ran from Artaud through the Living Theater). The remainder of the text attempts to prevent this type of misunderstanding. The constructed situation must be distinguished, like water from fire, from the antitheater or the happenings for which it might be confused. It feels like but is not theater. It resembles it only because situationism is still in an experimental phase and lacks new words:

> Naturally, the relationship between the director and the "experiencers" of the situation cannot become specialized. It is only a temporary subordination of one team of situationists to the leader of an isolated experiment. These perspectives, or their temporary vocabulary, must not lead us to believe that this is an extension of theater. Pirandello and Brecht revealed the destruction of the theatrical spectacle, and made other claims that go beyond this. It could be said that the construction of situations will replace theater only in the sense that the construction of life has always increasingly replaced religion.[10]

Two years later, other formulations would avoid the danger of confusion between the constructed situation and participatory theater by logically placing the construction of situations within a *totalizing* framework. Communication will only be authentic when it is total, in other words, when it involves the participation of each one of us. When we remain only spectators—passive, by definition—we remain embedded in the spectacle. In a constructed situation there are no spectators, it reduces them to action, failing which, it becomes experimental, and from the experimental it becomes art, the domain of individual, that is, separate, activity. This position had been clearly enunciated by 1960:

> Unlike the spectacle, realized situationist culture introduces total participation.
> Unlike preserved art, it introduces an organization of the lived moment, directly.
> Unlike fragmented art, it introduces a global practice that implicates simultaneously all the elements that can be used. It tends naturally to collective and, of course, anonymous production (at least to the extent that, *since works of art are not stored as merchandise,* this culture will not be dominated by the need to leave traces). . . .
> Unlike unilateral art, situationist culture will be an art of dialogue, an art of interaction. Artists—together with all visible culture—are now entirely separate from society, as they are separated from one another through competition. But even before this capitalist impasse, art was essentially unilateral, unanswered. It will transcend the insular reign of its primitivism to achieve complete communication.

Since everyone, at a higher stage, will become an artist, that is, inseparably producer-consumer of a total cultural creation, we will witness the rapid dissolution of the linear criteria of novelty. . . .

We will now usher in what will be, historically, the last craft. The role of situationism, of the professional amateur, the antispecialist, is still a kind of specialization up until the moment of economic and mental abundance, when everyone will become an "artist," in a sense that artists have not achieved: the construction of their own life.[11]

The question was how to avoid the trap of experimental art or the happenings so typical of the period. Situationism resolved this by the unquestioned embrace of totalization, by projecting the complete elimination of any possibility of the spectacle, of representation, of separation, of difference between private life and public space, between work and leisure. In the situationist utopia, everyone would be simultaneously producer and consumer of a total cultural creation. Affecting all aspects of life, this is the exact opposite of the spectacle and, consequently, requires its destruction to usher in revolution, where the crowd is reduced to action, rejecting its role as spectator, overcoming union representatives and parties (from the left), sacking the churches, the museums, the central committee headquarters, and Trotskyist institutions. The text just quoted, published in 1960, does not say so explicitly, but it leaves little room for experimental art.

Because beauty, in a sense, had to be total, it would be political or it would not be. The realization of authentic communication involves generalized subversion, through the suppression of the division of labor and all forms of specialization, including artistic and political. This brings us back to our starting point in evaluating the impact of the Lettrist International: art will be transcended totally or not at all. The break must be final. In other words, conceptions of the end of art are always conceptions of *totality*, for better or worse. This does not necessarily lead to totalitarianism, even if it were to occur. But it aims toward a principle of totality. It starts from the principle that there exists a totality that constitutes, in every sense of the word, the end of art once this is fated to destroy itself in an authentic form of communication. The authenticity and fullness of communication go hand in hand. Communication can only be authentic if it is based on openness, on what Breton called a language without reservations and without a remainder (of which automatic writing was supposedly the embodiment). The end of art is not a book in which everything will be said (in the Hegelian sense), but a total book infinitely open and, therefore, no longer having the form of a book. It might be compared with Mallarmé's impossible "Book," made by and for everyone. It consists in the transition to the possibility that everything can be said, that everything can be said by and for everyone, in keeping with Isidore Ducasse, so often quoted by the situationists, who felt that poetry should be made by everyone and not by individuals. The end of art as the situationists imagined it is the "work," or total book, a kind of Wagnerian *Gesamtkuntswerk* that dissolves into the crowd. This is the crowd as artist, reappropriating the poetry beyond all known artistic techniques, separate and specialized. This is *Gesamtkuntswerk* that is at once omnipresent and invisible because of its realization by and for everyone—there will no longer be spectators. The only totality possible is for nonspectators. The "unheard-of" techniques imagined by Pinot-Gallizio and other situationists need to be understood within the context of the end of art, for they serve as the utopian figures of that context. As such, they call to mind the "temple" dreamed of by the Saint-Simonians, a kind of precursor to the Wagnerian project and heart of the "New City" imagined at Ménilmontant, the meeting place not only of masculine and feminine, but also a place where a new form of communication would be developed, the synthesis of all the existing arts, from theater to the novel, painting, music, dance, and so on.[12] Every history of the avant-garde, which the situationists hoped to terminate once and for all, would revolve around this goal: an impossible *Gesamtkuntswerk* conceived as a communications and community operator that abolishes or dissolves itself in politics. Or, to be more precise: that oscillates between a political perspective and one that is often religious, obvious in the case of the "classical" nineteenth-century utopias, but also found in someone like Artaud. The problem that Debord and his colleagues struggled to resolve was the following: how to avoid the ritualization of art and allegiance to the various communist parties?

The term "spectacle" appears in the first sentence of the manifesto quoted earlier: "Unlike the spectacle, realized situationist culture introduces total participation." The concept of the spectacle was present in the first issues of *Internationale situationniste*, but it played a relatively minor role. Its rise to prominence, which culminated with the 1967 publication of *The Society of the Spectacle*, began with the decline of the experimental phase of situationism announced by the manifesto, that is, with the adoption by the situationists of a resolutely totalizing perspective. Situationist art is total communication, realized by and for everyone. In this sense, it is the opposite of the spectacle, which must be understood as a negative totality: the spectacle is that which *totally* prevents communication from taking place.

This "total participation" arises with the destruction of the total passivity characteristic of the spectacle. In other words, the concept of the spectacle is the *effect* of the situationist desire for transparency; it is the shadow cast by power over desire. It is the effect of a project for restoring communication, and as such is responsible for *all* the world's sins. It designates everything that prevents communication from occurring and is equivalent in all respects to the absence of communication, as noted by many of the first theses in *The Society of the Spectacle*. The spectacle is the "official language of generalized separation" (Thesis 3). "The spectacle is by definition immune from human activity, inaccessible to any projected review or correction. It is the opposite of dialogue. Wherever representation takes on an independent existence, the spectacle reestablishes its rule" (Thesis 18). The spectacle is the dissolution of genuine communication (Thesis 25); it appropriates communication, which will exist only in a one-way form controlled by power (Thesis 24). The proletarianization of the world does not occur through the division of labor alone but also, and inseparably from it, by the confiscation of communication and through separation: "The generalized separation of worker and product has spelled the end of any comprehensive view of the job done, as well as the end of direct personal communication between producers. As the accumulation of alienated products proceeds, and as the productive process gets more concentrated, consistency and communication become the exclusive assets of the system's managers. The triumph of an economic system founded on separation leads to the *proletarianization of the world*" (Thesis 26).

Clearly, the concept of the spectacle refers to several things at once (subjugation of the world to the economy, the fetishism of goods, reification, alienation, ideology, and specifically, how images, representations, entertainment prevent authentic life from coming into being), in keeping with the comments made by Debord himself: "The concept of the spectacle brings together and explains a wide range of apparently disparate phenomena" (Thesis 10). In this sense, it serves as the clearest sign of the situationists' adoption of a totalizing viewpoint after 1960–62, which was later embodied in Debord's most important book, in what might also be considered to be his *Book*, or what he himself considered to be his *Book*: a book that demands no further comment, even twenty or thirty years later, a book whose text cannot be altered, a book that says everything about everything.[13] *The Society of the Spectacle* begins with what I refer to as a "total Book effect." It is the effect of a totalizing perspective, it embodies that perspective, makes us aware of the negative totality created by the spectacle. And, in keeping with the negative character of the totality that is its subject, it makes use of the rhetorical methods of *irrefutability. The Society of the Spectacle* is, at bottom, anything but a "dialogue." It is as if it had been written by no one, by no "I," a book that makes abundant use of appropriation and seems to be addressed to no one at all.[14] "Not personalized, the volume, from which one is separated as the author, does not demand that any reader approach it," wrote Mallarmé, who was very familiar with literary communism.[15] Few have understood as well as Debord that this was the price to be paid for popularity.

POETRY APPROPRIATED BY EVERYONE

But is it really Debord who is on everyone's lips? Weren't they also mouthing everything Debord appropriated, as a result of which he too will be appropriated or, as some would have it, co-opted? There are a large number of appropriations, or *détournements* (quotes *modified* to varying degrees), in *The Society of the Spectacle,* and it is no accident. After the experimental-utopian phase of the early years, appropriation became the only "technique" of communication possible, the only one that provided any adequate guarantees of an antiartistic stance. Appropriation, which had been practiced and theorized since the lettrist period, became, after the departure of the artists, the alpha and omega of situationist anti-aesthetics. It reestablished a sense of continuity with the radical Lettrist International. It became the principal technique of total opposition to the spectacle.

Unlike the experimental techniques of art, it produced no new work of art. There is no utopia of *détournement,* which is limited to the act of appropriating existing speech and images, and to this extent does not even constitute a technique, but an antitechnique. Moreover, *détournement* is virtually accessible to anyone; it is poetry for the masses, the realization of Ducasse's wish, or, more exactly, its systematization, since the *Poésies* of Ducasse, the obscure communard plotter, were based on nothing so much as the technique of *détournement.* It represents the most important collective manifestation of the means of expression and communication. It is a principle for subverting the author, who must yield to the appropriator, to the first comer, whose appropriation is obviously itself vulnerable to subsequent appropriations. An appropriated text no longer has an author, which is what makes *détournement* such a radical technique for the disappearance of the author. And the majority of authors, even the most fervent partisans of the "death of the author," are careful to avoid venturing across the thin ice of *détournement,* through which they may disappear once and for all. It is interesting to note, therefore, that every issue of *Internationale situationniste* included a notice that all the reproductions were explicitly authorized for use. Help yourself, appropriate to your heart's content—not exactly what might be called a politics of the author.[16] *Détournement* is a belligerent act of appropriation, or, more exactly, of reappropriation: it uses what had been excluded through integration in the spectacle for the purpose of authentic communication, and does so through the simple act of appropriation it represents. Appropriating the means of the spectacle, winning back the territory of communication that had been lost or confiscated, and reinventing it are one and the same thing, at least until the revolution comes along. As long as the spectacle is dominant, authenticity is possible only in the war against the spectacle, in the acts of appropriation through which its destruction is brought about. It is through warfare, or at least a warlike politics of communication, that situationism escapes utopia. *Détournement* is a strategy for winning back lost territory, as is the *dérive,* which is also based on diversion, on the defunctionalization of urban thoroughfares, and, consequently, on the *détournement* of an urban space that has in this way become "reappropriable."

The situationists were careful to keep their distance from the linguistic turn through which many intellectuals during the sixties abandoned Sartre to work for the revolution of poetic language. As such, language was never a central element in their proposals. The most notable exception is found in an article signed by Mustapha Khayati, published in 1966 and titled "Captive Words (Preface to a Situationist Dictionary)" ("Les mots captifs [préface à un dictionnaire situationniste]"). It is an interesting text for its detailed and systematic survey of the risks of appropriation, and because, in using the figure of the dictionary, it reinscribed *détournement* in the context of a language that had to be reinvented. "To bestow a purer sense to the language of the horde," wrote Mallarmé.[17] The situationists were certainly involved in such a project, a project that would give the "horde" the words whose meaning had been appropriated by power. To give transparency back to language, to make it, once again, an instrument of authentic communication for use by the horde and even proletarians who seek revolution—those were the objectives of a "situationist dictionary." There could be no revolution without destroying the words of power, without reappropriating the meaning of the words appropriated by power in its attempt to establish a reign of lies. Situationist appropriation is, in fact, a return; it consists in reappropriating for itself what had been confiscated by power:

> It is impossible to get rid of a world without also getting rid of the language that both conceals and protects it, without stripping bare that language's truth. Just as power is ceaseless falsification and "social truth," so language is its constant safeguard and the Dictionary its all-purpose reference. All revolutionary praxis has sensed the need for a new semantic field and for the assertion of a new truth; from the *encyclopédistes* to the "critique of stilted language" (Stalin) (by Polish intellectuals in 1956), this necessity has not ceased to be felt. *Power resides in language*, which is the refuge of its police violence. All dialogue with power is violence, whether suffered or instigated. . . .
>
> Critique of the ruling language, its *détournement*, will become the continuous practice of new revolutionary theory.[18]

The situationists were not the first to be captured by the demon of lexicography, so prevalent among the nineteenth-century utopians (beginning with the Saint-Simonians, who dreamed of a universal language), and the raw material of a number of *Books* attempted by various literary madmen. But the situationists were not as naive as their predecessors. In 1966, they appeared to be vaccinated for good against the virus of utopia, and the "situationist dictionary" would be as open and fluid as the situationist cities of the future. In other words, there would be just as few of them: "Nevertheless, we know in advance that these very reasons do not in any way allow us to claim a permanent, legislated certainty; a definition is always open, it is never final."[19] Khayati is also very clear about the situationist rejection of all forms of the mathematically inspired universal language Descartes dreamed of, a dream he shared with the Saint-Simonians, all the Hoéné Wronskis of the world, Lacan, lost in his knots and mathemes, cyberneticians, and contemporary programmers. (The universal language of the cyberneticians is no more than a reassurance of "the longevity of bourgeois categories.")

If there exist precedents for the dictionary the situationists dreamed about, they will be found among writers, not among the utopian technocrats who attempted to establish, mathematically or otherwise, the meaning of words, but among those who struggled to liberate words and their meanings, to free them of subjugation, from Rimbaud to the surrealists and beyond. Mallarmé pretended to regret that the perfect language didn't exist, while revealing that poetry came about precisely from this "defect in languages," a kind of indirect remuneration. The situationists followed this line of argument with the idea of a dictionary that claims to be a project for radicalizing or systematizing the liberation of words that had been experimentally attempted by the various avant-gardes. That is why the situationist dictionary is not, strictly speaking, a dictionary and why it never was. It is an instrument of combat or warfare, intended to spread the insubordination of words, to give them back to the tribe, to the community, and to communication by restoring to them their use-value, by freeing them from laboring—what Bataille called the "work of words"—for the power structure:

> Our dictionary will be a sort of grid with which one could decipher pieces of information and tear off the ideological veil covering reality. We will provide potential translations that will allow the apprehension of different aspects of the society of the spectacle, and will show how the smallest clues (the smallest signs) contribute to its maintenance. It is in a way a bilingual dictionary, for each word possesses an "ideological" meaning from power and a real meaning, what we consider to correspond to real life in the present historical stage. We could also establish at every step the various positions of words in the social war. . . . The genuine appropriation of words that *work* cannot be achieved apart from the appropriation of work itself. The institution of liberated creative activity will simultaneously be the institution of genuine, finally liberated communication, and the transparency of human relations will replace the poverty of words under the old regime of opacity. Words will not stop *working* so long as men have not.[20]

The situationist dictionary is a bilingual dictionary that appropriates, overturns, translates the spectacular into the revolutionary. It is based on practice, it is the other side of the reappropriation of labor targeted by revolution: the means of production must be reappropriated, but so must the means of communication. Constantly reinvented, rearranged on the basis of real, historical life, at bottom it is created not through language but through speech, which is why it cannot really take the form of a dictionary. It no more belongs in a book than a situationist city would belong in a model by Constant (moreover, nothing is closer to architecture than the book). It only takes place when *enacted*. And, in that sense, it is not the heart of a revolution in poetic language but must supply the revolution with its poetry and even its poetics. It is anything but coincidental that *détournement*'s hour of glory—and that of the SI—occurred when poetry could be heard in the streets in May 1968, poetry that had been "theoretically" prepared between 1962 and 1968.

The Poetics of Revolution

In an April 1962 article from *Internationale situationniste*, we read "Communication never exists other than in joint action."[1] It is when the last artists were leaving that the SI finally decided on a rhetoric of action. It began to assume a much firmer political stance, similar to the one taken during the transition from the "first" to the "second" Lettrist International. In order for there to be communication, there must be not art, but action, and joint action at that, because we cannot communicate alone. Constant had left in the summer of 1960, Asger Jorn in April 1961. The majority of the German artists in the Spur group were thrown out in February 1962, and the Nashists followed a month later. The artists and model builders were gone. The principal leaders of the SI were now Debord, Michèle Bernstein, Attila Kotanyi (a Hungarian architect who had joined the SI in 1961), and Raoul Vaneigem, introduced to Debord by the communist philosopher Henri Lefebvre in 1960. The SI's "artistic" period was followed by what has been referred to as its "sociological" period.

Why "sociological"? There are at least three reasons for this. First, the totalizing perspective adopted by the SI led it to position itself much more explicitly within and in relation to society as a whole, which was judged to be generally dismal. What was at stake was not only the world of art and architecture, but the world in general, which had to change to prevent those who no longer wanted to be artists from becoming utopians. To make art a genuine part of life required the transformation of society and, consequently, an increasingly systematic awareness of every aspect of everyday life. This leads immediately to the second reason for the "sociological" turn: the notion of daily life. At the time, the term benefited from considerable attention from sociologists and became, between 1962 and 1968, one of the key terms in situationist discourse, if not the keystone of revolution as envisaged by the SI. It served as a common theme for several articles in *Internationale situationniste,* from the sixth issue forward (1961),[2] and was to become the focal point of that other situationist "classic," Raoul Vaneigem's *Revolution of Everyday Life,* which was published in 1967, the same year as *The Society of the Spectacle.*[3] Finally, and the third reason for referring to a "sociological" turn, the SI's outlook was now much more explicitly revolutionary. During the early sixties, the SI returned to the radicalism it had displayed during the *Potlatch* period. The reemergence of a radical stance was prompted by the overall political context, which also helped supply a more theoretical discourse (the war in Algeria, the beginnings of the Cuban Revolution, the rise to power of an anti-Stalinist extreme left). With the artists and architects now out of the picture, the transformation of society was no longer seen other than in terms of the proletarian revolution. The only real question was to determine which one, and this led the SI to initiate a dialogue with the various strains of Marxist thought (primarily the "heretical" Marxisms, which were critical of Leninism), as well as with the revolutionary organizations in which these were embodied.

With respect to the critique of everyday life, the influence of Henri Lefebvre's ideas on the new direction taken by Debord and his allies has often been stressed, especially the influence of his "theory of moments," which was formulated for the first time in 1947 in the *Critique of Everyday Life,*[4] then in 1958 in *La somme et le reste.*[5] This theory has so often been compared to the "construction of situations" developed by Debord and his followers that Henri Lefebvre was believed to be another misunderstood genius, forced to provide a personal record of his most important contributions to twentieth-century thought in a book of memoirs significantly titled *Le temps des méprises.*[6] In it we learn that not only was Lefebvre the source for nearly everything that was theorized under the name situationism, as he had been ten years earlier for Cobra, but that he had also been the trigger for the riots of May 1968. Apparently this resolved the great mystery of determining the individual single-handedly responsible for the events of that spring. But the survivors of Cobra will be no less astonished to learn that they were as much followers of Lefebvre as the insurgents of

May 1968. In reviewing back issues of *Cobra* and the other publications associated with the movement, the least that can be said is that Lefebvre is hardly a compelling presence (in fact, Christian Dotremont, certainly the least popular of the Cobra members among the situationists, seems to have been the only one to have read him). Although it may be possible to be a Lefebvrian without knowing it, it is far from certain that this would be a good indicator of the longevity of his work.

Lefebvre's influence on situationism requires some explanation. In a letter dated February 14, 1960, Debord wrote to the Belgian situationist Frankin that he was in the process of discovering in *La somme et le reste* the theory of moments, which he found interesting. He also said that Lefebvre had written to him on January 3, 1960, following the appearance of issue 3 of *Internationale situationniste*, and that he was planning to meet him.[7] What does this imply? That Debord did not meet Lefebvre in 1958, as the latter claims in interviews—another misunderstanding?—but two years later, that is, somewhat late to give much credibility to the legend of Lefebvre carrying the situationist infant to the baptismal font (especially when we recall everything that transpired since the origin of the Lettrist International)? Debord makes infrequent reference to Lefebvre before the fourth issue of *Internationale situationniste*, which appeared exactly four months after he met the philosopher. Lefebvre is explicitly referred to for the first time in the "Thèses sur la révolution culturelle" [Theses on cultural revolution], which appeared in the first issue of *Internationale situationniste*, signed by Debord. He was recognized as an original theorist (as was Lucien Goldmann somewhat later), and it is therefore reasonable to assume that Debord had read an article by Lefebvre written in 1957 titled "Le romantisme révolutionnaire," in which he corrected his earlier (1947) uncharitable attitude toward avant-gardes (especially surrealism) and modernism. But, as was the case in the following issues, Lefebvre's position was criticized from the outset. The risk of "revolutionary romanticism," the dangers of which Debord saw very clearly, was considered inadequate as a criterion for revolutionary action against culture:

> We are separated in practice from true control over the material power accumulated by our time. The communist revolution has not occurred, and we still live within the framework of the decomposition of the old cultural superstructures. Henri Lefebvre correctly sees that this contradiction is at the heart of the specifically modern discordance between the progressive individual and the world, and

calls the cultural tendency based on this discordance revolutionary-romantic. The defect in Lefebvre's conception lies in making the simple expression of discordance a sufficient criterion for revolutionary action within culture. Lefebvre renounces beforehand all experiments toward profound cultural change, while remaining satisfied with a content: awareness of the (still too remote) impossible-possible, which can be expressed no matter what form it takes within the framework of decomposition.[8]

Debord read Lefebvre, just as he read many other authors he never hesitated to make use of, but the impression given here is certainly not one of surprise. The terms of the debate are already in place. Debord would never be satisfied with "revolutionary romanticism," which was felt to be too *passive* (and a bit stale as well) in terms of revolutionary praxis. It could even be said that the SI's entire focus was based on the attempt to transcend the "revolutionary romanticism" that, to some extent, characterized the avant-gardes of the twenties and thirties (or those of the nineteenth century) and led them—one of the pitfalls of individualism—to waste their energies in trying to make impossible alliances with the Communist Party when it was decided that the time for collective action had arrived. This was a problem that Lefebvre was familiar with firsthand, given his contacts with the surrealists in the twenties, when he was leading the "Philosophies" group, and his later membership in the Communist Party, for which he was the star philosopher before being suspended from his starring role in 1958. In general, though, it is simply irresponsible to claim that all, or nearly all, situationist thought, including psychogeography, *détournement,* the transcendence of art, the criticism of avant-gardes, and especially the idea of the construction of situations, came from Lefebvre. And one looks in vain in the books Lefebvre had written at this time for the slightest development that is directly related to any aspect of the situationist movement, which was under way six years before *La somme et le reste* and the second version of the *Critique of Everyday Life* appeared, that is, long before the period when Lefebvre began to get interested in urbanism. So, to make him the spiritual father, or godfather, of situationism requires an element of spite, or at least a good deal of ignorance.[9]

In reading Debord's article on Lefebvre in *Internationale situationniste* 4, we are struck by the critical distance he establishes, which had not changed since the first issue of the review. The theory of moments is discussed and compared to the "construction of situations" in a way that makes any attempt to make a direct connection between the situationists and Lefebvre problematic, to say the least. In particular, Debord compares the logic— according to him purely temporal or event-driven—of Lefebvrian moments to the spatiotemporal logic of the construction of situations (as manifested primarily by psychogeography). In this same article he insists on what distinguishes the "natural" character of the Lefebvrian moment from the constructed, that is to say, artistic, character of the situation: "The situation, like the moment, 'can expand or contract in time.' But it seeks to establish itself on the objectivity of artistic production. Such artistic production is a radical break with durable works of art. It is inseparable from its immediate consumption, a use-value that is essentially foreign to preservation in the form of commodities."[10] This initial clarification is of considerable interest. It suggests that if, for Debord, art as we know it is outmoded, he still feels that one remains an artist as a "constructor of situations." Poetics, for Debord, is always associated with a conscious project, it does not occur spontaneously or naturally during special moments of everyday life, as suggested by Lefebvre (who compares it to being in love).[11] From this point of view, poetics also implies for Debord joint action and even a community. This was the whole point of the situationist movement, fundamentally incompatible with Lefebvre's sociological "spontaneity" flourishing in the shadow of a Stalinism that had never been entirely rejected. Is it necessary to add that Lefebvre was never a part of the Situationist International?

Although Debord's initial response to Lefebvre was critical, this did not prevent him from seeking a dialogue with someone he respected, then became friends with for two years. During this period, it is difficult to determine exactly what one owes to the other, given the amount of time they spent together in conversation. According to the situationists, the reason for the break between the two men seems to have been that Lefebvre had difficulty remembering his debt to Debord (as well as to Vaneigem and Kotanyi). One day he decided to publish an essay under his own name that had been formulated *by* or at least—and according to his own version of the facts—*with* the situationists on the Paris Commune. It was as if their rejection of copyright for articles published in *Internationale situationniste* provided blanket authorization, and to Lefebvre in particular, to appropriate, for personal benefit, thoughts and ideas that had until then been developed jointly according to Lefebvre, and without Lefebvre according to the situationists.[12] Did Lefebvre misunderstand the nature and rules of *détournement* or situationist policy on copyright? By Lefebvre's own admission, this was not his only error. And the argument he invoked in his defense—that he was intimately involved in their evaluation of the Paris Commune—only leads us to believe that Lefebvre was himself aware of the weakness of his arguments. He was quick to look for other reasons to explain the break with Debord. Of these, one involved a woman (it is well known that a hundred years of argument and conflict within the avant-garde can ultimately be reduced to affairs with women, which conceal so many others). Another, more obscure, had to do with the review *Arguments,* which was then about to cease publication, and which Debord is said to have wanted to replace with *Internationale situationniste,* once again thanks to the indispensable sponsorship of the inventor of May 1968.[13]

A few comments are in order concerning these disputes, to help resolve another misunderstanding, also associated with the "sociological" phase of the Situationist International. Just as it was said that Debord was influenced by Lefebvre, it was claimed that he owed nearly everything he wrote—especially *The Society of the Spectacle*—to the arguments developed by the group Socialisme ou Barbarie. This was one of the few "heretical" Marxist groups—anti-Bolshevik in other words—then active in France. It was a Trotskyist splinter group initially led by Claude Lefort, then by Cornelius Castoriadis (other members included Jean-François Lyotard and, more episodically, Gérard Genette).[14] For someone as attentive as Debord was to the concept of the gift, the authenticity of dialogue, and his own freedom, which made him particularly unreceptive to any form of intellectual submission, this claim would imply any number of unacknowledged borrowings and intellectual debts—unless we assume that Socialisme ou Barbarie itself owes everything to the *Critique of Everyday Life,* an assumption that to my knowledge even Lefebvre never made. In spite of his Stalinist connections (or his problems in severing them), he never cultivated close friendships with theoreticians of the far left and anti-Leninist left.

The dialogue with Socialisme ou Barbarie began in 1959. It took place primarily through Daniel Blanchard, alias Canjuers, with whom the leader of the SI signed a joint declaration that was to serve as a platform for the SI's possible collaboration with Socialisme ou Barbarie.[15] A tense political context, dominated by the de Gaulle "coup d'état," the war in Algeria, and the widespread strikes by Belgian miners during the winter of 1960–61, was the principal field for a potential joint action by the SI and Socialisme ou Barbarie. But there is little evidence that Debord sought out a dialogue or alliances with groups and individuals he respected but whose interests were dissimilar.[16] As in the 1930s, a period marked by antifascist struggles, there were united fronts and joint resistance movements. It was in this context that, between 1959 and 1961, Debord had a number of contacts with members of Socialisme ou Barbarie, participated in their discussions, and discovered a number of theoretical weapons that strengthened his own anti-Leninist and anti-Stalinist orientation. Although he seems to have been a formal member of Socialisme ou Barbarie, he maintained his distance from the group. He also did not get along well with Castoriadis, who was indifferent to the status of art. We have only to read *Potlatch* to see that Debord's anti-Leninism does not date from this encounter. Through Socialisme ou Barbarie he discovered a number of classic texts of heretical Marxism, as well as a systematic approach to the "workers' democracies" of Eastern Europe, which had been tirelessly scrutinized by the theoreticians of Socialisme ou Barbarie, who were searching for possible signs of a forthcoming anti-Stalinist revolution (such as the worker uprisings in Berlin in 1953 or the Polish uprisings of 1956). He had no trouble accepting a theory of revolution that assumed some form of working-class power based on the principle of self-management or the spontaneous organization of a revolutionary proletariat, rather than through the Leninist proletariat favored by the avant-garde, from which he had been alienated by his long-standing rejection of representations and delegations. But this is a far cry from saying that situationism, at least during its second phase, was inspired by Socialisme ou Barbarie.

If, in Lefebvre's case, it is still reasonable to claim that he and the situationists were on the same footing, that is, shared an interest in everyday life, it is precisely the lack of common ground that is so striking when we more closely examine the attempts at reconciliation between the SI and Socialisme ou Barbarie. In other words, and much more clearly than in the case of Lefebvre, what would lead to the break with Socialisme ou Barbarie (what might be termed a "soft break," without conflict or polemics, polite but firm) was the intransigence of the group to the poetic-cultural outlook that always characterized Debord and his work: on one side, a poetic project for the (re)construction of everyday life; on the other, arid speculations about the telltale signs of the decay of the Communist parties of Eastern Europe.[17] It would require a high degree of myopia regarding the unique problematic developed by Debord and the SI to view his encounter with the theoreticians of the far left as a decisive moment in his life. But such misunderstanding is inevitable as long as we insist in seeing him as a theoretician, or qualifying as "sociological" a period that was no less dominated than the previous one by a concern for poetics, by a project to reinvent communication.

Proof of this can be found in the well-known "conference" titled "Perspectives de modification conscientes dans la vie quotidienne," given two weeks after his break with Socialisme ou Barbarie. Debord recorded the talk on tape for the research group on everyday life led by Henri Lefebvre at the CNRS [Centre National de la Recherche Scientifique]. It was later published in *Internationale situationniste*.[18] Both the form and the title of the talk highlight the distance between Lefebvre's position and that of the situationists: the CNRS deserved a tape recorder, but not much more, and could hardly be considered part of the SI's strategic objectives.[19]

Here, it is a question of the *conscious* changes in perspective in everyday life. Debord's attitude was not that of a sociologist. His point of view implies a practice, even a poetics: everyday life should be changed the way situations are constructed. It is also important to bear in mind that Debord's perspective was totalizing, as it was already during the period when urbanism was defined, for this reason, as unitary. Making use of Lefebvre's definition of everyday life, wherein everyday life is what remains when we have extracted all specialized activities from lived experience, he introduces a reversal through which everyday life, the remainder of all activities, is assumed to be at the center of everything, because of which it is not specialized: "We must once more make everyday life the center of everything. Every project starts from there and every realization returns there to assume its true signification. Everyday life is the measure of everything: of the fulfillment, or rather nonfulfillment, of human relations; of the use of lived time, of the search for art; of revolutionary politics."[20]

Everyday life was the keystone of a totalizing perspective. Or, to be more accurate, it was the name of a totality to be re-created, to be won back in the face of the separation and privation imposed by the society of the spectacle. One could even say that the only constructed situation that entirely avoided the risk of being merely an event (or worse, a separate artwork that had degenerated into a happening or spectacle) was everyday life that had been totally (re)constructed. No longer the remainder of specialized activity, it would become the measure of all things by reappropriating specialized and separate activities. From this viewpoint, everyday life was the opposite of private life, which is the product of separation and specialization. Private life is everyday life deprived of everything, reduced to being only the remainder of specialized activities, deprived of itself and simultaneously abandoned to separation and the absence of communication: "The question has been raised: 'Private life is deprived of what?' Quite simply, of life, which is cruelly absent from it. People are as deprived as possible of communication and self-fulfillment. It would be preferable to say: deprived of the ability to create their own history, personally."[21] To make the transition from private life to everyday life meant reinventing forms of communication confiscated by the space-time of the society of the spectacle. "This society tends to atomize people into isolated consumers, to prevent communication. Everyday life thus becomes private life, the domain of separation and the spectacle."[22]

The stakes are certainly political and could only be accomplished by revolution, because so much was hanging in the balance. But this "so much" is also a matter of poetics, a question of *lifestyle,* or simply *style.* Debord himself seemed to hesitate to make such an apolitical claim, leaving his sentence—and the question of style—incomplete: "In responding positively to this question about the nature of poverty, arguments can only be formulated in the form of projects for enrichment: a project for a different lifestyle, or simply a style . . ."[23]

Moving from private life to a reinvented everyday life—revolution, in other words—was also a matter of poetics, a question of style. So, in spite of situationism's "sociological" turn and the mass departure of artists from the SI, Debord continued, after 1962, to position himself outside politics and literature in the traditional sense. He attempted to occupy a space that was always his own, where he continued to attempt to tie together the threads of revolution and poetry, here understood as a style of communication and a lifestyle. In the following issues of the magazine, there appeared several articles concerning this very point. More than ever, the SI clung to this border between poetry and revolution, whose *coincidence* in Berlin dada or the Congolese revolution was foreseen rather dramatically in certain published articles:

They try to make us forget the extent to which true dadaism was German dada, and the extent to which it was bound to the rise of the German revolution after the 1918 armistice. The necessity of such a connection has not changed for anyone who today assumes a new cultural position. It is simply that this novelty must be found *simultaneously* in both art and politics.

The simple anticommunication borrowed today from dadaism by the most reactionary defenders of established lies has no value at a time when it is urgent to create new communication on the simplest as well as the most complex levels of practice. The most worthy successor of dadaism, its legitimate successor, existed in the Congo in the summer of 1960. The spontaneous revolt of a people that had been kept, to a greater extent than elsewhere, in a state of infancy, just when the rationale—more alien than anywhere else—for its exploitation began to waver, led to the sudden appropriation of the external language of their masters through poetry and as a mode of action. The expression of the Congolese during this period deserves respectful consideration so that we may recognize the grandeur and effectiveness (for example, the role of the poet Lumumba) of the only communication possible, which, in all cases, makes common cause with the intervention in daily life, the transformation of the world.[24]

According to the SI, the Congolese revolution entailed the appropriation and reappropriation of the language of the masters, by which it coincided with the (re)invention of communication: poetry in action, poetry become action. The revolution helped fulfill what might have taken place with Berlin dada, the period when it was organically connected to the German Spartacist forces, if the latter had succeeded. In his *Préface à un dictionnaire situationniste,* Mustapha Khayati again returned to the opportunity given to German dadaism. This was credited with the exemplary project of claiming the right to say anything, but it failed to transform this "say everything" into "do everything." "'Saying everything' cannot exist without the freedom to do everything. Dada had a chance of fulfillment in *Spartakus,* in the revolutionary practice of the German proletariat. The latter's failure made the former's inevitable."[25] The reevaluation of dada by the situationists is an interesting one. By emphasizing Berlin rather than Zurich or Paris as its most authentic moment, they focused on the least spectacular, the least theatrical, the most obscure aspect, one is tempted to say, the one that disappeared completely with the failure of the Spartacist uprising. At the same time, they chose the part of dadaism that most resembled what the SI would become *two years later,* with and after the events of May 1968.

But Khayati's argument is also interesting from a theoretical point of view: saying everything is only possible if you can also do everything—the poetics of revolution as a form of pragmatics. To be able to say everything, speech must be immediately convertible into action, it must be performative, one must perform. The authenticity of communication is measured against action or joint action, without which speech is co-opted in representation, the open gateway to the spectacle. What is revolutionary speech? It is speech torn from representation, any form of representation, and *immediately* diverted into the practice it engenders through utterance. Debord's interest in the councilist theories developed by Socialisme ou Barbarie may also be the result of a specific relation to speech, the effect of a singular way of inhabiting or making use of language. It arises from his relation to representation (whether it be artistic, linguistic, or political), from a long-standing project to abolish all forms of mediation for the benefit of an absolute immediate.

In this context, an article that appeared in issue 8 of *Internationale situationniste*, in January 1963, titled "All the King's Men," is to my mind one of the most remarkable articles ever published in the review and one that most clearly expresses the SI's unique position at the juncture of politics and culture, one that was apparently quite remote from the concerns of Socialisme ou Barbarie. As in Khayati's "Captive Words," the point of departure here is the control of language by the power structure, which deprives it of its communicative function—its poetic force. There was no possible compatibility between state and communication: "Where there is communication, there is no state."[26] Power is based on the appropriation of language, a form of proletarianization. It forces language to give up its labor power—Bataille's idea of the "work of words."[27]

> Words work on behalf of the ruling organization of life. . . . Under power's supervision, language always designates something other than authentic lived experience. It is precisely there that the possibility of a total opposition resides. The confusion in the organization of language has become so great that communication imposed by power is unveiled as an imposture and a deception. . . .
>
> Power lives on stolen goods. It creates nothing, it recuperates. If it created the meaning of words, there would be no poetry, but solely useful "information." We could never confront one another within language, and every refusal would be outside it, would be purely lettrist. However, what is poetry if not the language in revolution, and as such inseparable from the revolutionary moments in world history as well as in the history of private life?[28]

Knowing this, it is easier to see why no "situationist dictionary" was ever published, for it would consist only of the totality of all the singular and historical reinventions of everyday life discovering its language and becoming communication. For Bataille, a dictionary that accounted for the work of words could only be realized in writing. For the situationists, it coincided with revolution, an infinitely open totality, and the (re)construction of individual lives. What is also surprising is the unexpected use of the term "lettrist," a sign of both continuity and evolution. Lettrism was a rejection of the dominant language, and in that sense was indisputably a poetic act. But it was an *external* rejection of language, a rejection that involved escaping (articulate) language, and it challenged the false appearance of communication demanded by the power structure with an absolute form, not of communication, but of noncommunication. As such, it could be considered the culmination of the history of modern poetry, described in "All the King's Men" as the history of insubordination, a rejection of a form of communication that had been falsified and confiscated by the power structure.

At this time, the SI's sociological phase was in full swing. But when we examine the situation more closely, we find that although the problem of art was now behind them, the same was not true of poetics (in the broad sense), which had become the focus of Debord's and his companions' concerns. An article such as "All the King's Men" suggests a much greater proximity between the SI and Tel Quel's *Théorie d'ensemble* (1968) than with the arguments advanced by Socialisme ou Barbarie.[29] It's hard not to think of Artaud—at least one aspect of his life—and many others who were later promoted by the adherents of the revolution of poetic language, when we read statements such as this: "Information is power's poetry (the counter-poetry of the maintenance of law and order). It is the media faking of what is. Conversely, poetry must be understood as immediate communication in reality and real modification of that reality. It is nothing other than liberated language, language that wins back its richness and, breaking its significations, at once recovers words, music, cries, gestures, painting, mathematics, events."[30] The situationist poetic is semiotics (in Julia Kristeva's sense, that is, to the extent it stands in opposition to the symbolic) in the service of politics.

The revolution in poetic language now implied revolution *tout court,* and therefore the end of poetry or literature as a specialized and separate activity. It implied the end, and, therefore, once again the Book: "liberat-ed" language is a kind of *Gesamtkunstwerk,* a "total" form of expression comprising every "separate" form of expression (such a project was quite explicit for someone like Artaud). Everything in the world, at least in the situationist world, is intended to culminate not in a beautiful Book, but in a beautiful revolution, which takes the place of the Book, which may be nothing other than the situationist figure of the Book or, if one prefers, the figure of the end of art. In 1960, Asger Jorn had already written that "once realized, communism will be the work of art transformed into the totality of everyday life."[31]

In any event, the fates of poetry and revolution were intimately con-nected with each other. It was through its ability to create events and their language simultaneously that poetry would reinvent itself and become revolution: "Rediscovering poetry can merge with reinventing revolution, as certain stages of the Mexican, Cuban, or Congolese revolutions quite ob-viously prove."[32] By definition, poetry produces revolution or, more accu-rately, is already revolution, but in the virtual state. It is an appeal to a real revolution that must, in some sense, be placed at its service, something the surrealists had never dared express: "It is not a question of putting poetry at the service of the revolution, but rather of putting revolution at the ser-vice of poetry."[33] This eliminated a considerable number of the debates and misunderstandings (especially with the Communist Party) that had been commonplace for avant-gardes and French intellectuals. Poetry is always at least the figure of revolution. It is the revolution in absentia, its shadow; it evokes its absence while repeating its promise: "Between revolutionary periods when the masses accede to poetry through action, we might imag-ine that circles of poetic adventure remain the only places where the totality of the revolution lives on, as an unfulfilled but immanent potentiality, as the shadow of an absent individual."[34]

The circles of poetic adventure are the circles of a temporarily absent revolution. They are communities in which the possibility of authentic communication is preserved and celebrated, while waiting for the crowd to declare itself, communities that will embody the "absent individual" of revolution to the extent that they themselves tend to disappear, to the ex-tent they do all in their power to escape the gaze of the spectacle whose vir-tual interruption they become: the obscurity of Mallarmé and Lautréamont, the clandestine existence of the lettrists of Saint-Germain-des-Prés, or of

Rimbaud and his friends. They are the trustees of revolution. "All have for an aim and as actual result, the immediate transparency of a certain communication, of mutual recognition, and of agreement."[35]

Poetry and revolution are both defined as actual communication, impersonal and necessarily collective. This is what made May 1968 the greatest poetic event of the twentieth century (as the Paris Commune was in the nineteenth, though bloodier). Every aspect of the situationist world is designed to culminate in the occupied streets of May 1968, the poetry of graffiti, the continuous debates held at the Odéon Theater and the Sorbonne, and especially the factory occupations by the workers described in 1969, in the last issue of *Internationale situationniste*, as "the *generalized critique* of all forms of alienation, all ideologies, and all aspects of the former organization of real life. . . . The *recognized desire* for dialogue, of completely free speech, the thirst for true community."[36] It is time to take a closer look at the role played by Debord and his followers in the events of May 1968.

From Strasbourg to Segovia

The revolution would take place through poetry, understood as the immediate reinvention of communication for and by everyone. During the early sixties, this was the position of the situationists, which Lefebvre would later reject after having been repudiated by his "young friends." One might as well assume, he said, that a violent general strike was possible. This was no doubt a misunderstanding, but Lefebvre was not the only one who failed to anticipate, theoretically or practically, May 1968. The situationists, who saw in those events a striking confirmation of their concept of revolution, did not forget to remind Lefebvre of his sagacity later on.[1]

The involvement of the SI in May 1968 is not just a matter of philosophical and political debate on the nature of revolution, for we know that the situationists were very concretely engaged in those events. But how much do we really know? There is no shortage of controversy about the nature and meaning of the events of that May. Some are associated with left-wing historiography, others with the anarchist tendencies that were so prevalent that spring. Some saw it as a prelude to insurrection, others as a crisis of government, others as a revolt against authority (against the father), possibly in conjunction with the arrival of an individualist and hedonist culture. These arguments are well known and I won't discuss them here. However, in the midst of the controversies, disagreement about the role played by the SI in the events of that year is one of the few absolutes. There are some historians of May 1968 who have literally never heard of the situationists. Others are willing to admit the existence of something like *The Society of the Spectacle* or *The Revolution of Everyday Life,* and that these were the bibles of many of the rioters, among whom the authors of those histories were not to be found. Hervé Hamon and Patrick Rotman, for example, the authors of *Génération,* gave them no more than a foot-note after many long chapters devoted to some of the leading figures of the French left.[2] Others—and this includes the situationist historiographers— saw only the situationists. More or less everyone agrees, notwithstanding the divergent interpretations of the overall situation, on the role played by Cohn-Bendit, July, Krivine, Geismar, and so on. But concerning the role of Debord and his colleagues, no one seems to know. Where were the situa-tionists in May 1968? According to the historians we have consulted, they were everywhere and nowhere.

There were never many situationists to begin with, and they were never interested in increasing their ranks—before, during, and especially after May 1968. They didn't recruit anyone; there were never situationist battal-ions the way there were Trotskyist and Maoist battalions, with their banners, flags, security staff, and megaphones. In 1966, shortly before the Strasbourg "scandal," the SI counted maybe a dozen members: Debord, Michèle Bern-stein (who quit in 1967, although she remained close to Debord for several years), Théo Frey, Édith Frey (kicked out in 1967), Jean Garnault (not yet the head of the "Garnaultin" plot of the following year), Anton Hartstein, Her-bert Holl, Mustapha Khayati, Ndjangani Lungela, Jeppesen Victor Martin, Donald Nicholson-Smith, Raoul Vaneigem, and René Viénet. This num-ber changed little over the next two to three years (but dropped considerably in the months immediately prior to the dissolution of the SI in 1971). Under these conditions, it would have been difficult to serve as a counterweight to the traditional leftist organizations with their considerably larger mem-ber base, who, unlike the SI, did everything they could to remain visible.

STRASBOURG

If we are to believe situationist historiography, the origins of May 1968 coincide with the moment the SI first went public as a revolution-ary force, that is with the SI's participation in the celebrated Strasbourg "scandal."[3] To force the issue somewhat, it could be said that May 1968 was nothing more than the manifestation of what had been conceived over the years within the circle of poetic adventure formed by Debord and his companions. There are reasons for this, and the statement can be understood in terms of the logic of Debord's thinking, as shown by some of his comments in the months and years following May 1968.

What was the Strasbourg scandal? Taking advantage of a crisis in the national student union, a handful of students at the University of Strasbourg who sympathized with the Situationist International managed, in May 1966, to get themselves elected to run the local student union, AFGES (Association Fédérative Générale des Étudiants de Strasbourg, a local affiliate of the Union Nationale des Étudiants de France). Their entire program was based on sabotaging the bourgeois university, which led to their decision to immediately dissolve AFGES (a reasonable idea from the situationist perspective). In this context, the Strasbourg students asked the Situationist International for its support. The SI responded favorably to their request by helping with the publication of a pamphlet titled *De la misère en milieu étudiant considérée sous ses aspects économique, politique, psychologique, sexuel et notamment intellectuel, et de quelques moyens pour y remédier* [On the poverty of student life, considered in its economic, political, psychological, sexual, and particularly intellectual aspects, and a modest proposal for its remedy] that was signed "by members of the Situationist International and the Strasbourg students." The pamphlet was written by Mustapha Khayati. Initially published in 1966 by AFGES, the pamphlet went through a large number of pirate editions before being republished in 1976 by Éditions Gérard Lebovici. The reprint led to new polemics between Debord and a number of ex-situationists, including Khayati and Vaneigem, who reproached Debord and Éditions Lebovici for appropriating a text that was the emblem of a collective and anonymous political culture.

Where did the events of May 1968 originate? According to situationist historiography, they are hidden in Strasbourg, in the obscure support provided by the SI to student sympathizers. In the beginning of May 1968 was the situationist word. The Strasbourg students, unable to write the pamphlet they had planned to produce with the SI, served as its mouthpiece, or at least that of its delegate.[4] The first half of "On the Poverty of Student Life" is an attack against student life and the university in general, described as a place of extreme alienation and subjugation to power, from which the students will free themselves only by joining the forces of global revolution. From its opening lines, the pamphlet seethes with contempt for those who are clearly the opposite of the lost children:

> The student is a stoic slave: the more chains authority heaps upon him, the freer he is in fantasy. He shares with his new family, the University, a belief in a curious kind of autonomy. Real independence, apparently, lies in a direct subservience to the two most powerful systems of social control: the family and the State. He is their well-behaved and grateful child, and like the submissive child he is over-eager to please. He celebrates all the values and mystifications of the system, devouring them with all the anxiety of the infant at the breast. Once, the old illusions had to be imposed on an aristocracy of labor; the petits cadres-to-be ingest them willingly under the guise of culture.[5]

The students were especially despicable—and, in fact, despised—because their submissiveness was in a sense their vocation, and especially because they took refuge in the illusion of an autonomous world of culture. To that extent, they were the most fervent pillars of the cultural state established during the Fifth Republic, which May 1968 shook to its core.[6] The second half of the pamphlet lays out the principal arguments defended by the SI at the time (critique of Leninism, defense of workers' councils, critique of the spectacle, transcendence of the commodity economy, abolition of work for free creative activity).

Printed at the expense of the Union des Étudiants de Strasbourg, controlled by the pro-situationists, the pamphlet was distributed in the fall of 1966 and caused a scandal not only among the university administration, but also in the press, which was outraged to see such radical and irresponsible bitterness. For the situationists, the scandal provided a considerable source of publicity and gave evidence as well of their tactical abilities. In a few days or weeks, their arguments, previously relatively confidential and limited to the readers of *Internationale situationniste,* were literally brought to the awareness of the public by the newspapers. "On the Poverty of Student Life" is, if not the first situationist manifesto, at least the first text in which the SI showed itself publicly. From university to university, then from country to country, in various new editions and translations (Martos provides a figure of three hundred thousand published copies), the little situationist pamphlet served, wherever it went, as a detonator.

"We brought fuel to the fire," Debord wrote in *In girum imus nocte.*[7] No false modesty here: the situationists were happy to manufacture the detonators for the bombs that already existed, allowing them to explode, or, to put it somewhat differently, to express themselves. They provided them with a voice (which is not the same thing as giving free expression to violence: situationism should not be confused with terrorism). They were not really concerned about the rest, and to search for situationists in Strasbourg or elsewhere, to assign them a responsibility they systematically waved aside, was pointless. This forced their accomplices in Strasbourg to openly refute the attacks by the press confusing them with the SI. Only the SI could speak for the SI, only the SI represented the SI (which amounts to escaping the mechanisms of political representation). In Strasbourg, the SI shone by its absence, that is, through its voice, which was scandalous, and inaudible to the enemy.[8] Initially, it provided an opposition movement with a voice, just as later it would continue to provide this (and other movements) with a *form of expression.* I'm thinking in particular of one of the formal means used by the situationists—the appropriation of comic strips (the text in the speech bubbles was systematically replaced)—which was also used in Strasbourg when the students returned to school in the fall of 1966, especially by one André Bertrand, the "author" of the mythical *Retour de la Colonne Durruti.* One of the panels shows an image of Lenin exclaiming: "And as for the JCR, I'll fuck them too."[9] Two cowboys discuss reification (they have been reading *The Society of the Spectacle*); two well-informed toothbrushes dismiss, back to back, fascists, Gaullists, Communists, and anarchists with the words: "Yes, it's true, all of them, consciously or not, are part of that old world we must now fight against."[10]

PARIS

The situation more or less returned to normal in Strasbourg the following year. The "Durruti Column" decided to turn its attention to Paris and was also seen in Nanterre. Thanks to the pro-situationist *"enragés"* (the best known of whom is René Riesel, he and Patrick Cheval were the only *enragés* to later become members of the SI), the toothbrushes showed up during the first part of a show that this time promised to be spectacular. During the preparations for the celebration, the situationists were obviously present, which is to say they shone by their absence, playing the role of advisors to the *enragés* and providing supplies of "On the Poverty

of Student Life" to all comers, including the Liaison des étudiants anar-
chistes [Anarchist Student Liaison], with the proviso that the pamphlets
be distributed during Professor Henri Lefebvre's classes.[11] Because of the
radical nature of their proposals, the *enragés* were soon marginalized at
Nanterre, where the initiative was quickly taken by the "Mouvement du
22 mars" [March 22 Movement], led by Daniel Cohn-Bendit. They left the
campus, but not without providing student agitators with forms of expression they had adopted from the situationists. Some of the graffiti they
splashed across the walls of the buildings in Nanterre before their departure were destined for glory: the ever-popular "Never work!" "Take your desires for reality," "Boredom is counterrevolutionary." Thus the *style* of May
1968 had already been established as early as March. Form preceded content, speech brought objects to life, nothing would take place that hadn't
been proposed. To paraphrase Mallarmé, "I say 'revolution' and there immediately rises the one absent from all bureaucratic bouquets." Because
the *enragés* left Nanterre the day the March 22 Movement came into being,
it is obvious that the controversial role of the situationists in triggering the
events of May 1968 is to be found in their ability to provide the student
movement with a sense of style, a singular voice, a new voice, one that had
literally never been heard before and was for many completely inaudible.

The situationists were the great stylists of May 1968, providing its formal
structure.[12] Their efficiency, indeed their success, was based on their art of
détournement, their sense of the unanswerable insult, their formal inven-
tiveness. They were able to provide forms of expression that anyone could
immediately reuse, appropriate, and develop for their own use. This under-
lies their techniques of appropriation and is why the situationists made
it a policy to reject copyright. It was one thing to provide the means of expression, but these are meaningless—at least from the revolutionary point
of view—if they are not at the same time techniques for sharing or trans-
mitting speech, for the *production of community.* The effectiveness of the
situationists was to have identified one with the other. They were stylists,
but revolutionaries as well, producing ready-to-wear for the month of May,
words that could circulate freely, without an author, without copyright, that
derived their effectiveness precisely from the fact that they lacked authorship, lacked authority.[13]

There is nothing more community oriented, even communist, than the
development of situationist slogans during May 1968. There is a certain

logic to the fact that the reverse of their future omnipresence on the walls of Paris can be found in the invisibility of the situationists, their absence, which has led some historians to deny them any role in the events of May. "The more famous our theses become, the more shadowy our own presence will be," Debord wrote at the time of the SI's dissolution.[14] The celebrity of our slogans depends on our ability to detach ourselves from the conflict, to not claim authorship, to return to the shadows of the authentic community being formed. The revolution came without a signature. In Strasbourg, Nanterre, and somewhat later at the occupied Sorbonne, when Debord was present, the situationists or their allies always began by supporting the most radical points of view.[15] Through the use of graffiti, pamphleteering, and radical slogans, they disseminated their ideas widely, only to withdraw from the scene when the majority refused to listen. They abandoned their weapons on the field of battle—slogans, which now made their own way, having been picked up and duplicated by others.

Where were the situationists in May 1968? They were on the barricades like almost everyone else (although not everyone was present during the most violent confrontations). Then they shifted their efforts to the Sorbonne, which they left very soon after, at the beginning of the first factory occupations that would lead to the spreading wildcat strike. They defended their "councilist" arguments by forming a "Conseil pour le maintien des occupations" [Council for maintaining occupations] (CMDO), settling into an office next door to the headquarters of the Maoists on the Rue d'Ulm, then in the basement of the École des Arts Décoratifs, custom-made for the stylists of revolution. But their presence was most felt wherever they were not, wherever they were not seen: in the many slogans they invented or for which they provided models, on posters, or in the appropriation of comic strips whose numbers continued to grow. They did not go to war as "political activists" (they never attempted to recruit, or swell the ranks of the workers, never led the marchers with a megaphone in hand), but rather as poets gifted in rhetorical disappearance and anger: through words (and puns) they reinscribed violence in a fundamentally symbolic structure.

The presence of situationists in the CMDO can be explained by their rapid disenchantment with the student revolt. The action now shifted to the wildcat strikes in the factories, the first signs of which appeared before the March 22 Movement (primarily in Nantes and Redon), and which took from the student disruptions the style they needed to become systematic.[16] Art, as well as the unions, had been relegated to the past. Representation, regardless of the genre, was not faring well; it was time for councilism. But claiming that the situationists militated within the CMDO does not make them easier to locate. This merely shifts the question to the extent that the CMDO was their creation (more exactly, the creation of members of the SI and their *"enragé"* accomplices), to the extent that, here too, they simply supplied fuel for the fire. But fire does not represent oil any more than the CMDO represented the striking workers. At most it helped them explode, in other words, to express themselves.

In fact, the CMDO may only have been the embodiment of a politics of communication that Debord had adopted years earlier. In terms of its internal operation, it was based on direct democracy, it had a continuous general meeting where anyone could express himself or herself freely (this was also the utopia of the first days of the occupation of the Sorbonne). There was no hierarchy, everyone had an equal say in discussions, decisions, and their execution. Those in charge of various tasks, who were designated by the general meeting, could be recalled at any time. Everything concerning delegation and representation was reduced to a state of ephemeral fragility.[17] In this sense, it represents a formal embodiment of the authentic dialogue Debord always claimed to favor, and the case of the CMDO was highly symbolic because dialogue was inseparable from mutual action, namely, support for the factory occupations. What did this support consist in? Basically, they provided the striking workers with *means of communication.*

The situationists initially served as liaisons between the various occupied factories, which they enabled to remain in contact with one another (especially since they had access to a number of cars that had been appropriated from their traditional isolationist function conferred by the society of the spectacle: just as any means of communication and transport can be appropriated).[18] They also—and for this reason their choice of the École des Arts Décoratifs is not irrelevant from a symbolic point of view—made a large number of posters covered with situationist slogans invented for the occasion, all of which defended workers' councils against the political parties and unions. Along with texts, images, and cars, you could appropriate a school of decorative arts (even though it appears that striking printers played a large part in producing the posters). The CMDO freely distributed the posters to the occupied factories. They published pamphlets and distributed a new wave of appropriated comic strips—the label or signature of the situationist contribution to the street decorations of May 1968.

The CMDO was about communication, poetry in action. "The recognized desire for dialogue, for completely free speech, the thirst for a real community found fertile ground in the buildings taken over for meetings and in the common struggle: telephones, among the very few technical means still functioning, and the movement of large numbers of emissaries and travelers—in Paris and in many other countries—between occupied buildings, factories, and general meetings embodied this real use of communication."[19] Genuine communication, emissaries, movement, and travel: Debord could just as easily have been speaking about his years in Saint-Germain-des-Prés, the celebrations in Florence, the adventures in Spain. He remained focused on circles of poetic adventure and privileged moments when the poetic becomes manifest.

SEGOVIA

I want to briefly skip ahead to 1980. By then the reaction had been under way for a number of years. The response had been swift and brutal in 1968, then became increasingly oppressive. The CMDO disappeared, the factories were busy with production, and many former leftists were getting ready for jobs in government. After the dissolution of the SI in 1971, Debord systematically chose exile and travel over the formation of new groups, whether political or avant-garde. There was little community involvement. He also refused to back the countless pro-situationist or, more generally, anarchist groups that multiplied during these years in France, Italy, Spain, and Portugal. Debord certainly had contacts with these movements but they were limited to specific individuals with whom he maintained professional or even friendly relations. He gave up any attempt to help such groups organize themselves or consolidate their forces, and never assumed a leadership position in any of them, although he was asked. On the contrary, he did everything he could during this period to escape their demands and even gave up using a phone. The SI was over. There was no question that the Debord of the seventies would support anyone, even indirectly, as he did during the period of the Strasbourg disruptions or the Nanterre *enragés*. Now, revolution was about autonomy, which few revolutionaries seemed to want, at least among those who tried to obtain

Debord's support. This was the position he would maintain from this point on; once Debord adopted a stance, he rarely changed his mind.

There was one important exception to this position, which was also an exception to the positions he had staked out during the seventies and eighties in contrast to the anarchists, who had chosen armed struggle. This was the 1980 appeal from Segovia, which should be seen in the context of Debord's relations with Tony Lopez Pintor, the "Andalusian," an anarchist he had met in 1978 and who introduced Debord to Spain. Debord's translation of Manrique is one sign of this attachment. The other is a translation he completed together with Alice Becker-Ho of a surprising text, dating from the Spanish civil war, entitled *Protestación en frente los liberatarios del presente y del futuro sobre las capitulaciones de 1937.*[20] It was the final

...tti Column, or rather a return to the source: this text, ...he Spanish civil war and the struggles among Stalinist, ...controlled anarchist factions, is associated with one of ...of European revolutionary struggle in the twentieth cen- ...ord was able to recognize something akin to his own po- ...on of Spain, its language, its passions, and its taste for ...rty required this (we know that the Spanish Republican ...he Communists did everything they could to undermine ...rchists—especially the celebrated CNT, which made the greatest contribution to the struggle against Franco's supporters).

In adopting Spain, Debord not only found, through Manrique, a father figure to mourn, but also a genealogy for the defunct Situationist International, which is to say that the Segovia appeal was not simply an accident. By the end of the seventies, Debord was in contact with Spanish anarchist groups (especially a group known as GAL, "Groupe autonome libertaire," which his friend Jaime Semprun was close to). They asked his help in supporting their comrades imprisoned in Segovia, who had been accused of armed robbery, theft, and in some cases murder. The accused, about fifty in all, were modern Robin Hoods. Some were innocent, victims of police provocation, but many others were guilty before the law. They had robbed, pillaged, blown up public buildings, courthouses, and railroad tracks, and they redistributed the take to strikers, the unemployed, and militant revolutionaries.

Debord agreed to help because, in his opinion, the imprisoned Spanish anarchists acted on their own and had not been manipulated. They too were "uncontrolled," and had no scores to settle with the now legal Communist Party represented in the Cortes, Spain's parliament, or with the CNT, which was no longer what it had been since it now played the game of union representation. But how could he help them? Significantly, his support took the form of an anonymous appeal from Segovia signed "international friends" (although he was the sole author), which was disseminated in its Spanish translation by anarchist networks.

The mass distribution of the appeal impressed the young Spanish government, which remained fragile and had no desire to confront the anarchists at a time when it was so concerned with the far right. Therefore, it decided to withdraw, out of fear of increased agitation. The accused from Segovia were released "for lack of evidence," the irony being that although the Spanish state was not at this time concerned about lack of evidence in condemning its enemies, in this specific case the evidence was available. The government simply closed its eyes.

The affair demonstrates Debord's remarkable tactical sense, together with a formidable ability to bluff, for behind the omnipresent and threatening posters that popularized the "Segovia appeal," there was nothing to back it up other than Guy Debord's indeterminate word. It was an exemplary operation, which speaks more forcefully than many others about Debord's "politics": his understanding of the uses of language for waging war, and the clandestinity and anonymity that speech required in order to become bellicose. There is little doubt that Debord's Segovia text was effective more because of the form in which it was made known than for its content alone, and such effectiveness would have been inconceivable if the text had been signed. Spanish democracy may still have been fragile in 1980, but it is hard to imagine it making an about-face solely because of Debord's name. It was his ability to enunciate the ghost of Spanish anarchism that made them take notice. Following the dreary Italian years, the Segovia appeal represented a final opportunity for committing his words to a cause (in the sense of committing troops to a battle). This seemed to mobilize Debord, as if, in 1980, revolution were still possible in Spain the way it had been in Paris in 1968: through words, slogans, and posters.

When the Segovia prisoners were acquitted for lack of evidence on November 26, the appeal appeared in a French "translation."[21] Debord denounced the silence observed by the various Spanish political factions (including the CNT) concerning the imprisoned anarchists. He saw this silence as proof of a belated reconciliation among the counterrevolutionary forces, who had united once before to crush what was to become the most powerful worker uprising in Europe. It is this silence that served to justify the appeal. Like so many other of Debord's writings or actions, this too was based on a heightened sense of the use of public space, of the implementation of a strategy of denunciation. Debord had written a great deal to condemn or to silence. In the case of Segovia, he wrote to overcome the silence, to publicly proclaim what was supposed to be ignored. Even though the government had closed its eyes to the anarchists' escape, it would have been dangerous to avoid publicizing the event:

> There is nothing judicial about this affair. It's a simple matter of relations of force. Since the government has such an obvious interest in avoiding mention of these comrades, it is sufficient that we force the discussions out into the open so that the government is forced to admit that it is in its immediate interest to free them rather than to keep them in prison. Whether the government chooses to arrive at this result by means of a trial in which their sentence is equivalent to the time they have already spent in jail, or by an amnesty, or by allowing them to escape, is without importance. However, we insist on the fact that, as long as popular opinion concerning their case is not sufficiently forceful and threatening, the escape favored by the authorities is dangerous. You are familiar with the "ley de fugas," and will see it applied on many occasions.[22]

The most important section of the book consists of texts written by the imprisoned anarchists, in which they state their autonomy. Obviously, all those texts, which are signed "Groupes autonomes" or not signed at all, are anonymous, as was the case in past struggles. A third section of the book contains songs about the prisoners of Segovia, appropriated Spanish folk songs given new lyrics for the occasion, whose author-aficionados are again Debord and Alice Becker-Ho. These are popular melodies that were given to a revolutionary people through their appropriation. From Strasbourg to Segovia, all of Debord's battles were similar, clothed in the same style.[23]

The Greater the Fame of Our Arguments, the Greater Our Obscurity

It has been said that Debord's style is insurrectional. This is especially true of his involvement in May 1968 and the Segovia appeals. Speech was not only used in the service of war or revolution, but itself became the site or nerve of warfare. Conversely, revolution will always be a matter of speech, of reinvented communication. The transition to the situationist act was, in concrete terms, a transition to speech, an assumption of speech, but a form of speech that dreams of its own *dissolution* in a pure revolutionary act (an uprising, a strike). A speech that abandons itself to its own perdition: Debord was always the lost child he started out as, and he always entertained the same dream of disappearance, of dissolution. It is this dream that led to the dissolution of the Situationist International, as if situationist discourse (specifically, the SI) in 1971 had no further reason to exist because of the rise to power of revolutionary struggles around the world. In this sense, the dissolution of the SI should also be understood as an image of Debord's relationship to his own speech and even to himself. It was a personal matter for him, as was the entire history of the SI.

"Never have we once been involved in anything either politicians of the most extreme left-wing variety or the most progressive-minded intellectuals get up to in the way of business, rivalries, and the company they keep. Now that we can moreover pride ourselves on having achieved the most revolting fame among this rabble, we fully intend to become *even more inaccessible,* even more clandestine. The more famous our theses become, the more shadowy our own presence will be."[1] Thus concluded the *Theses on the Situationist International and Its Time (Thèses sur l'Internationale situationniste et son temps),* which appeared a year after the SI's dissolution in 1971. Debord promoted the dissolution by creating a "split" within the SI. This brought into opposition those who wanted the SI to remain what it had always been, those who wanted to take advantage, at least according to Debord, of the fame it had garnered by its participation in May 1968, and those who refused to see the SI become an ideology or object of contemplation, who rejected the now prestigious role that the "reformist" spectacle of the early seventies tried to force it into. But it was Raoul Vaneigem who had become the primary target, ever since his promotion to the rank of head of the "navel gazers."[2] Debord had become frustrated trying to singlehandedly create a revolutionary organization for the greater good of others. The majority of the contributions to the final and voluminous issue of *Internationale situationniste* (September 1969) are by him, and when he challenged his companions to produce the next issue, nothing happened for two years. Supposedly power-hungry leaders are said to always behave in this manner, to make it impossible for others to follow in their footsteps so they can be criticized for their failure. In Debord's case, given the nature of the situationist adventure in general and the review in particular, and given the image he provides in his correspondence—that of a tireless leader who encouraged a motley assembly of companions with remarkable magnanimity—such an assumption makes little sense. Blaming Debord for the inability of the "navel gazers" to produce a thirteenth issue of *Internationale situationniste* is as relevant as attributing to him an outsized appetite for power. And he demonstrated his lack of interest in power *by creating the split in the SI,* by forming a splinter group with himself as its sole representative, or nearly so.

The splinter group was small, consisting of only two people: Debord and the Italian Gianfranco Sanguinetti, cosigner of the *Theses on the Situationist International and Its Time.* Cofounder of the Italian section of the SI during the years of unrest, 1969–72, Sanguinetti took refuge in France but was later thrown out. He did not play an active role in the final discussions that shook the SI. Although Debord had him sign a text of which he was the only "author," it was solely out of solidarity with him and his expulsion, which demonstrated that Sanguinetti was willing to make a personal sacrifice, unlike the "navel gazers." This solitude gave the desire for obscurity an immediately personal dimension: the process of liquidating the SI seems to have had more to do with Debord alone than its founding had. With the culmination of what was, if not the most spectacular, at least the most celebrated and best-known part of Debord's career, it was Debord and Debord alone who chose to return to the clandestine existence of the early years, who decided, once again, to disappear. The dissolute life of the years in Saint-Germain-des-Prés was mirrored by the dissolution of the Situationist International: "We will become even more inaccessible, even more clandestine. . . ."

Of course, the situationist adventure was collective. It was constructed through joint participation in a series of experiences and the sharing of talent, and a not negligible number of those who belonged to the group were—still are—brilliant individuals. However, I would like to advance the argument that the Situationist International came to an end, in every sense of the word, when it was dissolved by Debord in 1971. Not only did his adventure end with the demise of the SI, but this was his *goal.* The adventure was realized in and through its dissolution. "The more famous our theses become, the more shadowy our own presence will be." This was not an acknowledgment of failure but a gesture of exultation, which tied the success of the SI to the verbal disappearance of its members. The objective of the SI was to have taken place, it consisted in knowing how to disappear, or, better yet, knowing how to disappear in time, which would become one of its most important contributions to the revolutionary movement. In this sense, the SI should be considered, in every sense of the term, as the work or one of the works of Debord alone. At least, he found in the dissolution toward which it advanced the means to realize his passion for loss and obscurity that may or may not have been shared by other members of the SI. Return to obscurity, to idleness, blackout. For the SI the blackout finally arrived, and it didn't last twenty-four minutes, but an eternity. Never in the history of the avant-garde had there been such a triumphant moment of self-dissolution or self-destruction. Everything about the situationist world seemed designed to achieve this obscurity, which Debord's quote marks with a final celebrity.

Looking back on the fifteen years of activity of the Situationist International, in the eyes of those who remain impassioned by the history of the SI, my statement may appear gratuitous, or at least assign far too much importance to Debord's contribution to the SI. There were a number of other talented situationists: Constant, Khayati, Michèle Bernstein, Alexander Trocchi, Asger Jorn, Vaneigem, Pinot-Gallizio, Sanguinetti, and so on. And then, there were the "pro-situationists," the large number of groups espousing situationist arguments in France, Italy, Spain, and the United States, who were engaged in the political and artistic struggles of their time, in ways that were sometimes violent and radical. There was a situationist life after the dissolution of the SI and this would be an additional reason not to reduce it to the work of Debord alone.[3] And yet, the signs and reasons for believing this to be true are easy to find.

Those who are convinced that the SI not only existed but was made to exist may not realize that it did all it could to remain as clandestine as possible, that it had always coveted a relative secrecy, and when the time came to show itself publicly (May 1968, for example), it avoided proselytizing. Although it expelled many of its members, a far larger number never had the opportunity of being admitted. Even in its early years, and certainly once it had become well known, the SI never went out of its way to recruit anyone and had a habit of not accepting members. Many of Debord's letters explicitly confirm the shrewdness of such a policy, especially at the time of the

SI's break with the militant Socialisme ou Barbarie group, some of whose members appeared ready to join the SI (none were admitted). Bourseiller sees in this the proof that the SI was an elitist organization, as if the SI had a responsibility to be hospitable, as if it had failed to live up to some elementary democratic obligation by refusing newcomers, as if an organization that refuses to accept outsiders is necessarily elitist.

And what if the opposite were true? What if the SI rejected outsiders not out of elitism, in order to form one of those "societies of the strong" that a man like Caillois dreamed of, but because it always remained conscious of the possibility of its own disappearance, because it chose to exist on the ephemeral edge of its always imminent dissolution? The SI rejected the world of outsiders because it rejected *the world* and not, as is often believed in secret societies and the fantasies of Freemasons, to assume power, much less out of a desire to govern. There are lost children and then there are what should be called "lost organizations," in which the founders collaborate solely for the purpose of losing themselves together. The Lettrist International was unquestionably the group led by Debord that came closest to such an ideal, but the history of the SI can also be understood as a *return* to this incandescent point of departure, this somber melancholy. Increasingly, throughout its brief history, it became clandestine, inaccessible, as intransigent about requests for membership as it was about excluding members, and less preoccupied than ever about its own survival. When, in 1970, Debord took the initiative of organizing a split, he simply completed a process of dissolution that had been under way for years. The group he led, which had been more important to the "culture" of May 1968 than any other organization, three years later had no more than a half-dozen members. Compared to the Trotskyist and Maoist battalions, which it did not take long to dislodge from the heights, the number is obviously miniscule. But this is simply a tangible sign that, at least from Debord's point of view, it was never a question of keeping the SI around longer than necessary, much less of strengthening its ranks with large numbers of members.

Membership in the SI was primarily a question of capability, as Debord pointed out in 1963 in a letter to Raoul Vaneigem.[4] In this same letter Debord clearly connects the refusal to expand the organization with his distaste for expulsions. Given the reputation he had acquired, it should come as no surprise that this type of argument has gone relatively unnoticed: "I want to kill the fewest number of people possible (in every sense of the word 'kill,' metaphorical and concrete) and at the same time I want to minimize doing or experiencing what I dislike. And this holds true for the SI just as it does in the outside world."[5] The SI rejected recruitment not out of elitism but to avoid misunderstandings, awkward relationships (the insistence on knowing especially), harmful encounters, even murder. And it did so because it was the only way for those (especially Debord) who wanted to preserve their freedom and not distress others.

Naturally, there were numerous expulsions, but this does not make the SI an elitist or Stalinist organization. I have already shown the falsehoods behind the rumors of a Debord who was out for blood, a man who took a perverse pleasure in expelling people from the SI. The letter used as the epigraph of the second volume of his correspondence is essential for understanding that what was behind the expulsions was always the notion of freedom—of those expelled as well as of those who remained:

> Superficially, there are many signs of "authority" in my behavior (providing you forget that I have always been harsh with the outside world but only sometimes within the movement). But I feel I had, in almost every period, the means to make use of even greater authority (and certainly to benefit from it). The practice of expulsion seems to me absolutely contrary to the use of people: it forces them to be free alone—by remaining themselves—if they cannot participate in sharing a common freedom. And I rejected from the outset a large number of "faithful disciples" without allowing them the opportunity to join the SI and, as a result, to be expelled.[6]

Debord expelled a number of people. That much we know. Some of his contemporaries no doubt would have preferred that he make use of those who came to seek him out, that he become, like so many others, a kind of industrial producer of devout militants, unbeatable in the art of distributing pamphlets no one read and pleased to share in the friendly atmosphere found in small cells and at meetings. His correspondence shows that he did not lack generosity or patience, not only in conversation but in his actions, in the concrete support he gave to those he saw most often. It also shows that the majority of expulsions were not the product of a single individual who took advantage of his power but collective decisions (and frequently other situationists were far more interested than Debord in cleaning house). Finally, it suggests, especially when personal relationships were involved (not necessarily associated with the SI), that very often, when Debord decided to break with someone, he did it because he was fed up with giving, because the others were unable to play their part in the pot-latch he had proposed to them. The Debord of the last years of the SI was a man tired of the unilateral nature of the relationships his place within the situationist movement required him to maintain. As a result, he increasingly withdrew from any interaction with the younger generation, grew tired of being considerate to others. He was someone who had become indifferent to the fate of a group for which he had given his all.

The "agony" of the SI, which is described by Bourseiller as a quasi tragedy (similar to the way he described Debord's death), was in no way tragic for Debord. A number of people had grown accustomed to his generosity and refused to accept the fact that one day this might change. Instead of accepting the real reasons for the split, they attributed it to his incomprehensible and irrational character, the so-called Don Juanism of his friendship, because impotence (here, responding to the logic of the gift as a form of challenge) will always be the one thing that is not only widespread, but hidden. From the beginning of the Lettrist International to the final days of the Situationist International, Debord gave generously, but he also scrupulously exercised his right not to give, his right to separate from those who gave him nothing in return or with whom he disagreed. In short, he exercised his right to preserve or take back his freedom. Was he a Stalinist? Does the exercise of such a right have anything to do with the arbitrary purges and executions that resulted from the sordid confessions extorted during secret trials? Did Debord ever destroy those he broke off with or even have the power to do so? Did he ever exercise the slightest function in any institution that would have enabled him to settle accounts in this way? The very immediate connection that is sometimes made between the SI and the practice of expulsion is to a large extent based on the fact that all the expulsions were *public*. The reasons were given in most cases and were translated into political terms (never personal attacks). The SI exercised considerable transparency and visibility when it came to expelling people. That is why the explusions had nothing in common with the Stalinist purges; in fact, they were the exact opposite. Expulsion from the SI was all the more a public event in that it fundamentally meant being "expelled" into the public domain, implying the loss of the right and duty of clandestinity implied by inclusion in the SI. It is because they were openly discussed and their rationale made public that the expulsions could be thought of as a strategic weapon for the movement.[7]

There is another reason why the SI has always been accused of having a mania for expulsion. Other organizations expelled members, but the SI's expulsions were final. In this sense, they bore Debord's stamp, for his melancholy imprint could always be found on the groups he led. Breton expelled a number of people, but he also reconciled with many of them, apparently finding a certain charm in ambivalent relationships. The LI and the SI never reversed themselves: "there can be no turning back, no reconciliation" (the only exception, quite paradoxically, involved Ivan Chtcheglov, who, excluded from the LI, became a "situationist from afar" after his internment in a psychiatric institution). Debord was not fond of ambivalent relationships or compromise, he never changed his mind about those who disappointed or wounded him, he never negotiated with anyone. He always experienced his relationships with others on a personal level and precipitated breaks whenever they lacked passion. That is why it is possible to claim, at least to a certain extent, that the history of the LI and the SI is a kind of indefinitely repeated echo of the introductory "I don't think we'll ever see one another again" spoken at the beginning of *Howls for Sade*.

Expulsion played an essential role in the SI, far more than it did in other avant-garde groups, political or cultural. There was nothing accidental or tactical about it. Embedding expulsion and separation within a project that was both unitary and communitarian (to put an end to alienation, separation, and the lack of dialogue), it consigned to the past everything that was directly experienced, it isolated what was shared or could be shared within a past that was certainly glorious but always irreversible. The past for Debord was always absolute; he never reconciled with or came to terms with it. The systematic practice of expulsion, which Debord always insisted upon, without the least trace of guilt, was not part of a desire for power but a reflection of his melancholy, his interest in the passage of time. It accelerated the passage of time, it yoked the relation with the Other to the past and made the SI a group whose principal characteristic was to have had no other destiny than its past, a destiny that was finally realized at the time of its breakup.

It is worth noting that the many expulsions that littered the history of the SI left little trace, unlike the often very public breaks that typified other avant-garde groups.[8] Aside from the immediately public arguments brought about by conflict, those expelled rarely tried to settle scores and never engaged in personal attacks. They remained strangely loyal to what they had been and discreet about the SI's activities in general, as well as their own participation. They never let the cat out of the bag. Conversely, we can explain their behavior by their lack of interest in making public something that might not necessarily reveal them in the best light. I have already suggested that impotence is not the easiest thing to admit. The same is true of seduction or fascination, or, more trivially, the insistence on knowing the raw material of nearly all group undertakings, with which Debord systematically refused to comply. But regardless of the reason for their exclusion, those who were expelled became tacit accomplices by their silence, as if they supported, although belatedly, a process of disappearance in which they lived up to the role they had been asked to play. Because they never complained or offered a different version of the facts, because they remained silent, they became living proof that dissolution was the SI's destiny. More generally, having done nothing to reappropriate the history of the SI for themselves, or the LI before it, they also confirmed what I suggested earlier: to the extent that dissolution was its destiny, we can consider the SI as the work, or one of the works, of Debord alone, whose proclivities always tended toward organizations that were lost or fated to become lost. Or, because it would be absurd to claim that Debord was the only member of the SI, we can consider the SI to be a work *signed* by Debord alone.

After all, what would have prevented those who were expelled from giving their own version of the period of Saint-Germain-des-Prés, or writing their own panegyric? What prevents them from doing so now? It's remarkable that we had to wait until the appearance of *In girum imus nocte* and *Panegyric,* that we had to wait for Debord to impose *his* legend, so that in its shadow, others, using it like a stepping stone, would remember their own experiences and write their own memoirs. I am not the first to suggest that the SI is the work (one of the works) of Debord alone. In claiming this, I am not overlooking the support of the other members, but Debord's signature is all over the SI. Debord was allowed to sign the SI's activities, and there is no reason to be shocked by this or to accuse Debord or his successors, his editors, the media, or even the bourgeoisie as a whole, of having appropriated an experience that belonged to the public domain, putting in its place the legend of one man. All those who could have signed for Debord—if they hadn't broken with him—let him sign, recognized this as a kind of right (there were, it is true, protests when "On the Poverty of Student Life" was reprinted by Champ Libre). He was granted the right of expulsion and the right of signature, which is fully consistent with the decision to dissolve the SI made by Debord when he organized the "split." From this point of view, it is obvious that the dissolution and, later, the narratives and new editions were the countersignature of what had initially been his work, of what had initially borne his signature, his stamp, and the characteristics of his style.

As mentioned in chapter 1, Debord published his *Mémoires* at the time the SI was founded, and followed up in 1959 with his film *On the Passage of a Few Persons.* The SI was all well and good, but real life was somewhere else: it was where it always *had been,* in an absolute past. This indicates considerable skepticism just when he took the initiative to create a new group that existed, from the time of its foundation, in the shadow of an experience that was irrevocably over. In any case, the situationist years can never be compared with the Saint-Germain-des-Prés years. *Panegyric* skips them entirely and *In girum imus nocte* covers them in one or two pages: the clandestine meetings that took place in all the ports of Europe cannot conceal the fact that they often provided the opportunity for lengthy discussions, breaks, and conflicts. In the story of revolution they deserve no more than a footnote. Almost nothing remains of them except for Asger Jorn, the dead friend mentioned in *In girum imus nocte* and, for the last time, in the second volume of *Panegyric.* And we should not overlook Debord's complaints and increasingly targeted criticisms of the SI's activities, and his unwillingness to assume the responsibility for publishing *Internationale situationniste* by himself during its final years. Some of his letters indicate that he was, if not eager, at least relieved to be done with the SI.[9]

Under these conditions, it is hardly an exaggeration to claim that the SI's greatest success occurred when it dissolved itself. It was in precisely these terms that, ten years after May 1968, Debord, in *In girum imus nocte,* referred to the SI. In 1978, the outlook for revolution had been considerably dampened. There had been an assault and it was very beautiful, because nothing can ever resemble the past. What remained was the fact that because of their "training," in every sense comparable to the Light Brigade that had been sent to the front to fight the Russian Imperial Army during the Crimean War, Debord and his comrades held the line, regardless of the losses suffered. The following text was spoken over sequences taken from *The Charge of the Light Brigade* by Michael Curtiz:

It's a beautiful moment when an assault against the world order is set in motion.

From its almost imperceptible beginning you already know that, whatever happens, very soon nothing will ever again be the same as it was.

The charge begins slowly, picks up speed, passes the point of no return, and irrevocably collides with what seemed unassailable: the bulwark which was so solid and well defended, but which is also destined to be shaken and thrown into disorder. That is what we did, emerging from the night, raising once again the banner of the "good old cause" and marching forward under the cannon fire of time.

Along the way many of us died or were taken prisoner; many others were wounded and permanently put out of action; and certain elements even let themselves slip to the rear out of lack of courage; but I believe I can say that our formation as a whole never swerved from its line until it plunged into the very core of destruction.[10]

The assault took place, shaking up the old world order and provoking disorder. Were they victorious? Debord is careful not to answer the question. However, he makes it clear that the situationists' "Light Brigade" did not return from battle. That is why it was necessary for the man who led the charge to prevent himself from becoming the Lord Raglan of May 1968: "I have never quite understood those who have so often reproached me for having squandered this fine troop in a senseless assault, perhaps even out of some sort of Neronian self-indulgence."[11] This is followed by several comments about the lack of strategic knowledge on the part of those who accused him of having allowed his followers to get caught up in the May 1968 riots. I want to quote only his concluding remarks, which should convince the skeptics that the real destiny of the Situationist International was its disappearance, at least from Debord's perspective:

To listen to those who seem to be complaining that the battle was begun without waiting for them, the main result was the fact that an avant-garde was sacrificed and completely pulverized in the collision. In my opinion that was precisely its purpose.

Avant-gardes have only one time; and the best thing that can happen to them is to have enlivened their time without outliving it. After them, operations move onto a vaster terrain. Too often have we seen such elite troops, after they have accomplished some valiant exploit, remain on hand to parade with their medals and then turn against the cause they previously supported. Nothing of this sort need be feared from those whose attack has carried them to the point of dissolution.[12]

Avant-gardes are made to dissolve in the spring sun, and war is made to be fought rather than to be won. It may even be made to be lost if that's the only way of avoiding memorial day parades. In 1978, situationism was as unconcerned as ever with maintaining some sort of privileged position on the radical left. The point is *to serve one's time,* to fight to consign the current order to the past, or at least to undermine its legitimacy, providing one is prepared to fade away, to disappear in the accelerated passage of time, whose possibility is represented by revolution. The Situationist International made war so a period of time would pass and so it too would pass. It deserved to dissolve, just as Debord deserved his inaccessibility and ever deeper immersion into a clandestine life.

I have advanced the thesis that the SI moved *essentially* and not accidentally toward its dissolution and that it is in this sense that its activities were "signed" by Debord. It achieved fulfillment in the obscurity of its members or, more specifically, in their ever deepening obscurity. Dissolution was the final stage of a process that had always led the group toward its own disappearance, in which its only perspective had been the desire to melt into the invisibility of the proletarian future. The message was clear by 1962. The situationists were fish who were invisible in the popular waters:

> We are totally popular. We address only those problems that remain unresolved throughout the population as a whole. Situationist theory is already in the people the way a fish is in water. In reply to those who believe that the SI has constructed a speculative fortress, we affirm, on the contrary, that we will dissolve into the population that lives our project at every moment, although they experience it initially in the form of want and repression.[13]

Situationism tended toward invisibility for the sake of popularity: it was invisible because popular, popular because invisible. Its destiny was to fulfill itself, which is to say to dissolve itself, in the people. It was here that it found its destiny because, like Mallarmé's crowd, the people are slow to proclaim their presence. There is a shortage of situationism among them, they experience it in the form of what they need to manifest themselves, which also explains why the situationists were so intent on obscurity and invisibility. Ten years later, the *Theses on the Situationist International and Its Time* stated this clearly. Here, Debord affirmed the absolute identity of situationism and the modern revolutionary movement, whose reappearance everything, especially the events of May 1968, seemed to point to. The proletariat is situationist, situationism is proletarian, here and now, immediately. And this immediacy leaves no room for the various proletarian messianic movements the far left thrived on. It is incompatible with the construction of any revolutionary party that is preparing a better future as it is with the imaginary alliances among Maoist worker-priests and the working classes:

> What are called "situationist ideas" are merely the initial ideas of the period that is witnessing the reappearance of the modern revolutionary movement. . . . The SI's success lay simply in voicing "the real movement that abolishes the existing state of things" and *in knowing how to voice it.* . . . In the last analysis, it is not therefore a matter of a theory *of the SI, but of the theory of the proletariat.*
>
> We gave voice to the ideas *that were necessarily already present* in these proletarian minds, and by doing so we helped to activate those ideas, as well as to make critical action more theoretically aware and more determined to make time its own. . . . The *repressed side* of proletarian critique has emerged, it has acquired a memory and a language. It has undertaken the *judgment of the world.* . . .
>
> The occupations movement was the rough sketch of a "situationist" revolution, but it was no more than a rough sketch both as practice of revolution and as a situationist consciousness of history. It was at that moment internationally that a generation began to be situationist.[14]

Debord scuttled the SI to avoid any aporia associated with the process of transmission. At the moment of its dissolution, he claimed, in a kind of proud show of strength or final challenge short-circuiting any form of revolutionary messianism, that the transmission *had taken place,* that situationism was now present wherever true revolutionary struggle could be found, that the proof of its existence and vitality lay in the very obscurity of those who founded it. Where was situationism? Where was Debord? He was hidden in those proletarian heads or in the movement to occupy the factories during May 1968. In fact, he was so well hidden that no one seemed to be aware of his presence, and the fact that those proletarian heads eventually forgot they were situationists changes nothing. Situationism conceives of itself and realizes itself as the dissolution or dissemination of the discourse that embodies it, in a people yet to appear, who were prefigured in the most revolutionary practices (and only those) of May 1968. "Where I was, there revolution will be." Situationism occurs where there are no longer any situationists (at least not officially), for their contemplative and substantial presence becomes an obstacle to the real struggle and, ultimately, to the revolution itself:

The dreariest ones talked about fun, while the most resigned talked about passion. Membership in the SI, even in its contemplative form, was to be proof enough of all this, with which nobody otherwise would have dreamt of crediting them. Although numerous observers, policemen or others, denouncing the direct presence of the SI in umpteen rebellious activities that are developing very well along their own lines right across the world, may have given people the impression that every member of the SI was working twenty hours a day to revolutionize the planet, we should stress here the falseness of this image. History will, on the contrary, show the considerable *economy of forces* by means of which the SI managed to do what it did. So that when we say that some situationists were doing really too little, this should be taken to mean that they were literally doing next to nothing.[15]

Ironically, the forces of repression were more familiar with situationism than the situationists themselves. They were able to identify it in the many subversive acts attributed (rightly or wrongly) to the situationists. A situationist was, more than ever, someone who is not where we think he is, who knows how to disappear, who knows how to vanish behind the struggles of those who are situationists without knowing it. He is someone who shares with Debord the old desire to be forgotten. Debord points out potential candidates in an article that appeared in the last issue of *Internationale situationniste*, titled "Qu'est-ce qu'un situationniste?" [What is a situationist?] (as if the question was no longer self-evident):

> Those who, not being members of the SI, want others to believe they are, will immediately be treated as *suspect* by their entourage. As for all the others, those who are not conducting, somewhere in the world, an organized effort in conjunction with the SI, the best thing those "situationist" revolutionaries can do is to retain for themselves (and therefore, for the rising proletarian movement) whatever they found good about us, in terms of outlook and in terms of method. That means not bringing us up as a reference but, on the contrary, *forgetting us a little*.[16]

Dissolution: a situationist who reveals himself is suspect. To truly be a situationist, one must forget situationism in general, and Debord in particular, whose desire for obscurity was fulfilled. Real revolutionaries know how to make themselves forgotten, disappear, lose themselves. Their fame resides only in their vocation for obscurity, the standard against which their subversive potential must be measured. Debord did all he could to succeed in this (he had been in training for almost a quarter century), not without some success when we consider the widely varied assessments of the role and influence of the situationists in the events of May 1968. At the time, there were some people who knew nothing of the SI, others who knew nothing but the SI, and a range of positions in between these two extremes. Such a divergence of opinion can be attributed to the instinct for obscurity on the part of Debord and his companions: their lack of visibility does not mean they were not active, quite the contrary. Concerning the role of the situationists in May 1968, and especially his personal role, Debord was careful to reveal little. *The Real Split in the International* can even be read as a work intended *to avoid answering* the question, to avoid revealing anything about the actual political effectiveness of the situationists, identifying situationism with the revolutionary struggles taking place around the world.

For the revolution to happen, you need to change scales, look beyond Paris, view the world from afar by telescope, as if you were on the moon; rest assured you won't be able to find the, now miniscule, situationists, especially the contemplative ones. And with time comes obscurity and absence. In *In girum imus nocte*, the Paris of May 1968 is evoked in a few sentences, and not a word is mentioned in *Panegyric*. Compared with the attention given to the clandestine years of Saint-Germain-des-Prés in these works, this is surprising coming from someone who presented himself as the most legitimate disturber of the public order. But the golden age of Saint-Germain-des-Prés had been clandestine, unlike the events of May 1968. And later, what was needed was to rediscover that clandestinity and not continue May 1968 or yield to visibility, as some members of the SI wanted. Insurrection rises from the shadows and out of obscurity, far from the well-mannered Stalinist or Trotskyist organizers, which is why it must, of necessity, return to the shadows. It is the negative that comes to light, foreseeable only by those who have already lived it (the only ones able to write about or predict it): "If many people did what we wrote, it's because we essentially wrote the negative that so many others had experienced before us, and that we experienced as well."[17] Pro-situationists, try harder if you want to be obscure.

We can rephrase this somewhat differently. I have a great deal of difficulty in seeing Debord's life in general and the dissolution of the SI in particular as the failure that many commentators claim them to be. Was the SI a failure? What should it have become? What should its leaders have done? What exactly is Debord being criticized for (and, consequently, what do we want of him, what are we asking of him)? For having placed himself within the framework of revolution or for having rejected that framework? For having produced a "theory" appropriate to the society of the sixties and seventies, or for failing to produce a revolutionary theory modified for the 1990s? By what right does a period in which revolution is the least of worries, even when it feigns a critical stance against the "society of the spectacle," reproach someone who had the lucidity to change his point of view? Is it possible to speak of the situationist adventure (as perhaps of the avant-garde adventure in general) without giving in to the pathos of failure and co-optation, to the "agony," the "fatal collapse," the "end of illusion" (as if Debord had ever had illusions), or the "final cycle?"[18] After all, all it would take to prove the "late" Debord wrong would be to make a revolution.

The Last Guardian

Villiers de l'Isle-Adam warned us that by playing at being a ghost, we are liable to become one. In a similar manner, situationism may have succeeded all too well in hiding itself—certainly far better than Breton, as shown by the second surrealist *Manifesto*. It's not even clear that situationism had a future, given the current lack of perspective in differentiating between poetics and revolution. Revolution at the service of poetry, poetry at the service of revolution? Which poetry? Which revolution? This was the most important question advanced by the SI, a question it never backed away from. It dissolved itself rather than settle down. In truth, there was no situationist art. The revolution alone would have been a form of situationist art. The situationists wanted to restore communication and community. Because they didn't succeed, they preferred to disappear. They chose to live outside society rather than accept compromise and disavowal.

Some critics have postulated a kind of post-SI and post–*Society of the Spectacle* Debord, reduced to irrelevance or to being no more than a mere stylist (which is another form of irrelevance). As for the myth of Debord as "theoretician," although the criticism is understandable, it has little meaning when we take into account his concern for form and communication, which he carried with him throughout his life. Naturally, Debord's point of view in his last books is no longer revolutionary, but he is hardly to blame that such a perspective disappeared from sight.

However, the desire for true communication and, consequently, the criticism of the false appearances of communication never left him, although it assumed a form nearly opposite that prevalent during his situationist years. The fact that he stopped suggesting ways of subverting society does not imply that he was reconciled to it or had become more tolerant. The Debord of *Comments on the Society of the Spectacle,* for example, did not forget the plan for a situationist dictionary begun in the sixties. He was still a lexicographer, still determined to use the words of the spectacle against it, to expose their use in promoting lies, dissimulation, and disinformation, in denouncing their unacknowledged *work.* The only thing missing in these last texts is the appeal to a collective form for reinventing communication. The time when it seemed possible to return to the tribe its words, purified of their lies, seemed quite remote, as remote as the "tabula rasa" of the situationist cultural revolution through which the memory of older times would be abolished.

In his later work, Debord insisted upon, as he had during the fifties and sixties, the disappearance of communication. He believed that communication could only get worse because the spectacle now had the means to impose its truth absolutely, pushing aside all the others, including any undesirable scientific truths. And it now had the means because it had destroyed community, because there was no longer, strictly speaking, a place in which dialogue could occur and verities could be contradicted:

> Spectacular power can similarly deny whatever it likes, once or three times over, and change the subject; knowing full well there is no danger of any riposte, in its own space or any other. For the agora, the general community, has gone, along with communities restricted to intermediary bodies or to independent institutions, to salons or cafés, or to workers in a single company. There is no place left where people can discuss the realities which concern them, because they can never lastingly free themselves from the crushing presence of media discourse and of the various forces organized to relay it.[1]

What does dialogue become when truth has fled beyond all the Lembergs and Cracows of the world? Its opposite, its ghost, the false appearance of speech, an absolutely unilateral form of "communication" that prevents any reappropriation, or appropriation, and a horde of communications specialists who are paid to keep it that way. At the same time, the meaning of appropriation changes profoundly from the moment any revolutionary or communitarian outlook disappears. It loses its function as a revolutionary technique of communication. It is now used on behalf of an idea of memory, of history, or even of the preservation of language, all of which are threatened with being submerged and destroyed by the progress of the spectacular. When the situationists were active, the abolition of the past and of culture as a whole was revolutionary. Now, power works to abolish history and the past: "How drastically any absolute power will suppress history depends on the extent of its imperious interests or obligations, and especially on its practical capacity to execute its aims,"[2] Debord wrote in *Comments on the Society of the Spectacle,* adding, a few pages later: "All usurpers have shared this aim: to make us forget that *they have only just arrived.*"

Power attempts to abolish history, the way it tries to destroy the search for truth in all its forms, especially through the use of information technology. This at last provides an opportunity to do away not only with history, but also with any genuine critical culture, and, by extension, with a culture of reading and even a culture of speech, an art of conversation, one of whose last practitioners Debord flattered himself as being: "Thus it is hardly surprising that children should enthusiastically start their education at an early age with the Absolute Knowledge of computer science; while they are still unable to read, for reading demands making judgments at every line; and is the only access to the wealth of pre-spectacular human experience. Conversation is now almost dead, and soon so too will be those who knew how to speak."[3]

In a world assumed to be subsumed in a kind of permanent and generalized brainwashing, Debord positions himself, according to the expression used by Claude Rabant, as the *last guardian.*[4] It is up to him to preserve language as the substrate of speech, starting from a position of authentic dialogue, and to save culture from the destruction to which it has been consigned by the spectacle.[5] Appropriation is no more than a sign or vestige of a vanished culture, with which only Debord was familiar, because he had lived it in exemplary fashion (with his life being deeply woven into its fabric), and therefore it is his responsibility to serve as its witness. Appropriation was transformed into citation, it was flanked by quotation marks for improved recognizability. In *Panegyric,* Debord explained this, with his typical disdain, in the following terms:

> I will have to make rather extensive use of quotations. Never, I believe, to lend authority to a particular argument but only to show fully of what stuff this adven-

ture and I are made. Quotations are useful in periods of ignorance or obscurantist beliefs. Allusions, without quotation marks, to other texts known to be very famous, as in classical Chinese poetry, Shakespeare, or Lautréamont, should be reserved for times richer in minds capable of recognizing the original phrase and the distance its new application has introduced. Today, when irony itself is not always understood, there is the risk of the phrase being confidently attributed to oneself and, moreover, being hastily and incorrectly reproduced.[6]

Having become a guardian of culture during a period of ignorance and obscurantism, Debord also became a guardian of *style,* that formal arrangement of language that enables it to endure. Those who adopt the style of the spoken word, he wrote in *Panegyric,* can neither write nor speak, nor can their readers. Writing well and speaking well were, for Debord, a matter of natural distinction, since his life was distinct from that of his contemporaries, who spoke only the language of the spectacle. Style is indeed the man, even the men Debord decided to ignore:

> In contrast, I for my part am going to write without affectation or fatigue, as the most normal and easiest thing in the world, in the language I have learned and, in most circumstances, spoken. It's not up to me to change it. The Gypsies rightly contend that one is never obliged to speak the truth except in one's own language; in the enemy's language the lie must reign. Another advantage: by referring to the vast corpus of classic texts that have appeared in French throughout the five centuries before my birth, but especially in the last two, it will always be easy to properly translate me into any future idiom, even when French has become a dead language.[7]

Debord's writing will last eternally, well beyond the death of a French language standardized through globalization, the prevalence of English, and computer technology, which are more or less one and the same thing. Debord is the guardian of a dead, or nearly dead, language, of which his contemporaries are increasingly ignorant or contemptuous, and which has, as a result, become the language of the enemy that Debord intends to remain. This is obviously why he now gets so much enjoyment out of proclaiming his liking for it. Classical French has become, in the society of the spectacle, an almost secret language, a language that society is no longer able to understand or speak, like argot, Romany, or the language of Villon and his friends, a sample of which Debord deliberately reproduces in *Panegyric.*[8] For lack of a situationist tribe, or the support of the crowd, it was up to Debord to make use of the classical style that came so naturally to him.

Style would be used to overcome the defects of nearly dead languages, to testify to the destruction of language and culture. The literary status of Debord's work hinges on his use of style, which is inseparable from a return to memory. Gone is the situationist utopia of authentic communication; now it is singularization by and through writing that returns, in the form of mourning for the community, just as verse for Mallarmé is a temporary replacement for an improbable perfect language (and for an improbable community as well). Debord's style is a politics of communication continued through literary means, or one that has returned to its poetic origins—which the avant-gardes, including situationism, have never entirely abandoned.

Does this mean that, in the end, Debord became the writer he always was, or always wanted to be, or even that he must be considered a great writer? It's a question I can't answer, not knowing what a great writer might be. But the least we can say is that opinions vary about this and will continue to diverge long after the day Debord is reissued by the Bibliothèque de la Pléiade. He continues to divide opinion even today—which certainly wouldn't displease him. In contrast to the praise accorded his "great art" by Philippe Sollers, there are those who feel that his resurrection is a creation ex nihilo—by Sollers himself and by those who cling to a political Debord and reject his descent into literature. There are still others who believe that he never really wrote anything, that he never had the experience of what Blanchot called the "great impropriety" of writing.[9] I hope I have shown that such a debate serves no real purpose. Even during his most radical years, those during which the question of art appeared to have been abandoned, situationism, as a project of "total" communication, continued to maintain a connection with poetic desires, if not the oldest historically, then at least the oldest in the avant-garde. From this perspective, Debord's ties to literature—which do not necessarily make him a writer—are all the more indisputable in that they were always present. He never made a choice between poetics and politics. Rather, he chose to articulate them, never abandoning one for the other but continuing to explore the passage that connects them, the ultimate Northwest Passage of the avant-garde. This is as true of the situationist period as it was for the lettrist period. It remains to be shown that this is equally true for the work Debord produced in the last years of his life.

4. STRATEGY

The Moving Surface of the River of Time

The lost children (the expression is of military origin) are the product of war. In an earlier chapter I discussed Debord's affinity for lost children and why he preferred war to peace. What is certain is that his affinity was deliberate. He was a man who enjoyed confrontation and favored battles from which the combatants never returned. And he did so because they were an opportunity, even the condition, for loss. Ultimately, war and loss amount to the same thing, they are two faces of the same hunger for the irrevocable, for experiences that are lost forever, for periods of unrest and change. Loss *is* war, but experienced from within.

War is present from beginning to end in Debord's work, it is one of its fundamental themes. Images of warfare are scattered throughout his films. The virtual script of *Howls for Sade* refers to images of a line of troops from the Army of India during the nineteenth century, then a battleship from the battle of Tsushima (during the Russo-Japanese War of 1905); there are pictures of parachutes opening, numerous scenes of riots, the bodies of young men killed in the streets of Athens, and the French infantry in Indochina. *On the Passage of Several Persons* contains footage of confrontations between Japanese workers and police, the English police pushing back protesters, images of the Algerian war, a cavalry charge in the streets of a city. In *Critique of Separation* we see an officer holding his sword, rioters in the Congo being hit with rifle butts, squadrons during maneuvers, West Point cadets in old uniforms, a riot in the courtyard of an American prison. In *The*

Society of the Spectacle, nuclear submarines make their first appearance in avant-garde film, along with aircraft carriers shooting missiles, scenes of the war in Vietnam, a still of the Russian civil war, the Watts riots, the insurrection in Budapest, an excerpt from *For Whom the Bell Tolls*, the Kronstadt sailors, the Civil War. *In girum imus nocte* focuses more openly on a certain type of popular fiction, on the heroes of our childhood: Robin Hood, Zorro, General Custer, Prince Valliant. Debord also uses footage from *The Charge of the Light Brigade*, Michael Curtiz's 1936 film about the Battle of Balaklava, a famous episode of the Crimean War, where Lord Raglan sent the men of the light brigade to their death against the Russian troops.

These are images of war that have been appropriated from archives or other films and always skewed in relation to the text, which is about (at least apparently) something else: Debord's personal experience, the Saint-Germain-des-Prés years, struggles in which he participated, or his critical attitude toward society. There is nothing original about them; most of the time they are stereotypes, images that have been seen before. But that does not mean they are insignificant: all, or nearly all, refer to civil (or colonial) wars, uprisings that have been violently repressed, and revolutions that are not always successful. There is no question of Debord's fondness for lost battles, for battles that have become legendary for pitting dissimilar forces against one another. Strung end to end, they constitute a kind of collective memory of uprisings and revolts that have punctuated the history of the world, an overview of its deepest wounds. They all refer, directly or indirectly, to class struggles, to confrontations between those who have everything and those who have nothing. Nearly all of them refer to uncertain battles on which the fate of humanity hinges, where freedom or servitude are decided. With the exception of the images of the Russo-Japanese War in *Howls for Sade*, there is no footage of wars between equally matched powers: there is none of the First or Second World Wars, for example.[1]

These are images of history and disruption: they are signs of Debord's interest in situations of conflict, which is confirmed by the majority of his texts. As early as *Mémoires*, he framed his life within a context of warfare and legend, with allusions to the various combats fought by the Knights of the Round Table. Other works reprise that same legendary register, describing lettrist activities in similar terms, especially *In girum imus nocte* and *Panegyric*, which add to the aura of the warrior devoted to perdition that of the criminal: Debord was also one of those who frequented the "dangerous classes." The years spent in Saint-Germain-des-Prés were haunted by the memory of Villon, the poet-bandit and his companions, and *In girum imus nocte* also "quotes" at length from *Children of Paradise*, with Lacenaire, the criminal who would have preferred a brilliant literary success to the glory he obtained from his crimes. Debord was also fond of Marcel Carné's *Les visiteurs du soir*: the story of a devil who sends his children (good-looking, seductive, and lost) to earth to sow division and conflict. This film is also quoted in *In girum imus nocte,* and there are allusions to it in all of Debord's work.

Debord the warrior, Debord the criminal, Debord the divider. What if books like *The Society of the Spectacle* and *Comments on the Society of the Spectacle* were themselves, by way of Marx and the class struggle, the effect of such an imagined world? What if they served as the theoretical version of a polemical and conflict-laden vision of the world that was always the center of his experience, and that to a large extent constituted its center? This would be another shock to pure theory and an additional reason to avoid cutting Debord into slices, leaving aside those felt to be unworthy of the theoretician we want him to have been. Is it really important to contrast *The Society of the Spectacle* or the *Comments* with autobiographical works such as the *Considerations on the Assassination of Gérard Lebovici,* "*Cette mauvaise réputation,*" or even *Panegyric,* which are so often seen as the product of wounded narcissism? Instead, I want to advance the hypothesis that there is no bitterness in Debord's last books, that *Panegyric* is one of the most remarkable examples of serenity in the entire history of French autobiography. Such books were written to reaffirm a polemical vision of the world: precisely so that this would not be perceived as merely a vision or a theory, but would be embodied in an experience—words, a style—simultaneously singular and exemplary, which would often assume the form of a challenge.

Comments on the Society of the Spectacle and *Panegyric* should be thought of as the back and front of a single project, through which writing is used on behalf of war or conflict (which is not the same thing as using it on behalf of the unachieved revolution, as it was understood by the surrealists). In this sense, the images of warfare scattered throughout Debord's work (especially his films) reveal his *strategic* conception of writing as the index of an imaginary that makes use of language for conflict and polemic (the "insurrectional" style of the years of the Situationist International is only one aspect of this).

In *Panegyric* it is quite clear that Debord's interest in strategy is inseparable from his interest in war in general and memoirs of battle: "I have been very interested in war, in the theorists of strategy but also in recollections of battles or the many other conflicts history mentions—surface eddies on the river of time. I am not unaware that war is the domain of danger and disappointment, perhaps even more so than the other sides of life. This consideration has not, however, diminished the attraction I have felt for that particular side."[2] An attraction to strategy, war, upheaval, danger, and disappointment, an attraction to the movement on the surface of the river of time. The many images of rivers found in *In girum imus nocte* are, therefore, also images of war, whether the Seine in Paris, the Arno in Florence, or the canals of Venice, where the movement is reversed: we flow along them, we become ephemeral, passing, the warrior whose trace time will erase. The poetics of war is a poetics of passage, including the final passage (we can never step twice into the same river and, similarly, we can never fight the same war twice). The attraction to the flow of time and the attraction to war are one and the same; they coincide in the images of water, of surface movement. Ten years before *Panegyric, In girum imus nocte* suggested as much:

> The sensation of the passing of time has always been vivid for me, and I have been attracted by it just as others are allured by dizzying heights or by water. In this sense I have loved my era, which has seen the end of all existing security and the dissolution of everything that was socially ordained. These are pleasures that the practice of the greatest art would not have given me.
>
> As for what we have done, how could the present outcome be assessed? The landscape we are now traversing has been devastated by a war this society is waging against itself, against its own potentialities. The uglification of everything was probably an inevitable price of the conflict. If we have begun to win, it is because the enemy has pushed its mistakes so far.[3]

Baudelaire, the goldsmith of melancholy, said that beauty was what fell immediately into memory. Debord could easily have accepted this description by modifying it slightly: beauty exists in the *transition* from what is to what was, in the fall of the old world not only into memory but also, and especially, into oblivion. What he loves most about the world is that it passes, that it flows and is destroyed. Debord is an artist of transition: he believes in the beauty of the fall, believes that the war that caused it was worth more than any work of art. And that is why he is not, strictly speaking, an artist, to the extent that art is remembrance, a re-creation of what was. "These are pleasures that the practice of the greatest art would not have given me." Unlike war, great art establishes, retains, immortalizes—those are the least of its faults.

But Debord loved his world for its moral instability, its movement, its disturbances, in which any sense of safety and certainty was lost. We cannot reproach his work for not being better than it is, for it is as good as he wanted it to be: it is an archive of loss, an archive of the flow imposed on time by war. He loved his world because it was at war with itself and it was in that war, and possibly only in it, that he found himself, that he found his place. War joined him to his world, allowed him to love it, independently of the question of knowing who would be victorious. For, although he was at times a triumphalist, as in 1971 when he wrote the *Theses on the Situationist International and Its Time,* which announced its imminent victory around the world, he also accepted the fact that there would be struggles whose outcome was uncertain. He even accepted defeat, if only out of disgust with the grand and stately parades of war veterans. It was the fate of the Light Brigade to destroy itself during a charge of great beauty, just as it was the fate of the SI to dissolve itself, to lose itself, and, possibly, to begin to win by losing itself, by disappearing beneath the moving river of time.

Descriptions of Battle

THE IMAGINARY WARRIOR

The historians and commentators of May 1968 disagree about many things. However, very few of them saw it as a civil war, with troop movements and brigade charges. If there was a war, no one knew about it and it must have been the mildest civil war reported in the history of the modern world. It would be tempting to conclude that the wars conducted by Guy Debord, and May 1968 in particular, were imaginary wars, and the parts of *In girum imus nocte* devoted to the events that took place in May, or the pages of *Panegyric* on the golden age of lettrism, are above all the sign of his desire to become part of his own legend. By assimilating the situationists to the Light Brigade massacred in the Crimea, or the lettrists to the brigands of Villon's time, Debord made himself the subject of his own film. It was as if he were a kind of modern Don Quixote,[1] an imaginary general, as Argan was an imaginary invalid. It has also been suggested that although there may be nothing wrong with thinking of oneself as the head of a band of warriors at the age of twenty, it would be ridiculous to maintain such a position in adulthood, as was assumed to be the case with Debord when he made *In girum imus nocte*. The criticism obviously reveals a sense of confusion between childhood and a lost childhood, which is designed to last. Are we certain that those who live out their lost childhood are trying to reach adulthood? In any case, Debord finished his film by warning us that we would never achieve wisdom. Others—like those who reproached him for the childishness of his imaginary warrior—wanted to see him as well behaved, a theoretician, a former child who had become an adult, the manager of a small, and equally docile, revolutionary business, possibly even publishing a small-circulation review. They were careful to avoid explaining why an imaginary literary warrior should limit himself to childhood, when other fabulists—certainly no less imaginary or ridiculous when you think of it—were exempt from retirement and allowed to continue their immodest behavior until senility was upon them, sometimes even beyond.

In any event, whatever imagined life there was, it is important to understand it. It is not because Argan is a hypochondriac that he is healthy, quite the opposite, since it's obvious that he's doing badly. The battle scenes in Debord's narratives certainly possess a legendary quality, as do the references to the underworld of Saint-Germain-des-Prés. In this sense, they are, without question, imaginary, but this imaginary produces real *effects*, like any imagined world, and I am not even thinking of the effects Debord may have had on others, the ways he intervened in other people's lives to change them, his seductive powers, or his ability to convince. I am thinking of the effects his imagination may have had on the way he conducted his own life. He would not be the first person to have lived his life in terms of the legend he decided to become. By playing at being a ghost, we become one. In Debord's case, we can also say that by playing at being a warrior, he ended up waging war, at least in his own way. I would even venture that our interest in Debord (what he was as much as what he wrote) is connected to this ability to realize an imaginary warrior, to give it unique consistency and form—to embody it. His detractors are not wrong to attack him for this:

without his fascination with war and its trappings, Debord would no longer be Debord.

THE MILITANT

How was such an imagined world embodied? I am not referring to Debord's activities as a militant, even though these were real and it would be a mistake to overlook them. He often paid the price for his actions, but, after all, he was not alone and many others ran far greater risks. He was a rebel in 1951, always on the edge of illegality, hanging around with deserters, (petty) crooks, at least one "murderer," abducting not only texts and images but minors as well. He was clearly on the outs with society, rejected the dominant order—but without sacrificing himself through confrontation, as some of his clearly more suicidal companions did. As early as the lettrist period, the political positions he assumed, especially in *Potlatch*, were always clear and radical, and remained so during the situationist period and beyond; he certainly didn't lack courage.

Debord always rejected the order imposed by capitalism and imperialism, as well as all forms of communism connected with the Leninist-Stalinist movement, or any form of representation of the proletariat by an avantgarde. More generally, he was opposed to state structures, regardless of their nature. We saw in the preceding chapter that, in the early sixties, in the wake of Socialisme ou Barbarie, he clearly came out in favor of workers' councils that would deprive the self-proclaimed representatives of the working class of their monopoly, which at the time included quite a large number of people. During the Algerian War, he signed the famous *Déclaration sur le droit à l'insoumission* [Declaration on the Right to Insubordination]. He was not one of the first signatories, but joined them as soon as he became aware of the manifesto and was asked to sign. When he was accused, along with a number of other signatories, he claimed to have helped draft the declaration (more specifically, he claimed co-responsibility) as a sign of solidarity. All of this is well known. But it nonetheless remains part of a verbal war that drew little attention from the "enemy," except for the publication of the Algerian *Déclaration*. But in this case the government dropped its investigation, primarily through the efforts of Jean-Paul Sartre, who was too famous to arrest ("On n'emprisonne pas Voltaire"). We can assume that, for Debord, this was just one more reason to despise Sartre, whose fame transformed the war into a comedy.[2]

Earlier, I discussed the role of the situationists in May 1968, which they imprinted with their own style. Obviously, an interest in form does not preclude an interest in insurrection. Debord fought on the barricades (primarily the violent confrontations of May 10 and 11 on the Rue Mouffetard), but here too, he was not alone, as he was not alone at the Sorbonne, or the Council, when he insisted on continuing the occupation of the universities. Debord's commitments were real enough. He always liked fighting and had no hesitation about getting involved, not only in the streets of Paris in May 1968, but sometimes in the local cafés.

When, during the summer of 1968, the wind shifted and the government began its campaign of repression against the most subversive activities, he had good reason to anticipate the danger and take refuge in Belgium or in the countryside with those companions who were the most compromised. But in general the situationists were not the first target of the post–May 1968 repression, which was directed primarily against militant Maoists and Trotskyists (never having had any "official" existence, the SI was never directly associated with any of the organizations that had been banned by the government).[3]

In the years following May 1968, Italy was far closer to civil war than France. After the hiatus in Belgium and to escape the multiple aftershocks of the Paris uprising (not just the repression but the incessant and stifling demands resulting from his "celebrity," and the way the city had been deprived of everything that had made it habitable for him), Debord decided to live in Italy for a time. This was in 1972, immediately following the dissolution of the SI. In 1969, his friends Gianfranco Sanguinetti and Paolo Salvadori created an Italian section of the SI. This was the last and certainly the most "political" of the SI sections, the farthest removed from any artistic concerns (there was a world of difference between the earlier German and Scandinavian sections and the new Italian section). In Italy, situationist ideas, spread by the new section (as well as by a number of libertarian groups), appeared to have greater resonance with the working class. Wildcat strikes and sabotage, outside the control of unions or the Communist Party, multiplied around the country. It's not hard to imagine the appeal the climate of insurrection held for Debord during those years, which are sometimes described as the "years of lead," because of the terrorist shadows that continued to hover over them. Whether or not it claimed to follow situationist ideas, the libertarian or far-left movement was often not far from implementing them. It had a foot in armed struggle, sometimes more than a foot, and it was in this context of widespread illegality that terrorist phenomena were defined.

It is much easier to acknowledge now than thirty years ago that it was because of this mood of insurrection that the Italian government, through the secret services and a handful of questionable Masonic lodges, "produced"— at least partly, through manipulation and infiltration—terrorism and the many subsequent attacks intended to frighten the population and encourage them to demand government protection. Against the dangers of armed struggle, against uncontrolled and uncontrollable libertarians, nothing is as useful as a good, apparently red, brigade and a few bombs exploding in railroad stations at rush hour. In any case, this was Debord's initial opinion, and he always tried to distinguish between the legitimate armed struggle of true revolutionaries and their terrorist caricature.[4]

Nonetheless, the Italy in which Debord chose to live was unquestionably a dangerous place to be. Like his accomplices, and because of his reputation, he was constantly under surveillance and suspected of participating in some of the most violent attacks. Those around him were arrested or even murdered, although their death was often disguised as an accident. He knew that he and many of his friends were being monitored around the clock, that antigovernment groups were being infiltrated and members turned, and that "comrades" who were arrested and then released could not be trusted. Debord lived through all this, lived within it. He supported and even helped many of the Italian insurgents, who were sometimes sought by the police, sometimes went underground (and not only in Italy). Through all this Debord managed to carefully maintain his distance from terrorism, but he was a man under suspicion. Eventually, he had to leave the country. Although Italy may have been close to open warfare, it would have to take place without Debord. But it is important to recognize that, as far as the type of "hard" warfare typified by the Red Brigades was concerned, he wanted no part of it. In 1978, he had no qualms about breaking with Gianfranco Sanguinetti—the last situationist, expelled from France, and a cosigner of the famous 1971 *Theses on the Situationist International and Its Time*—when, following a disagreement over how to interpret the activities of Italian terrorists (at the time, the Aldo Moro affair was in all the papers), he suspected him of being complacent toward terrorism.[5]

So much for the Italian campaign. Later, while traveling between Arles,

Spain, Italy, Paris, and, increasingly, Champot, Debord continued to maintain contact with far-left groups, especially the Spanish anarchist movement. But his commitment remained primarily verbal (except in the case of the Segovia affair). He never took action (but what action, exactly? That was the crux of the problem).[6] He never took up arms, never committed any holdups, and, in fact, was never arrested. I do not question his courage, or the behavior of his contemporaries, or even the example they may have set. However, I am not sure that enumerating the facts will convince many readers that Debord's life was one of constant warfare.

So, what about Debord the warrior? He may be better hidden than he appears, even more obscure. We won't find him in the battles fought by the Lettrist International (from 1952 to 1958), or later by the Situationist International (from 1958 to 1971)—at least these are not sufficient to make him a warrior. In spite of their military connotation, the "artistic" avant-gardes— and the groups Debord led were part of the avant-garde even when they tried to transcend it—rarely engaged in war, other than to do battle with the art world and its institutions. That is what they are there for, there is little disagreement about this. It's what we expect of them, with a handful of unanticipated seasonal scandals thrown in for good measure. Consequently, theirs is a *good war,* since that is what the art of the twentieth century experienced, a century that was profoundly anchored in the avant-garde tradition (and a tradition is what it has become). But is there anything less warlike than the avant-garde? Debord was so convinced of this that he became interested only in transcending the avant-garde, seeing it dissolved by converting it into a Light Brigade. He accepted the avant-garde only on condition that it would be sacrificed, destroyed through war, something it was little accustomed to.

ON STRIKE

As a warrior Debord was hardly more visible than when he intentionally tried to disappear from sight. His militant and avant-garde activities were real enough, but did they make him a warrior, did they create "Debord," confer upon him the renown some critics have claimed was the only thing he was interested in? Can one construct a legend through militant activity? It's not clear, even though the activities were far from negligible. There were many European revolutionaries, some of whom had taken action, who considered Debord a partner, a theoretical support, or simply a good listener.

Clearly, he was an intellectual, but a revolutionary intellectual, choosing his partners and correspondents on the basis of the struggles he felt to be important. He conversed with these men and women at length, hardly at all with anyone else. It is important to bear this in mind when trying to understand the context in which Debord tried to situate himself, for he was never *simply* an intellectual, in the sense in which he no doubt would have defined the term: someone officially engaged in the production of ideas.

Nor was he *simply* an artist or writer: he had ideas, a style, an art, but they were always placed within a strategic perspective, that of someone who found the world a bad place and decided to struggle against it, regardless of his literary or philosophical references. The division between the writer and the militant is inappropriate, at least in Debord's case. Neither of the two areas of specialization interested him in and of itself: only the transition from one to the other, the articulation of war and poetry. Instead of asking about his literary models and what he owes to them, we should focus on the battles fought by the writers he admired and asked that we read from *his* point of view. After all, they were not born classics. They too found the world in which they lived to be offensive, they too rejected it, fought against it.

There are elements of Debord in Cardinal de Retz, in Baudelaire (another lost child), in Rimbaud, in Lautréamont the appropriator, who disappeared during the Paris Commune, in Mallarmé, the adept of rhetorical disappearance, who said the only bomb he was familiar with was a book.[7] But this does not mean that Debord tried to imitate those he admired, or to prolong their experience, much less produce a body of work that would be as good as, or possibly better than, theirs. In this sense, we could say that he represents an accident of modernism. He understood the risks better than others, he admired its tutelary figures (Baudelaire, Lautréamont, Mallarmé, etc.), as well as its avant-garde continuation in the twentieth century (from Breton to Isou and beyond). But with Debord the tradition is derailed. It is deflected from its destiny: the "strike against society" so important to Mallarmé changed its meaning completely; it underwent a kind of amplification or enhancement. Obviously, the change did not imply a resumption of work or an attempt to resocialize the situation of the writer (at the time, this was approximately Sartre's reaction), but, on the contrary, a generalization of the idea that one should "never work."

Everything in the situationist world was designed to produce a general strike carrying away everything in its path—writers and literature included. In that sense, Debord is the modernist myth of the writer-as-negative-force become reality, cut off from his literary embodiment and, therefore, the destruction or deconstruction of the myth. This doesn't mean he no longer writes or that his writing does not have literary qualities, but that it is suspended from its mythmaking function, its task of bringing the writer into being as the myth of absolute social negativity. Here, we can only say that Debord knew how to make use of literature, and to use it well. It was never a substitute or reserve for political struggle, a reserve his contemporaries frequently viewed in terms of the "death of the author," under cover of which one could continue to write—consistent with the myth, consistent with the self-evangelical logic that assumes the inevitability of such death. This—rhetorical—death was not Debord's strong point because, to a greater extent than nearly all his contemporaries, he lived it, he embodied it.[8] He was an author who renounced his calling and simultaneously disqualified the most prestigious of contemporary myths conferring on the writer his problematic legitimacy. A general strike, not only against society, but against literature. Between the militant and the writer was the strategist, who saw writing only as a tool of war, something that could create or complement conflict, as fire brought to oil, a detonator for a stationary explosive.

DEBORD AND ROUSSEAU

Having rejected the enticements of the "death of the author," it was no great leap for Debord to also reject any form of "essential solitude," nor did he manifest the sorrowful acceptance of privation in all the forms it is generally associated with. This is true, and certainly obvious, for the lettrist and situationist periods, but it is equally true of the years following the dissolution of the SI; moreover, he wrote a great deal during this period.

Debord did not withdraw from the world in 1972 or later out of anger at the failure of the revolution he was supposed to have predicted, periodically conveying his resentment to his contemporaries from the depths of his splendid solitude. There was no temptation in the desert for Debord. Although he decided to leave Paris after the SI dissolved, he did so because he could live better elsewhere. But in Florence, Seville, later in Venice and even Champot, Debord remained what he had always been. He continued to lead the life he always wanted to lead, he continued to exercise his right to freedom, he remained a social being. Nothing could be more inaccurate than to accuse him of being bad-tempered, to describe him as an avatar of Alceste.[9]

Debord was not Alceste, unable to leave Célimène's antechamber for the desert he dreamed of, unable to separate from her. It's one thing to develop an undying hatred for the human race and hang around as long as possible to tell them about it; it's another to enjoy conflict, strategy, secret undertakings, plots. Debord was not a misanthrope; he was not filled with hate, never had much time to hate. That requires a good memory and immobility (Alceste never moved), and Debord was someone with a fondness for forgetfulness and mobility. On the whole, we could even claim the contrary. For Debord, war was a way of loving, if not the human race, at least the time he lived in, a way of showing his enthusiasm for it and of generating enthusiasm by introducing division and conflict—an evening visitor, a devil's emissary who falls in love with the world. Debord's melancholy was too combative and too joyful for an ill-tempered man. Although he often found himself on the losing side, he did not, like Alceste, take pleasure in losing to prove that society is unjust, when it *should be just*. He knew it was unjust, but rather than complain about it and cling gloriously to that complaint, he continued to fight, even in his personal life, using the means of justice supplied by the "enemy" whenever he was directly involved. (After the murder of Gérard Lebovici, Debord went to court and won.) And finally, since we are talking about Alceste, although Debord enjoyed fighting, he also enjoyed love, and, unlike the atrabilious lover, he never waited patiently in the wings. He loved and was loved in turn, and was happy in love. His love affairs were often associated with the battles he fought and formed with them the obverse and reverse of the same life of adventure. "But I, not being that type of person, can only tell of 'the knights and ladies, the arms and loves, the gallant conversations and bold adventures' of a unique era."[10] Few atrabilious men seem to have been as happy and as free in love, and the final pages of Schiffter's book, where he tries to show that Debord was wrong to be a libertarian rather than a libertine, are especially unconvincing.

Ultimately, the question of whether or not Debord was a misanthrope or ill-humored would be academic (what point would there be in comparing someone who had lived to a fictional character?) if behind this comparison there wasn't the more consequential and consistent figure of Jean-Jacques

Rousseau, whose affection for Alceste is well known (he reproached Molière for ridiculing him, personally, by creating the character of Alceste). This is obviously the crux of Schiffter's remarks, for he views Debord as a kind of modern Rousseau (Schiffter, as appearances would have it, dislikes Rousseau, whom he sees as a man filled with bitterness and resentment). To my knowledge, there is no explicit reference to Rousseau in Debord's work, and it is unlikely he would have appreciated certain aspects of Rousseau's life, such as his maudlin forbearance. But this does not prevent him from effectively being a Rousseauist. I have already pointed out the role played by the use of a rhetoric of exemplarity and sincerity, with which Rousseau introduced the modern form of autobiography.[11] Moreover, Debord's work in general (and *The Society of the Spectacle* in particular) is based on a metaphysics. As is also often the case with Rousseau, it postulates a golden age, a humanity originally transparent to itself, whose fundamentally communitarian nature has not been destroyed by the rule of commodities. There is much in common between this position and elements of the *Discourse on Inequality* (just as the desire for authentic communication lies at the heart of the *Essay on the Origin of Languages*). Finally, we can follow Schiffter when he claims that both Debord and Rousseau possess a fundamental suspicion of the visible, or, more accurately, a suspicion of any suggested fantasies associated with images, or artifice (the famous twenty-four minutes of silent black screen also scream out in favor of Rousseau).[12]

In spite of their differences—intellectual, stylistic, and personal—we can state, hypothetically at least, that Debord was a modern Rousseau, as Schiffter maintains. But we must also recognize that, for someone trying to demonstrate Debord's lack of importance, the comparison is not the most convincing. For if the question of his historical status remains open, Rousseau's place is well established, and favorably for him. Everyone is entitled to their personal opinion of Rousseau, but that's not really the issue here. In the history of ideas in modern Europe, few works have had as much impact as his—literary, anthropological, pedagogical, and especially political. The revolutionaries of the Convention were not mistaken about this, nor later the socialist thinkers, whether "romantics," utopians, or self-proclaimed scientific socialists (is Marx even conceivable without Rousseau?), or the various later avant-gardes as they oscillated between Fourierism and primitivism.[13]

If Rousseau did not stop producing effects, it's because his was, precisely, an art of effects—in every sense of the term. He was sufficiently brilliant to have a profound impact on the history of ideas, and managed to produce a break with the past by inventing a form of social critique that played an essential role in subsequent thought—as if everything had changed after Rousseau. His critics have behaved as if he were damned by his contradictions, between, for example, his praise of immediacy and his use of the most sophisticated literary means, his recycling of the eighteenth-century novel, and so on. But this says nothing about Rousseau's formidable capacity to produce effects, to attract readers, to make use of what he recycled—appropriated—for his own use. It is possible that every science of effects, every strategy entails an art of *détournement,* and it is as absurd to imagine a Rousseau unconscious of the effects produced by his books (or trying not to produce them) as it is to claim that Debord simply copied the *Theses on Feuerbach.* All things considered, Schiffter's comparison is not so far off the mark. But it favors Debord, even though this was certainly not his intention. If Debord is our modern Rousseau, we are forced to acknowledge that he must have inherited at least some sense of *intervention,* of that ability to disrupt the sense of continuity and articulate a social critique that is so radical that it completely reconfigures the terms of the debates and conflicts of an era.

In other words, what Debord "inherited" from Rousseau was essentially a science of the effects of speech, an art of polemics, which should be understood here not only in its customary and relatively superficial sense (even if, in this sense, Debord wrote polemical texts), but also in a more fundamental, even foundational, sense. So, where is Debord the warrior? He is hidden in his words, in his capacity to use them to divide, to provoke conflict, and to create difference. It could even be said that Debord radicalized Rousseau's method by emphasizing division rather than reconciliation. His work enables us to read, or read more easily, what is profoundly "bellicose" in Rousseau's work. It is interesting to note that while some of Debord's books (especially *The Society of the Spectacle*) do not exclude a melancholic regret for a golden age, nothing in them resembles Rousseau's idea of a social contract, or the adventures of Saint-Preux and Julie. There were no situationists in Clarens. On the contrary, everything in Debord's world seems made to result in war, a (more) passionate and certainly not a more reasonable life. The overlap between Rousseau and Debord lies in their oscillation between melancholy, which gives rise to the feeling of loss or separation (the sentiment of a vanished golden age), and a "paranoiac" position through which both men behave as if they were the "last man." Necessarily alone against the world, the last man reappropriates whatever has been lost—the authenticity of communication, for example, but I am not sure that this is merely an example.

I put the term "paranoia" in quotes, but use it in a positive sense.[14] It designates not only something like the "sense of the enemy" that characterizes real strategies (political, military), but also, in Rousseau as well as Debord, a conflict-laden vision of the world. And this vision assumes a relationship of confrontation between an ego whose singularity is conferred by confrontation and, more or less, the rest of the world. It is in this capacity of taking upon oneself such confrontation, of embodying it, of becoming part of it as a subject that the possibility arises of a social critique as radical and comprehensive as was Rousseau's in his lifetime, and as Debord's is now.

Where do accurate, or at least new, theories come from? From a subjective effort, individual invention, the reinvention of a relationship between the subject and the world. In saying this, I am not maintaining that the social critique offered by Debord is true. It is probably no more or less true than that of Rousseau, but, as we know, the proof of the pudding is in the eating. As with Rousseau, it is important to recognize that Debord had the ability to produce effects, the ability to reconfigure the contemporary field of social criticism, in which the majority of the "themes" he developed, from *The Society of the Spectacle* to *Comments on the Society of the Spectacle,* occupy a central place. Appropriated or not, falsified or not, they are on nearly everyone's tongue. It's possible that there is a point where unanimity for or against oneself amounts to exactly the same thing, and it's possible that today Debord has reached that point. He may even be the only one to have reached it, but he could only have done so alone. And it is not as easy as it seems. Not everyone can become Rousseau; there is a personal price to be paid in getting there.

How to Be Disliked

To assume the burdens of confrontation, to make the class struggle or historical battles in general a conflict between oneself and the world, a

personal matter, is something Debord pursued throughout his life. It was
this that formed the kernel of his legend, or, if you prefer, that created the
legend, that caused a specific form of revolutionary practice to be associated with an individual or a name. The Maoist left, less heroic and following an imperative of self-abnegation, even sacrifice of the personality,
thought it would be able to join the proletarians in the factories and share
their struggles. With Debord, it was the opposite, a kind of incorporation
of the proletariat in whose name Debord would make war, but alone, thus
making himself not only the measure of all things, but allowing himself the
possibility of a comprehensive refutation of the world. The challenge was
absolute: "There is nothing more natural than to consider everything from
the standpoint of oneself, taken as the center of the world; one finds oneself thus capable of condemning the world without even bothering to hear
its deceitful chatter."[1] To make oneself the center of the world while negat-
ing that world, ignoring it: it is not the tranquil—or ironic—assumption
of megalomania that is so surprising in this passage, but the lucidity of
the irrevocably discordant nature of such a position. You want war? Then
make yourself the center of the world, for this is a position others are sure
to argue with. You are certain to annoy everyone, because everyone would
like to be in your shoes. The center of the world is the most disputed position, the most *untenable* position there is. Anyone who tries to appropriate
it must know that, sooner or later, he will trigger a war.

Debord, of course, knew this, which is why he did it. At the heart of all
his works, written or otherwise, at the heart of his legend, there is the will
to stand out, to make a difference, to offend. He offended others by pretending to be the center of the world, and he occupied that center because
he was someone who offended everyone. As far as Debord was concerned,
this was his principal achievement, his true *art*: "I have merited the universal hatred of the society of my time, and I would have been annoyed to
have any other merits in the eyes of such a society. But I have noticed that
it is in the cinema that I have aroused the most extreme and unanimous
outrage. I have even been plagiarized much less in this domain than elsewhere, up until now at least. My very existence as a filmmaker remains a
generally refuted hypothesis."[2] Debord rejoiced in giving offense. His art
is an art of offense, something he claimed publicly or symbolically. In any
event, this is what he always tried to accomplish and, apparently, it is what

he did best, right from the start. In *Panegyric* he takes the trouble to specify that he began his campaign of offense not in 1968, but in 1952: "I think rather it is what I did in 1952 that has been disliked for so long."[3]

Debord has been offending people ever since his symbolic birth in 1952, and that is why he gave particular offense in his films, for this birth coincides with the release of *Howls for Sade*, an exemplary and legendary gesture of the destruction of cinema, the source of nearly universal rejection, the object of unanimous indignation, as was true of all the films that followed. These films aroused such profound disgust that, for once, no one plagiarized him; it is his existence as a filmmaker that is rejected. The epitome of hatred may consist in its concealment, a conspiracy of silence being the worst form of hatred. Debord the filmmaker was particularly offensive and proud of it: others stopped plagiarizing him, there was no flattery through imitation. This may have been the reason he chose filmmaking as his only "profession," as his only public identity.

Profession: public offender. He precipitated his contemporaries into obscurity and anger. It was Gérard Lebovici who became the producer of his films and who even bought a small theater to project, round-the-clock, his friend's films, and only those. No one did more to help Debord offend others than Gérard Lebovici, no one was more supportive of his art of offense, or identified as much with it, made it his own. Is this the real reason, after Lebovici's murder in 1984, Debord withdrew all his films from circulation, as an homage to the man who had, for more than ten years, given him the means to fight his wars, to continue to offend?

But the art of giving offense is obviously not simply the result of Debord's being a filmmaker. The man who wrote *"Cette mauvaise réputation . . ."* indicated, on the very first page of the book, that he never made an effort to please. And the author of *Panegyric* was very satisfied to have deprived the world of his talents, of anything the world might have approved of. He succeeded so well in this that his world appears to long for a sense of disorder that he alone attempted to bring about, thus ensuring his "singular folly":

> I will say that I have always made a point of giving the vague impression that I had great intellectual, even artistic, qualities of which I preferred to deprive my era, which did not seem to deserve to use them. There have always been people to regret this absence and, paradoxically, to help me maintain it. If this has turned out well, it is only because I have never sought out anyone, anywhere. My

entourage has been composed only of those who came of their own accord and were capable of getting themselves accepted. Has even one other person dared to behave like me, in this era? It must also be acknowledged that the degradation of all existing conditions occurred at precisely the same moment, as if to justify my singular folly.[4]

In keeping with his desire to offend, Debord made himself, at least mythically, the object of a universal hatred that helped ensure his singularity. What better way to be unique than to make oneself hated by everyone? What better way to make oneself hated than to promote one's singularity— one's life as a cautionary tale? This is what it means to make oneself the center of the world. But then we must go the distance, never give up, never compromise, never grow reconciled, or change our mind about our peers, who we have decided, once and for all, are not really our peers. In other words, a declaration of war on the human race is fundamentally performative. It gives rise to the hostility it evokes or convokes. It provides its reality, the way a simple avowal gives love its consistency, makes it something real rather than an imaginary sentiment. Like love, hate must be declared openly. It doesn't require actions to come into being. Giving offense is a form of speech, an art.

Debord proudly acknowledged that he was not disagreeable only as a filmmaker, but his most unforgivable "crimes" are relatively vague. In *In girum imus nocte,* they coincide generally with what was needed to overturn the world: "For my part, if I have succeeded in being so deplorable in the cinema, it is because I have been much more criminal elsewhere. From the very beginning I have devoted myself to overthrowing this society, and I have acted accordingly."[5] That is all we are going to learn. And in a passage in *Panegyric* where Debord presents himself, via Gondi (Cardinal de Retz), as a "disturber of the peace," he is not even sure that the crimes—"of a new kind"—have been carried out. Debord is content to have imagined them: "I have never really aspired to any sort of virtue, except perhaps to that of having thought that only a few crimes of a new type, which could certainly not have been cited in the past, might not be unworthy of me; and to that of not having changed, after such a bad start."[6]

New crimes. These seem to coincide with a discourse used to describe more than to acknowledge them. They are inseparable, absolutely linked to a discourse (writing, film) given over to the hostility of the Other by refusing to recognize him. Debord always claimed to be irrevocably different from his peers, never saw himself in them, never acknowledged them. He aligned himself with the "I alone" of Rousseau's *Confessions* and possibly with his claim of authenticity, but certainly not his belief that he "knew men," having determined once and for all not only not to know them but to break with them and turn a deaf ear to their deceitful speech. Not to know men, not to acknowledge them, not to acknowledge oneself in them or be acknowledged by them—it was in these terms that his art of annoyance could be described. It consisted in an attempt—which could be described as folly, as he himself said—to escape a dialectic of identification and avoid the tribute such a dialectic pays to the imaginary. Singularity is the degree zero of identification. It is bound by an identity that owes nothing to the Other and does not wish to be acknowledged. If we are fascinated by Debord, it is because he decided one day not to be like us, or never to be identified in such a manner, to escape the fundamental *visibility* by which someone is acknowledged as such. An iconoclast not only "theoretically" but also in his own (inter)subjectivity, Debord's most fundamental desire was that between himself and the rest of the world there would be no image or imaginary allowing them to acknowledge one another. A book such as *The Society of the Spectacle*—and this is the source of its enigmatic force—projects onto the world a rejection of appearances, which may also be a rejection of one's self-image, a rejection of what is irrevocably alienating in any process of identification. Debord possesses a desire for absolute singularity (which is also a desire for absolute liberty) that consists in identifying only with oneself and, consequently, never expecting anything from the Other. "I don't claim to resemble any other person," we read in *Panegyric*,[7] and in a passage in *"Cette mauvaise réputation . . . ,"* where he attacks Régis Debray, Debord significantly compares two fundamental aspects of his art of displeasure: "I expected nothing. At every moment I identified only with myself; and especially with no 'ism,' no ideology, no project. My time has been the present."[8]

Singularity is an art of the present, an art that leaves behind no trace or image, an art of avoiding images, of not walking in them, to paraphrase Saint Augustine. To displease means *to ask for nothing*. "I have never sought out anyone." Debord's history reflects the interruption of the imaginary, the refusal to ask for anything. Debord never sought anyone out, never asked anything of anyone. That is why he serves as his own authority and disqualifies

any judgment of himself from the start. Because he never tried to please
and, consequently, never became visible to others (to please is to make oneself visible, to succeed in making others love our self-image), his opinion
of himself never took into account the opinions of others. This is the true
meaning of *Panegyric*, an autobiographical text, but also, and especially, an
unreserved eulogy of a life that tried to be exemplary in every respect, a eulogy without distance, free of blame or criticism, in keeping with the definition by Littré at the beginning of the book. The epigraph is confirmed by
the one in the first chapter, where we read: "disdaining to justify his accusations or eulogies; adopting without examination and without that critical spirit so necessary to the historian, the false judgments of prejudice,
of rivalry or enmity, and the exaggerations of spite or bad feeling; . . . never
quoting any witness but himself, nor better authority than his own asser-
tions."[9] *Panegyric* leaves no room for the gaze of the Other, it disqualifies it
from the start. The book was made to displease because Debord's project
was designed to be acknowledged for its absolute singularity—"I am what I
am." With Debord, there is no other *point of view* but his own: "In the same
way, I believe people will have to rest content with the history I am now
going to present. Because no one, for a long time to come, will have the
audacity to undertake to demonstrate, on any aspect, the contrary of what
I will say, whether it be a matter of finding the slightest inexact element in
the facts or of maintaining another point of view on them."[10]

Panegyric reveals, retrospectively, that *In girum imus nocte* is a kind of
prototype *Panegyric*: "As for myself, I have never regretted anything I have
done; and being as I am, I must confess that I remain completely incapable of imagining how I could have done anything any differently."[11] I did
what I did or what I could, I am what I am, and unable to *imagine* anything
else. It was as if Debord lacked the ability to identify with himself, or with
something like an ego ideal. A breakdown of the imagination, as if his ego
was his ideal. Under these circumstances, there is no room for the Other,
given that the construction of an ego ideal always involves the exposure of
the ego to the gaze of the Other as well as the exposure of the Other to our
gaze. Such an Other is in the position of no longer seeing, no longer judging, no longer being able to play the superego. Regardless of whether he
likes it or not.

But these are only books, you might claim, and they have nothing to do
with life. Can we be so sure? Certainly, they are words, but Debord paid a

personal price precisely so he might avoid turning his writing into a stream of empty persifflage. In this, an area that was so vital to the totality of avant-garde practice in the twentieth century, he succeeded better than others, in fact, better than all the others.[12] Could he have written what he wrote, present himself as he did, if he had allowed himself to be dependent on others, like everyone else, if he had established the least contractual relation with them, if he had received a salary (which he never did), or collected Social Security, or agreed to receive medical care, even once in his life, in a hospital (something he always stubbornly refused), or had sought to take his place, like so many others, in an institution that confers recognition and prestige?[13] Could he have written what he did if he hadn't been someone who never asked for anything, hadn't been someone who made no contractual commitment, a man free of any relationship other than emotional? It is still hard to imagine: Debord's life and work are one and the same thing.

In any case, it is this situation that gave so much weight to Debord's publication, shortly before his death, of the film contracts made with the companies run by Gérard Lebovici, which were collected in a small book titled, appropriately, *Des contrats*.[14] Still a curiosity among Debord's literary output, the book generally went unnoticed or was targeted for its so-called cynicism, given the lopsided nature of the contracts in question. These entail few if any obligations from Debord and a great number from the production companies run by his friend. Was this simply cynical? Aren't those contracts the proof that, for Debord, a contract had no meaning unless it had succumbed to friendship, to desire, to the gift that cannot be calculated, to the potlatch? It is important to read the "Justifications" that precede the contracts themselves, the first of which is for *The Society of the Spectacle* (1973), the second for *In girum imus nocte* (1977), and the third for a film on the history of Spain that Debord never made. For this film he limited himself to collecting funds to conduct an on-site feasibility "study" (an attentive reading of this, deliberately ironic, contract reveals that the film will never be made):

> There is no equality in such contracts; and it is precisely this unique quality that makes them so honorable. They have chosen what they prefer in everything. All of them are prepared *to inspire confidence on one side only*: the one who alone could lay claim to admiration.

The artist is not obligated to explain how he would go about completing some kind of apparently insoluble exploit, which as a result could only surprise. To announce, veridically, the title of a work, whose treatment no one would be able even to imagine, is the greatest concession that can be made. And similar information will, subsequently, preferably be eliminated. Finally, even more perfectly negative, a third film was chosen in advance so it would never be made; and this film would turn out to be consummately ironic. Moreover, all these contracts were carefully calculated to satisfy whatever element of luxury there was in my needs, while remaining uncontrollable from every point of view; and without ever revealing too much, even implicitly. *Sólo vivimos dos dias* ("We only have two days to live"). It is a principle that is hardly favorable to financial speculation.[15]

Only Debord's producer was bound by the signed contracts. As for the author, they literally served as a blank check. There was nothing to do but trust him, although the producer was responsible for supplying all the guaranties (rights, payment). They denied him any right of inspection over what would be produced: only a friend like Lebovici would have agreed to such conditions—or such nonconditions. The films for which Debord signed contracts are *unimaginable* for others, even his producers. Consequently, he could never bind himself contractually to them, because they could never imagine the product the contract covered. One can only do without a contract when negotiating with one's peers, and Debord didn't have any. He was a filmmaker without qualities, and without titles. With the second contract, even providing a title was too much of a concession; for it would say too much, would allow the imagination to wander too freely, and assign too much importance to the gaze of the Other (the contract for what would become *In girum imus nocte* simply states: "Sixth film by Guy Debord"). And with the third, even making the film was too much. Debord asked for nothing, which is also why he owed nothing other than a pure object of desire (in this sense, he was not indifferent to the fact that it involved a planned film on Spain, a country that had become known as a land of passion), without a name, without a title, without any reality other than that *given* by the producer. Ultimately, this third contract simply certifies that Debord owes nothing to anyone, even when he receives funding to make a film, even when he signs a contract to that end.

This is the privilege of glory, of those who have succeeded in achieving a sense of renown, those who are admired without asking to be admired. We cannot bind celebrity the way we do a name. Celebrity has no place in a contract. It is honored with gifts and freedom, not obligations. Nor was it without significance that this was nearly the last act in Debord's life, an act that served as a final homage to Gérard Lebovici.

One of the very last sentences written by Debord, with which he concludes his "Justifications," is also about Lebovici, the perfect partner for his potlatch: "A man named Boggio, in *Le Monde*, who wanted to expose, as informatively as possible, Lebovici's murder, indicated that the producer had gradually 'distanced himself from the norm socially accepted in his professional milieu.' We could just as easily say that he became celebrated by doing so." In the shadow of Debord's celebrity and outside any norm (legal, contractual), Lebovici ensured his own. His own fame consisted in recognizing what was unique about Debord's fame, that is, in recognizing it without being able to acknowledge it as belonging to an equal. This is the fundamental paradox represented by these contracts, which are anything but.

Refutations

Offending others brings up the question of self-image, or, more accurately, its rejection, the refusal to give the Other any hold on you. What makes us pleasing to one another is not only the images we present to each other, but that we resemble one another, that we are alike. Take away those images and you take away resemblance and are left only with singularities, a war of singularities. Perhaps now we can get a better idea of why, officially, Debord had to be a filmmaker rather than a writer or something else. For him, an image was a strategic weapon, its destruction was part of a campaign in a war he waged, and film was, in a sense, the bunker that had to be captured. *Howls for Sade,* howls against humanity. The war began with a film designed to offend, which deprived the viewers of images—of pleasure—as well as any possibility of acknowledgment or identification, whether of themselves or of the "author." "Cinema is dead. There can be no more films. Let's move on to the discussion."

Let's move on to the discussion and, possibly, to conflict, to combat. The virtual declaration of the aforementioned filmmaker is indeed a declaration of war addressed to the all-too-human viewer, who is dismissed as such. A Debord film is a way of establishing a hostile relationship with the public. Twenty-six years after this first film, and even if *In girum imus nocte* was no longer given over to a black screen and absolute silence, Debord still doesn't seem to feel much affection for the viewer, for he begins the film as follows: "I will make no concessions to the public in this film."[1] All the same, it's a remarkable statement, for it not only suggests an a priori relationship of conflict between the filmmaker and his public, but, since his initial position serves as a statement of intent, that the purpose of the film is to provoke hostility. It is as if *In girum imus nocte* was essentially a declaration of war. I will make no concessions to the public, there will be no reconciliation, we will share no pleasing or beautiful image, for the public does not deserve to be addressed by me: "this particular public, which has been so totally deprived of freedom and which has tolerated every sort of abuse, deserves less than any other to be treated gently."[2]

I am what I am and the public is what it is. And just as I refer only to myself, being the center of the world, I refer the public to itself. *In girum imus nocte* begins with a series of mirror images of the public: a "modern employee" in her bath with her son, a clothing store with two customers, a "working" couple in their living room playing with their children, a couple welcoming another couple in their home and playing Monopoly with them, and so on. Debord identifies only with himself and makes films in which the viewers are forced to identify with themselves. It is easier to understand how the first part of *In girum imus nocte* relates to the second, devoted to Debord's autobiographical narrative. The public, which doesn't deserve any pleasant images, which is convened only to forgo an imaginary, as we might say someone forgoes dessert, has access to the Debord legend because it doesn't concern them, because it can only disappoint their expectations, because it was made to offend, to leave them out of the picture: "Thus, instead of adding one more film to the thousands of commonplace films, I prefer to explain why I shall do nothing of the sort. I am going to replace the frivolous adventurers typically recounted by the cinema with the examination of an important subject: myself."[3] Why does Debord have recourse to his autobiography? Why does he speak about himself? So he won't have to speak about the others, not to the others or for them. For Debord, autobiography is used to disqualify the gaze of the Other; it is a fundamental *refutation* of the viewer or reader.

I emphasize the word *refutation* because Debord used it in the title of his first explicit work on "refutation," *Refutation of all the Judgments, Pro or Con, Thus Far Rendered on the Film "The Society of the Spectacle,"* made in

1975. The film attacks the reviews of the film version of *The Society of the Spectacle* that appeared in newspapers and magazines—a film that had been made and shown two years earlier—while at the same time bringing us up to date about the Portuguese revolution and the joint program of the French left, still shining like a new penny, for which, and this should come as no surprise, Debord harbored little enthusiasm.

As the title indicates, the refutation does not target any particular judgment, but all the judgments, all the opinions concerning *The Society of the Spectacle*, about which no one is authorized to speak: "Those who claim to like my film have liked too many other things to be capable of liking it; and those who say they don't like it have also accepted too many other things for their judgment to have the slightest significance."[4] Debord's works were not made to be seen, to be viewed the way you would a film, at least if viewing implies judgment, positive or negative. All those who think they have a right to watch *The Society of the Spectacle* are mistaken. They have seen too much already, they have liked too much, they have liked too many images. The only unobjectionable viewer is the one who, having never seen anything and continuing to see nothing while watching *The Society of the Spectacle*, would be fully outside the spectacle, to the point of no longer being a viewer at all. Silence or the failure to express an opinion in a newspaper or magazine does not absolve one from being disqualified. The silent viewer has no more legitimacy than some "pen pusher." By keeping silent, you can escape the ridicule that comes with revealing your lack of intelligence, but you will be suspect all the more for maintaining the superior form of hostility that the conspiracy of silence represents. In a sense, the viewer is rebuffed the moment he sees *The Society of the Spectacle* as a film, for what is at stake is the negation of the spectacle: "In a freer and more truthful future, people will look back in amazement at the idea that penpushers hired by the system of spectacular lies could imagine themselves qualified to offer their smug opinions on the merits and defects of a film that is a negation of the spectacle."[5]

The only possible point of view on a film such as this, the only one that enables you to understand it, is the negation of the spectacle (the negation of the society that produces the spectacle or produces itself as spectacle, of which cinema and the position of the viewer as we understand them are only the effect or symptom). Debord implies that it is impossible for the film to be judged from a cinematic point of view. Those who attempt this do so to hide their opposition to the conception of society advanced by Debord, to erase the reality of the war he is conducting, and especially to avoid revealing their actual loyalties: "They are attempting to disguise as a mere disagreement between different conceptions of cinema what is actually a conflict between different conceptions of society, and an open war within the existing society."[6]

The Society of the Spectacle and the *Refutation of all Judgments* were not made to be liked, or even to be viewed and evaluated according to some cinematic aesthetic. Take it or leave it, they were made solely to be understood, and could only be understood by adopting Debord's viewpoint, which coincided with that of revolution (which, in Portugal, was on the point of failing after the so-called Carnation Revolution): "There are people who understand, and others who do not understand, that the class struggle in Portugal has from the very beginning been dominated by a direct confrontation between the revolutionary workers organized in autonomous assemblies and the Stalinist bureaucracy allied with a few defeated generals. Those who understand such things will understand my film; and I don't make films for those who don't understand such things, or who make it their business to prevent others from understanding."[7] *The Society of the Spectacle* is addressed to those who understand, to those who have adopted a revolutionary attitude and for whom the film cannot be questioned, since it is beyond any reservations, any objections, even any form of appreciation viewers might have—attitudes through which the enemies of the revolution betray themselves, whether cinephiles or not. But because it is hard to understand why those who have adopted a revolutionary attitude would need a film inviting them to make revolution, it becomes obvious that the goal of Debord's film is above all to divide, to exclude, and to establish a relationship of intransigent confrontation with the viewer. For this reason as well, Debord, good strategist that he was, decided to make *The Society of the Spectacle* into a film. In doing so, he brought contradiction to a painful point within the system, the point he had started from twenty years earlier, by attacking society at the heart of its love for images rather than making use of a book that had become, in the society of the spectacle, a weapon of secondary importance.

If Debord made a film about his "major work," it was not to add pictures to his arguments, much less to illustrate them, but to make more noise (to howl louder, as in his first film), to heighten conflict, to publicize the war he was waging, to heighten contradiction, and to *infuriate* the public. The filmed version of *The Society of the Spectacle* coincides, significantly, with the enemy's co-optation of its first, print version:

> Most of these commentators are now fawningly praising the excellence of my book, as if they were capable of reading it and as if they had already welcomed its publication in 1967 with the same respect. They generally complain, however, that I have abused their indulgence by bringing the book to the screen. The blow is all the more painful because they had never dreamed that such an extravagance was possible. Their anger confirms the fact that the appearance of such a critique in a film upsets them even more than in a book. Here, as elsewhere, they are being forced into a defensive struggle, on a second front.[8]

Film as a tool for waging war. The true meaning of the film version of *The Society of the Spectacle* may be found in *Refutation of All Judgments*, as if Debord's only goal in filming *The Society of the Spectacle* was to have an effect, that is, to generate judgments and opinions he could subsequently refute. Debord's cinema was strategic. He did not make films to give people something to see but to force his enemies to reveal themselves and to repulse their attacks.

The images in *The Society of the Spectacle* are as unoriginal, as appropriated as those used previously. Sometimes they are the same. Debord's films are literally without a subject, not just because they block any kind of interpretable content for discussion but because they do not involve an author who presents images or texts he has signed and will answer for. A strategic art is one that is rigorously impersonal, and to look for Debord in his films could, in his eyes, only be a sign of bad faith, an intent to escape the pure confrontation his art embodies: "Faced with an unusual number of innovations and an insolence that is utterly beyond their comprehension, these avant-garde consumers vainly try to rationalize a ground for approval by attributing these fascinating eccentricities to a nonexistent individual lyricism."[9] The avant-garde consumer looks for a subject that, although it may not be directly addressed to him, at least represents him; he searches for the trace of an author, for lyricism. But Debord's films, and possibly all of his work, paradoxically including the most autobiographical, are "insolent" precisely because there is nothing lyrical about them, in the sense that no subject ever presents itself to the gaze of the Other, never exposes itself to the Other. No subject signs them, no subject assumes responsibility for them, or agrees to answer for what has been filmed or written. They are supreme examples of *détournement* (who would sign an appropriated text?), but Debord's "irresponsibility" is not limited to appropriation.

The strategy of refutation at work shares in this same irresponsibility, the same desire to deny the viewer or reader a space for interpretation or exchange, to force upon him the immediacy of confrontation and involve him in a war he would prefer to forget. A war that remains clandestine, invisible. All the better if it is unlikely that the revolutionary crowds in whose name Debord expresses himself would enter the movie house on Rue Cujas to see *The Society of the Spectacle* or *Refutation of All Judgments*. Why would they see a film that was made only for those who understand its revolutionary point of view, which is to say, for them, since they have already understood it? The real viewers of Debord's films are those who remain in shadow, the absent crowds for a black screen: "He also regrets that a mind of my quality has limited its expression to a 'cinema ghetto' where the masses will have little chance to see it. This argument does not convince me. I prefer to remain in obscurity with these masses, rather than to consent to harangue them under the artificial floodlights manipulated by their hypnotizers."[10] Mallarmé wrote that he was not of the present, "for lack of a declaration by the crowd."[11] For Debord, crowds exist, providing one removes the artificial light imposed on them by their "hypnotizers." They exist, providing they can remain, like him, in the shadows. We could even say they exist as a knowledge of shadow: knowing how to remain obscure, to remain a shadowy being. Similarly, the present exists as well: but it is the present of invisible wars and revolutions, which, most of the time, become visible only to fail, in Portugal and everywhere else. It's not entirely true that Debord identified only with himself, since the crowds in the shadows were him as well, were Debord identifying with revolution. "I prefer to remain in obscurity with these masses." I alone know my heart and understand revolution. Rousseau makes you cognizant of your humanity, Debord makes you cognizant of war. To read his books or watch his films is to receive, live, a letter from the revolution. What gift will you give in return, and to whom?

The *Refutation of All Judgments* is the first of a genre proposed by Debord. In 1982, a year after the release of *In girum imus nocte* (and four years after it was made), the process was resumed, but purified and radicalized. In general, Debord was not very interested in process. He continuously transformed his battle technique and developed new forms of action. Instead of refutation, this turned out to be an unknown form of *"poubellication"* (junk publication). Judgments of the film are not, strictly speaking, refuted, but simply consigned to a pamphlet, whose title explains what Debord is after: "Ordures et décombres déballés à la sortie du film *In girum imus nocte et consumimur igni.*"[12] The cover page further states, not without irony: "from various authorized sources."

Like most of Champ Libre's books, the print quality was outstanding and the book appeared with the customary light-blue cover. An homage to the enemy: a public display of trash—clever, and a bit insane. There was no author's name indicated. Speech belonged to the enemy. There was no question of Debord confusing his with theirs. He was careful to make sure that even the title wasn't his. In fact, it was a *"détournement"* of a sign ("garbage and waste") visible in the street from Debord's apartment in Arles. More than ever, his "strategic" art was impersonal, and Debord was even less inclined to initiate a dialogue with the enemy or accept the least amount of criticism, or interpretation. Anyone who looked for it fell symbolically into the garbage cans visible from his windows, without any further discussion, without any explanation of their ultimate disgrace, regardless of their enthusiasm, admiration, contempt, or incomprehension of *In girum imus nocte.* Obviously, his biggest enthusiasts were the ones most disconcerted by this. They believed their unconditional acceptance would afford them a degree of *recognition* from Debord, that it would make them accomplices.[13] Obviously, they were wrong, because Debord never asked anything from them, least of all their agreement.

Considerations on an Assassination

It took the murder of Debord's friend, publisher, and producer, Gérard Lebovici, for him to abandon *poubellication* for a more conventional form of refutation. The attacks by the press to which he was subjected in the days after the murder affected him too *personally.* He was forced to abandon his silence as a unique historical figure and engage in a polemic. But that was not all. The *Comments on the Society of the Spectacle,* which appeared three years later, must also be understood in light of Lebovici's murder and the insinuations that followed. They give a more theoretical form to a response that the affair as a whole made necessary. But for the moment, Debord had to try to stop the most personal attacks: "Since I find myself, as much by nature as by the singular place I occupy in society and in contemporary history, very far removed from any kind of personal polemic, it would require something this unfortunate and despicable to draw me out of my habitual and disdainful silence, and to oblige me this time to 'answer a fool according to his own folly, lest he be wise in his own conceit.'"[1]

Debord met Gérard Lebovici in 1971, during the republication of *The Society of the Spectacle*, after having broken with his first publisher, Buchet-Chastel.[2] Born in 1932 (about the same time as Debord) into an Italian Jewish family, Lebovici was also a lost boy whose mother had been murdered in Auschwitz and whose father died from grief. Even as a young man he became an important figure in French cinema, where he was active first as an impresario, then as a producer and distributor.[3] The events of May 1968 and his left-wing sympathies turned him into something of an enigma, complacently described as such in the press at the time of his murder, which has yet to be solved.

It is hard to explain how a rich impresario and film producer wound up rubbing elbows with the radical left and becoming a publisher in the process. Through his involvement in the events of May 1968, Lebovici met Gérard Guégan, who suggested they start a libertarian publishing company. This turned out to be Champ Libre, which began in 1968 with the publication of a book by Guégan on the history of banditry in France. As a beginning, it does possess a certain piquancy, for at the time of Lebovici's death, the press speculated about a possible connection with the entourage of Jacques Mesrine, the ephemeral public enemy number one, whose book *L'instinct de mort* Champ Libre had just published. For the press, it was as if the publication of a history of banditry could only have one possible conclusion.

As a publisher and "sponsor of the far left," Lebovici met Debord in 1971, having learned that he was looking for a new home for *The Society of the Spectacle*. The two men soon became close friends. I place no faith in the claim that Lebovici was following Debord's orders, drawn in by his new friendships into some vaguely terrorist network that was both fatal and diabolical. It is clear, however, that the effect of their friendship radicalized not only Lebovici's political position but also his behavior. He began to adopt Debord's style, especially his pronounced and systematic use of the most unforgivable, the most cutting insults, at least when it came to the management of Champ Libre.

It's hard to measure Debord's influence on the history of Champ Libre.

He always refused to participate in any formal capacity, never went to their offices, and saw himself as a strictly private adviser. He also refused to assume any responsibility in Lebovici's 1974 decision to sack his employees (Gérard Guégan, Raphaël Sorin, Jean-Yves Guiomar, and Alain Le Saux), who assumed Debord had had a hand in their dismissal. Yet, it is certain that, after 1971, Lebovici gradually put Champ Libre at Debord's disposal. Debord clearly marked the publishing house with his style and his signature, made it his own, the way he had done earlier with the SI. The famous Champ Libre *Correspondance* is proof of this, as well as the house's editorial policy, and even more so its (anti)media policy. A publishing company that has no publicity department, that *asks nothing* of the press, and even had a tendency to silence the press, to deny it any authority, seems to have been custom-made for Debord.

From 1971 until his death, Lebovici was not only Debord's friend and the publisher of his books (as well as a number of texts related to the situationist movement and its history), but also the producer of his last three films.[4] But then Lebovici did something that was considered unacceptable on the part of a serious film producer. In 1983 he purchased a theater in the Latin Quarter to show only, and continuously, Debord's films. This was the famous Studio Cujas, which must have been the least profitable movie house in the history of French cinema. At the time, Lebovici was considered a kind of double of Debord. His generosity, coupled with their complicity, was seen as inexplicable, and highly suspect. It never occurred to those who felt it necessary to express an opinion on this mystery that Lebovici's attitude may have been based on the sense of gift giving that served as a kind of personal ethic for Debord. No one ever hypothesized that if the movie impresario was seduced by the revolutionary, if he admired him, he would do everything he could to be admired in turn, primarily by showing a heightened sense of potlatch, which he practiced in accordance with its principles, that is, with excess. Very few of those who had met Debord, few of those who wanted to move forward with him, were capable of any equivalent gesture. Lebovici published Debord's books, produced his films, including those that were never even made, gave him a theater, possibly even a publishing house. Given who he was, and his means, he must have felt this was appropriate, that it would satisfy Debord's challenge and his friendship for him. It was for this reason that Debord, after his friend's

murder and the subsequent uproar, decided to engage in a "potlatch of destruction" by withdrawing all his films from circulation. It was as if they
had belonged to Lebovici, as if they were now to be set aside for his grave.
An exemplary response given to a man who had been an exemplary friend:
Debord, officially a filmmaker, sacrificed nothing less than his entire body
of work for his friend, at least its most visible part, and the only part he
could remove from public view.

On March 5, 1984, Lebovici was ambushed in an underground parking
lot on Avenue Foch and shot several times. We still don't know his reason
for going there. The last piece of information we have is that he received a
phone call from Sabine Mesrine—or someone posing as her—the daughter of Jacques Mesrine. Naturally, the police investigated Mesrine, but the
investigation led nowhere, as was true of all the other leads. There was talk
of some obscure connection with the criminal underworld, bootleg videos,
and especially—and this is where Debord comes in—connections with the
European terrorist movement. To these various hypotheses, none of which
have ever been confirmed, should be added the "situationist" claim of his
assassination by the French secret service.[5] However, the press presented Lebovici's assassination as the murder of a man of mystery, the victim of some obscure plot. Reduced to rumor and speculation, journalists,
from across almost the entire political spectrum (ranging from *Minute* to
L'Humanité), focused on the most visible aspect of the story, at least the
one most openly acknowledged—his connection with Guy Debord, a man
who was himself sufficiently secretive to be highly suspect (if he led a clandestine life, he must have had something to hide). The press was unanimous in its finding: you can't have a mystery without a mystery man, just
as you can't have smoke without fire. And since the enigmatic Lebovici was
dead, it was his friend—his damned soul—who held the rope. The number of insinuations grew. The key to the mystery lay with the obscure and
Mephistophelean Debord and Lebovici's shady situationist acquaintances,
who were conveniently confused with terrorist causes by the media. After
that it was merely a short step to the assumption that the wealthy Lebovici
had been financing the Red Brigades (wasn't his wife Italian?), or "Action
Directe," or even German terrorists, finally being swept up in some deadly
plot. By the time he tried to extricate himself, it was too late. This was the
story maintained by the inimitable *France-Soir* (March 13, 1984):

Gérard Lebovici was, on the other hand, a very important provider of funds for certain ultra-leftist cliques, all under the sphere of influence of the "situationist" movement that came out of May 1968. . . . Why not imagine that this impresario-patron had suddenly desired to cut off or reduce the aid that he was going to give them? In such a case, this decision would have been greeted by anger, even violence by those affected. . . . Certain followers of the situationist movement have been very close to terrorist groups like "Direct Action," which for a long time has maintained very close ties with "Prima Linea," the Italian organization that was the rival to the Red Brigades. This is the infamous "Italian trail." In this vein, some people have pointed out that Madame Lebovici-Floriana is the daughter of a dental surgeon from Turin."[6]

The article is hardly surprising given that the press, in a democratic society, has astonishing leeway in printing pretty much what it wants. What's more, it's only a hypothesis ("Why not imagine . . ."). Le Monde sang the same refrain: Lebovici was supposedly "killed for having gained control of the situation, for having refused, just this once, what one was sure he would accept."[7] The only difference with *France-Soir* is that *Le Monde* abandoned the terrorist track to focus on the direct influence of Debord, who is supposed to have pushed Lebovici too far, especially vis-à-vis the movie industry, distancing himself more and more from "the norm that is socially acceptable for his professional milieu."[8] At this stage of such a scientific inquiry, it's hard to tell if Lebovici was murdered by Debord or by assassins on his payroll because he refused to cooperate, or by the "cinema milieu," which decided—almost legitimately—to put an end to his dangerous *dérive*. It didn't matter much because it was Debord who found himself accused, if not of being the murderer, at least of being the man responsible for the crime.

We could multiply the examples. The number of accusations and contradictory insinuations assembled by Debord in his *Considerations on the Assassination of Gérard Lebovici* is impressive. It was almost too easy for him not only to refute what the press was saying about him but to illustrate his claims about the practice of falsification at the heart of the system of the spectacle (three years later, this would be one of the key arguments of *Comments on the Society of the Spectacle*).

With his usual skill as a polemicist, he makes use of acid irony and scathing humor. It has been said of the *Considerations* that, in terms of Debord's theoretical works, it is a minor book, a resentful book by someone who had nothing more to say. Assuming this to be true, we still have to acknowledge that that "nothing" is especially brilliant here. However, why assume Debord wrote *Considerations* to say something, since it is so obvious that the book was written to *expose* enemy speech, to expose the lies, the spite, and the slander, and to refute them as well—to silence them?

With *Considerations on the Assassination of Gérard Lebovici,* Debord has written a book that functions like an amplifier, concentrating and accumulating, and will enable the enemy to see for itself the extent of its own falsehoods. "Never have so many false witnesses surrounded a man so obscure," he writes at the beginning of the book.[9] It is less an exercise in appropriation than one of commentary turned back on the source, and the exercise was no less *impersonal* than his other efforts, in spite of appearances. As was the case with *"Cette mauvaise réputation..."* (1993) and part of the projected *Ordures et décombres,* Debord accomplished here what so many writers dreamed of: no longer existing in the first but the third person, becoming a more or less legendary "he," a "nonperson," as the linguists say. That is why it is particularly inappropriate to reproach the writer he never wanted to be for having nothing to say. An elocutionary disappearance that has become real, an "I" really replaced by an Other, the abandonment of fictions and myths. Debord allows another to speak for him, an Other who is not fictional, who does not "write," who is not a writer, does not produce literature. And if his "I" returns, it certainly does not do so to claim that he is an Other, but, on the contrary, to attack that Other, to refute its gaze and deny it any authority.

Wherever the Other sees me, I must succeed in destroying it. Debord's way of reasoning would run something like that, and can help us understand his lack of interest in psychoanalysis (which has so often served as a theoretical imaginary or source of legitimation for the century's writers). Because the circumstances in which the *Considerations* were written are obviously not the first episode in this war between Debord and the world, this could be restated as: I am where the Other seeks to destroy me with false witnesses and false images because I have always removed myself from its gaze, because my singular work is to have succeeded in escaping it. I am, but only as a force of refutation and destruction of the Other's falsifying gaze. Here as elsewhere it is not a question of talking with the enemy, or getting him to recognize you by forcing him to acknowledge a more accurate image of yourself, but only of shutting him up. Proof of this comes in the form of Debord's reaction when he sued the newspapers for defamation and won: "The defamers were ordered to pay me a certain amount of money, and in addition to have published at their expense each one of these libel judgments in three newspapers of my choice. But I do not wish to choose any newspaper, finding them all of equal value. I do not have a better opinion of their readers, and I am not interested in rectifying their reports on me. The only thing that I could not allow this time was to let them say whatever they wanted."[10] Not to let them say whatever they wanted, force the enemy to remain silent. Beyond the suggestions of Debord's responsibility in Lebovici's murder, the attempts to photograph him at the time of the affair, already mentioned earlier, assume an emblematic value.[11] They illustrate, in a highly accurate manner, the strategy at work in this book:

> Dozens of photographers, in groups or individually, and even some cameramen, stationed themselves in front of my windows for several weeks, waiting to get a picture of me on the sly. It is comforting to note that all the time spent by these incompetents came to nothing, with only one exception—after months of trying, someone managed to get a blurry, and not very interesting silhouette taken through a telephoto lens by infiltrating the house next door. The photograph, coupled with some hateful commentary, was then published in *Paris-Match*.[12]

There are slanderers and there are photographers, and they are the same. Debord wrote *Considerations* to reduce the first to silence, and he published a photograph of himself to expose the derisive character of the photographic pursuit of celebrity. In general, it was a question of not giving a toehold to the gaze of the Other, to prevent a photograph from being taken, on the sly or otherwise; to remain in control of what one is by proffering one's own image, photographic if need be, to the fuzzy and lying images taken by the enemy. Such is the strategy described by Debord to get away from photojournalists, and it's also the strategy of the entire book. Presumably, in this way the reader is led far from considerations having an immediate relationship to the murder of Gérard Lebovici. The true "subject" of this book is, in the end, Debord himself, who, symbolically assassinated by the press, takes the place of his friend. In essence, it is about his singular battle with the rest of the universe, his refusal to appear, and his art of giving offense, the magnitude of which he reminds us of in this book: "I have succeeded in universally displeasing, and in a way that is always new."[13] To some extent, the two murders amount to the same thing, aside from the fact that Debord was harder to kill. The feeling of slippage is reinforced, or even inferred, by the fact that while he accumulated press excerpts about Lebovici's death, he selected the ones that concerned him most personally. I don't wish to deny the reality of the accusations to which Debord was subjected; however, we cannot reduce all of the press commentary about Lebovici's death to a defamation campaign against Debord. In this sense, Lebovici is again Debord's double, as was so often claimed when he (or Debord) was reproached for adopting his epistolary style and prejudices, or buying the movie theater, Studio Cujas. Lebovici may have been Debord's *agent*, but not in the way he worked as an agent for movie stars; from 1971 to 1984, he was identified not with directing but with implementing Debord's singular combat. It should not then be surprising that Debord also felt himself the target of the bullets fired in the parking garage on Avenue Foch, and it makes sense that he decided to leave for the countryside at this time.

It has been suggested that Lebovici's murder affected Debord so deeply that it served as a turning point in his life, the final turning point, the beginning of the end, that after the struggles conducted through Champ Libre, he was in some sense "finished," without illusions, without support, and with nothing else to say. No one has ever specified what the beginning of the end is supposed to mean, because the assumption of some "final failure" in the case of Debord is considered to be self-evident. But what failure are we talking about? Of what end was Lebovici's murder the beginning? And what about the books written after 1985, nearly half of Debord's written output? Has anyone ever really questioned the fact that Debord wrote more after his friend's death than ever before, or that he was never so much a writer as he was in those last years of his life? I admit I have difficulty viewing this as a failure of some kind, except, of course, in the sense of making Debord responsible for the disappearance of a revolutionary perspective on a global scale.

Against Interpretation

Far from being a minor work, *Considerations on the Assassination of Gérard Lebovici* is one of the finest examples of the strategy of refutation. Debord made use of it again in 1993 when he wrote *"Cette mauvaise réputation . . ."*. This time the refutation is explicitly directed at general criticisms of Debord. The book is not tied to any specific event, as in the Lebovici affair, and does not try to disqualify public criticism about a specific work, as with the *Refutation of All Judgments*. Debord now responds, point by point, citing at length the most important articles ("the most shocking examples," he calls them) that appeared about him and his work between 1988 and 1992. His response is designed to show their inanity and falsity. Debord again reviews his past behavior, as if enthralled by the displeasing image he has worked so hard to produce, fascinated by the hated "he" he has so well succeeded in becoming for others. Between him and his critics, there is without doubt a complicit temperamental incompatibility. It's a war that had been going on for a long time and will continue until the end of time, and *"Cette mauvaise réputation . . ."* is the final scene.

Between 1988 and 1992—and this is one of the reasons Debord again made use of the technique—his situation, his image, had changed considerably. After roughly ten years of relative silence, which he broke only to attack his enemies at the time of the Lebovici affair, he published, one after the other, two books that received considerable attention. *Comments on the Society of the Spectacle* (1988) and *Panegyric* (1989) mark Debord's return on the "intellectual scene."[1] He had never before received so much recognition or been as popular. His notoriety now extended beyond the pro-situationist milieu, which did not always take kindly to no longer being his exclusive audience. Moreover, Debord was beginning to be thought of as a writer rather than a "man of politics." The moment of recognition had arrived, and with it the time for commentary. The change of status was confirmed by his change of publisher, now Gallimard, about which rivers of ink have been spilled.[2] In other words, and as the Lebovici affair shows, the production of misleading and deceptive speech was on the rise and was intolerable, both in principle and especially because so much of it was malicious. That someone might be proud of his art of giving offense, that he might accept the bad reputation he had been saddled with is one thing, but that's no reason he should forgo aggravating it by refuting the judgments of those who *created* that reputation for him. In fact, the failure to rebuff them could be seen as an authorization to continue to make such judgments. Debord stuck to his bad reputation in every sense of the word. Proof of this can be found in the fact that the book contains only unfavorable articles and carefully omits the most praiseworthy judgments (those of Sollers, for one, who, moreover, is referred to only in the most ambiguous terms, for comments that appeared in *L'Humanité*: "In the November 5, 1992, issue of *L'Humanité*, . . . some flattering comments were made about me. But these are unimportant because they were made by Philippe Sollers").[3] Just as the Lebovici affair became, as far as Debord was considered, a personal matter, the comments he reproduced in *"Cette mauvaise réputation . . ."* transform the criticism of Debord's work into a systematic act of accusation and falsification.

"Cette mauvaise réputation . . ." follows the same principles as Debord's previous books. Here too he appears—one last time—as a man who rejects any allegiance to the gaze of the Other, any recognition of and by the Other. Moreover, it is significant that this was the only "previously unpublished" book by Debord to be published by Gallimard. It was as if, having entered the central bank of French literature, and now recognized as a writer, Debord did everything he could to exhaust his symbolic capital as quickly as possible, so he would not have to live up to any possible expectations as an author. He published a book consisting, for the most part, of other people's comments, based on a process that even for him wasn't original (it was basically the same procedure he had used for *Considerations*). It was disappointing, and many commentators were disappointed. This time, they claimed, Debord really had nothing left to say. *"Cette mauvaise réputation . . ."* is such a truly disappointing book that its critics nearly overlooked the unforgivable co-optation of such a mediocre author by Gallimard.

But how could they recognize someone who had never identified with anyone but himself, who had never competed with anyone, as he explicitly stated?[4] Debord never compared himself to or subjugated himself to anyone, there was never any common standard between himself and others. *"Cette mauvaise réputation . . ."* is based on the same idea of singularity and, if you like, of infallibility as his previous "autobiographical" books: "I am certain that everything I did was for the best," he writes, and he still refuses to make the slightest concession.[5] And if he is certain, it's because, given who he is, he couldn't have done otherwise ("I" is certainly not an Other): "On the other hand, I feel it was, in a way, impossible for me to fail, since, unable to do anything else, I did what I had to do."[6] This self-fulfilling belief is true of *The Society of the Spectacle*. Throughout the book, Debord is one with his major work. A quarter of a century later, he feels that the book still responds to the requirement of not being visibly false and, at the same time, being completely unacceptable; therefore it is still nearly perfect: "A book capable of responding simultaneously to 'these two requirements' seemed to me, for the most part, flawless. Those who refused to accept the book deceived themselves. And I don't see how else I could have done any better, given who I am."[7]

"Given who I am." It is these words, with which Debord concluded his refutation of his reputation, that the press continued to harp on. I did what I did, I said what I had to say, I won't change a comma; likewise, I am what I am, my image belongs to me. "What need do they have to 'portray' me? Haven't I, in my writing, provided the best portrait that could ever be made, assuming there was even the slightest necessity for the portrait in question?"[8] These are the terms of this final act of refutation, the final challenge, which seems to me no different from those that preceded it. Debord addressed the most direct attacks, as well as the most elaborate interpretations. He reaffirms (if we follow his arguments in the order in which he presents them) his intent not to "succeed," his indifference to power—including the power that supposedly forced him to maintain his obscurity or clandestinity, the power he would have had as the "leader" of a party (a power he would not have made good use of)—his interest in "style" or language, his lack of interest in work and money, his love of freedom, his desire to live the way he wanted, his role in the battles fought by the Situationist International, and so on. He defends himself against the charge of having published under a pseudonym, refutes the claim that he was "paranoid," and attacks, at length, Gérard Guégan's recollection in his memoirs of the reissue of *The Society of the Spectacle* by Champ Libre, while ironically conceding that he spoke truthfully on one point, namely, that in 1992 he was sixty years old. Finally, we learn that he is an expert in the trafficking and exhibition of fake Chinese antiques, and relatively unenthusiastic about the new world order that followed the fall of the Berlin Wall. From Bosnia to Walesa, Iraq to Yeltsin, and from Algeria to the televised landing in Mogadishu, this order not only demonstrated who he was, but also the validity of Debord's theses, whose relevance we continue to challenge.

Debord's point about all this never changes: he continues to refuse to talk to the enemy. Knowing this, it's easier to understand his bias in what is presented as an act of self-defense and accusation, why he omits anything that would be to his advantage, anything by which he would succeed in being pleasant. His word does not need to be interpreted. It says what it says, it says who he is. Interpreting it, commenting on it rather than drawing the obvious conclusions, is to refuse to listen, it's the beginning step in going over to the side of the enemy. Even in *Considerations on the Assassination of Gérard Lebovici,* he concluded with a claim that must—it's now or never—be taken at face value: "I do not think I am as 'enigmatic' as they like to say. I even believe that I am at times easy to understand."[9] How can we understand Debord? We need to take him at his word. There is nothing equivocal about him, nothing enigmatic, and therefore nothing to interpret. From this point of view, any interpretation is parasitic, in both senses of the word: it interferes with clarity, with the purity of a meaning that is easy to understand for anyone who wants to understand it, and it is a form of appropriation. Anyone who comments on Debord's work does so to enhance his own standing rather than to draw the inevitable conclusions of what he has read. His offense is to assume that Debord's work is literature.

Here, we are at the heart of a certain relationship to discourse or speech, for neither *Considerations on the Assassination of Gérard Lebovici* nor *"Cette mauvaise réputation . . ."* is a minor work; on the contrary, they are symptomatic. Debord's writing has the fervor of immediacy. Not only must recognition of and by the Other not occur through images, which are always misleading, but it must not occur through writing either, which is just as misleading once we acknowledge its interpretability. At least this was the case with the public Debord, the person he chose to become in his books and films. We must not give speech the opportunity to become part of an imaginary, part of a falsifying interpretation. We must act immediately or, to be more precise, speech must no longer serve as an act of mediation, but as an immediate act carried out by precipitating speech as pure effect. Speech is not made for dialogue but to *cut,* to be immediately understood, to encourage a second immediacy not only with respect to its content but also with respect to the consequences to be drawn—or it should be rejected at once. The passion of immediacy is the passion for passion, it assumes either absolute complicity (the complicity of warriors as well as lovers) or the refutation and destruction of the Other—war, in other words.

Based on this relationship to speech, a *poetics of invective* could be deduced. Its natural terrain would include reviews, pamphlets, posters, as well as *open* letters. It becomes increasingly clear, with the gradual publication of Debord's correspondence, that many of his letters are friendly, warm, and generous. Few of them resemble his published letters, which reveal a rich sense of invective and are obviously not intended to attenuate his bad reputation.

The letter is a preferred medium for disavowal and invective, providing it is published. It is initially conceived as open (even though it may take time before this happens). Its bite is greater when it has been published, when it brings to public attention something that should have remained private. It cancels the Other, the person to whom the letter was initially addressed, by "denouncing" him publicly, generally without the recipient's awareness. It indicates a refusal or interruption of any possibility of dialogue. Having received an accusatory letter, there is nothing to say, nothing to repeat. The letter cuts like a knife, is unacceptable. The only possible response is another thrust of the knife, wound for wound. The charm and effectiveness of this technique can be verified in the two volumes of Champ Libre's *Correspondance,* in which Debord was involved in more than the obvious sense.[10] [These should not be confused with the five volumes of Debord's correspondence, published by Fayard. Champ Libre published two volumes of its own correspondence, which included letters by Debord, Lebovici, and others.—*Trans.*]

Many of the letters, not all of which are polemical, were indeed written by Debord (to Gianfranco Sanguinetti, Jaime Semprun, or Georges Kiejman), although this is far from self-evident in the case of a publishing house such as Champ Libre, whose relationship with Debord was supposedly only amicable and professional. A number of old scores were settled through these letters, Debord's naturally, but they were supported with admirable solidarity by Gérard Lebovici. Finally, even Lebovici's letters, in which Debord is not the main subject, relate to him stylistically, through the use of a form of insult that is no longer novel. Here, too, Lebovici is indeed Debord's spokesman. Some commentators have gone so far as to claim that Lebovici's letters were, if not written by Debord, at least dictated, inspired, or suggested by him, while others (including one Julien Loiseau, whose book Lebovici had summarily refused to publish), experts in the poetics of invective, claim to see marked differences between the two styles, as shown by the following letter: "I can see that you make free use of such contempt, believing you are imitating the great Debord in doing so. You lack his verve and literary style. Nor do you possess his foresight, and, to be perfectly honest, you have never participated in any International. And if you really knew how to read, as you would have people believe, you would realize that although Debord often made use of invective, he never made use of contempt, even less toward his enemies than toward anyone else."[11]

It was the supreme insult: you are not as good as Debord at giving offense. Should we believe Julien Loiseau's claim that Lebovici wrote as Debord dictated? We could resolve the contradiction by deciding that Lebovici was not a good copyist, or that Julien Loiseau lacked perspicacity, as shown in the same letter: "I would be surprised if you were to publish this letter in volume 2 of *Correspondance,* a book that the world proletariat will continue to wait for, undoubtedly. At least you won't be able to toy with me like an actor in your play, and you should let the readers content themselves with something duller." Unless Loiseau, as a clever strategist, was writing specifically so that what he wrote would appear in volume 2: after all, being known as an enemy of Lebovici or Debord was an enviable position. In any case, it was a status, a job in what Loiseau perspicuously describes as a "play," or spectacle, one of the most entertaining spectacles produced by the far left (which is rarely very entertaining).

These were some of the charms of vituperative correspondence. You could play the role of the enemy alongside a handful of stars (the singer Renaud, Patrick Manchette, Georges Kiejman, Christian Bourgois, Yves Florenne) and a large number of (former) regulars (Gérard Guégan, Mustapha Khayati, Jaime Semprun, Jacques Baynac). Some excelled in death threats (primarily Paolo Salvadori, who also made use of a certain degree of violence in monitoring the fate of Debord's work in Italy). Lebovici himself was characterized by his lightning-fast return of service (or offers of service), which generally arrested any further exchanges, while Debord's specialty was a patiently constructed correspondence, the slow but irreversible destabilization of the adversary, who discovers, much too late, that he is playing—and losing—the game.

Debord's work consisted essentially in a form of speech that deflected any form of interpretation, or any response at all, for that matter, like a shouted insult, asking nothing more than its own realization, or its dissolution in a common struggle (this was the fate of the SI in particular). This could be said to be the heart of Debord's oeuvre and is what makes it uncertain that such an oeuvre exists. The desire for immediacy that animates his work carries it beyond itself, precipitates it into a kind of idleness ("Never work!"). It starts from a refusal to create a body of work, to leave traces, to provide something to read or see; it presents itself as pure action, exists here and now, an ephemeral movement on the surface of the river. Which is why we can say that situationism was essentially Debord's oeuvre become act, that situationism was an enactment—among other things—of *Debord*'s desire for immediacy. Proof comes in the form of the almost total silence observed by those who were Debord's accomplices at the time. It was as if they knew only too well that situationism had relied upon the enactment of Debord's trenchant speech. Because they all (or nearly all) had, one day or another, been skewered by it, they were forced to remain silent. It is significant that in a book such as *"Cette mauvaise réputation ..."*, intended to refute the judgment of his enemies, Debord also cautioned, as if in passing, those of his former companions who risked interpreting or describing their situationist past: "Two or three imposters below the threshold of the media have sometimes claimed they knew me then, but naturally they had nothing to say. For myself, I had nothing to say in return to them, preferring instead to attack someone authentic who one day dared try his hand at the game. None of those whose names have appeared in *I.S.* have ever clearly exposed anything since then."[12] Situationism was built around the acceptance of bellicose speech, which disqualified in advance any commentary that was not as cutting, any observations, any historical consideration implying a different viewpoint.

From this perspective, it is interesting to see how situationist historiography has developed. The *Histoire de l'Internationale situationniste* by Jean-François Martos, for example, strictly limits itself to existing documents, to what are called, and for good reason, *instruments*.[13] Martos does not provide any commentary for the documents, never attempts to interpret them. He limits himself to providing simple paraphrases to connect the documents, which are presented chronologically—a nearly unending repetition of what had been said in *Potlatch* and in *Internationale situationniste,* in Debord's books, even in the first works of situationist historiography, such as René Viénet's *Enragés et situationnistes dans le mouvement des occupations,* concerning the events of May 1968.[14] "Nothing will remain without being uttered," wrote Mallarmé. The situationist history assumes that nothing other than insults will remain, and also that there is nothing else to add, nothing to say about what has been said. If more needs to be said, if Martos's *Histoire de l'internationale situationniste* is needed, as Viénet's and a few other books were, it is primarily to refute the enemy's version of the same events, so that there is no further confusion between the authentic revolutionary movement of May 1968, in which the situationists took part, like fish to water, and the spectacular and petit bourgeois student agitation with which nearly everyone blindly identified. Situationist historiography exists to denounce false witnesses and not to explain an event or series of events, as would be the case with traditional historiography. Here, too, the problem is not one of comprehension. In its situationist version, history is not more enigmatic or difficult to understand than a book by Debord, and, like his books and films, exists only for those who understand and have chosen sides. It actively participates in this choice, serves as a battleground, just one act among the many other acts and deeds it evokes to ensure its self-creation and the continuation of combat. Its truth is the truth of the revolutionary desire it seeks to embody, a desire that ignores the existence of opposing arguments or different points of view. It is a truth that ignores even the most rudimentary argumentation. The lack of nuance in situationist historiography is the result of its revolutionary purity. Like Debord, the revolution does not exist to please or convince its adversaries of the academic honorability of the discourse that describes it. And anyone who finds fault with Viénet's or Martos's books, those who reproach them for their lack of objectivity or lack of information, or even their lack of culture, do so in bad faith. By not limiting themselves to what has taken place, the critics reveal their wish that the past had been otherwise, they reveal their counterrevolutionary intent.

The letter Debord wrote to Martos when Martos sent him the completed manuscript for his *Histoire de l'internationale situationniste* is, in this sense, important. Debord suggested one or two "reformulations" and asked Martos to correct some quotes that he had reported incorrectly (or were incorrectly attributed). However, he did not offer any comments, any arguments, any interpretation, for the simple reason that Martos's "history" didn't offer any; it merely reaffirmed the point of view adopted by the SI: "Aside from this, I feel everything is correct. There is nothing to add. To use a Latin phrase: *Nihil obstat. Ergo: imprimatur.*"[15] Since Martos hadn't added anything, Debord wouldn't either, and would give his imprimatur (which is difficult to contest), leaving a good number of readers perplexed. But what else was a spectacular reader for? What would be the point in telling him everything or explaining everything?

Nothing to add, nothing to question, nothing to interpret concerning anything I have done or said. Twenty-five years after its appearance (and virtually much more), *The Society of the Spectacle* is still a "faultless book." Not even a comma needs to be changed, and anyone who attempts the slightest modification would immediately pay the price: like Buchet in 1971, when it tried to add a subtitle, or like the many translators who were regularly and publicly discredited by Debord, as in the "Preface" to the fourth Italian edition of *The Society of the Spectacle* (1979). He criticized the translations of his books in the harshest terms and it appears that he occasionally had his "good" translators do the work for him. Complaining about all the bad translations of his book, he wrote, concerning the Italian versions:

> There was nothing worse than the situation in Italy, where, in 1968, the publisher De Donato issued the most monstrous [translation] of all, which has only been partially improved upon by the two rival translations that followed. Moreover, Paolo Salvadori, having gone to find those responsible for this excess in their of-fices, struck them and literally spat in their faces, for this is naturally the way good translators act when they meet bad ones. It suffices to say that the fourth Italian translation, which is by Salvadori, is excellent.[16]

How do we recognize a good translator? By his ability to punch a bad one and spit in his face. Translators are divided into two camps, like everyone else, for that matter, and they demonstrate their excellence by striking the enemy, namely, translators who misrepresent. Beware those who allow themselves the least interpretation, the slightest deviation from a book as unassailable as *The Society of the Spectacle*: "There is not a word to be changed in this book in which, apart from three or four typographic mistakes, nothing has been corrected in the course of the dozen or so reprints it has known in France."[17] How is it possible to translate without changing a word? By slugging anyone who makes such changes, who is nothing but a spokesperson for those who are unable to read, for those unable to understand, to whom *The Society of the Spectacle* is not even *addressed*. You are not my audience, Debord says. The revolution confines discourse to a two-fold bind: "As a matter of fact, I believe that there is nobody in the world capable of being interested in my book apart from those who are enemies of the existing social order and who act efficaciously, starting from this position."[18] Are you one of those who does not understand *The Society of the Spectacle* or finds fault with it, although it is without fault, and nothing is easier to understand? You are mistaken if you believe the book is intended for you; you are wrong in taking yourself for an Italian worker instead of the enemy:

> On the other hand, to my knowledge it is in the factories of Italy that this book has found for the moment its best readers. The workers of Italy—who can be held up as an example to their comrades in all countries for their absenteeism, their wildcat strikes that no particular concession can manage to appease, their lucid refusal of work, and their contempt for the law and for all Statist parties—know the subject well enough by practice to have been able to benefit from the theses of *The Society of the Spectacle,* even when they read nothing but mediocre translations of them.[19]

Debord's information on the struggles in Italy may have come from Gianfranco Sanguinetti. Sanguinetti, in the letter that would lead to the break between the two friends (because of his refusal to explain his hedging on the question of terrorism), goes on at some length concerning what was known as "the first Strasbourg of the factories" in Italy. "Situationist workers" had caused the Motta and Alemagna food manufacturers to go bankrupt, first through a series of wildcat strikes, then by making public the actual content of their food products, and, as if that was not enough, by publicly declaring that they would piss and spit in the manufactured products or encourage the other workers to multiply the number of days they called in sick. Finally, they demanded extravagant indemnities when they were fired, these being calculated on the basis of the damage they could have caused in the following three months if they had remained on the job.[20]

The question arises, then, of why—or for whom—a fourth, finally excellent, translation of *The Society of the Spectacle* was made. Certainly not for petit bourgeois intellectuals, who would have no better understanding of it than of the earlier versions, because they didn't want to understand and because it wasn't intended for them in the first place. But nor was it made for the Italian workers, since they had already begun to act, since even the most mediocre, the most "monstrous" translations were sufficient for them to piss on Motta's *panettone.* So it's reasonable to doubt whether they needed to read Debord to be situationists. The best reader is still someone who has no need for the book, someone who is a situationist by nature, who understands before the book exists, who grasps the sense *before* it's correctly transmitted. The literal meaning on which Debord insists is not the literal meaning understood by linguists and philologists. It is a meaning that exists *prior* to itself, which is already there, in spite of the imperfections and falsifications of the translations, to the extent that one is situated within the perspective of revolution. The true literal meaning is the revolutionary meaning. Similarly, we can say that Debord has always addressed himself to an earlier reader, capable of understanding so quickly that he can do without reading. The real reader of *The Society of the Spectacle* is ahead of the book that is intended for him, in advance of it, as if he had already read it.[21] This anteriority of the reader is, paradoxically, what ensures such a book its posterity. Being fault-free and irrefutable, it will continue to be, if not read for all eternity, then at least until the next revolution, contrary to nearly all other books, which are ephemeral effects of the spectacle: "I flatter myself on being one of the very rare contemporary examples of someone who has written without being immediately contradicted by events, and I do not mean contradicted a hundred or a thousand times, like the others, but not once. I have no doubt that all my theses will continue to be confirmed until the end of the century and even beyond."[22]

The Society of the Spectacle is beyond criticism, it is a book in which everything that needs to be said has been said. It is *the* book, or the Book, Debord's version of the old dream of the total book that would contain the world, a book encompassing the world. Comprised by the book in every sense of the word, it is the world itself that becomes the commentary on the book—in fact, the only one possible (although not necessary). From now on, the world is nothing but the writing of the pages that are still missing, but anticipated, from *The Society of the Spectacle*:

> In fact, it fell on spectacular society itself to add something this book, I believe, had no need of: stronger and more convincing proofs and examples. We have been able to witness the falsification, like a sticky fog that accumulates along the ground of everyday existence, thicken and descend, down to the fabrication of the most trivial things. We have witnessed the technological and police control of men and natural forces aspire to the absolute, including "telematic" madness, a control whose mistakes are growing as quickly as its means. We have witnessed the State lie develop in itself and for itself, having so well forgotten its uneasy link with truth and plausibility that it can forget and replace itself from hour to hour.[23]

The Society of the Spectacle is *the* book not only because it says everything, but because it's a book that, once become reality in the world, will ultimately be the work of everyone, as Mallarmé and Lautréamont had hoped. There would no longer be a need for Debord the author, no need for him to add or remove anything. The society of the spectacle itself will do the work, it will continue indefinitely to write the missing chapters, it will itself serve as the truest commentary and the most infinite. Increasing falsification will confirm that with *The Society of the Spectacle* everything has been said once and for all, especially when falsification affects the text itself or its author.

It is often said—often for the wrong reasons or out of ignorance—that Debord was a one-book writer (clearly, with *The Society of the Spectacle* in mind). Obviously, this is wrong in the sense we would ordinarily understand the statement, which is more a symptom than anything else. It's true that there is at the heart of Debord's work something like a "Book effect" (a will to totality, to say everything, to pack everything into a single book), which is embodied in *The Society of the Spectacle.* That is why this book has continued, ever since its publication, to produce the effects we are familiar with. And Debord has been content to manage those effects, repeat them, intensify them in all his book and films. Paradoxically, it is because he wrote other books, which reaffirmed that everything had been said and that there was nothing more to say, that Debord may have become a one-book writer.[24]

Shadows, Secrets, and Mirrors

The *Préface à la quatrième édition italienne de "La Société du spectacle"* was reissued in 1992 by Gallimard along with *Commentaires sur la société du spectacle,* published for the first time in 1988 by Champ Libre. There is nothing accidental about the choice of publisher, which certainly had Debord's approval. The progress of spectacular power, whose description appears in the *Comments,* was already announced in 1979, primarily in the excerpt from the preface to the fourth Italian edition cited earlier. More generally, with *Comments on the Society of the Spectacle,* Debord wrote his most "Italian," his most "Florentine" book, and therefore it was only logical to republish this preface, which in many respects is a first version of the book.

Why Italian? Because at the heart of the description of the progress made by spectacular power, we find the ineffable P2 group (Potere Due), that is, the attempt to create a secret, parallel Italian government, presented by Debord as a model of all forms of modern government. Italy therefore has the privilege (with France) of being in the forefront of the integrated spectacle, the synthesis of two older forms of the spectacle described in *The Society of the Spectacle*: the diffuse spectacle of capitalist democracies, of which the United States is the model, and the concentrated spectacle of fascist or Stalinist dictatorships. Why Florentine? Because the essence of the integrated spectacle is to have succeeded in establishing a completely *fallacious* universe, in which lies, falsehoods, perjury, the tactical use of rumors and disinformation, secret services, plots, and even assassinations can be multiplied with complete impunity, as in Renaissance Florence.

The end of democracy and a return to Machiavellian tyranny, not to the spectacular dictatorships of old but to a world of obscure intrigue, one characteristically Florentine: power does not come from the barrel of a gun but in a vial of poison, preferably invisible and radioactive. For Debord, we have entered the era of generalized secrecy, unchallenged falsehood, and the perpetual present. It's a world from which all truth, all memory (and with it all history), even all speech have been banished. "All usurpers have shared this aim: to make us forget that *they have only just arrived,*" he wrote.[1] They work to erase history, to promote false witnesses in the media and elsewhere, to ignore opinion and public debate, to create not only widespread amnesia but illiteracy and aphasia as well. Soon, thanks to improvements in computer technology, no one will be able to read, judge, interpret, or even talk.[2]

It was already known that spectacular power was capable of causing the disappearance of towns and communities, and of using sophisticated methods of exploitation. Now, it promotes itself as the essence of communication, if not the essence of humanity. It destroys speech and its celebration in the art of conversation, which has been replaced by the omnipresent "language of the spectacle." This now constitutes the only choice individuals have, condemned to sacrifice their individuality, their personality, their singularity: "He will essentially follow the language of the spectacle, for it is the only one he is familiar with."[3] The world described by Debord is a dehumanized world in which speech, with its dialectic of truth and lies, has been replaced by a semblance of speech that is all lies, a world in which one lie hides another, in a process of infinite regress. It is made of trompe l'oeil and pretense. Manipulation is absolute, which assumes that those who govern are themselves manipulated by others, who are themselves manipulated in turn, without their awareness, and on and on. The political scene consists of puppets manipulated by other puppets manipulated by other puppets, who will always remain invisible.

This was the reason behind the lamentable coup attempt by Colonel Tejero in Spain in 1981: "Often domination will protect itself by *false attacks*, whose media coverage covers up the true operation. Such was the case with the bizarre assault on the Spanish Cortes by Tejero and his civil guards in 1981, whose failure had to hide another more modern, that is to say more disguised *pronunciamento*, which succeeded."[4] What more modern and hidden *pronunciamento* is Debord talking about here? The strengthening of democracy in Spain following the coup attempt? The fact that Spain became shortly after a social democracy and did not relapse into civil war? Did Felipe González manipulate Tejero to prevent the imminent triumph of the revolution, and by what obscure forces was he manipulated? It is easy to get lost in the swirl of conjecture, but that may be precisely what power wants.

The model or emblem of the era of the integrated spectacle would, of course, be the Mafia. The epoch was decidedly Italian: "The Mafia is not an outsider in this world; it is perfectly at home. Indeed, in the integrated spectacle it stands as the model of all advanced commercial enterprises."[5] Or the secret services—another kind of mafia—which cannot simply be reduced to the official secret services used by governments. It could even be said that their only function is to dissimulate the "true" secret services, primarily by spectacularly bungling certain operations, as the French secret service brilliantly succeeded in doing in the *Rainbow Warrior* affair (1985).[6] There are many secret services, they are part of the state, but they are also private. Because they are, by definition, secret, it is impossible to know who belongs to them, which amounts to saying that everyone is part of them, in one way or another. We are all secret agents, we all work, the majority of the time without realizing it, at promoting the obscure triumph of spectacular power, which ensures our collaboration by sharing certain false confidences with us, specifically created for the occasion. The secret services are sometimes accomplices and sometimes rivals, sometimes they defend the same interests, sometimes they do not. Sometimes they don't even know what interests they are defending, becoming, like all of us, the victims of the absence of memory and historical knowledge that characterizes modern states: "To this list of the triumphs of power we should, however, add one result which has proved negative: once the running of a state involves a permanent and massive shortage of historical knowledge, that state can no longer be led strategically."[7]

This deficit of memory resulted from a very important reversal of perspective. It could be said that *Comments on the Society of the Spectacle* postulates an unrepresentable enemy.[8] That's certainly true, but it constitutes merely the first step in the analysis and the mechanism set up by Debord. For if the enemy has become invisible, the enemy of the enemy has as well. From one point of view, spectacular power triumphs, it is omnipresent, and all the more so because it is invisible. But from another point of view, this triumph is blind. It doesn't realize that its own enemy, far from seeking invisibility and clandestinity, has simply ceased to exist. Or, although it may realize this, it produces false enemies, such as "terrorists," but also theoreticians, as if to prevent the real enemies from returning:

> Its principal present contradiction, finally, is that it is spying on, infiltrating and pressuring *an absent entity*: that which is supposed to be trying to subvert the social order. But where can it actually be seen at work? Certainly conditions have never been so seriously revolutionary, but it is only governments who think so. Negation has been so thoroughly deprived of its thought that it was dispersed long ago. Because of this it remains only a vague, yet highly disturbing threat, and surveillance in its turn has been deprived of its preferred field of activity. Surveillance and intervention are thus rightly led by the present exigencies determining their terms of engagement to operate on the very terrain of this threat in order to combat it *in advance*. This is why surveillance has an interest in organizing poles of negation itself, which it can instruct with more than the discredited means of the spectacle, so as to manipulate, not terrorists this time, but theories.[9]

There has been much discussion over the past few years over whether the theory of revolution found in *The Society of the Spectacle* is still relevant, and very well-reasoned arguments have been proposed to show that it isn't, or never was, or has become obsolete through the emergence of new communications technologies. There is obviously much less talk about what a theory of revolution adapted to the contemporary world should look like. This is probably why one of the fundamental arguments in *Comments on the Society of the Spectacle* is so rarely mentioned: while the conditions *are* revolutionary, given the number of means available to the world's leaders to destroy humanity, the *perspective* of revolution has completely disappeared. Negativity has disappeared, the power structure no longer has any enemies, which means that it has to create its own, usually in the form of romantic red brigades and mild-mannered theorists who write doctorates on subversion. This is the integrated spectacle, from which nothing escapes. Debord was aware of this, and after trying not only to conceptualize but to make revolution, he became, in a sense, the theorist of its absence. And this makes him especially unbearable to those today who make revolution their theoretical stock-in-trade.

Was Debord a theorist of a now impossible revolution? He was probably no more a theoretician than he was twenty years earlier, and *Comments on the Society of the Spectacle* serves as a complex mechanism containing at least a third stage, in which it is Debord himself who returns, in his singularity. War is now made with the assistance of phantom secret services, the enemy itself becomes a ghost, and consequently war a kind of game. "This struggle is also a game," wrote Debord:[10] invisible secret services against equally invisible enemies, this is what the integrated spectacle has become. Obviously, the cards it deals are marked and transform the world into a vast illusion. The only true enemy, the only one who doesn't play the game, is Debord himself, who does not fail to remind us who he is and that he is alone. No one but him could have written his *Comments*:

> An anti-spectacular notoriety has become something extremely rare. I myself am one of the last people to retain one, having never had any other. But it has also become extraordinarily suspect. Society has officially declared itself to be spectacular. To be known outside spectacular relations is already to be known as an enemy of society. . . .
>
> These *Comments* may one day serve in the writing of a history of the spectacle, without any doubt the most important event to have occurred this century, and the one for which the fewest explanations have been ventured. In other circumstances, I think I could have considered myself altogether satisfied with my first work on this subject, and left others to consider future developments. But in the present situation, it seemed unlikely that anyone else would do it.[11]

Concerning the *Comments*, Debord has been criticized for falling into Epimenides' paradox: since a property of the integrated spectacle is that it is totalizing, if not totalitarian, no one could take advantage of the extraterritoriality needed to criticize it.[12] Yet it is precisely this right of extraterritoriality that Debord assumes, which is what gives his *Comments* their singularity and beauty: they engage us in an untenable discourse, unjustifiable, or at least unjustified, whose authority is self-generated. And given the fragility and unverifiable nature of some of his hypotheses (the one concerning Tejero's *pronunciamento,* for example, or that of the "assembly-line production" of assassinations shown by the murders of Kennedy, Aldo Moro, and Olof Palme), we may ask if this isn't the crux of the matter: the gradual development of a position of extraterritoriality, an unassailable position about which, once again, there is nothing more to say. It's important to remember that the *Comments* are nearly contemporary with *Panegyric* (which appeared a year later), making them two sides of the same strategy of refutation of the Other (of the enemy), of the same search for singularity. In *Panegyric,* Debord became an impenetrable fortress against the Other, whose gaze is refuted in advance and in principle. He becomes someone who will have done his utmost to offend humanity and withdraw from it. In the *Comments,* he becomes the pure gaze directed from without at the enemy's empty fortress: a destructive gaze that undoes all the trompe l'oeil of the enemy in question, that sees it in its invisibility, that pulverizes like a laser beam its gimcrack house of cards and reveals its absence of humanity.

The Debord of the *Comments* became humanity itself; he swallowed the world, was the last man, the only one who did not lie in a universe marked by complete dishonesty, the only one who knew how to write, read, interpret the world, and speak a language other than the language of the spectacle. To reproach him for his affection for extraterritoriality or the unverifiability of his arguments is to have misunderstood his book. This extraterritoriality is something he claims, a challenge that is comparable in every respect to the one he advanced a year later in *Panegyric.* And in the dehumanized world he describes, it's hard to see who might be authorized to verify his arguments. All the same, we can assume that with the elements of logic and philosophy at his disposal, Debord must have realized that he had *proved* nothing. For in doing so, in trying to prove his claims, he would have had to accept the rules for speech and dialogue, seek out the consent of the Other, recognize it or recognize its right to review the arguments he had developed. Such recognition was no more relevant to the *Comments* than to any of his other books. Because the world was divided into two camps (even if the combatants had become invisible), roughly half the readers of the book could be placed in the enemy camp, with whom there could never be any question of dialogue. The ironically low figure for the number

STRATEGY | 263

of anticipated readers confirms the fact that the *Comments* were not made
to be read any more than they attempted to prove anything:

> These *Comments* are sure to be welcomed by fifty or sixty people, a large number
> given the times in which we live and the gravity of the matters under discussion.
> But then, of course, in some circles I am considered to be an authority. It must
> also be borne in mind that a good half of this interested elite will consist of people
> who devote themselves to maintaining the spectacular system of domination,
> and the other half of people who persist in doing quite the opposite. Having,
> then, to take account of readers who are both attentive and diversely influential,
> I obviously cannot speak with complete freedom. Above all, I must take care not
> to give too much information to just anybody.[13]

There was no reason to write verifiable arguments. Those who wanted to
destroy the domination of the spectacle understood in advance what was at
stake, and to supply others—his enemies—with proof of his claims would
be an amateurish mistake for someone as adept at strategy as Debord. The
first, and most elementary, rule was obviously to avoid showing your hand
to your opponent, to avoid giving away too much information. The second consisted in making use of the enemy's weapons, turning them against
him, which Debord did exceedingly well. To the totalitarianism of spectacular domination he presented a discourse that was equally totalizing. He
condemned the whole world, without allowing the least opportunity for
a response, and he made use of secrecy and decoys—not without irony—
which he indicated at the very start of the book: "Our unfortunate times
thus compel me, once again, to write in a new way. Some elements will
be intentionally omitted; and the plan will have to remain rather unclear.
Readers will encounter certain decoys, like the very hallmark of the era. As
long as certain pages are interpolated here and there, the overall meaning
may appear: just as secret clauses have very often been added to whatever
treaties may openly stipulate; just as some chemical agents only reveal their
hidden properties when they are combined with others."[14] The strategy of
exposition described here, with its omissions and secret clauses, strangely
resembles what will be described throughout the *Comments*: "The real influences remain hidden, and the ultimate aims can barely be suspected
and almost never understood."[15] In order to denounce a society in the grip
of a multiplicity of secret services, Debord became a secret agent himself,
which wasn't too difficult given his experience in clandestinity, which he

made good use of. In this context, he succeeded better than all the others. He knew everything, was a kind of ironic Hercule Poirot in a plot between government and Mafia, who succeeds in escaping from the sophisticated labyrinths of spectacular domination but deprives us of the final chapter, who keeps his reasoning process hidden and limits himself, like the enemy, to insinuation, overblown examples, and gross generalizations. It is as if he had himself become an adept at disinformation, assuming it functions the way it is described: "Unlike the straightforward lie, disinformation must inevitably contain a degree of truth but one deliberately manipulated by an artful enemy."[16]

What if that "artful enemy" were Debord? What if he himself was playing a game, the game of a secret agent who has infiltrated the other side, adopting their strategy and techniques to improve his chances of success? The *Comments* would then be a strategic demonstration of how to combat the totalitarianism of the generalized spectacle using its own weapons (the only ones possible, since governments alone continue to believe in the existence of real enemies, since the totalitarian logic of the spectacle has disbanded the revolutionary forces, now condemned to an extraterritorial totalitarianism). From this viewpoint, the book is part challenge, part game, like so many other aspects of the work and of Debord's strategy. *This struggle is also a game*: war is also a game, which is one more reason to enjoy it.

If this is the case, the technique of using the enemy's weapons had been tested once before in *Véridique rapport sur les dernières chances de sauver le capitalisme en Italie*.[17] Written in 1975 by Gianfranco Sanguinetti, then associated with Debord—and passing himself off as a cynical capitalist under the pseudonym Censor—the book describes the comparative advantages of the strategy of historical compromise and state terrorism. It received considerable attention in Italy. Everyone fell for Sanguinetti's ruse, at least until he showed his hand and revealed the author's true identity. Everyone was duped, and everyone, from the Christian Democrats to the Communist Party (most probably the principal target of the attack), found reasons to criticize Censor's frankness about the prevailing cynicism in politics, which was precisely the desired effect. Another case of fire added to oil, but in this case the fire was disguised as water. It was an exercise in pure strategy, in which the role of the strategist of the defunct SI was considerable. Behind Censor was Sanguinetti, but behind Sanguinetti was Debord, or at least his style, in every sense of the term: his understanding of formulaic statements, his acerbic wit, his sense of intervention—and arguments that he had been making for years. Is it so surprising that he hastened to translate Censor's book into French?

The Game of War, Gondi

Games play a role in *Comments on the Society of the Spectacle* just as they do in Censor's book and in many other books by Debord. Although he did not earn his living playing poker, as he claims in *Panegyric,* Debord loved gambling and organized his life as a big game. This predilection for games appears in his declarations of war and in the challenges he issued; they were a way of adding excitement to his life. War was exciting and beautiful because it was a game, even a superior kind of game. The *dérive* and *détournement* (of cultural artifacts as well as minors) are another kind of game, and not so different from war. Debord's life revolved around games, seduction and warfare, provocation and dissimulation, labyrinths of various kinds, and even catacombs where the knights of the lettrist round table played a game of "whoever loses (himself) wins." The situationist project was ludic above all else. It consisted in making game playing an integral part of life, of making life a game, and in this sense it certainly contributed to turning May 1968 into the festival many intended it to be instead of a series of street battles and violent confrontations.

Where was Debord in all this? He was hidden in the center of a rotating triangle, whose apexes changed constantly: warfare, games, and literature (poetry). Each apex shifted the others, or took its place. Warfare consisted in inventing the words capable of destroying the enemy; it had to be as beautiful as a chivalric epic, make use of the fine arts and poetry. It took place not only in the street, but in books—which were explosive in their own way. Game playing turned into warfare, becoming the "great game," embodied in life. But it had to be more than just a game: having an enemy rather than a mere opponent is what made it exciting. The same was true of literature, which had more to do with strategy than with aesthetics, and oscillated between warfare and games. It incorporated a principle of aggression and a rejection of the reader, and was intended to dissolve in the construction of lived situations. In both cases, the reader was displaced, shifted, deprived of the suspicious charms of passive aesthetic contemplation. The choice was his to make: become a partner or an enemy.

There are few pictures of Debord writing. There is one in volume 2 of *Panegyric*, taken when he was writing *The Society of the Spectacle*. In the others he is smoking, drinking, hugging or walking with some young girl, or doing nothing. Apparently, Debord was not very interested in cultivating an image of himself as a writer. However, he did promote his image as a game player, for in the next-to-last section of the book (1977–84), he can be seen with Alice Becker-Ho playing the "Game of War" he invented in 1977 (shots of the game also appear in *In girum imus nocte*).[1]

Many writers have been gamblers, but few have designed strategy games. The "Game of War" is played on a checkerboard of five hundred squares (25 × 20). There are two opposing armies of equal force, consisting of a number of regiments of infantry, cavalry, and artillery, with forts and arsenals. The terrain on which they play is partly mountainous and there are specific rules of engagement, offensive and defensive coefficients of force, and so on. The goal of each player is to destroy the opponent's army through various maneuvers and battles, while protecting his own resources and means of communication. The game is supposed to incorporate all the tactical and strategic recommendations described by Clausewitz on the basis of eighteenth-century warfare, the French Revolution, and Napoléon's campaigns. Because of its complexity, it is not as efficient as other better-known (but less realistic) games of strategy, from chess to Go. It does reflect Debord's interest in a certain type of "classical" military strategy, which can be implemented using his game. The fact alone of creating a game on the basis of the theories of Clausewitz rather than contemporary military strategy is significant. It was strategy in the pure state that interested him, and this had nothing to do with contemporary techniques of mass destruction. Moreover, no one would have the bad taste to describe computerized nuclear destruction as being part of the art of warfare, whereas in Clausewitz's day, and Napoléon's, war was still an art. There was an element of game play in warfare, at least from the point of view of those who analyzed it retrospectively.

Few writers have invented games, and fewer still have turned a match into a book, as Debord did in 1987, shortly before writing his strategic *Comments on the Society of the Spectacle*.[2] Debord was less a writer than a game player; he published matches rather than texts, and published them with his game partner, who was also the woman he lived with. He played rather than wrote, made writing a kind of game and a form of warfare, inscribing his life in a strategic rather than a literary constellation:

> And so I have studied the logic of war. Moreover, I succeeded, a long time ago, in presenting the basics of its movements on a rather simple board game: the forces in contention as well as the contradictory necessities imposed on the operations of each of the two parties. I have played this game and, in the often difficult conduct of my life, I have drawn a few lessons from it—I also set myself rules of the game for this life, and I have followed them. The surprises of this Kriegspiel seem inexhaustible; and I fear that this may well be the only one of my works that anyone will dare acknowledge as having some value.[3]

With his "war game" Debord formalized his rules for living. It was his most *autobiographical* work, the only one that would be recognized as a work, because it was inexhaustible. Debord's effort was one of the most systematic attempts in the history of literature to focus on the conjunction of a science of writing and a science of strategy, possibly even an attempt to do better in this field than the predecessors he so admired: "It must be acknowledged that those amongst us who have been able to perform wonders with writing have often shown less evidence of expertise in the command of war. The trials and tribulations met with on this terrain are now innumerable."[4] This key passage is followed by a series of examples of relatively unsuccessful combinations of literature and soldiering (Vauvenargues, Gondi, Charles d'Orléans, Thucydides, even Clausewitz, who is considered a writer for the occasion), and some fairly successful ones (Saint-Simon, Stendhal attacking an Austrian battery, Cervantes, resolute in the face of the Turks at Lepanto, and finally Dante, who killed his adversary at Campaldino).

There is nothing decorative in the many quotes on military strategy or history found in Debord's books. They are the best indications of his "artistic" geography, the terrain he intends to occupy. Where others quote Flaubert, Proust, Mallarmé, or Joyce as the flashing lights of their desire for literature, Debord quotes, as exponents of the strategic vanishing point of his art, Clausewitz, Machiavelli, Thucidydes, Herodotus, Xenophon, and others who witnessed or played a role in great battles. The same is true of Baltasar Gracián (1601–58), a rebel Spanish Jesuit, whose *L'homme de cour, Le héros, L'homme universel,* and *Le politique Dom Ferdinand le Catholique* were all published in translation by Champ Libre.[5] Generally, Gracián is described as a moralist, a moralist of disillusion (the title of one of his most famous books, *L'homme détrompé*, suggests this). Obviously, this would interest Debord, illusion being one of the things in his life he worked hard to avoid. But what is most striking, especially in *L'homme de cour*, is the strategic, or simply relational, dimension of the book. Gracián's morality is not strictly speaking charitable; in fact, it is singularly immoral. It is a science of the effects of behavior and speech, puts others in the position of being enemies, or at the very least assumes the existence of a relation of force with them. It teaches us how to scheme, how to dissimulate, how to deceive, how to exploit the enemy's weaknesses and get the best of him. It is a morality without pity, like war. Written in impeccably baroque style, sometimes criticized for its affectation and verbosity, it was certain to please Debord, for it is obvious that the "man of the court" could only survive by becoming an enemy of the court.[6]

It is impossible to discuss the "game of war" without mentioning Gondi, the Cardinal de Retz, whose *Mémoires* accompanied Debord throughout his life. In *"Cette mauvaise réputation . . ."*, he denies writing like the Cardinal de Retz, and he is certainly right. The article in *Actuel* that discusses this stylistic scoop is careful to avoid specifying just how Debord resembles Retz. However, there are many reasons for Debord to have admired the man. He was one of the principal participants in the civil war of the Fronde, which was the last battle fought (and lost) by the aristocracy against absolute monarchy, the final expression of an aristocratic form of sovereignty (as Corneille understood it) in the face of the advent of the "spectacular" power of Louis XIV. He played a central role because, as coadjutor of the archbishop of Paris, his uncle, he "held" Paris, and was capable, depending on the circumstances, of calming the people of Paris or, on the contrary, of organizing an uprising. He was involved body and soul in the barricades of 1648 (a distant reflection of the street battles and barricades of 1968). Debord admired the man for his interest in strategy, his talent for intrigues that were often so sophisticated that his closest colleagues sometimes lost the thread (he would have been an enthusiastic reader of the *Comments*), his boldness, his sense of defiance, and his unswerving opposition if not to the king, at least to Mazarin. Like so many others in Debord's universe, he was a magnificent and proud loser, choosing flight and exile rather than yielding to the advances of Mazarin and the court. For Gondi, no going back or reconciliation was possible. But he was primarily a writer, a memorialist. He was able to retrospectively convert a failed political career into a legend, into a formidable piece of theater, in which he plays the principal role as one might expect. And it is the role of a gambler rather than a warrior. He seems to have enjoyed the maneuvering and plots in which he participated (often taking the initiative) for their own sake rather than for the sake of victory (which we find, in reading his *Mémoires*, continued to elude him). In 1956, when Debord had just turned twenty-five, it was this aspect of Retz's personality that he emphasized. It was the retrospective mythologizing of the gambler's life that seduced him, as shown by a note in *Potlatch*:

> In the latest book on Retz (published by Albin Michel), Mr. Pierre-Georges Lorris, without abandoning the most conventional moralism in judging his subject, does do justice to the ridiculous explanation of his behavior as being a sign of ambition: "From defeat to defeat, the *Mémoires* proceed, until the final disaster. . . . His *Mémoires* do not manifest the despondency of the conquered, but the amusement of a gambler. . . . Retz achieved the only goal he set himself."
>
> The extraordinary ludic value of Gondi's life, and of the Fronde in which he was the most significant participant, remain to be analyzed from a truly modern perspective.[7]

Retz was a gambler, a game player. He played at war (the way others play poker or chess), risking his life, escaping prison, and going into exile. In his *Mémoires*, each action is reinterpreted in tactical and strategic terms, and it is through its style, irony, and humor that the book becomes something beautiful. But style, as they say, is the man; it is not created ex nihilo, but develops through living. Retz's life had to be ludic so that the *Mémoires* could be as well. Style is the man, and it is the man who appeals to, who presents his life to another, turns it into a legend, playing his last hand and issuing his last challenge. When does a life begin to be written? From the outset it can position itself as a function of the legend or the exemplary narrative it will one day become. The principal difference between Retz and Debord was that Debord seems to have been aware of the legendary nature of his life much earlier than Retz. But then, Gondi couldn't read the *Mémoires* of the Cardinal de Retz when he was twenty.

CONCLUSION
DEBORD, AGAINST TYPE

Calm block here fallen from obscure disaster,
Let this granite at least mark the boundaries evermore
To the dark flights of Blasphemy hurled to the future.

Debord never set an example. He was no one's student, never followed anyone, and did nothing that would encourage a following of his own. It's not clear he wanted to be read, at least not by just anyone. Everything points to the fact that he did everything he could to avoid being a leader, and he succeeded. He erased his tracks. The only ones that remained were those he decided to leave behind. All in all, he was an example of someone who should not be followed, and was exemplary only because he could not be followed, because he invented a life for himself that was impossible to imitate. It was a life of actions, of words, writing, and images, all of which express his love of singularity and freedom. Inimitable.

It would be even harder to "be like" Debord by becoming a theoretician, by repeating his "theses," by detaching what he thought and wrote from the singularity of a lifetime or a stated position, by failing to invent the life one must live to bring about another theory, capable of *reflecting its era* (to use Debord's expression) with its necessary ambiguity. The era, tired of the wordplay that has served as theory for the past twenty or thirty years, has discovered that it lacks theories. In its search for a new Marx, it wonders whether Debord will do, hesitates, weighs the pros and cons (mostly deciding against), sees that nothing is available, and grows depressed. But what it may be missing is experience, that sense of freedom and defiance that characterized Debord. What is missing is less the aptitude for theory than a sense of the poetic—as I have used the term throughout this book with reference to Debord. It is remarkable that, among those who now claim to admire what he wrote, there are many writers, some of whom were his friends (often discreet), but few "theorists"—philosophers, sociologists, political scientists, or media scholars. In one way or another, he continues to irritate many of them, and I believe he does so for the same reason that he interests writers and artists: because, in everything he has written, we find an insistence on style, on singularity, on whatever situates him effectively within a poetic rather than a theoretical framework.

It is pointless, therefore, to read Debord in the hope of finding something. The revolution he worked for was a form of haute couture. "There was a neighborhood where the negative held court." He added the forms, sumptuous, even sumptuary, with his defiance and his potlatches. That does not mean that we should place his books back on the shelves among the belles lettres, relieved and charmed that nothing in them concerns us. Debord the writer and Debord the theorist were never in opposition. After all, many of his theses are still relevant and supported by current events. As he himself noted in his preface to the fourth Italian edition of *The Society of the Spectacle,* history has been in a hurry not only to confirm many of his findings but also to write a few pages or chapters that were missing.

In reading Debord it is important to keep in mind the role of game playing, defiance, and style. It is important to remember, though, that his style—of life as well as literary—is inseparable from his lucid, even pitiless, analysis of the society of his time, and these have always reinforced one another in his work. Molière suggests somewhere that lovers detect a wealth of charms in even the ugliest of mistresses. To see that ugliness requires the complete absence of complacency that has always characterized Debord and enabled him to reject *as a whole* the society of his time. The truth we are prepared to admit about the world depends on our love for it, and, more specifically, what we ask of it. Debord never asked anything of it, and that is why he could say what so many others knew but could not say, carefully avoiding drawing the obvious conclusions.

As a whole (calm block, fallen from obscure disaster): this is a critical element in the contemporary intellectual environment, which supports the kind of specific or regional intellectual once imagined by Foucault (today, every cause has its specialists, not to mention its official bureaucrats, and temporary workers). One of the first theses of the society of the spectacle states that "the concept of the spectacle brings together and explains a wide range of apparently disparate phenomena."[1] Debord's approach was unifying, totalizing, which is what makes it so radical. Someone recently asked, on a French radio program,[2] why the ecology movement was no longer interested in him, why it didn't make him one of their spokespersons—this, with the slight condescension found when discussing a political movement so naively Rousseauian, with which it is anything but innocent to associate someone like Debord (whom it is hard to imagine as some bucolic ecologist, this man so stubbornly, notwithstanding Champot, committed to the metropolis and the encounters it promoted). The misunderstanding is worth consideration. There is no denying that Debord's writings have shown a heightened awareness of the various ways chosen by the world to destroy the environment. More than forty years ago, he denounced automobile culture, the industrialization of food, and modern urbanism. Later he took an interest in the Chernobyl disaster, especially the astonishing mendacity associated with the situation. And it is not hard to imagine him writing about the diseases affecting European cattle and the people who eat them. Society seems to be doing its best to honor him by confirming his arguments on the tyrannical rule of the commodity. But if he showed relatively little interest in ecological issues, it was obviously because they were not ready to be conceptualized as a whole. What would Debord have been to the ecological movement stripped of what was most essential about him, without his rejection of capitalism and the state, without his vision or his mourning for the world, and without his style, none of which are compatible with government-sponsored environmental protection programs?

As a whole: what's true for ecology is true for all the other applied disciplines in *The Society of the Spectacle* and the *Comments*, which it would be wrong to interpret as treatises on political science or media studies. This is an important point: the spectacle Debord described is not an object of study for political scientists or sociologists. It is not restricted to stereotypes about television paralyzing our faculty of judgment, or platitudes about what is sometimes referred to as the politics of the spectacle, or the arrival of the information society and virtual communities. Nor can it be reduced to the landing of GIs on the shores of Mogadishu filmed lived by CNN. That (which is far from an isolated example) is at best a symptom of the spectacle, and often acknowledged as such by Debord, but in an offhand way.

The symptoms of the spectacle's domination are much more global, the rule of the commodity absolute. Debord responded to this with an equally absolute rejection (that is, freed of all obligations). The concept of the spectacle cannot be parceled out to specialists—which has not, of course, prevented them from grabbing what they could. But what does that leave us with? Not much, at least not much that we don't already know. The truth is true, and at the same time unbearable, desperate, only when it is expressed as a totality. By revealing only partial truths, we repress the whole, replacing it with a series of clichés. Debord wanted to speak the whole truth, like many of those who served as his models. Or, more specifically, he cared that everything that could be said was said. He conceived of his actions, as I have suggested throughout this book, as those of an *analyst* of society (appropriating Freud for that purpose). He became the smuggler or trustee of a fundamentally impersonal truth that "works," travels, and manifests itself most effectively when we don't want to know, when it is strongly resisted, contested. This is the truth against which all social and cultural agencies are supposed to protect us, the way neurosis and its symptoms hold our unconscious desires in check. So, if there has recently been something like a return to Debord, this should be viewed the same way we view the return of the repressed.

As was the case with Freud, Debord's position represents a stunning show of force, but it was obviously not the same, neurosis and its compromises not being his specialty. One can reject his arguments or counter his diagnosis of the self-destructive nature of the society of the spectacle with the euphoric vision of a democratic society freed of its chains by the wonders of the market economy. We can assume that the world he claims has distanced itself through representation—a multitude of representations and mediations—will one day provide us with a sense of immediacy, one that is in a way freely offered, through the Internet, the ultimate guarantor of authentic communication. But there are two sides to every coin, and counterstudies and counterstatistics are not in short supply. Does that mean we have put Debord's arguments to rest? I'm not so sure.

Conversely, will anyone be able to authenticate, declaiming passages from *The Society of the Spectacle*, the bitter accusations of the misdeeds of a form of economic globalization that is, in truth, as old as capitalist economy itself? Or by energetically railing against the power of the media or public opinion? I'm not so certain, for the simple reason that Debord's arguments were advanced neither to be refuted nor confirmed, at least not in this context, where they experience a contagious lifelessness whether they are promoted or attacked. The truth of his arguments is the truth of his attack, his absolute disqualification of the gaze of the Other; it is the truth of *a refusal,* and that cannot be discussed or refuted. It simply is, uniquely itself, and can only be acknowledged—at least that's what I've tried to do in this book. Agreement and disagreement, along with the procession of minor identifications and appropriations that accompany them, are then almost secondary. They become articles of faith, matters of belief, and everyone believes what it is in his interest to believe—or what he imagines to be his interest.

I'm not saying that all ideas, all opinions are valid, that all are equally true or false, which would have the advantage of allowing me to dispense with them one and all. But how do we distinguish among them? What are the conditions of possibility for truth? For Debord, the truth was to be found wherever nothing stood in the way, where there was *nothing left* to stand in the way. It was something won by fighting, the pot in a high-stakes game (the spectacle is also a lie). What does a man think when he has nothing at stake, when he aspires to nothing, no title, no form of recognition? What truth can he offer when he believes in nothing because he has no interest in living it out, identifies only with himself? This is the question that his work leaves with us. It is the form of demonstration promoted by Debord, a kind of Monsieur Teste of revolution.

What is it about Debord's ideas that makes them so radical? It is the fact that he paid a personal price, that he remained resolute throughout his life, was able to use poetry—his work as well as his life—to foster the rejection of society and the search for absolute freedom. It is because those ideas are based on an ethics, a morality of demoralization, which contrasts strangely with the self-righteousness and moralism that are currently prevalent. And, to quote an expression found in *In girum imus nocte,* it is the belief that "If nothing is true, everything is permitted," a position it is difficult to achieve or sustain. It is not easy to realize one's desire. It is not easy to live like Debord. It is not easy to think like him or even with him. Which is why it is not easy to forget him.

NOTES

Introduction

1. Guy Debord (G. D.), *In girum imus nocte et consumimur igni* (1978), in *Complete Cinematic Works*, translated and edited by Ken Knabb (Oakland, Calif.: AK Press, 2003), 187. This was Debord's last film.

2. By "understand Debord" I do not mean something like a "more intimate portrayal of Guy Debord." This book is an attempt to understand why Debord wrote what he wrote and filmed what he filmed, that is, to situate him accurately within the history of nineteenth- and twentieth-century avant-gardes. To do this I have obviously reviewed all his work, and examined the available commentaries and documents about Debord and the groups he led. I have also interviewed some of the people who were close to him, to try to capture something like the spirit of his time. Finally, I made use of my own resources, in the sense that this book develops some of the ideas found in my previous work on Mallarmé, on the avant-garde, and more generally on the unstable boundary between biography and literature.

1. Lost Children

ORIGINS

1. G. D., *Howls for Sade*, in *Complete Cinematic Works*, translated and edited by Ken Knabb (Oakland, Calif.: AK Press, 2003), 110.

2. G. D., *Critique of Separation*, in *Complete Cinematic Works*, 35.

3. G. D., *In girum imus nocte et consumimur igni*, in *Complete Cinematic Works*, 152.

4. G. D., *Panegyric*, vols. 1 and 2, translated by James Brook and John McHale (New York: Verso, 2004), 11; originally published as *Panégyrique* (Paris: Fayard, 1997).

5. In a letter to Ivan Chtcheglov, dated September 2, 1964, Debord wrote what appears to be completely in line with his feelings about money: "But if I had been

rich, I would have found no better way to ruin myself than to finance our enterprise and to be more generous to our friends, who genuinely deserve it" (*Correspondance*, vol. 2 [Paris: Fayard, 2001], 298).

6. For additional details on Debord's childhood and family, see the recent biography by Christophe Bourseiller, *Vie et mort de Guy Debord* (Paris: Plon, 1999).

7. Ibid., 22–23.

8. Ibid., 24.

9. Ibid., 25.

10. G. D., "*Cette mauvaise réputation . . .*" (Paris: Gallimard, 1993), 24.

11. Ibid.

SCRATCHED NEGATIVES AND THE GAME OF APPEARANCES

1. Based on a letter from Gil Wolman, one of Debord's closest friends during the lettrist period (1951–58), Christophe Bourseiller (*Vie et mort de Guy Debord*, 68–69) refers to a suicide attempt using gas that supposedly took place during the summer of 1953, but which has not been confirmed. The same letter is also referred to by Len Bracken, in his biography of Debord, *Guy Debord—Revolutionary: A Critical Biography* (Venice, Calif.: Feral House, 1997). In fact, it is likely that during the summer of 1953, Debord was simply ill. Whatever may have occurred, it seems to me that to suggest that the (false) suicide attempt of 1953 was a "premonition" (the word used by Bourseiller) of the 1994 suicide is highly speculative. Bracken explicitly rejects this idea (29–30).

2. *Internationale situationniste* 1 (1958) (Paris: Champ Libre, 1975), 19. This text, signed with the pseudonym Gilles Ivain, was written in 1953, and it is indeed by Ivan Chtcheglov, one of Debord's friends during the lettrist period, as indicated in a note added in 1958: "The Lettrist International had, in October 1953, adopted this report on urbanism by Gilles Ivain, which was a decisive element in the new direction taken by the experimental avant-garde at that time" (ibid., 20). For Ivan Chtcheglov's future and role in the movement, see chapter 2, "Cartes du Tendre."

3. *Potlatch* 23 (1955), republished in *Guy Debord présente Potlatch (1954–1957)* (Paris: Gallimard, "Folio" collection, 1996), 205.

4. G. D., *Panegyric*, translated by James Brook and John McHale (New York: Verso, 2004).

5. According to Greil Marcus, *Lipstick Traces: A Secret History of the Twentieth Century* (Cambridge: Harvard University Press, 1989), 324. Marcus's comments on these individuals—and especially Debord—are some of the most inspired (and inspiring) in what is by far the most original book devoted to the early part of Debord's life and work (the lettrist period, from 1951 to 1958).

6. See chapter 2, "The End of Art."

7. Marcus, *Lipstick Traces*, 328.

8. G. D., *Correspondance*, vol. 1 (Paris: Fayard, 1999), 24.

9. Gil Wolman, *L'Anticoncept*, reprinted in Gérard Berreby, ed., *Documents relatifs à la fondation de l'Internationale situationniste* (Paris: Allia, 1985), 102–3.

10. G. D., *La Société du spectacle* (Paris: Buchet-Chastel, 1967); translated as *The Society of the Spectacle* by Donald Nicholson-Smith (New York: Zone Books, 1994).

11. Jorge Manrique, *Stances sur la mort de son père* (Paris: Champ Libre, 1980; Cognac: Le temps qu'il fait, 1996).

12. On the Lebovici affair, see chapter 4, "Considerations on an Assassination."

13. This photograph is now one of the best known of Debord. It has appeared in print many times, as is appropriate for an official portrait. Significantly, it appears in volume 2 of *Panegyric*, where it is placed at the beginning of the section of the book titled "1984," a period that was always associated for Debord with the turmoil caused by the murder of Gérard Lebovici.

14. G. D., *Considerations on the Assassination of Gérard Lebovici*, translated and with an introduction by Robert Greene (Los Angeles: TamTam Books, 2001), 48–49. Originally published as *Considérations sur l'assassinat de Gérard Lebovici* (Paris: Éditions Gérard Lebovici, 1985).

PASSING THROUGH LETTRISM

1. Jean-François Martos, *Histoire de l'Internationale situationniste* (Paris: Éditions Gérard Lebovici, 1989), 11. In all fairness, it is important to note that on the following pages Martos returns once or twice to the achievements of the "old guard" of lettrism. However, this did not change much in the overall assessment of the movement.

2. *Documents relatifs à la fondation de l'Internationale situationniste*, edited by Gérard Berreby (Paris: Allia, 1985), 147.

3. Ibid., 149.

4. A sign of the times. Debord's success and the somewhat muted feelings he now arouses have led to the republication—for those interested in settling old scores—of all Isidore Isou's writings about Debord and the Situationist International (see Isidore Isou, *Contre l'Internationale situationniste* (Paris: Éditions Hors Commerce–d'art, 2001).

5. The two texts were republished in *Documents relatifs à la fondation de l'Internationale situationniste*, 85–123. A complete edition of *Ion* is once again available from the publisher Jean-Paul Rocher (Paris, 1999).

HAVING BOARDED AT NIGHT THE LIGHTEST OF CRAFTS

1. G. D., *Contre le cinéma* (Aarhus, Denmark: Scandinavian Institute of Comparative Vandalism, 1964).

2. G. D., *Complete Cinematic Works*, translated and edited by Ken Knabb (Oakland, Calif.: AK Press, 2003), 1–11.

3. Ibid., 2. We note in passing the appearance of "Ernest" in Debord's name. Ernest will be his most faithful traveling companion throughout the lettrist period. In spite of the apparent parody in its use, and however discreet (nothing like Jean-Isidore Goldstein becoming Isidore Isou), it does indicate that between Guy Debord and "Guy Debord" there exists a difference that is both imperceptible and fundamental.

In other words, any appearance, any process of becoming public (or a filmmaker, or a writer) transforms the status of the proper name, brings it into the space of recognition of which this second name, Ernest, is the ironic index.

4. Ibid. Once again, there is ambiguity in the reference to Debord's birth. He was indeed born in 1931, but the structure of the sentence distances him from the date and assimilates him to the year 1951, the year Guy Debord really became himself— "Guy-Ernest Debord."

5. This was Philippe Sollers's hypothesis, which he presented in an interview published in *Le Monde* (August 24, 2000), during the release of *Sade* by Benoît Jacquot, a film that is, on the contrary, very much engaged in Sade's appearance. At the same time, it is clear that what is unique about *Howls for Sade* is that *it is not about* Sade, or at least that, in 1952, it disappointed the expectations of a public that, through exposure to the surrealists, Bataille, Blanchot, and Klossowski, knew the classical avant-garde like the back of its hand.

6. G. D., *Complete Cinematic Works*, 1.

7. *Documents relatifs à la fondation de l'Internationale situationniste*, edited by Gérard Berreby (Paris: Allia, 1985), 113.

8. Ibid., 113–14.

9. In its imaginary version, *Howls for Sade* indicated the presence of a sequence from a boxing match, without any further information. However, it is difficult not to "see" this as an homage to the legendary boxing matches Cravan fought in Paris and Spain, and which are probably a more important part of his work than his writings. On Cravan's life, see Maria Luïsa Boras, *Cravan, une stratégie du scandale* (Paris: Éditions Jean-Michel Place, 1996).

10. G. D., *Panegyric*, translated by James Brook and John McHale (New York: Verso, 2004), 12.

11. Cravan and Lautréamont. The names are obviously both pseudonyms, two histories of breaking with one's family, followed by disappearance and re(birth). Cravan and Lautréamont owe nothing to anyone, even through their names.

12. G .D., *Panegyric*, 22.

13. G. D., *Complete Cinematic Works*, 6.

14. G. D., *Panegyric*, 6.

15. G. D., *Complete Cinematic Works*, 149.

16. In her *Pour Guy Debord*, Cécile Guilbert comments on this. She writes that "style is never form. Every powerful idea finds the conditions for its formulation naturally. The power of style is simply power" ([Paris: Gallimard, 1996], 64). A few pages further on she quotes an expression of Debord taken from *Thèses sur l'Internationale situationniste* (1971): "To know how to write, you need to have read, and to know how to read, you must know how to live" (83–84).

17. At present there are three (to which must be added the biographical indications scattered throughout numerous other books): Len Bracken's *Guy Debord— Revolutionary* is more energetically hagiographic than Bourseiller's, whose intent, which he explained in several radio and television interviews when his book was

published, was to "demythologize the icons of May 1968." This is no doubt a praiseworthy goal, but one wonders if he didn't succeed a little too well. Was it really necessary to throw out the lost baby with the bathwater of May 1968? Andrew Hussey's *The Game of War: The Life and Death of Guy Debord* (London: Jonathan Cape, 2001) owes a great deal to Bourseiller, in more ways than one. It doesn't add more to what we know, but less: a thick layer of vulgarity, another of spite, and a third of incoherence. We can only hope that Hussey's book remains unparalleled.

18. The following have already appeared: Jean-Michel Mension, *La tribu,* interviews with Gérard Berreby and Francesco Milo (Paris: Allia, 1998); Ralph Rumney, *The Consul,* translated by Malcolm Imrie (San Francisco: City Lights, 2002; originally published as *Le consul,* interviews with Gérard Berreby, in collaboration with Giulio Minghini and Chantal Osterreicher [Paris: Allia, 1999]).

19. In 1960 Michèle Bernstein published her first novel, *Tous les chevaux du roi* (Buchet-Chastel), and in 1961, *La nuit,* which was presented as the "Nouveau Roman" version of the first. She always insisted that she wrote these books strictly out of financial necessity. The autobiographical and a fortiori biographical dimension of these texts remains extremely problematic.

20. See, for example, the first part of Jean-Marie Apostolidès's *Les tombeaux de Guy Debord* (Paris: Exils, 1999). The book is especially illuminating when read in conjunction with Bourseiller's biography, which Apostolidès was unfortunately unaware of at the time.

I WANTED TO SPEAK THE BEAUTIFUL LANGUAGE OF MY CENTURY

1. G. D., *Mémoires,* preface, "Attestations" (Paris: Belles-Lettres/Pauvert, 1993).

2. To be thorough, we should add the London Psychogeographical Association, whose only member was Ralph Rumney, the fourth person to be excluded from the Situationist International.

3. See chapter 2.

4. Jean-Marie Apostolidès, *Les tombeaux de Guy Debord* (Paris: Exils, 1999), 87ff.

THE GOLDEN AGE

1. In fact, the transition or change of personnel took place with the fourth (and last) issue of *Internationale lettriste* (June 1954), which appeared the same month as the first issue of *Potlatch* (June 22, 1954).

2. Jean-Michel Mension, *La tribu* (Paris: Allia, 1998).

3. G. D., *Panegyric,* translated by James Brook and John McHale (New York: Verso, 2004), 21, 23.

4. G. D., *In girum imus nocte et consumimur igni,* in *Complete Cinematic Works,* translated and edited by Ken Knabb (Oakland, Calif.: AK Press, 2003), 162. Referring to the names I mentioned earlier, no member of the Lettrist International ever had a good reputation, not even—and this explains why—a reputation. Debord was the only one to have succeeded in gaining one, and his was not good.

5. The passerby in question is a certain Buffier, a photographer, who published

a postcard with the image of Debord's inscription accompanied by the caption "Superfluous advice." Debord returned to this episode in a letter dated June 27, 1963 (*Correspondance*, vol. 2 [Paris: Fayard, 2001], 244), addressed to the Cercle de la Librairie, which, quite seriously, demanded payment for republication in *Internationale situationniste* of the inscription in question. We can imagine the scathing satire in Debord's reply; he amused himself by threatening the complainants with having Buffier's card removed from sale because it misappropriated the meaning of his work.

6. G. D., *Panegyric*, vol. 1, 23.

7. Ibid., 24.

8. Ghislain de Marbaix was also one of the rare few to appear in a photograph in volume 2 of *Panegyric*. His picture is accompanied by a quotation from the "Belle leçon aux enfants perdus" by François Villon: a legend for a legendary character, whom Debord always considered one of his friends.

9. The only manifesto the Lettrist International ever really produced was a half page in *Internationale lettriste 2*. See *Documents relatifs à la fondation de l'Internationale situationniste*, edited by Gérard Berreby (Paris: Allia, 1985), 154.

10. See "My Child, My Sister . . ." in this chapter.

11. See Mension, *La tribu*, 54.

BERNARD, BERNARD, THIS BLOOM OF YOUTH WILL NOT LAST FOREVER

1. Debord's meeting with Asger Jorn was important in several ways. Friendship most of all, but also for helping to found the Situationist International, which in large part owes its internationalism to Jorn, and finally in terms of material resources. Jorn provided financing for Debord's films between 1959 and 1961, as well as for *Internationale situationniste*, the review that was "international" between 1958 and 1969, and which was considered, at least from the point of view of the far left, as relatively lavish. Jorn's financial support of the Situationist International continued well beyond the point when he withdrew from the group in 1961. And Jorn would later claim such support as his specific contribution to the activities of the SI.

2. G. D., *Complete Cinematic Works*, translated and edited by Ken Knabb (Oakland, Calif.: AK Press, 2003), 14.

3. Ibid., 15.

4. Ibid., 16.

5. Ibid., 22.

6. Ibid., 16.

7. Ibid., 17.

8. Ibid., 22. In the book, image and text are accompanied by a marginal description that reads as follows: "The previously seen tracking shot (across the café) is repeated, this time with the worst take, without any cuts, and with a succession of defects—people intruding into the field of vision, lens reflections, camera shadows—ending with a swish pan shot."

9. Ibid., 19.

10. Ibid., 29.

11. Ibid., 32.

12. Ibid., 35.

13. Ibid., 38.

14. Ibid., 33.

15. Twenty-seven of the forty-five expulsions from the Situationist International that were meticulously cataloged by Jean-Jacques Raspaud and Jean-Pierre Voyer took place between 1958 and 1962. See their *L'Internationale situationniste: Protagonistes/ Chronologies/Bibliographie, avec un index des noms insultés* (Paris: Champ Libre, 1972).

16. G. D., *Complete Cinematic Works*, 175.

17. Ibid., 152ff. for the following quotes.

18. Ibid., 161.

19. Ibid., 168.

20. Ibid., 169.

21. G. D., *Panegyric*, translated by James Brook and John McHale (New York: Verso, 2004), 26. To be precise, this was the next-to-last evocation of Saint-Germain-des-Prés, the last being the exclusively visual remembrance in volume 2 of *Panegyric*.

22. The still of Alice Becker-Ho and Céleste is reproduced at the end of the "text" of *In girum imus nocte* (see *Complete Cinematic Works*, 201). Part of the same image (the one with Alice Becker-Ho) also appears in volume 2 of *Panegyric*, following two photographs associated with Florence.

23. G. D., *Complete Cinematic Works*, 186.

24. G. D., *Panegyric*, 41.

25. G. D., *In girum imus nocte*, in *Complete Cinematic Works*, 187. That Debord was thinking here, via Lorenzaccio, not only of Machiavelli, which is hardly surprising in someone as concerned with strategy as he, but also of Dante (and we often forget the extent to which he was engaged in the political struggles of Florence), is confirmed by the use of the pseudonym Cavalcanti (the leader of the party to which Dante belonged) in his correspondence at this time, especially with Gianfranco Sanguinetti (see *Correspondance*, vol. 2 [Paris: Champ Libre, 1981], 97ff.).

26. There are abundant signs of Debord's interest in the baroque: his penchant for fluidity, mobility, his passion for unstable historical periods that are often associated with the baroque, his preference for a city like Venice, or a writer like Baltasar Gracián, or baroque music, especially the use, in the film version of *The Society of the Spectacle*, of a very beautiful sonata by Michel Corette. Considered as part of the baroque movement, Corette was for a while the official musician of the Prince de Condé, in other words, the Fronde (which, through Cardinal de Retz, would continue to play an important role in Debord's mental landscape).

27. See chapter 1, "Origins."

28. G. D., *Complete Cinematic Works*, 155.

29. Ibid., 156.

30. Ibid., 189.

31. Ibid., 164. Omar Khayyám, a Persian mathematician who lived approximately from 1050 to 1123, also developed a reputation as a poet. Some of his poems were blasphemous and circulated clandestinely.

32. Ibid., 165.

33. G. D., *Panegyric*, 3.

34. G. D., *Complete Cinematic Works*, 29.

35. Ibid., 30.

36. There are one or two references to childhood in Debord's correspondence, primarily in a letter to Ivan Chtcheglov (the most seriously "lost child" of Debord's former companions), which ends, with little connection to what went before, with the following: "And the happy days of summer, remembering one's own childhood." See *Correspondance*, vol. 2, 277.

37. *International situationniste* 1, 8. This text, which was published in 1958, in the first issue of *I.S.*, appeared in the unsigned group "editorial." Although there is nothing to indicate that this editorial and the anonymous texts in the newsletter were written exclusively by Debord, the consensus today considers his role in their writing to have been significant—even preponderant.

38. G. D., *Complete Cinematic Works*, 14.

39. Ibid., 36.

40. G. D., *Panegyric*, 29.

41. Ibid., 30.

42. See Michel Surya, "Le cadavre surfait de... (Debord et la littérature)," *Lignes* 31 (1997).

MY CHILD, MY SISTER . . .

1. Frédéric Schiffter, *Guy Debord, l'atrabilaire* (Biarritz: Éditions Distance, 1997).

2. Jean-Marc Apostolidès, *Les tombeaux de Guy Debord* (Paris: Exils, 1999).

3. The fortunes and misfortunes of the psychocriticism of the writer's spouse: one doesn't always win and sometimes always loses. *Tous les chevaux du roi* is the story of a ménage à trois: Gilles, supposedly a kind of Debord disguised as Valmont, Geneviève, his faithful companion and something of a Merteuil, and the young Carole, whom Gilles-Valmont-Debord falls in love with. Apostolidès assumes that Carole (that is, the Cécile-Tourvel of *Tous les chevaux du roi*) is the beautiful Éliane Papaï. Hardly. Bourseiller reveals that she is in fact the lovely Michèle Mochot-Bréhat. In itself this is not all that important, just one name substituted for another. However, it is highly doubtful that for Debord there was no difference between Éliane Papaï, whose picture is scattered throughout his books and films, and Michèle Mochot-Bréhat, who is almost never shown. There is also the fact that Debord's affair with Michèle Mochot-Bréhat did not end after a few months, as in *Tous les chevaux du roi* (where Valmont-Gilles-Debord hurries to return to Merteuil-Geneviève-Bernstein), but in 1984, nearly a quarter of a century later. This is a Valmont who has become

faithful to Cécile and to Madame de Tourvel. All things considered, it is easy to see that the stories are quite different.

4. Guy Debord and Michèle Bernstein were married in 1954 and divorced in 1972. From 1964 until the end of his life, Debord lived with Alice Becker-Ho, whom he married in 1972.

5. G. D., *Correspondance*, vol. 2 (Paris: Champ Libre, 1981), 147.

6. G. D., *Complete Cinematic Works*, translated and edited by Ken Knabb (Oakland, Calif.: AK Press, 2003), 165.

7. G. D., *Panegyric*, translated by James Brook and John McHale (New York: Verso, 2004), 41.

8. G. D., *Complete Cinematic Works*, 186.

9. Alice Becker-Ho, *D'azur au triangle vidé de sable* (Cognac: Le temps qu'il fait, 1998), 17–18.

NO TURNING BACK

1. G. D., *Complete Cinematic Works*, translated and edited by Ken Knabb (Oakland, Calif.: AK Press, 2003), 161.

2. Ibid., 175.

3. Ibid., 155.

4. See chapter 2, "The Poetics of the *Dérive.*"

5. G. D., *Complete Cinematic Works*, 177.

6. Ibid., 178.

7. In the last issue of *Internationale situationniste* (1969), written almost entirely by Debord, it seems, we can still read about this in terms of the occupation movement, which, like the labyrinth of the Saint-Germain-des-Prés years, entailed the opening up of space, the circulation of travelers: "The recognized desire of dialogue, of completely free speech, the interest in genuine community, had found their footing in the buildings used for meetings and in the shared struggle: telephones, among the few technical devices still in operation, and the wandering of so many emissaries and travelers, in Paris and other countries, between occupied sites, factories, and gatherings, served as the carrier for this genuine use of communication" (*Internationale situationniste* 12 [Paris: Fayard, 1997], 3).

8. G. D., *Complete Cinematic Works*, 183.

9. Ibid., 185.

10. Ibid., 187.

11. G. D., *Panegyric*, translated by James Brook and John McHale (New York: Verso, 2004), 40.

12. Ibid., 42.

13. Ibid., 44.

14. G. D., *Complete Cinematic Works*, 193.

15. Jorge Manrique, *Stances sur la mort de son père* (Paris: Champ Libre, 1980; Cognac: Le temps qu'il fait, 1996), 73. English translations from *Hispanic Anthology:*

Poems Translated from the Spanish by English and North American Poets, collected and arranged by Thomas Walsh (New York: G. P. Putnam's Sons, 1920); see also Frank A. Dominguez, *Love and Remembrance: The Poetry of Jorge Manrique (Studies in Romance Languages)* (Lexington: University Press of Kentucky, 1988).

16. Manrique, *Stances sur la mort de son père*, 75.

17. I am again unable to conceal my disagreement with Jean-Marie Apostolidès (*Les tombeaux de Guy Debord* [Paris: Exils, 1999], 128–36), who, after reading the same *Couplets*, comes to the astounding conclusion that, for Debord, the only good father (whose elegy he writes) is a dead one, according to the most accepted Oedipal schemata—as if it were a question of the child taking his place, as if all rivalry would cease with his death. But nowhere in Debord's work or life, aside from the episode with Isidore Isou, who cannot seriously be taken for a father figure, is there any sign of rivalry with a paternal figure. Are we again going to drag poor Breton out of his grave for the occasion? If there is one thing Debord never wanted to be, and never was, for anyone, it was a father. So one has to ask why would he want to take the place of his own? Lost children have no father and do not aspire to fatherhood. They break with the genealogy of heredity, they are without a heritage or a memory. Apostolidès's hypothesis is untenable, especially when it leads him to imagine a kind of slippage concerning Gérard Lebovici, Debord's friend, assassinated in 1984, who would thus have had the dubious privilege of changing status from a living brother to a dead father, all because of an epitaph by Jorge Manrique that was placed on his grave.

WHATEVER WAS DIRECTLY EXPERIENCED HAS BEEN DISTANCED THROUGH REPRESENTATION

1. G. D., *Panegyric*, translated by James Brook and John McHale (New York: Verso, 2004), 17.

2. G. D., *Complete Cinematic Works*, translated and edited by Ken Knabb (Oakland, Calif.: AK Press, 2003), 150–51.

3. Ibid., 151.

4. Other films emphasize one of these two aspects (autobiography in the case of *Howls for Sade* and *On the Passage of a Few Persons through a Rather Brief Unity of Time*, and theory or social criticism in the case of *The Society of the Spectacle* and *Refutation of All the Judgments, Pro or Con, Thus Far Rendered on the Film The Society of the Spectacle*). It is important to note, however, that with the images, especially those in *The Society of the Spectacle*, this "genre" difference tends to blur, because a certain number of elements (scenes of war or uprisings, quotes from other films, portraits of Debord's companions) can be found in all of Debord's films: the images he chose challenge, in their own way, the separation between the different types of speech.

5. In this sense, the most useful book to have come out recently is Anselm Jappe's *Guy Debord*, translated from the French by Donald Nicholson-Smith (Berkeley: University of California Press, 1999).

6. See chapter 4, "The Game of War, Gondi."

7. Anselm Jappe (*Guy Debord*, 176) identifies a number of these appropriations, especially those Debord has made use of from the writings of Hegel and Marx. There are others as well, especially Freud. In *The Society of the Spectacle*, the principle of *détournement* is clearly indicated in the quote—accurate for once—from a passage of Ducasse's *Poésies*, an homage to the first appropriator (who therefore cannot be appropriated): "Ideas improve. The meaning of words has a part in the improvement. Plagiarism is necessary. Progress demands it. Staying close to an author's phrasing, plagiarism exploits his expressions, erases false ideas, replaces them with correct ideas" (Thesis 207).

2. An Art without Works

THE END OF ART :: Homage to Lettrism

1. Éliane Brau, *Le situationnisme ou la nouvelle Internationale* (Paris: Nouvelles éditions Debresse, 1968, 64). Concerning Éliane Brau, see chapter 1.

2. Anselm Jappe, *Guy Debord*, translated by Donald Nicholson-Smith (Berkeley: University of California Press, 1999), 52ff.

3. See Greil Marcus, *Lipstick Traces: A Secret History of the Twentieth Century* (Cambridge: Harvard University Press, 1989), 246ff.

4. Gabriel Pomerand (his real name was Pomerans) was a Polish Jewish refugee who was nineteen at the time. He met Isou in 1945 and was his most faithful lieutenant during the early years of lettrism. He was excluded from the lettrist movement in 1956, became addicted to opium, and committed suicide in 1972.

5. See Raymond Queneau, *Les enfants du limon* (Paris: Gallimard, 1937).

6. According to Éliane Brau, *Le situationnisme ou la nouvelle Internationale*, 73.

7. Aside from Gabriel Pomerand, there was Maurice Lemaître (born Moïse Bismuth), who remained his most loyal flag bearer until the final hours of lettrism and, consequently, one of the fiercest enemies of Debord, whom he referred to as a Nazi. *International situationniste* responded much more politely by calling him an "excrement" and "eternal."

8. In his introduction to *La mécanique des femmes*, Isou challenges the authorities to arrest him, primarily because he had gone much farther in terms of subversion with the publication of *La dictature lettriste* and his *Introduction à une nouvelle poésie et une nouvelle musique*. But a lettrist scandal could never equal a sex scandal. Maybe this is the reason why Isou resigned himself to becoming a sexual recidivist, publishing, in 1960, an *Initiation à la haute volupté*, banned in 1977.

9. For additional details on Michel Mourre's life, see Greil Marcus, *Lipstick Traces*, 279–310, and especially Mourre's autobiography, which was published in 1951 (Paris: Julliard). Written immediately after the scandal in Notre-Dame and his (re)conversion to the Catholic faith, *Malgré le blasphème* is presented explicitly as the story of the failure of his life.

10. G. D., *Complete Cinematic Works*, translated and edited by Ken Knabb (Oakland, Calif.: AK Press, 2003), 163.

11. See Isou's *Traité d'économie nucléaire: le soulèvement de la jeunesse* (Paris, 1949).

12. All the historians of dadaism have certainly noticed this, as did the former dadaists themselves, who were, during the years of the Cabaret Voltaire, the Messieurs Jourdains of onomatopoeic poetry. The dadaist Raoul Hausmann pointed this out in a letter to Debord in March 1963: "If Isidore Isou claims to be the first to have made lettrist poems, he should learn about Ball's stories in his 1916 diary and the statements by Schwitters in *G* in 1923. As for Lemaître, he published a drawing in *Ur* in 1947 that he simply copied from a drawing of a North American Indian, published in 1912. . . . All of lettrist painting is nothing but an imitation of my *Poèmes-Affiches* and *Tableaux-Écritures* of 1918 to 1923" (letter quoted in G. D., *Correspondance*, vol. 2 [Paris: Fayard, 2001], 204 n. 3). The only question that can seriously be asked is whether the borrowings of lettrism were conscious—and consciously dissimulated—or if there is a kind of constellation of texts and positions worked out by Isou that "naturally" resulted, that is to say, in good faith, in the repetition of many aspects of the dadaist adventure.

13. Concerning the function of sharing in automatic writing, see Vincent Kaufmann, *Poétique des groupes littéraires: Avant-gardes 1920–1970* (Paris: Presses Universitaires de France, 1997), 27ff.

14. The references to total art, rebaptized "integral art" for the circumstances, and to Wagner are explicit in a text signed by Gil Wolman and C. P. Matricon titled "Pour une mort synthétique," which appeared in the lettrist review *Ur—Cahiers pour un dictat culturel* (1951): "What is known as integral art is art as being whenever it has functioned as a stimulus acting through all of man's senses simultaneously.

OBJECTION: If a man is affected by an art that is translated into the auditory and visual planes, etc., he must, to interpret this art as a Whole, integrate these different planes into a totality. But since integration is the mode of thought and since you deny the possibility of thought to such a man in such a position, what happens in the case of an art that is not integrated by the intellect?

RESPONSE: Precisely. Integral art is an art that replaces man's intellect in him. In his attitude, man is art outside himself. His EGO and the being of integral art are ONE.

OBJECTION: Others (including Wagner) have also looked for this integral art.

RESPONSE: Their failure stems from the fact that they have *added* music + painting + poetry, etc. Integral art *multiplies*: music × painting × poetry" (reproduced in Gérard Berreby, ed., *Documents relatifs à la fondation de l'Internationale situationniste (1948–1957)* [Paris: Allia, 1985], 136).

This is simple enough. It would have been sufficient for Wagner to multiply instead of add for him to achieve his goal, to end segregated artistic practices. It is noteworthy that Wolman's solution resolves, radically and logically, the difficult question of the role of the subject with respect to the total work of art. So that he is not *stationary*, so that everything is funneled through "integral art," the subject has only to blend with it. We also find, from the perspective of a genealogy of the *Gesamt-kunstwerk* leading from the utopians and Wagner to the situationists, the decisive role—a kind of missing link—played by Kurt Schwitters (the Schwitters of the Merz-bau, for example).

A Disfigured Lettrism

15. Besides Debord, the official members, those who signed the communiqués of the Lettrist International, included: Serge Berna, Jean-Louis Brau, Gil Wolman, all three of whom were cofounders of the Lettrist International along with Debord, and Sarah Shouaf, Pierre-Joël Berlé, Mohamed Dahou, Jean-Michel Mension, Éliane Papaï, Françoise Lejare, someone named Leibé, and a certain Linda. In the third newsletter, the names Gaëtan M. Langlais and Bull appear. D. Brau, who one suspects may not be unrelated to Jean-Louis Brau, appeared at some point. In the fourth and final newsletter of the Lettrist International, which came out in June 1954, Henry de Béarn, André-Frank Conord, Jacques Fillon, Gilles Ivain (Ivan Chtcheglov), and Patrick Straram made their official appearance and were for a time the principal protagonists—at least initially—of *Potlatch,* along with Michèle Bernstein. Many of the members of the Lettrist International (Brau, Mension, Langlais, Papaï, Lejare, Shouaf) were around during the Saint-Germain-des-Prés years but were not part of the second group of international lettrists.

16. Republished in *Documents relatifs à la fondation de l'Internationale situationniste,* 154.

17. *Guy Debord présente Potlatch (1954–1957)* (Paris: Éditions Gérard Lebovici, 1985; republished by Gallimard, "Folio" [1996], 8). All quotes from *Potlatch* are from this reprint.

18. See, for example, *Potlatch* 8, where there is an article titled "Pour la guerre civile au Maroc" (ibid., 56).

19. See chapter 3, "The Last Guardian," note 8.

Co-optation

20. *Guy Debord présente Potlatch,* 9.

21. Ibid., 41–42.

22. *Internationale situationniste* 5 (1958–69) (Paris: Fayard, 1997) 11.

23. Who remembers them today? The signifier was then the objective ally of a proletariat whose enemy was difficult to make out. Was it the bourgeoisie or the signified? It was another name for the mythical Marxist use-value that had to be restored to the dignity a treacherous exchange value had robbed it of. Those who wish to refresh their memory may want to consult the *Théorie d'ensemble* published by Tel Quel (Paris: Seuil, 1968).

24. Debord had, in his own way, ensured this, by insulting Claude and Antoine Gallimard in an issue of *Internationale situationniste* 12 (115–16). To my knowledge, this is the only time in the history of situationism that insults were addressed to two (or even three) generations of the same family. One can't help but wonder about the

fact that the run of *Internationale situationniste* concluded with these insults, that these were literally the last words in the publication. "You've been screwed. Forget us." I don't know to what extent, twenty years later, those who signed this letter have been forgotten, but it is clear that there must exist publishers who are less forgetful, more vindictive, and less co-optive.

25. I am alluding here to the strange recommendations in favor of *Comments on the Society of the Spectacle* that appeared in September 1988 in the *Lettre du Livre Club du Labyrinthe,* a small review associated with the Groupe de Recherche et d'Étude sur la Civilisation Européenne (GRECE) led by Alain de Benoist, as well as the appropriation of those same *Comments* by a certain Pierre Guillaume, former Socio-Barbarian who had become a Holocaust revisionist and denier (*Annales d'histoire révisionniste* 5 [1988]). Concerning the latter, given the existence of a disagreement between Debord and several members of the group Socialisme ou Barbarie (active, like the SI, during the early sixties), including Guillaume, we can assume a much more personal settling of scores to be the motive. Note that Debord was read—and appreciated—during the nineties by Maurras's successors (see, for example, François Huguenin, "*La Société du spectacle* et *Commentaires sur la société du spectacle* de Guy Debord," *Réaction* 7 [fall 1992]).

26. We would expect no less of Jean-François Martos and others. However, I would have expected a somewhat more nuanced description of the literary and artistic scene of the 1950s from Anselm Jappe, who simply remarks that "On the literary front, the well-worn values, the Mauriacs and Gides, remained firmly in place" (*Guy Debord,* 50). Jappe's summary is a bit succinct.

27. It was standard practice for the Lettrist International to insult Breton. But this did not prevent its members from also referring to surrealism as constituting the starting point for their own activities, within a context of aesthetic rejection. Any number of *Potlatch* texts state this explicitly: "Only a hostility predicated on bad faith leads some people to confuse us with a phase of poetic expression—or its negation—which matters little to us, as much as any *historical* form that writing may have assumed. It is as clumsy to limit our role to that of partisans of some mediocre aesthetic as it is to denounce us, as has been done, for being drug users or gangsters. We have said repeatedly that the demands once made by surrealism—to refer only to this system—should be considered a *minimum* and their urgency not lost sight of" (*Guy Debord présente Potlatch,* 44). Significantly, the first issue of *Internationale situationniste* opened, three years later, with an article titled "Amère victoire du surréalisme" [Bitter victory of surrealism], which, while being a somewhat reserved acknowledgment of surrealism and its accomplishments, confirmed its value as a minimalist program, to be taken up and then surpassed.

One Step Back

28. *Potlatch* 28, 263, reprinted in *Guy Debord and the Situationist International: Texts and Documents,* edited by Tom McDonough (Cambridge: MIT Press, 2002), 26.

29. Ibid., 25–27.

CARTES DU TENDRE

1. During the fifties, when Debord was writing his *Mémoires*, the authors of the Nouveau Roman, and Robbe-Grillet in particular, were some of the favorite targets of lettrist sarcasm. Their existence was irrefutable proof of the death of art hidden behind the appearances of survival. We also find, in this context, that the Nouveau Roman was, along with the New Wave, the last avant-garde (in the broadest and most commonly accepted sense of the term) Debord would do battle with. The rise to power, during the following decade, of Tel Quel left him indifferent, primarily because of the amount of distance he had put between himself and the Parisian avant-garde scene.

2. It is still being developed by the military, satellites having replaced explorers and surveyors.

3. Christophe Bourseiller, *Vie et mort de Guy Debord* (Paris: Plon, 1999), 76–77.

4. *Potlatch* 2 (1954), (Paris: Gallimard, 1996), 21.

5. See, for example, *Correspondance*, vol. 2 (Paris: Fayard, 2001), 207, 219.

6. Ibid., 236–237.

7. Ibid., 265. In the third section of *Mémoires* is a small photograph of Ivan Chtcheglov, significantly placed immediately before Debord's development of the theme of psychogeography. As far as can be determined, the reference is to the page referred to in the dedication. *Panegyric*, volume 2, also contains two pictures of him, one of which is placed opposite an excerpt from *The Naked City*.

8. Gilles Ivain, "Formulaire pour un urbanisme nouveau," *Internationale situationniste* 1, 15–20, and "Lettres de loin," *Internationale situationniste* 9 (Paris: Fayard, 1997), 38–40.

9. G. D., *Complete Cinematic Works*, translated and edited by Ken Knabb (Oakland, Calif.: AK Press, 2003), 170.

THE POETICS OF THE *DÉRIVE*

1. G. D., "Théorie de la dérive," *Internationale situationniste* 2 (Paris: Fayard, 1997), 19–20. This text appeared initially in 1956 in *Les Lèvres nues* 9, a review associated with the Belgian "revolutionary" surrealist movement, which, after the war, refused to abandon a revolutionary political viewpoint, unlike the now classical (not to say academic) surrealism of Breton, who with time became increasingly less interested in strictly political engagement. *Les Lèvres nues* was edited in Belgium by Marcel Mariën, whom Debord and Wolman met in 1952 during a stopover in Brussels. The lettrists published a large number of texts in Brussels. Aside from *Potlatch*, their own review from 1954 to 1957, *Les Lèvres nues* was the only publication in which they participated. The fact that it was a "dissident" surrealist review, which attempted to restore to surrealism the radicality it had lost during its official period (the Breton period), is also significant. *Les Lèvres nues* is in one sense the proof of a certain kinship between lettrism and surrealism. Genealogically, Mariën's review was the missing link between Breton and Debord.

2. The existence of this relationship becomes even more obvious after reading some of Debord's letters containing reports of *"dérives"* that are unquestionably surrealist in tone. I am thinking in particular of a beautiful letter dated October 31, 1960, addressed to Patrick Straram (a former lettrist who had left for Canada but with whom Debord continued to correspond for several years). In it Debord relates the events of a rather bizarre, alcohol-laced evening, which he then compares to Malcolm Lowry's *Under the Volcano*: "So, Lowry's influential game, for someone who submits to it under favorable conditions (?), is sufficient to forcefully reveal *significant* incidents that otherwise would have gone unnoticed, and certainly not have been understood as such—, and first of all to reveal, as their center, the meaning of the entire day, this *dérive*. A meaning that was not premeditated or self-evident" (*Correspondance*, vol. 2, 42). In this same letter he also mentions, although more briefly, another *dérive*, about which Debord merely remarks: *"Dérive* incredibly hurried and containing an odd leitmotif, irrational and external, the reappearance of signs related to Van Gogh's death." Much more clearly than in the official reports, here the *dérive*, as is often the case with surrealist experiments, is associated with . . . the sign, with the ability to recognize a meaning beyond the absence of meaning. Finally, given the scarcity of "personal" narratives in Debord's correspondence, it is remarkable that they appear to be prompted by reports of the *dérive*. Here the *dérive* appears more clearly as a space ripe for the deployment of authenticity or subjectivity.

3. It is easy to convince oneself of this by rereading *Nadja* or the first chapters of *L'amour fou*, in which the objectification of desire appears explicitly as the result of a process or, more specifically, a collective ramble. *Nadja* was also a book that Breton had wanted to expose to life, "left ajar, like doors," according to his well-known expression, so one could make the transition from book to life: "I hope, in any case, that the presentation of some dozen observations of this order as well as what follows will be of a nature to send some men rushing out into the street, after making them aware, if not of the non-existence, at least of the crucial inadequacy of any so-called categorical self-evaluation, of any action which requires a continuous application and which can be premeditated" (*Nadja*, translated by Richard Howard [New York: Grove Press, 1960], 59). Concerning *Nadja* and *Le paysan de Paris* as invitations to the *dérive*: The differences with a book such as *Mémoires* are less obvious than it may appear and have a lot to do with the artistic "bad faith" of the surrealists, for if they bet on the city, if they made appeals to "run down into the street," their literary ulterior motives were never very far. The books "left ajar, like doors" remain books, and the doors left ajar to life can also be crossed in the opposite direction.

4. *Internationale situationniste* 1, 15.

5. Ibid., 19.

6. Recall that in the "Preface to a Modern Mythology," which serves as an introduction to *Le paysan de Paris*, and in the first pages of the book, Aragon explicitly extols, as a precursor of a new mythology, a Paris that is fast disappearing through accelerated modernization, boulevards replacing the emblematic *passages* and their erotic shadow plays. In keeping with the Baudelairean tradition, the Paris of modern

myth is primarily a Paris devoted to disappearance. The fate of the passages, whatever they might be, is to pass away.

7. Many of these places are explicitly described in two "Comptes rendus de dérives," which were published in the same issue of *Les Lèvres nues* as the "Theory of the dérive." Debord seems to have been the only one to have participated in both *dérive* actions.

8. I am alluding to the book by Louis Chevalier, *L'assassinat de Paris* (Paris: Calman-Lévy, 1977); *The Assassination of Paris*, translated by David P. Jordan (Chicago: University of Chicago Press, 1994).

9. According to the fragmentary reports of the *dérive* found in the *Correspondance*, it seems absolutely clear that *dérive* and sobriety were completely incompatible.

10. The term *"dérive"* itself has military origins. In terms of strategy, it refers to a "calculated action determined by the absence of a proper locus." For Clausewitz, it was an "art of weakness," and for von Bülow a "maneuver within the enemy's field of vision." See Tom McDonough, "Situationist Space," *October* 67 (winter, 1994): n. 45, reprinted in Tom McDonough, ed., *Guy Debord and the Situationist International* (Cambridge: MIT Press, 2002).

11. For additional details on the relation of the lettrists and the situationists to "functionalist" urbanism, see Simon Sadler, *The Situationist City* (Cambridge, Mass., and London: MIT Press, 1998).

12. Roger Callois, "Paris, mythe moderne," in *Le mythe et l'homme* (Paris: Gallimard, 1938). In this sense, although there is little that connects them directly, Caillois at least shares with Debord a certain contempt for poetry and literature in general, which are guilty of ineffectiveness and impotence, and whose only hope would be to rediscover the power of myth. The return to myth, which is a return to power, to effectiveness, inevitably involves idleness, the abandonment of literature strictly speaking.

13. G. D., "Théorie de la dérive," 22.

14. Even the two "Comptes rendus de dérive" published in *Les Lèvres nues* (see note 7), the only ones published, to my knowledge, are written as "objectively" as possible and limit themselves to an external description of the events that occurred during the *dérive*. At no time do they discuss what the participants actually experienced.

15. G. D., *Critique of Separation*, in *Complete Cinematic Works*, translated and edited by Ken Knabb (Oakland, Calif.: AK Press, 2003), 33.

16. G. D., *The Society of the Spectacle*, translated by Donald Nicholson-Smith (New York: Zone Books, 1994), thesis 172.

17. Ibid., thesis 168.

PSYCHOGEOGRAPHY AND PSYCHOANALYSIS

1. Gilles Ivain, "Formulaire pour un urbanisme nouveau," *Internationale situationniste* 1, 18.

2. The situationist *dérive* was simply one aspect of what Anthony Vidler referred to as the "architectural uncanny," in *The Architectural Uncanny* (Cambridge, Mass., and London: MIT Press, 1992).

3. Gilles Ivain, "Formulaire pour un urbanisme nouveau," 18.

4. Ibid.

5. *Internationale situationniste* 9, 38.

6. *Internationale situationniste* 1, 11.

7. Aside from the explicit reference to psychoanalysis in this 1958 text, we find that the period of "constructing situations" coincided with the rapid growth, during the fifties and sixties, of a series of experimental forms of psychotherapy that challenged the techniques of separation of conventional psychiatry and served to focus criticism on everyday life in its totality: group therapy, psychodrama, role-playing, the emergence of various forms of "antipsychiatry," and so on. Among them, psychogeography represents a radical and wild version (in the sense of wild analysis), totalizing, without limits or borders, without safeguards.

8. The reference to Leiris, who in 1958 had already published *Scratches* and *Scraps,* is interesting because the writer positioned himself at the crossroads of all the then-current avant-gardes. He began as a surrealist but drifted toward Bataille. And, like Bataille, he had been in analysis, before making autobiography a means of—naturally, interminable—self-analysis. At the same time, he was close to Sartre and, more generally, through his ethnographic activities, to the anticolonialist political movement.

9. In a letter sent in 1963 to the (young) German situationist Uwe Lausen, who was practically the only survivor of the German section, Debord wrote the following, which significantly relates the question of subjectivity to the expression "passage through life" (always movement, mobility, drift): "We no longer wish to talk about whether a review is or is not necessary, if theory is or is not boring or somewhat impractical. We no longer want to have to prove that we are concerned about (and even before all else, with the weapons of all those mediations) our personal adventures in our passage through life. We feel we are at the center of the problem of subjectivity. And a thousand times more 'artists' (or successors of the old artistic world) than someone like Prem [an ephemeral German situationist]" (*Correspondance,* vol. 2, 216–17).

10. It is in these terms that Lacan's work was so amiably described, in this case in association with Heidegger: "Heidegger and Lacan employ, without any other reason than to dazzle the public, the obscure disintegration of language they found in the final phase of modern poetic writing (where this disintegration has had a profound meaning). They emulated this style, with the maximum of literary talent, but in their particular 'discipline.' It is the supposed seriousness of the philosopher or psychoanalyst that validates the obscurity that has been so roundly criticized, as a gratuitous game detrimental to the reader's comfort, in our most contemporary poets. In return, obscurity, which is here truly hollow and pompous, hides the vacuity of their ideas and allows both men to stage a cultural *show* out of a succession of those old philosophizing forms of *disconnected thinking,* which for years have been separated from thought, petrified and moribund. Their modernism is decked out like Pompeii" (*Internationale situationniste* 10, 63–64).

11. *Potlatch* 7, 51.

UNITARY URBANISM: BETWEEN UTOPIA AND ARCHITECTURE

1. Gilles Ivain, "Formulaire pour un urbanisme nouveau," *Internationale situationniste* 1, 19.

2. See Simon Sadler, *The Situationist City* (Cambridge, Mass., and London: MIT Press, 1998).

3. During the early Lettrist International period, Louis II of Bavaria became one of the symbols of psychogeography, along with Piranese, Claude Lorrain, the postman Ferdinand Cheval, Arthur Cravan, Jack the Ripper, and others—all of them devoted psychogeographers, a label attributed to them the way the surrealist label had been assigned to others in a different era: "Louis II of Bavaria is a psychogeographer among royalty" (*Potlatch* 2, 20). The reference to Louis II is even more significant in that it also presages, via Wagner, who was his protégé, the problematic of the *Gesamtkunstwerk* (see chapter 3, "Means of Communication").

4. Concerning the Saint-Simonians, see Henry-René d'Allemagne, *Les saint-simoniens, 1827–1832* (Paris, 1930), 302ff.

5. Gilles Ivain, "Formulaire pour un urbanisme nouveau," 16.

6. *Potlatch* 5, 37–38. There is something arbitrary and outrageous in the lettrist accusations against Le Corbusier, who, after having been the originator of functionalism during the period between the two world wars, would become, during the fifties and sixties, one of its harshest critics (Asger Jorn acknowledged this in the first articles he wrote for *Internationale situationniste*).

7. See Michel Foucault, *Discipline and Punish*, translated by Alan Sheridan (New York: Vintage Books, 1995). There is no sign of any rapport between Foucault and Debord, who seem to have ignored one another, for numerous reasons easy to imagine, associated with their different social and professional positions, lifestyles, means of intervention, and the focus of their thought. However, between the "later" Foucault, the one who analyzed the mechanics of surveillance characteristic of power, and Debord's stubborn resolution to remove himself from any power conceived as spectacle—the gaze that nothing escapes—the incompatibility is not as absolute as might be imagined. For Debord, as for Foucault, power is in the last resort the ability to see and be seen, as suggested by Martin Jay in *Downcast Eyes: The Denigration of Vision in Twentieth-Century French Thought* (Berkeley: University of California Press, 1994), chap. 7.

8. *Potlatch* 27, 243–45. Elsewhere in the same issue there is a list of participants of the festival, whose turpitude and baseness were revealed for all to see—a throwback to the heyday of surrealism. Prominent on the list are the names Béjart, César, Ionesco, the inevitable Isou, Messiaen, Stockhausen, Prévert, Tardieu, Tinguely.

9. In other words, anti-Bretonian surrealism, in which the lettrists themselves participated a few years later, collaborating with Marcel Mariën on *Les Lèvres nues*. Revolutionary surrealism played a brief transitional role between the surrealist movement and the situationist movement, by way of Cobra on the one hand, and the Lettrist International on the other. ·

10. This dimension of the Cobra project was already evident in the manifesto of the Dutch experimental group written by Constant in 1948 and published in the first issue of *Reflex*: "The historical influence of the upper classes has increasingly pushed art into a position of dependence, accessible only to exceptionally gifted intellects, alone capable of deriving some freedom from formalism. In this way an individualist culture has been constructed, which is condemned along with the society that produced it, its conventions no longer offering any opportunity for imagination and desire, even preventing man's vital expression. . . . A popular art cannot currently correspond to the conceptions of the people, for the people, to the extent it does not actively participate in artistic creation, can only conceive of historically imposed formalisms. What characterizes popular art is its vital expression, direct and collective. . . . A new freedom will be born that will allow mankind to satisfy its desire to create. Through this development the professional artist will lose his privileged position. This explains the resistance of contemporary artists" (this text was republished in a French translation in *Documents relatifs à la fondation de l'Internationale situationniste*, edited by Gérard Berreby [Paris: Allia, 1985], 31–33). Clearly, all the future situationist statements concerning an authentically popular and collective art, and the subsequent disappearance of individual art, did not spring out of nowhere. They originated in the "revolutionary surrealist" movement of the immediate postwar period, which, paradoxically, was more active in northern Europe than in France, where it was harder to separate surrealism from Breton.

The "popular culture" referred to by Constant and Cobra would again remain an unfulfilled wish. The members of Cobra were artists and, like artists in other avant-garde movements, they signed their works, their "collectives" rarely surpassing more than two individuals (as in the case of Jorn and Dotremont). However, we can assume that the popular culture that constituted one of Cobra's goals made its way into the style of the works produced by its members. It is true that in general this was, if not immediately, at least easily accessible, and did not require prior knowledge of art from the viewer. The principle of spontaneity on which their works were based was just as true of their reception.

11. Asger Jorn, "Pour la forme," *Internationale situationniste* (Paris, 1958), republished in *Documents relatifs à la fondation de l'Internationale situationniste*, 413–14.

12. Neither Asger Jorn nor the situationists at a later date had a monopoly on antifunctionalism. Throughout the fifties and sixties, the idea could be traced to a number of experiments that fell along the border between art and architecture. To some extent, it even determined the border between the two: for artists, utopia, for architects, concrete projects that were professionally and technically acceptable. The emergence of situationism is contemporary with a movement that strongly contested functionalism and engaged architects such as Peter and Alison Smithson, Gill and Bill Howell, and John Voelcker, who, together with the Dutch architects Aldo Van Eyck (a friend of Constant) and Jacob Bakema, Georges Candilis from France, Giancarlo De Carlo from Italy, and Shadrach Woods from the United States, formed

"Team 10." At the International Congress of Modern Architecture (CIAM) in 1956, the group established itself as being strongly critical of functionalism. For additional information on this subject, see Simon Sadler, *The Situationist City*, 22ff.

13. For a time, those contacts remained informal and were based, for the most part, on the personal friendship between Debord and Jorn. They didn't become official until 1957, when the LI sent Gil Woman to the Congress of the International Movement for an Imaginist Bauhaus in Alba. Their "official" status was entirely relative, however, because the congress, like the one in 1957 devoted to the foundation of the SI, was attended by no more than a handful of individuals who apparently spent as much time drinking as they did on political and artistic conspiracy.

14. This age difference is interesting and rather atypical in the history of avant-garde groups, which have been, for the most part, the result of contemporaries trying to usurp an earlier generation. Nothing of the kind occurred in the meeting between Jorn (or the painter Pinot-Gallizio) and Debord, who was never one for Oedipal relationships.

Unitary Urbanism

15. *Internationale situationniste* 1, 17.

16. Ibid., 24. Concerning the debate introduced by Constant, there is a discrepancy between the apparently highly acrimonious public debates—those reported in *Internationale situationniste*—and the much more nuanced positions illustrated by the exchange of letters among the principal protagonists. For example, the debate over theory between Constant and Debord (supported by Jorn) in *Internationale situationniste* does not occupy the same place in their exchange of letters at this time (at least judging by Debord's letters). This confirms the proposal advanced earlier that the public space, and it alone, was inevitably one of conflict for Debord. On another level, one may wonder whether the lack of true debate in the letters shouldn't be attributed to the evasiveness of Constant, who sometimes gives the impression of having joined the SI only to let them know that he wanted out as soon as possible.

17. Ibid.

18. Before the break with Pinot-Gallizio, whose involvement in the art world was incompatible with the situationist project, many situationists admired and defended the principles of his "industrial painting." Pinot-Gallizio made paintings by the meter, and his production was unlimited. It was a compelling illustration of inflation in the art market, and had the added benefit of doing away with problems of format (he cut off whatever length of painting the buyer wanted to purchase), "period," inspiration, authenticity, reproduction, gallery openings, and so on.

19. *Internationale situationniste* 3 (December 1959), 32.

20. Ibid., 34.

21. In referring to the Grail, I am not forgetting that it was the term used by Debord at this time (in his *Mémoires*) to describe the quest of the earlier lettrist-drifters, as if for him the fourth dimension of pure poetry was the poetry experienced

during the *dérive*, experienced through the soles of one's feet rather than in an amusement park, even a situationist one.

22. *Internationale situationniste* 5, 10. Later, Pinot-Gallizio was partially redeemed because of his behavior, even though this did not result in his reentry into the SI, something that never happened and never would happen. Debord was not someone interested in reconciliation. From the point of view of the SI, Pinot-Gallizio was one of the most sympathetic among the expelled, certainly more sympathetic than Constant, who, although he was never expelled, decided to quit shortly after the departure of Pinot-Gallizio and some others. I discuss these individual situationist histories because they confirm the relatively fluid and random nature of its foundations. Someone like Pinot-Gallizio may not have remained long in the SI, but he could have. Maybe Constant should have been expelled before deciding to leave. Was their position that much different than Jorn's? Jorn himself quit the SI a few months later to prevent his prestige as an artist from overshadowing the situationist rejection of art. But, like Constant and several others, he resumed painting and exhibited with a clear conscience. Throughout all this he remained close friends with Debord and continued to finance the activities of the SI. Jorn had no trouble returning to where he had left off as an artist, for he had never abandoned his earlier interests, even during his situationist period. Between 1958 and 1961, he exhibited and collaborated with a number of individuals who were at least as suspect as those who triggered Pinot-Gallizio's expulsion. Debord never said much about this, dogmatism being apparently of less interest to him than the quality of a relationship, the reciprocity of generosity. These incidents demonstrate just how hard it to is to keep utopia squarely in sight when you lose faith in a fourth dimension, whether pure poetry or something else. It is difficult to adhere to the kind of limit represented by utopia without succumbing to either of the two "specializations" that have always been the nightmare of avant-gardes, including the situationists: art and politics.

23. *Internationale situationniste* 3, 12; reprinted as "Unitary Urbanism at the End of the 1950s," translated by Thomas Y. Levin, in *On the Passage of a Few People through a Rather Brief Moment in Time: The Situationist International, 1957–1992*, edited by Elisabeth Sussman (Cambridge: MIT Press, 1989), 143.

24. Ibid., 144.

25. Ibid.

The New Babylon

26. Ibid., 38; "A Different City for a Different Life," translated by John Shepley, in *Guy Debord and the Situationist International: Texts and Documents*, edited by Tom McDonough (Cambridge: MIT Press, 2002), 96.

27. West Berlin, closer to Paris, was another example. Its center, rebuilt at this time, was supposedly one of the great successes of modern architecture. This is significant because, at this time, German situationists were joining the SI in force.

28. In doing so, he resumed the attack on Le Corbusier, one of the first to imagine constructions built on columns. Constant was also greatly inspired by the work

of architects such as Yona Friedman, founder of spatial urbanism, and, in 1957, the "Groupe d'études d'architecture mobile" (GEAM), in which Constant participated.

29. *Internationale situationniste* 3, 39–40; McDonough, *Guy Debord and the Situationist International*, 99.

30. "Description de la zone jaune," *Internationale situationniste* 4, 24.

31. See Jean-Jacques Raspaud and Jean-Pierre Voyer, *L'Internationale situationniste: Protagonistes/Chronologie/Bibliographie* (avec un index des noms insultés) (Paris: Champ Libre, 1972), 16.

32. *Internationale situationniste* 7, 26–27.

33. The official reason for Jorn's departure, apparently at Debord's request, was his fame as an artist, which was felt to be incompatible with situationism's antiart position. Jorn subsequently continued to work from time to time with *Internationale situationniste* (under the pseudonym Georges Keller, as if to mark the now subterranean nature of his situationism) and to support the SI financially—he said this support was his specific contribution to the movement. Clearly, his friendship got the better of his principles. However, Jorn's position was uncommon given that any break with the SI was in general absolutely final. The SI reminded Constant of this when he asked to withdraw from the group temporarily. This is important given that the SI came into being after the meeting between Debord, the antiartist, and Jorn, the artist, and that all the conflicts that divided the group were, in a sense, present from the beginning. Without Debord and Jorn's deep friendship and feelings of mutual esteem, which were capable of overcoming differences of position that were insurmountable in other cases, it is likely that the SI would never have seen the light of day.

3. The Light Brigade

MEANS OF COMMUNICATION :: From the Abeyance of Meaning to Transparency

1. G. D., *The Society of the Spectacle*, translated by Donald Nicholson-Smith (New York: Zone Books, 1994), thesis 187.

2. Ibid., thesis 191.

3. There is a reference to the Northwest Passage in Debord's *Mémoires* concerning the earliest psychogeographic experiments with the *dérive*. As such, the best way of finding it is to continue to look for it: art enters life in exemplary fashion when it commits life to psychogeographic exploration.

4. I am thinking especially of the Sartre of the last chapter of *What Is Literature?* who expects the future proletarian revolution to assign the writer the place he deserves by granting him the freedom to speak to everyone, to have all of humanity as his audience, and to no longer be condemned to writing for the (petite) bourgeoisie alone.

5. In France, there really was no other claimant to the title of the last avant-garde, other than Tel Quel, which survived the SI for about a decade. The question

remains whether this was an avant-garde in the strict sense of the term. It was never Tel Quel's aim to transcend art in order to make common cause with an authentic form of communication, and the group was only marginally "communitarian."

6. In many respects, *The Society of the Spectacle* is a reflection of the fall, in the sense understood by Rousseau in the *Confessions* (but also in the two *Essays*), and even, as often happens when one starts down this path, a reflection on multiple and ever-repeating *falls*. If you begin with the fall, you generally continue falling, at least until you find yourself on the terra firma of primitive society, nomadic and proto-communist, one that has never known the division of labor, or the exploitation and alienation through which the lie is substituted for authentic communication, transparency, and lost innocence. We are subject to the reign of the spectacle. But since when? That story is more difficult to unravel and demonstrates that the concept of the spectacle is harder to locate historically than it seems and, consequently, it may be less a question of a concept than of the way Debord positioned himself.

From Urbanism to Totality

7. *Internationale situationniste* 3, 38.

8. "Those who think the automobile is eternal have not considered, even from a narrowly technological point of view, other forms of future transport. For example, certain models of helicopter designed for individuals and currently being tested by the U.S. Army will probably be in use by civilians within twenty years" (ibid., 36).

9. *Internationale situationniste* 1, 12.

10. Ibid.

11. *Internationale situationniste* 4, 37–38.

12. "Today, a temple will rise . . . larger than the Greek circus or the antique theater . . . ; it will rise and open its heart to the theater, to the pulpit, to the forum, to the novel, while allowing them to develop. . . . From those two harmonious forms the new drama will be born: tradition, the past, convention will be solemnly glorified and the genius of humankind will preside there; but, through woman's inspiration, prophecy, the future, the extraordinary will cast their dazzling colors and their saintly exuberance upon it. Painting, music, coordinated gestures, elocution, rhymed language, and decoration; dance, pantomime, improvisation, free verse will combine to fill every heart with enthusiasm" (quoted by Henry-René d'Allemagne, *Les saints-simoniens, 1827–1837* [Paris, 1930], 305).

13. See chapter 4, "Against Interpretation."

14. Within the society of the spectacle, as within the book that describes it, no dialogue is possible, or even desirable, the enemy being, by definition, not made to be recognized. The rhetoric of *The Society of the Spectacle* or of Debord in general, who displayed unusual perseverance in this, can be characterized by this attitude of total negativity, just as we describe someone who refuses to engage in a dialogue as displaying negative behavior.

15. Stéphane Mallarmé, "Action Restricted," in *Selected Poetry and Prose*, ed-

ited by Mary Ann Caws (New York: New Directions Publishing Corporation, 1982), 80; *Œuvres complètes* (Paris: Gallimard, "Bibliothèque de la Pléiade," 1945), 372.

Poetry Appropriated by Everyone

16. The first issue of *Internationale situationniste* contained the following notice, which appeared regularly in all subsequent issues: "This publication is collectively written. The few articles written and signed individually should be considered the joint effort of our comrades and as particular expressions of collective research. We are opposed to the survival of forms such as the literary review or art magazine. All the texts published in *Internationale situationniste* can be freely reproduced, translated, or adapted without indicating the source."

17. Stéphane Mallarmé, "The Tomb of Edgar Poe," in *Stéphane Mallarmé: Collected Poems*, translated and with a commentary by Henry Weinfield (Berkeley: University of California Press, 1996), 71; "Le tombeau d'Edgar Poe," in *Œuvres complètes*, 70.

18. Tom McDonough, ed., *Guy Debord and the Situationist International: Texts and Documents* (Cambridge: MIT Press, 2002), 173. (This text originally appeared in *Internationale situationniste* 10, 50.)

19. Ibid., 173.

20. Ibid., 179.

THE POETICS OF REVOLUTION

1. *Internationale situationniste* 7, 21.

2. See "Perspectives de modifications conscientes dans la vie quotidienne," which is a transcription of the text of the taped speech Debord gave during a seminar by Henri Lefebvre, and "Banalités de base" by Raoul Vaneigem, which appeared in issues 7 and 8 of *Internationale situationniste*.

3. The "Banalités de base" served as an early draft of the book.

4. Henri Lefebvre, *Critique of Everyday Life*, translated by John Moore, with a preface by Michel Trebitsch (London and New York: Verso, 1991). A modified version, adapted in several places to account for the social and political changes that had occurred in France since the book's first publication (Grasset, 1947), appeared in 1958 from Éditions de L'Arche. This was followed in 1961 by a second volume (which contained the chapter on the theory of moments).

5. Henri Lefebvre, *La somme et le reste* (Paris: Minuit, 1958).

6. Henri Lefebvre, *Le temps des méprises* (Paris: Stock, 1975).

7. G. D., *Correspondance*, vol. 1, 312–13.

8. *Internationale situationniste* 1, 21, quoted in Tom McDonough, ed., *Guy Debord and the Situationist International: Texts and Documents* (Cambridge: MIT Press, 2002), 62. In issue 3 of *Internationale situationniste*, the tone was considerably more critical. With respect to the praise of "revolutionary romanticism," which served as the backbone for Lefebvre's ideas about the chances of cultural revolution

in *La somme et le reste*, the following appears: "But here we are approaching the science fiction of revolutionary thought, preached in *Arguments*, which is bold enough
to engage millennia of history but incapable of offering a single novel idea between
now and the end of the century; and naturally teamed up in the present with the
worst exhumations of neo-reformism" (*Internationale situationniste* 3, 5). The conclusion is obvious and appears a page later: "For revolutionaries there is no turning
back. The world of expression, regardless of its content, is already outdated." Apparently, Debord was not terribly excited about the youthful enthusiasms Lefebvre
had revised and corrected. With respect to his relationship with the situationists,
he was very much on the outside looking in. After all, it was Lefebvre who wrote to
Debord, and, in fact, he did so after the article quoted earlier in which Debord pulls
no punches. The situationists never sought Lefebvre out.

9. Bourseiller writes that Lefebvre enjoyed an excellent *literary (sic)* reputation,
which allowed him to introduce the situationists to the leading luminaries of the
day. But his list of VIPs is limited to Raoul Vaneigem, whom Lefebvre introduced to
Debord (Christophe Bourseiller, *Vie et mort de Guy Debord* [Paris: Plon, 1999], 129).
So it was through Lefebvre the poet that Debord met the well-known (at the time)
poet Vaneigem, thanks to which his own career as a poet was supposed to have taken
off. This has to be one of the most misunderstood pages in the history of French
poetry.

10. *Internationale situationniste* 4, 10–11.

11. In the second volume of the *Critique of Everyday Life*, Lefebvre estimates that
the "discovery" of everyday life (his oeuvre, therefore) is at least as important as the discovery of the unconscious was in Freud's time. The comparison suggests, and many of
Lefebvre's arguments are effectively directed at demonstrating this, that everyday
life assumes the role of the socially repressed. Consequently, it serves as a kind of unconscious that will be impossible, by definition, to consciously construct. Everyday
life is the psychopathology of social life. It is hard to imagine Debord, so attached to
the possibility of the conscious construction of lived experience, being seduced by
such an idea.

12. Lefebvre's text appeared in *Arguments* 27–28 (1962). The text by Debord,
Vaneigem, and Kotanyi was republished in 1971, initially in *Internationale situationniste* 12, 246, with the title "14 thèses sur la Commune." We can therefore exactly
measure the extent of Lefebvre's theft. In any case, in the history of situationism this
was the only time an accusation of plagiarism was made, and there is no reason it
would have been made against Lefebvre if it were unfounded. Debord was never
short of arguments for attacking his enemies or former allies, and it is hard to understand why he would have needed to resort to an accusation of plagiarism if Lefebvre's behavior hadn't justified it. It is worth noting in passing that the friendship
between the two men, which lasted for two years, does not square very well with
the image of an intolerant, uncompromising Debord. After all, Lefebvre had still not
severed all his connections to the Communist Party, or with the review *Arguments*,
which had been clearly proscribed by the SI. As for his academic connections, he

never even considered severing them. If Debord's objective had been to break with the man, there were a number of reasons or pretexts for doing so.

13. Concerning this matter, or at least Lefebvre's point of view on it, see Lefebvre, *Le temps des méprises*. The picture of Guy Debord taking over the review *Arguments* leaves the reader perplexed. Not only do we look in vain for any trace of such a project in Debord's writings (including the correspondence), but it is important to remember that *Arguments* and those who contributed to it were, from the very beginning of the SI, the object of particularly fierce criticism (it was as bad to be an *"argumentiste"* as it was a "Nashist"), a factor that led, two years *before* the break with Lefebvre, to the following statement: "The Council has decided that anyone who collaborates with the review *Arguments* after January 1, 1961, will under no circumstances be admitted to the situationists at any time in the future" (*Internationale situationniste* 5, 13). This means that Lefebvre could not have been unaware of what he was doing by publishing the work of the situationists, beneath his signature, in the last issue of the review. And the claim that Debord conspired to take over the review is as credible as it would be to claim that he was conspiring to take over *Les Temps modernes* or *Paris-Match*.

14. Taking its inspiration from the German, Italian, and Dutch "communist left" of the twenties and thirties, which was inspired by theorists such as Karl Korsch, Paul Mattick, Hermann Gorter, and Anton Pannekoek, after 1946 Socialisme ou Barbarie adopted their principal claim, namely, that the communist revolution was betrayed not only by the Stalinists (as the Trotskyists claimed), but by Lenin and the Bolsheviks as well, who were equally guilty of having abandoned the dictatorship of the proletariat in favor of a dictatorship of the party over the proletariat.

15. This document is titled *Préliminaires pour une définition de l'unité du programme révolutionnaire*. It has been republished in an appendix to a short book by Daniel Blanchard titled *Debord, dans le bruit et la cataracte du temps* (Paris: Sens & Tonka, 2000). It is not only a firsthand account of the relations between the SI and Socialisme ou Barbarie, but an analysis, in some ways remarkable, of what should be called the meaning of form in Debord and the connection between this meaning and revolution.

16. We find little evidence because it does not really correlate with the image of a leader hungry for power and purity, whose only satisfaction lay in exclusivity. Everything, however, points to the fact that Debord's relations with the Socialisme ou Barbarie group were extremely normal, limited to discussions, debates, joint projects. And when it was found that there were disagreements or simply a lack of interest, they separated without further ado. It was on the basis of a similar image of Debord that he was accused of having stolen his ideas from Socialisme ou Barbarie and Lefebvre: because they refused to acknowledge that he was a man of dialogue, partial to gift giving and exchanges, it was claimed that everything he obtained from others was stolen from them. Conversely, it seems self-evident, when we adopt this perspective, that no one owes anything to Debord. He plagiarized and stole, regardless of what the texts say, or don't say. But because no one has successfully shown

what texts Debord stole from, his accusers have recently settled on the accusation of "oral" theft. Debord owes everything not to Lefebvre's books, but to the notes he supposedly took, with the feverish industriousness characteristic of him, at Lefebvre's seminar, or possibly even through the tape recorder he used for his presentation at the seminar, which would have been used to rob the oracle Lefebvre of his every word. Reading *Le temps des méprises*, we find that the philosopher saw fire where there was no smoke.

17. To these reasons, which I consider essential, should be added others, equally important at this time. Debord looked askance at the disparity between the arguments of Socialisme ou Barbarie on worker self-management and the structure of the organization itself, or those like it. In a long letter he sent in May 1961 to the group Pouvoir Ouvrier (which had split off from Socialisme ou Barbarie), to explain why he was pulling out, he referred to the organization as one of "teachers" and "students," or "actors" and "spectators," and the "oppressive separation of roles" (*Correspondance*, vol. 2, 82–88). Ten years after his decision not to go to college, Debord still appears disenchanted with a group that was essentially associated with the student movement and a handful of teachers who—as he put it—were simply working overtime.

18. G. D., "Perspectives de modification conscientes dans la vie quotidienne," *Internationale situationniste* 6, 20–27. Debord's talk is dated May 17, 1961.

19. Debord discussed his choice in the opening paragraphs of his talk: "It is therefore desirable to reveal, by a slight displacement of the customary forms, that this too is everyday life. Of course, distribution of these words on tape does not exactly illustrate the integration of technology in an everyday world that is marginal to the technological world, but makes use of the simplest opportunity to break with the appearances of pseudocollaboration, of factitious dialogue, which is instituted between the speaker 'in person' and his audience. This slight disruption of comfort can serve to bring into focus, in questioning everyday life (an otherwise entirely abstract inquiry), the seminar itself, as well as so many other arrangements of the use of time, or objects, arrangements that are claimed to be 'normal,' that we don't even see; and that ultimately condition us" (ibid., 20). Debord's attitude toward communication is consistently negative. In this context, his gesture is itself a construction of a situation, or, more accurately, the critical construction of an antisituation—a denunciation of present appearances by the duplication of technological artifice.

20. Ibid., 21.

21. Ibid., 24.

22. Ibid., 23.

23. Ibid., 24.

24. *Internationale situationniste* 7 (1962), 22–23.

25. McDonough, *Guy Debord and the Situationist International*, 176. This article originally appeared in *Internationale situationniste* 10 (1966), 51–52.

26. "All the King's Men," *Internationale situationniste* 8 (1963), 30.

27. The claim about the "work of words" occurs in an article devoted to imagining a kind of dictionary that would take into account this work (see the short article,

"Informe," in Georges Bataille, *Œuvres complètes*, vol. 1 [Paris: Gallimard, 1970], 217). With this concept, Bataille also attacked, as is often the case, what he considered the idealist poetics of the surrealists, who favored wordplay, words "making love," to use Breton's expression from the first *Surrealist Manifesto*. But the point of departure for "All the King's Men" is also an explicit rejection of the surrealist position, as well as other amateurs of the signifier: "Contrary to what clever men may claim, words don't play. They don't make love as Breton thought, other than in dreams" (*Internationale situationniste* 8, 29).

28. *Internationale situationniste* 8, 29–30; McDonough, *Guy Debord and the Situationist International*, 153–54.

29. I am not trying to directly compare two groups that were historically the two last avant-garde groups in France. I simply want to point out that the linguistic, poetic, and political concerns of the situationists overlapped with the configuration and logic characteristic of avant-gardes in general. Their position with respect to Tel Quel's research (at this point mostly in the future) is ironically apparent in a photograph illustrating "All the King's Men," which represents "L'Algérie et l'écriture" [Algeria and writing]. In it we see an automobile covered with slogans in favor of the FLN [National Liberation Front]. Beneath the image is a quote from Roland Barthes, taken from *Writing Degree Zero*, affirming that "Writing is precisely this compromise between freedom and remembrance, it is this recollecting freedom that remembers and is free only in the gesture of choice, but is no longer so within duration. True, today I can select such and such mode of writing, and in so doing assert my freedom, aspire to the freshness of novelty or to a tradition; but I am already no longer able to develop it within duration without gradually becoming a prisoner of someone else's words and even of my own" (*Writing Degree Zero*, translated by Annette Lavers and Colin Smith [New York: Hill and Wang, 1977], 16–17). As such, even an *"argumentiste"* such as Barthes [Barthes was one of the editors of the French review *Arguments—Trans.*] can be appropriated. All it takes is to turn him into a caption for a picture of an Opel made poetic by the FLN.

30. *Internationale situationniste* 8, 31; McDonough, *Guy Debord and the Situationist International*, 154.

31. Asger Jorn, *Critique de la politique économique* (Brussels, 1960).

32. "All the King's Men," 31; McDonough, *Guy Debord and the Situationist International*, 155.

33. McDonough, *Guy Debord and the Situationist International*, 156.

34. Ibid., 155.

35. Ibid.

36. *Internationale situationniste* 12 (1969), 3.

FROM STRASBOURG TO SEGOVIA

1. *Internationale situationniste* 12, 6.

2. Hervé Hamon and Patrick Rotman, *Génération*, 2 vols. (Paris: Seuil, 1987, 1988). *Génération* is very typical, which is to say, very contradictory, in that it is one of the most comprehensive and most thoroughly documented books about May 1968.

However, it is only after four hundred pages on the archaeology of May 1968 that we meet the situationists, who are briefly surveyed in about ten pages. Here we learn that *The Society of the Spectacle* and *The Revolution of Everyday Life* were the true bibles of the insurrection, something that nothing in the book's four hundred previous pages or the nine hundred following pages would lead us to suspect.

Strasbourg

3. See Jean-François Martos, *Histoire de l'Internationale situationniste* (Paris: Éditions Gérard Lebovici, 1989); Pascal Dumontier, *Les situationnistes et mai 68: Théorie et pratique de la révolution (1966–1972)* (Paris: Éditions Gérard Lebovici, 1990); and René Viénet, *Enragés et situationnistes dans le mouvement des occupations* (Paris: Gallimard, [1968] 1998).

4. The polemics that broke out in 1976 between Debord and Gérard Lebovici on the one hand, and Khayati and Vaneigem on the other, at the time of the republication by Champ Libre of the famous pamphlet, suggest that, from Lebovici's point of view in any case, and no doubt also Debord's, Khayati, who was himself a mouthpiece, would have acted only as a representative of the SI. And it would be, at the very least, problematic to attribute to him a number of the theses on the society of the spectacle that were found several months later in the book of that title. Concerning the pamphlet, see the *Correspondance,* published by Éditions Champ Libre, vol. 1 (1978), 31ff.

5. *De la misère en milieu étudiant considérée sous ses aspects économique, politique, psychologique, sexuel et notamment intellectuel, et de quelques moyens pour y remédier* (Paris: Champ Libre, 1976), 13–14; reprinted as "On the Poverty of Student Life," in *Beneath the Paving Stones: Situationists and the Beach, May 1968,* texts collected by Dark Star (Oakland, Calif.: AK Press, 2001), 10.

6. This is an argument put forth by Marc Fumaroli, not someone known to harbor situationist sympathies (see *L'État culturel: Essai sur une religion moderne* [Paris: Éditions de Fallois, 1992]).

7. G. D., *Complete Cinematic Works,* translated and edited by Ken Knabb (Oakland, Calif.: AK Press, 2003), 173.

8. Inaudible and therefore incomprehensible, if we are to believe the press, which made repeated comparisons between the authors of the pamphlet "On the Poverty of Student Life" and "beatniks," hippies, and performance artists at happenings.

9. Quoted by Pascal Dumontier, *Les situationnistes et mai 68: Théorie et pratique de la révolution (1966–1972)* (Paris: Éditions Gérard Lebovici, 1990), 86. Here JCR means Revolutionary Communist Youth [Alain Krivine's Trotskyist group.—*Trans.*].

10. Ibid.

Paris

11. The anarchists refused to settle matters between the situationists and Henri Lefebvre, and relations between the two groups remained unchanged from this point on.

12. The situationists were always concerned with perfecting form. This is one of the things that characterized their review. *Internationale situationniste* always made an effort to be attractive, using bright, metallized covers, interesting typography, carefully designed layouts, and well-written texts. This differed significantly from the majority of far-left publications.

13. In the immediate follow-up to the events of May 1968, there appeared a work signed by Walter Lewino, with photos by Jo Shnapp: *L'imagination au pouvoir* (Paris: Le Terrain vague, 1968). It is a book of images, consisting of photographs of inscriptions, slogans, and so on, legible or visible on the walls of Paris around May 1968. Lewino, who had known Debord for several years but was never involved in SI affairs, donated half the royalties from the work to the SI. His distance from the organization merely served to give his gesture more weight: that of recognizing the "authorial" function of the situationists in developing the anonymous and collective forms of mural expression that appeared during the May 1968 revolt.

14. *La véritable scission dans l'Internationale situationniste* (Paris: Champ Libre, 1972; expanded edition, Paris: Fayard, 1998), 80; *The Real Split in the International: Theses on the Situationist International and Its Time* (London: Pluto Press, 2003), 76.

15. The situationists were at the first barricades set up in May and, shortly after, were part of the occupation of the Sorbonne, which they left after a few days, their arguments being espoused by a minority of students. They took advantage of this brief moment at the heart of the university to popularize their methods of expression, covering the walls with slogans: "Comrades! Humanity will only be happy when the last bureaucrat has been hung with the guts of the last capitalist," "Down with the little brat from Nazareth," "Dechristianize the Sorbonne at once!" "My desires are my reality because I believe in the reality of my desires."

16. "The workers, who as always had good reasons for being dissatisfied, started the wildcat strike because they caught wind of the revolutionary situation created by new forms of sabotage in the university and the successive mistakes made by the government in its response. They were obviously as indifferent as we were to the forms or reforms of university life, but certainly not to the critique of culture, of the environment, and of everyday life under advanced capitalism, a critique that spread very quickly after the first tear in the university veil" (*Internationale situationniste* 12, 8; this was the last issue of the SI's review and certainly the most important). For Debord, the student revolt had remained *formal*. It merely produced forms of sabotage that became revolutionary only when taken up by the workers in the occupied factories.

17. On the CMDO, see Pascal Dumontier, *Les situationnistes et mai 68,* 135ff.

18. There are, however, *détournements* that are not situationist at all: for example, those involving airplanes. All explosions are not created equal: the situationists never confused oil and kerosene.

19. *Internationale situationniste* 12, 3–4.

Segovia

20. *Protestation devant les libertaires du présent et du futur sur les capitulations de 1937 par un "incontrôlé" de la Colonne de fer,* translated from the Spanish by two unauthorized "aficionados," bilingual edition (Paris: Champ Libre, 1979).

21. *Appels de la prison de Ségovie,* through the coordination of autonomous Spanish groups (Paris: Champ Libre, 1980).

22. Ibid., 17. [The "ley de fugas," or fugitive law, permitted the assassination of detainees who attempted to flee.—*Trans.*]

23. The "aficionados" were also planning to produce—again with the support of Gérard Lebovici—a record containing some twenty appropriated popular songs, and had convinced the singer Mara Jerez to record them, at least in principle. She changed her mind, however, and the record was never produced. See Debord's *Correspondance,* vol. 2 (Paris: Champ Libre, 1981), 87–94.

THE GREATER THE FAME OF OUR ARGUMENTS, THE GREATER OUR OBSCURITY

1. G. D., *La véritable scission dans l'Internationale situationniste* (Paris: Champ Libre, 1972; expanded edition, Paris: Fayard, 1998), 79–80; *The Real Split in the International: Theses on the Situationist International and Its Time,* translated by John McHale (London: Pluto Press, 2003), 71.

2. This had been latent ever since May 1968, when the unfortunate Vaneigem was absent for the early, explosive weeks of the uprising, having felt it was not worthwhile to cancel his vacation reservations for Costa Brava. The tensions between him and Debord finally burst into the open.

3. On the life, or lives, of situationism after 1972, see the book by Laurent Chollet: *L'insurrection situationniste* (Paris: Dagorno, 2000). The book provides important information on a number of "affiliations" leading to more recent activities of the anarchist, or post-avant-garde, movement. The book does not avoid the risk of confusion, however. Some of the individuals mentioned are unlikely to be pleased to discover that they are agents of situationist insurrection. But although today it is possible, up to a point, to be a situationist without knowing it, we are better able to understand Debord's decision to dissolve the SI in 1971.

4. "First, it seems we are also thinking that membership in the SI (the fact of being, practically speaking, a situationist) is inseparable from a certain *capability.* This 'capability' obviously cannot be determined beforehand because it is, *to a certain extent,* fluid and differs somewhat among each of the individuals engaged in this complex task; because it is *historic* and will vary with the different stages of our actions; finally because there is no question of treating it as *being fixed once and for all* for each of our correspondents. Nor is it a question of waiting for the SI to provide completely, or even to a large extent, this capability to a correspondent. The SI can only engage in discussion on the basis of the practical dialogue that is already possi-

ble, it cannot become a 'primary school,' if only because *there are other urgent*—but more agreeable—*matters*" (G. D., *Correspondance*, vol. 2, 238).

5. Ibid., 240. In the same vein, Debord wrote "Therefore, it is even more important to avoid wounding people. To avoid establishing awkward relationships" (239).

6. Ibid., 156. Dated August 23, 1962, this letter could only have been addressed to Asger Jorn, as a kind of QED.

7. "It was never an SI practice to expel someone without lengthy deliberation, unless *everyone* knew the reasons. In a word, we know that this is a serious weapon (and we did this only because it is a *serious weapon,* without which we could never have maintained and developed our base. The idea of expulsion is not some kind of stupid joke for us)" (letter to Alexander Trocchi, April 22, 1963, ibid., 211).

8. This does not mean that the SI and Debord were never attacked. But the attacks, especially the most violent, the most hateful, almost always came from outside the SI, from individuals who were hostile to it, many because they had been denied membership.

9. In a letter to Paolo Salvadori dated December 11, 1984, Debord brought up the difference between his relationship with Gérard Lebovici and his relationships within the SI in the following terms: "That is to say that, just as I did not formally owe anything to Gérard, he obviously owed me nothing in turn. This is quite different from the relationships you saw in the SI, which I had no trouble doing without after having lived them for more than twenty years, for the final years had been difficult" (Jean-François Martos, *Correspondance avec Guy Debord* [Paris: Le Fin mot de l'histoire, 1998]). What is a group? It is something that requires the need for mutual obligations, that deprives you of freedom, something true friends do not.

10. G. D., *Complete Cinematic Works,* translated and edited by Ken Knabb (Oakland, Calif.: AK Press, 2003), 178–79.

11. Ibid., 179.

12. Ibid., 181–82.

13. *Internationale situationniste* 7, 17.

14. *The Real Split in the International,* 6–11. The analysis of the revolutionary nature of May 1968 and the role played in those events by the SI remained unchanged in 1971 from the months immediately following the events themselves, the only difference being that, in 1971, Debord's analysis occurred within the framework of a Situationist International that had been dissolved. Proof of this can be found in the final issue of *Internationale situationniste* (September 1969), which was devoted entirely to an assessment of May 1968. The fact that the dissolution of the SI changed nearly nothing compared to the 1969 analysis is in itself remarkable. It is as if, in 1969, the analysis included the possibility of dissolution, as if the role of the SI was over with its contribution to May 1968. By 1968, and possibly before, Debord's attitude toward the SI was the same as it was following its dissolution.

15. G. D., *The Real Split in the International,* 58–59.

16. *Internationale situationniste* 12, 83.

17. Ibid., 5.

18. These are some of the expressions used by Bourseiller *(Vie et mort de Guy Debord)*, but he is obviously not the only one to focus on Debord's failures. Under the heading of the "final cycle," the mix of lost illusions and accelerated process of co-optation, the biographer points to the support provided by Philippe Sollers, the move to Gallimard, and, as a preliminary to the final tragedy, predating the suicide it could only serve to prefigure, the Canal Plus broadcast about Debord that took place on January 9, 1995, a few weeks after his death. The first part of the broadcast consisted of the film Debord made in 1994 with Brigitte Cornand, titled *Guy Debord: son art et son temps,* and the second part of *La Société du spectacle* [The Society of the Spectacle] and *Réfutation de tous les jugements* [Refutation of all the Judgments]. Bourseiller describes the broadcast, which appeared at 10:10 p.m. on an encrypted channel, as Debord's "televised apotheosis," that is, as the last banderilla thrust into the revolutionary's side by the society of the spectacle in pursuit of its work of destruction-co-optation. After all, what could be more logical than an assassinated Debord hastening to his suicide. Brigitte Cornand suggests as much by carefully failing to mention that the text added at the end of the show at the request of Alice Becker-Ho to explain the circumstances of Debord's death was provided by his companion, thereby implying that the film was a statement from beyond the (televised) grave by Debord, who had supposedly planned his suicide for a long time.

THE LAST GUARDIAN

1. G. D., *Comments on the Society of the Spectacle,* translated by Malcolm Imrie (London: Verso, 2002), 19.

2. Ibid., 14.

3. Ibid., 29.

4. Claude Rabant, "Le dernier gardien," *Lignes* (May 31, 1997).

5. On this subject, see Cécile Guilbert, *Pour Guy Debord* (Paris: Gallimard, 1996), and her insightful comments on the meaning of the critique of the spectacle during the period of "information technology's absolute knowledge." The problem with information technology is not so much that one day computers will replace speech but that there are more and more people who accord them this power, who believe not only that translation, but also irony and even subtlety in general, will in the near future be available on the software market. Will we die of laughter or boredom?

6. G. D., *Panegyric,* vol. 1, translated by James Brook and John McHale (New York: Verso, 2004), 8. It is to the changing times that we must also attribute Debord's plan to republish a "critical" edition of *In girum imus nocte,* containing a list of all the appropriated texts and their sources: a transition from appropriation to quotation, as required by the current "period of ignorance." This critical edition would serve as an exemplary response to those who, never having understood the principle of *détournement,* accuse Debord of theft or dealing in stolen cultural goods. Debord, however, was never very interested in cultural games for intellectually backward graduate students.

7. Ibid., 9–10.

8. "I will speak of what we were then in the argot of Villon's accomplices, which is certainly no longer an impenetrable secret language. On the contrary, it is generally accessible to people in the know. But I will thus put in the inevitable criminological dimension at a reassuring philological distance" (ibid., 24). Concerning Romany, it's hard to know the extent of Debord's interest. However, Alice Becker-Ho's interest is more certain, because in 1990 and 1994 she published two studies designed to demonstrate the importance of the language of the Gypsies, who came to Europe in the fifteenth century, in creating the argot of the "dangerous classes" of that time and beyond. It was through Romany that the secret language of the dangerous classes was established, a language as impenetrable to the enemy and the government of the time as Classical French soon would be for spectacular authority. See Alice Becker-Ho, *Les princes du jargon* (Paris: Éditions Gérard Lebovici, 1990; reprinted, Paris: Gallimard, 1995) and *L'essence du jargon* (Paris: Gallimard, 1994). The Gypsy is the last figure to be faithful to the words of the tribe, words snatched to perform the forced labor imposed on them by the spectacle.

9. This position has been defended in the review *Lignes*, no. 31 (1997), and especially in the articles by Michel Surya and Francis Marmande.

4. Strategy

THE MOVING SURFACE OF THE RIVER OF TIME

1. Debord's silence about the Second World War has been pointed out before, a silence considered suspect by some commentators. Conversely, there is speculation that the Second World War was the source of his enthusiasm for revolt (this is the hypothesis advanced by Len Bracken, *Guy Debord—Revolutionary: A Critical Biography* [Venice, Calif.: Feral House, 1997]). The argument is hardly credible, however, because Debord was a child between nine and fourteen years of age at the time. He was relatively secure during the war, and did not experience any significant privation. Apparently, none of those close to Debord were victims of the war. For the same reason, Debord's silence about the conflict should come as no surpise. He only spoke about his own experiences, and only about those he felt were exemplary in his life, and he simply did not experience the Second World War. What about Debord the theoretician? What do we expect him to say? What we already know about the Nazis, the concentration camps, genocide? Debord never showed the slightest inclination to drape himself in the flags of a universal good conscience, which were so necessary to the public position of many intellectuals. There are no signs in him of the guilt or bad conscience that were so essential for others to continue writing after Auschwitz. Debord never had need of such moral stratagems to be able to write (a little), or to devote himself to idleness.

2. G. D., *Panegyric,* translated by James Brook and John McHale (New York: Verso, 2004), 55.

3. G. D., *Complete Cinematic Works,* translated and edited by Ken Knabb (Oakland, Calif.: AK Press, 2003), 189–90.

DESCRIPTIONS OF BATTLE :: The Imaginary Warrior

1. This is the position maintained by Frédéric Schiffter in his *Guy Debord l'atrabilaire* (Biarritz: Éditions Distance, 1997), 68.

The Militant

2. In a letter sent to Maurice Wyckaert, Debord refers to the *Déclaration* as something relatively important: "A highly decisive and serious conflict has finally begun" (*Correspondance,* vol. 2, 17). A few days later, he gave a detailed explanation of his position in a letter to Patrick Straram. He described the majority of the signers as the usual "left-wing club," that is, as the "worst enemies of any revolutionary effort (Sartre, Nadeau, Mascolo, and the reheated surrealists)," while pointing out, as in his letter to Wyckaert, the tenseness of the situation and the scope of the repressive measures employed by the government, which led him to consider going into hiding: "The question has been raised about going into hiding, fairly seriously. I don't know when *I.S.* 5 will appear. I have already hidden some papers in a more secure location. We are at one of those moments of political tension (can the government reverse itself, temporarily?) when anything can happen" (21–24).

3. This can be seen as proof of the SI's insignificance or of its tactical intelligence. A good revolutionary organization is one that can't be dissolved by the government, but decides—alone—when to disband.

4. Debord discussed at length the situation in Italy during the seventies in *Comments on the Society of the Spectacle* (1988), when all the ramifications of the notorious P2 group (Potere Due) began to come to light. What was for some a paranoid fantasy in 1988—and even more so ten or fifteen years earlier—became, six years later, the quasi-official version of history.

5. The details of the 1978 break can be read in the appendix to volume 2 of the *Correspondance* (Champ Libre). At the time of the kidnapping and assassination of Aldo Moro, Debord sent Sanguinetti a letter, signed with the pseudonym Cavalcanti (Dante's friend), in which he explained his arguments about the "Red Brigade," which, Debord felt, was taking orders from the Italian secret service. Sanguinetti responded with a long letter, also signed with a pseudonym, in which he presented a refutation of the claim of manipulation advanced by Debord, which demanded that Sanguinetti explain himself. Sanguinetti's silence sealed the break between the two men.

6. In the history of recent artistic and political avant-gardes, taking action almost always meant going beyond words, speech, and writing, in order to act, to take up arms—which, mysteriously, always became nothing more than pens. The history of the imagined world of the writer-revolver, in all its variations, has yet to be written. From Sartre, who would have been content to see writers using their pen as well as a revolver—that is, those who knew how to shoot—to Breton and his fundamental surrealist act (firing randomly into a crowd), which unites action and psychotic

acting out, to acts of terrorism, which some people criticized Debord for turning away from. But how can we fail to see that terrorism contradicted everything about Debord's *work*, given his sense of poetry and the meaning he assigns to poetic practice, the necessary conjunction of lived experience and speech?

On Strike

7. Subpoenaed as a witness for the defense in the trial of the writer Félix Fénéon, who was accused of planning anarchist attacks, Mallarmé is said to have stated that Fénéon and his accomplices were angels of purity and that, in any event, he was unfamiliar with "any bomb other than a book." Is it surprising that Debord tracked down this statement and was especially fond of it? Doesn't it put Mallarmé exactly where he intended to be? Did Debord dream of other bombs besides those made out of books, words, and slogans painted on walls in May 1968? More generally, we can say that Debord's debt to Mallarmé has been underestimated, possibly hidden by the obvious connection to Ducasse, the tutelary figure of appropriation. This did not prevent Debord from reading Mallarmé, whom he admired, not only because of the anarchist leanings of a man who is often made out to be a symbolist lost in the game of letters, but also because he perceived, with remarkable lucidity, the challenge to the legitimacy of all poetry found in Mallarmé's work, and because he perceived its destructive scope (in *Panegyric* he refers to the famous line "Destruction was my Beatrice"). And most important, there was no way Debord could not be aware of the Mallarméan belief in obscurity, which is not only an art of stylistic complexity, but an art of disappearance as well, an art of impersonality, an art of the "false appearance of the present." Like Mallarmé, he favored "going on strike against society," which caused an outpouring of comment from Sartre. But unlike Mallarmé, he never tried to save appearances. He was not a polite professor of English, who took a strange pleasure in posing, clowning, and social simulacra, all of which he was aware of, feigning death and making it a point of honor to "send the living his calling card, stanzas or a sonnet, to avoid being stoned by them, should they suspect him of knowing they did not exist." Debord was not polite. In fact, he insisted on not sending the "living" his calling card. He did all he could, through insult, to tell them they did not exist, that they were the ones who were dead, knowing that, if that were the case, he would be stoned by them. Mallarmé isolated himself from the living by pretending to be dead; Debord isolated himself from the dead by pretending to be alive, claiming he was alive, and sometimes even claiming he was the only one alive. Raoul Vaneigem, in 1989, long after his break with Debord, but still in keeping with the situationist spirit, wrote a book titled *Adresse aux vivants sur la mort qui les gouverne et les moyens de s'en débarrasser* (Paris: Seghers, 1990). Even though the book was written twenty years after the situationist adventure, the title could be read, emblematically, as a kind of situationist speech. Vaneigem suggests that his text is the exact opposite of the modernist position: it marks the transition from an address to the dead to an address to the living.

8. The death of the author, said to have been invented by Mallarmé and then

transmitted during the sixties to Blanchot, was popularized by Roland Barthes in 1968 in his article of the same name, "La mort de l'auteur" (*Manteia*, 1968) [reprinted as "The Death of the Author," in *The Rustle of Language* (New York: Farrar, Straus and Giroux, 1986)]. Debord was contemporary with a modernist culture of the death of the author, but he never adopted the rhetoric, apparently preferring more tangible forms of disappearance and perdition. This did not prevent proximity, if not complicity, with the ideas of someone such as Barthes (*Writing Degree Zero*, for example) or even Blanchot. With respect to Blanchot, not only did Debord cross paths with him (without ever having met him) at the time of the "Manifeste des 121," but he shared with him an ethics of the refusal of representation. This led both men to reject the mediatization of their own image, and they drew similar political conclusions. I am thinking primarily of certain texts by Blanchot on May 1968, which sometimes have an astonishingly situationist ring to them. This is particularly true of the writing on May 1968 found in *The Unavowable Community*, translated by Pierre Joris (Barrytown, N.Y.: Station Hill Press, 1988): "Saying it was more important than what was said. Poetry was an everyday affair. 'Spontaneous' communication, in the sense that it seemed to hold back nothing, was nothing else than communication communicating with its transparent, immediate self, in spite of the fights, the debates, the controversies, where calculating intelligence expressed itself less than a nearly pure effervescence (at any rate, an effervescence without contempt, neither highbrow nor lowbrow). Because of that, one could have the presentiment that with authority overthrown or, rather, neglected, a sort of *communism* declared itself, a communism of a kind never experienced before and which no ideology was able to recuperate or claim as its own" (30).

Debord and Rousseau

9. See Frédéric Schiffter, *Guy Debord l'atrabiliaire*, 14.

10. G. D., *Complete Cinematic Works*, translated and edited by Ken Knabb (Oakland, Calif.: AK Press, 2003), 152.

11. See chapter 1, "Having Boarded at Night the Lightest of Crafts."

12. This should come as no surprise in light of the dialogue, critical but obvious, between Sade and Rousseau.

13. And sometimes they combined Fourierism with primitivism. This was the case with the postsituationist Vaneigem. A book such as *Adresse aux vivants . . .* announced the arrival of a truly libertarian morality, combined with a return to an age of gathering. Similar themes were developed by Vaneigem in other books, especially *Le livre des plaisirs* (Encre, 1979) (republished, Labor, 1993 and 1998). I am not saying that these "isms" characterized situationism or Debord's thought, having previously remarked on his lack of interest in utopian thought. It is important to understand that the arguments developed later by Vaneigem are not so different from those he developed in *The Revolution of Everyday Life*, and that they constitute one of the possible developments of situationism, a development that accentuated Rousseauian pregnance.

14. Over the past few years, especially in connection with *Comments on the Society of the Spectacle*, there has been frequent discussion of Debord's paranoia. During this period of a relaxation in revolutionary fervor, such a statement is like a condemnation without appeal, as if it would be madness for someone today to think not only that enemies existed but that those enemies were also his enemies. Yet, there has been little explanation of what this is supposed to mean exactly. Is it a clinical diagnosis? Are they trying to suggest that Debord was psychotic, that he should have been, if not institutionalized, at least treated? To my knowledge, no one has risked making such claims, which obviously require fairly extensive knowledge of the subject. So Debord was paranoid, although he was in good health. Such diagnoses generally serve to disqualify or refute. Debord was paranoid; therefore, whatever he said was false. Note, however, that the learned clinicians who are satisfied with such a position are often the ones who grow indignant when the same clinical categories are used to describe other authors. Debord was paranoid, but Artaud was always in good mental health, as everything Rodez has written has demonstrated. For my part, I employ the term, with all the equivocation it entails, as I employed it elsewhere with respect to Artaud, because, in cases like those of Debord and Rousseau, it is symbolically productive (that is, capable of producing effects) to assume a "paranoid" position, whose condition of possibility is that it not be confused with delusion.

HOW TO BE DISLIKED

1. G. D., *Panegyric*, translated by James Brook and John McHale (New York: Verso, 2004), 7.

2. G. D., *In girum imus nocte*, in *Complete Cinematic Works*, translated and edited by Ken Knabb (Oakland, Calif.: AK Press, 2003), 146–47.

3. G. D., *Panegyric*, 22.

4. Ibid., 16.

5. G. D., *Complete Cinematic Works*, 148.

6. G. D., *Panegyric*, vol. 1, 17.

7. Ibid., p. 8.

8. G. D., *"Cette mauvaise réputation . . ."* (Paris: Gallimard, 1993), 100.

9. G. D., *Panegyric*, 1. This is an excerpt from the *Examen critique de l'ouvrage de M. le comte Philippe de Ségur* by Général Gourgaud, in other words, a settling of accounts between two former generals of the Empire, since Gourgaud did not support the analysis of the strategic errors made by Napoléon during the Russian campaign. The story ended in a duel between Gourgaud and Ségur during which Ségur was wounded.

10. Ibid., 11.

11. G. D., *Complete Cinematic Works*, 169.

12. One could also rewrite the history of the twentieth-century avant-garde as a series of variations on a theme: paying a personal price. Political, even military, engagements would go hand in hand with the most varied forms of drug addiction,

the most provocative forms of debauchery, fantasies of oversocialization, the overvaluation of writing as such, a handful of successful suicides, and so on. The entire history of the avant-garde can be read as a series of more or less successful conjunctions of doing and saying; and in this game, Debord was one of the most skillful, one of the most productive.

13. Significantly, Debord chose to be self-taught, to avoid the standard methods of recognition (of debts) that constitute the very heart of the institutions devoted to intellectual life (and perhaps not only those). He found his teachers in the books he loved and used. Lautréamont, Gondi, Clausewitz, Marx, Sun Tzu. But because he never had a role in academic life, he had nothing to thank them for, not to mention that he had never asked them for anything in the first place. One can have teachers without having debts.

14. G. D., *Des contrats* (Cognac: Le temps qu'il fait, 1995). Published in February 1995, barely three months after Debord's suicide, the book was conceived by him and intended for publication, as shown by a letter to the editor, dated November 27, 1994, three days before his death.

15. Ibid., 7–8.

REFUTATIONS

1. G. D., *Complete Cinematic Works,* translated and edited by Ken Knabb (Oakland, Calif.: AK Press, 2003), 133.

2. Ibid.

3. Ibid., 149.

4. Ibid., 113.

5. Ibid., 115.

6. Ibid., 116.

7. Ibid., 118.

8. Ibid., 115.

9. Ibid., 118–19.

10. G. D., *Refutation of All Judgments,* in ibid., 123.

11. Stéphane Mallarmé, *Œuvres complètes* (Paris: Gallimard, "Bibliothèque de la Pléiade," 1945), 372.

12. Paris, Champ Libre, 1982. The text reads: "Garbage and waste unleashed upon the release of the film *In girum imus nocte et consumimur igni.*"

13. This is particularly true of the article by Hélène Hazera (*Libération,* June 3, 1981), who, with impressive goodwill, littered her piece with positive sentiments and quotes. She reveals not the least sign of reservation, abandons any form of critical ethics involving a modicum of distance. A perfect article whose only fault is its existence. Other articles were less naive about the risks they ran: their authors had seen *Refutation of All Judgments* and knew that they had been too fond of other things, but this did not prevent them from appreciating *In girum imus nocte* and writing about it, often in very convincing terms. I am thinking primarily of the article by Louis Seguin (*La Quinzaine littéraire,* July 1, 1981), which includes some fine pas-

sages about the way Debord filmed Venice, and the articles by Pascal Bonitzer and Alain Badiou. Debord the filmmaker would not have lacked perspicacious viewers or critics if he had not done everything in his power not to have them, to eliminate any possibility of dialogue.

CONSIDERATIONS ON AN ASSASSINATION

1. G. D., *Considerations on the Assassination of Gérard Lebovici*, translated and with an introduction by Robert Greene (Los Angeles: TamTam Books, 2001), 2.

2. Buchet-Chastel had republished *The Society of the Spectacle*, adding, without consulting Debord, "theory of situationism" as a subtitle. From Debord's point of view, this was not only unacceptable but also contradictory. The *Thèses sur l'Internationale situationniste et son temps*, which dates from the same period, was written to refute this subtitle, to refute the idea that a theory of situationism existed, to refute those who took situationism in general, and *The Society of the Spectacle* in particular, to be a theory, a form of revolutionary ready-to-wear. His outrage was such that Debord sued Buchet, which refused to free him of his contractual obligations until forced to do so.

3. His agency represented Jean-Paul Belmondo, Catherine Deneuve, and Yves Montand. Among other films, he produced (with Artmedia, then with Soprofilms) *The Name of the Rose, The Last Metro, Mon oncle d'Amérique, The Wild Child, La balance, Fort-Sagane.*

4. After Lebovici's death, Debord stayed with Champ Libre as long as Floriana Lebovici, Gérard's wife, who had been its official manager, remained with the company. When she died in 1991, Debord broke with the heirs (Lebovici's sons), who transformed Champ Libre/Gérard Lebovici into Ivrea publishers.

5. Debord had dissolved the SI thirteen years earlier and the claim was not really his. It can't be excluded, but given Lebovici's talent for offense, which was almost as great as Debord's, given the number of enemies he had made, it's not really necessary. Debord explains this in a letter to Paolo Salvadori (and Jean-François Martos), who introduced the secret service theory (see Jean-François Martos, *Correspondance avec Guy Debord* [Paris: Le Fin mot de l'histoire, 1998], 191–92).

6. Quoted in G. D., *Considerations on the Assassination of Gérard Lebovici*, 13.

7. Ibid., 43.

8. Ibid., 41.

9. Ibid., 2.

10. Ibid., 72.

11. See chapter 1, "Scratched Negatives and the Game of Appearances."

12. G. D., *Considerations on the Assassination of Gérard Lebovici*, 46.

13. Ibid., 31.

AGAINST INTERPRETATION

1. I have not overlooked the fact that during those ten years of "silence," there appeared three films, which were shown almost without interruption since 1983.

But can you really exist on the "intellectual scene" by making films? The scene is piously devoted to the printed word, which is no doubt why Debord was so disinterested in it for so long, preferring film to writing. He was never pious or faithful to the book.

2. The transition to Gallimard was made possible by Jean-Jacques Pauvert. He suggested that he serve as Debord's "literary agent" when Debord broke with Gérard Lebovici's heirs and found himself without a publisher. He made it known in the press that he was looking for a publisher sufficiently independent to support him in his battle against the society of the spectacle. There is much that could be said about the way Debord went about finding a publisher: his way of publicly announcing what so many others dissimulated, and his absolute indifference to "public relations." He found himself effectively isolated and without a publisher, never having maintained any kind of relationship with a publisher, aside from Gérard Lebovici, and, after Lebovici's death in 1990, with his widow, Floriana Lebovici.

This was far from insignificant, especially when we consider that such a change of publisher did not fail to provoke the obvious criticisms: that Debord had himself been "co-opted," integrated into a cultural legacy he had rejected for so long, and during his lifetime, that is to say, with his complicity, thus betraying the fact that his entire career was one long attempt to cultivate his image as a writer. I have already pointed out the extent to which the argument about co-optation leaves me indifferent. Then, there is another possibility: What if Debord really was a great writer, a great formal inventor? What if his work possessed that sense of singularity that is the mark of great literature?

There is another element to the story, an important one, because it concerns Gallimard, which had been so copiously insulted in the pages of *Internationale situationniste,* and novelist Philippe Sollers. Although Sollers had nothing to do with the change of publishers, he was one of the first to recognize Debord the artist, and he was obviously not opposed to his moving to Gallimard. Concerning the legacy of Debord's acceptance, Sollers's articles about him, especially one of the earliest, which appeared in *Le Monde* at the time of the publication of *Panégyrique* in 1989, played a decisive role. They contributed enormously to Debord's being read outside the situationist circle and in ways that he had not been read before. Naturally, some people saw this support as merely aggravating existing critiques of Debord, as well as of Sollers. One had left his well-deserved obscurity only because the other was looking for a new straight man, a short-lived infatuation without which nothing would have happened. The problem is that it did happen, and the infatuation lasted at least ten years. Still, it's a lot for someone who has been reproached so often for his infidelity to the causes he has espoused. It is also worth noting that there was much in common between Sollers's "libertinage" and Debord's art of strategy—for example, the interest in play, their rejection of anything that resembled moral fundamentalism, and the rejection of all forms of self-righteousness, which took the place of a political viewpoint for many of their contemporaries. We would be wrong to think that Sollers's goal was to win acceptance: the proof is that he ended up hardly better off than Debord.

3. G. D., *"Cette mauvaise réputation . . ."* (Paris: Gallimard, 1993), 108.

4. Ibid., 14.

5. Ibid., 50.

6. Ibid., 13.

7. Ibid., 128–29.

8. Ibid., 32.

9. G. D., *Considerations on the Assassination of Gérard Lebovici*, translated and with an introduction by Robert Greene (Los Angeles: TamTam Books, 2001), 79.

10. Jean-Marie Apostilidès refers to writing's "plurality." See *Les tombeaux de Guy Debord*, (Paris: Exils, 1999), 105.

11. G. D., *Correspondance*, vol. 2 (Paris: Champ Libre, 1981), 66.

12. G. D., *"Cette mauvaise réputation . . . ,"* 61.

13. Jean-François Martos, *Histoire de l'Internationale situationniste* (Paris: Éditions Gérard Lebovici, 1989).

14. René Viénet, *Enragés et situationnistes dans le mouvement des occupations* (Paris: Gallimard, [1968] 1998). Viénet was soon after expelled from the SI. When Debord later referred to this book, he never forgot to specify that it was signed Viénet, thereby leaving the door open to all sorts of speculation about its true author (the book was supposedly written collectively by Debord, Vaneigem, Khayati, and Riesel, as well as Viénet, who limited himself to gathering the documentation). Perhaps we should not be too quick to take Debord at his word when he claims never to have written under a pseudonym: there are a number of ways of writing pseudonymously. There are less astute ways to display cunning or confuse the notions of authorship and authority than using the name of an accomplice whose existence is known.

15. Jean-François Martos, *Correspondance avec Guy Debord* (Paris: Le Fin mot de l'histoire, 1998), 110.

16. G. D., *Commentaires sur la société du spectacle*, followed by *Préface à la quatrième édition italienne de "La Société du spectacle"* (Paris: Gallimard, 1992), 93; translated as *Preface to the Fourth Italian Edition of "The Society of the Spectacle,"* revised edition by Michael Prigent and Lucy Forsyth (London: Chronos Publications, 1983), 1.

17. Ibid., 7.

18. Ibid., 3.

19. Ibid., 4.

20. See G. D., *Correspondance*, vol. 2, 114–16.

21. The earlier reader could also be what Raoul Vaneigem (who, in 1972, was still approximately on the same wavelength as Debord, in spite of his expulsion in extremis from the SI) called the "anti-reader" in the "Toast to revolutionary workers," which was added in 1972 to his *Revolution of Everyday Life*: "The main theses of the *Traité de savoir-vivre* must now find corroboration of a concrete sort in the actions of

its anti-readers: not in the shape of student agitation but in the shape of total revolution" (*The Revolution of Everyday Life*, 2d edition, translated by Donald Nicholson-Smith [London: Rebel Press/Seattle: Left Bank Books, 1994], 277).

22. G. D., *Preface to the Fourth Italian Edition of "The Society of the Spectacle,"* 101.

23. Ibid., 101–2.

24. I have already had occasion to emphasize the other forms assumed by this desire for totality: primarily the situationist utopia of total and authentic communication, which may possibly be embodied in architecture. During the last month of his life, Debord worked, with all the intensity disease and pain allowed, on an *Apologie*, which was destroyed according to his own wishes after his death. Apparently, it would have consisted of a kind of infinite extension of the principles at work in *Panegyric*, volume 1. Debord's *Apologie* would have been *Panegyric* raised to the height of a Book, and at the same time *Panegyric* would appear as a minor version of the Book, as a complete fragment indicating its position. Certainly, it would have been very beautiful.

SHADOWS, SECRETS, AND MIRRORS

1. G. D., *Comments on the Society of the Spectacle*, translated by Malcolm Imrie (London: Verso, 2002), 16.

2. See chapter 3, "The Last Guardian."

3. G. D., *Comments on the Society of the Spectacle*, 31.

4. Ibid., 55.

5. Ibid., 67.

6. This was an attempt by the French secret services in New Zealand to sabotage a ship that had been chartered by Greenpeace, the ecological organization, to obstruct French nuclear tests in the Pacific.

7. G. D., *Comments on the Society of the Spectacle*, 20.

8. See Laurent Jenny, "L'ennemi infigurable," *Critique*, no. 509 (October 1989).

9. G. D., *Comments on the Society of the Spectacle*, 84.

10. Ibid., 81.

11. Ibid., 18 and 73.

12. Marc Lebiez, "L'illusoire et le ludique," *Les Temps modernes*, no. 128 (November 1989).

13. G. D., *Comments on the Society of the Spectacle*, 1.

14. Ibid., 2.

15. Ibid., 83.

16. Ibid., 45.

17. Translated from the Italian by Guy Debord (Paris: Champ Libre, 1976).

THE GAME OF WAR, GONDI

1. One of the frames is reproduced in G. D., *Complete Cinematic Works*, translated and edited by Ken Knabb (Oakland, Calif.: AK Press, 2003), 194. The "Game of

War" invented by Debord was published in 1977 by the Société des Jeux Stratégiques et Historiques.

2. See Alice Becker-Ho and Guy Debord, *Le "Jeu de la guerre": Relevé des positions successives de toutes les forces au cours d'une partie* (Paris: Éditions Gérard Lebovici, 1987).

3. G. D., *Panegyric*, translated by James Brook and John McHale (New York: Verso, 2004), 55.

4. Ibid., 56.

5. As well as a number of works by Clausewitz.

6. Like Debord, Gracián was also fond of fragments, short, lapidary texts that strike like a stone or a bullet.

7. *Potlatch* 26, 242.

Conclusion

1. G. D., *The Society of the Spectacle*, translated by Donald Nicholson-Smith (New York: Zone Books, 1994), Thesis 10.

2. *France-Culture*, June 10, 2000.

BIBLIOGRAPHY

Works by Guy Debord

"Prolégomènes à tout cinéma futur," followed by an early script for *Howls for Sade*, in *Ion*, Paris, 1952; reproduced in Gérard Berreby, ed., *Documents relatifs à la fondation de l'Internationale situationniste*. Paris: Allia, 1985. 109–23.

"Rapport sur la construction des situations et sur les conditions de l'organisation et de l'action de la tendance situationniste international" (July 1957); reproduced in Gérard Berreby, ed., *Documents relatifs à la fondation de l'Internationale situationniste*. Paris: Allia, 1985. 607–20. Reprint, Paris: Mille et une nuits, 2000. "Report on the Construction of Situations and on the International Situationist Tendency's Conditions of Organization and Action." In *The Situationist International Anthology*, translated and edited by Ken Knabb. Berkeley: Bureau of Public Secrets, 1981 and 1989.

Mémoires (1952–53). Copenhagen: L'Internationale situationniste, 1959; reprint, Paris: Belles-Lettres/Pauvert, 1994, with a previously unpublished preface ("Attestations").

With Asger Jorn. *Fin de Copenhague*. Copenhagen: Permild and Rosengreen, 1957; Paris: Allia, 1986.

Contre le cinéma. Aarhus, Denmark: Scandinavian Institute of Comparative Vandalism, 1964.

"Le Déclin et la chute de la société spectaculaire-marchande." This was first published in English as *The Decline and Fall of the "Spectacular" Commodity-Economy* (Paris: International Situationniste, December 1965), translated by Donald Nicholson-Smith and subsequently in French in *Internationale situationniste* 10 (March 1966); reprinted in Paris by Les Belles Lettres/Pauvert in 1993. Reprinted in *Beneath the Paving Stones: Situationists and the Beach, May 1968*. San Francisco: AK Press/Dark Star, 2001.

La Société du spectacle. Paris: Buchet-Chastel, 1967. *The Society of the Spectacle*, translated by Donald Nicholson-Smith. New York: Zone Books, 1994.

With Gianfranco Sanguinetti. *La véritable scission dans l'Internationale: thèses sur l'Internationale Situationniste et son temps.* Paris: Champ Libre, 1972. 147 pp. Reprint, Paris: Librairie Arthème Fayard, 1998. *The Real Split in the International: Theses on the Situationist International and Its Time.* Translated by John McHale. London: Pluto Press, 2003.

Translation of Gianfranco Sanguinetti, *Rapporto veridico sulle ultime opportunità di salvare il capitalismo* as *Véridique rapport sur les dernières chances de sauver le capitalisme en Italie.* Paris: Champ Libre, 1976.

Œuvres cinématographiques complètes, 1952–1978. Paris: Champ Libre, 1978; reprint, Paris: Gallimard in 1994. *Complete Cinematic Works,* translated and edited by Ken Knabb. Oakland, Calif.: AK Press, 2003.

Préface à la quatrième édition italienne de "La Société du spectacle." Paris: Champ Libre, 1979. Reprinted with *Commentaires sur la société du spectacle.* Paris: Gallimard, 1992; Gallimard, "Folio" collection, 1996. Translated into English as *Preface to the Fourth Italian Edition of "The Society of the Spectacle"* by Frances Parker and Michael Forsyth. London: Chronos Publications, 1979. Revised edition by Michael Prigent and Lucy Forsyth. London: Chronos Publications, 1983.

Protestation devant les libertaires du présent et du futur sur les capitulations de 1937 par un "incontrôlé" de la Colonne de fer. Traduit de l'espagnol par deux "aficionados" sans qualités. Bilingual edition. Paris: Champ Libre, 1979.

Stances sur la mort de son père. Translation of Jorge Manrique's *Coplas de Don Jorge Manrique por la muerte de su padre.* Paris: Champ Libre, 1980; Cognac: Le temps qu'il fait, 1996.

Translation of *Appels de la prison de Ségovie* by the Coordination of Autonomous Groups in Spain. Paris: Champ Libre, 1980.

Ordures et décombres déballés à la sortie du film «In girum imus nocte et consumimur igni" (by authorized sources). Paris: Champ Libre, 1982; republished 1999 by Gallimard with the critical edition of *In girum imus nocte et consumimur igni.*

Considérations sur l'assassinat de Gérard Lebovici. Paris: Éditions Gérard Lebovici/Champ Libre, 1985; Paris: Gallimard, 1993. *Considerations on the Assassination of Gérard Lebovici,* translated and with an introduction by Robert Greene. Los Angeles: TamTam Books, 2001.

With Alice Becker-Ho. *Le "Jeu de la guerre": Relevé des positions successives de toutes les forces au cours d'une partie.* Paris: Éditions Gérard Lebovici, 1987.

Commentaires sur la société du spectacle. Paris: Éditions Gérard Lebovici, 1988; Paris: Gallimard, 1992. *Comments on the Society of the Spectacle.* Translated by Malcolm Imrie. New York: Verso, 2002.

Panégyrique. Vol. 1. Paris: Éditions Gérard Lebovici/Champ Libre, 1989; Paris: Gallimard, 1993. Vol. 2. Paris: Librarie Arthème Fayard, 1997. *Panegyric.* Vols. 1 and 2, translated by James Brook and John McHale. New York: Verso, 2004.

In girum imus nocte et consumimur igni. Critical edition. Paris: Éditions Gérard Lebovici, 1990; Paris: Gallimard, 1999.

"Cette mauvaise réputation . . .". Paris: Gallimard, 1993.

Des contrats. Cognac: Le temps qu'il fait, 1995.

Correspondance, vol. 1: June 1957–August 1960. Paris: Fayard, 1999.

Correspondance, vol. 2: September 1960–December 1964. Paris: Fayard, 2001.

Correspondance, vol. 3: January 1965–December 1968. Paris: Fayard, 2003.

Correspondance, vol. 4: January 1969–December 1972. Paris: Fayard, 2004.

Correspondance, vol. 5: January 1973–December 1978. Paris: Fayard, 2005.

Le Marquis de Sade a des yeux de fille. Paris: Fayard, 2004 (unpublished letters from 1949 to 1954).

ARTICLES (SIGNED AND UNSIGNED)

Potlatch. 1954–57. Reproduced in Gérard Berreby, ed., *Documents relatifs à la fondation de l'Internationale situationniste.* Paris: Allia, 1985; new edition: *Guy Debord présente Potlatch (1954–1957).* Paris: Gallimard, "Folio" collection, 1996.

Les Lèvres nues. Republished, Paris: Éditions Plasma, 1978.

Internationale situationniste. 1958–69; reprint, Paris: Champ Libre, 1975, and Paris: Fayard, 1997.

LETTERS

Debord, Guy. *Correspondance.* Vol. 1. Paris: Champ Libre, 1978; vol. 2. Paris: Champ Libre, 1981; reprint, Paris: Ivrea, 1996.

Martos, Jean-François. *Correspondance avec Guy Debord.* Paris: Le Fin mot de l'histoire, 1998.

FILMOGRAPHY

Hurlements en faveur de Sade. 35 mm, black and white, 80 minutes. Films lettristes, 1952.

Sur le passage de quelques personnes à travers une assez courte unité de temps. 35 mm, black and white, 20 minutes. Dansk-Fransk Experimentalfilmskompagni, 1959.

Critique de la Séparation. 35 mm, black and white, 20 minutes. Dansk-Fransk Experimentalfilmskompagni, 1961.

La Société du spectacle. 35 mm, black and white, 90 minutes. Paris: Simar Films, 1973.

Réfutation de tous les jugements, tant élogieux qu'hostiles, qui ont été jusqu'ici portés sur le film "La Société du spectacle." 35 mm, black and white, 20 minutes. Paris: Simar Films, 1975.

In girum imus nocte et consumimur igni. 35 mm, black and white, 105 minutes. Paris: Simar Films, 1978.

Guy Debord, son art et son temps, by Guy Debord and Brigitte Cornand. Video, black and white, 60 minutes. Canal Plus, 1994; first screening January 9, 1995.

On Debord: *Guy Debord, une étrange guerre,* by Emmanuel Descombes and Philippe Sollers, 2000 (made for television).

Critical Works on Guy Debord and the Situationist Movement

Agamben, Giorgio, Mirella Bandini, and Enrico Ghezzi. *Retour au futur? Des situationnistes.* Marseilles: Via Valeriano, 1990.

Apostolidès, Jean-Marie. *Les tombeaux de Guy Debord.* Paris: Exils, 1999.

Ball, Edward. "The Great Sideshow of the Situationist International." *Yale French Studies* 73 (1987).

Bandini, Mirella. *L'esthétique, le politique: de Cobra à l'Internationale situationniste, 1948–1957.* Marseilles: Sulliver/Via Valeriano, 1998.

Blanchard, Daniel. *Debord, dans le bruit de la cataracte du temps,* followed by *Préliminaires pour une définition de l'unité du programme révolutionnaire* by P. Canjuers and G.-E. Debord. Paris: Sens & Tonka, 2000.

Bourseiller, Christophe. *Vie et mort de Guy Debord.* Paris: Plon, 1999.

Bracken, Len. *Guy Debord—Revolutionary: A Critical Biography.* Venice, Calif.: Feral House, 1997.

Brau, Éliane. *Le situationnisme ou la nouvelle Internationale.* Paris: Nouvelles éditions Debresse, 1968.

Chollet, Laurent. *L'insurrection situationniste.* Paris: Dagorno, 2000.

Dumontier, Pascal. *Les situationnistes et mai 68: Théorie et pratique de la révolution (1966–1972).* Paris: Éditions Gérard Lebovici, 1990.

Ford, Simon. *The Realization and Suppression of the Situationist International: An Annotated Bibliography 1972–1992.* Edinburgh and San Francisco: AK Press, 1994.

Gombin, Richard. *Les origines du gauchisme.* Paris: Seuil, "Points-Politique," 1971.

Gonzalvez, Shigenobu. *Guy Debord ou la beauté du négatif.* Paris: Mille et une nuits, 1998.

Guilbert, Cécile. *Pour Guy Debord.* Paris: Gallimard, 1996.

Hussey, Andrew. *The Game of War: The Life and Death of Guy Debord.* London: Jonathan Cape, 2001.

Jacobs, David, and Christopher Winks. *At Dusk: The Situationist Movement in Historical Perspective.* Berkeley: Perspectives, 1975.

Jappe, Anselm. *Guy Debord.* Translated by Donald Nicholson-Smith, foreword by T. J. Clark. Berkeley: University of California Press, 1999.

———. "Sic transit gloria artis: Theorien über das Ende der Kunst bei Theodor W. Adorno und Guy Debord." *Krisis* 15 (1995).

———. "Politik des Spektakels—Spektakel der Politik: Zur Aktualität der Theorie von Guy Debord." *Krisis* 20 (1998).

Jay, Martin. *Downcast Eyes: The Denigration of Vision in Twentieth-Century French Thought.* Berkeley: University of California Press, 1994.

Jenny, Laurent. "L'ennemi infigurable." *Critique,* no. 509 (October 1989).

Jorn, Asger. "Guy Debord et le problème du maudit." Preface to *Guy Debord: Contre le cinéma.* Aarhus, Denmark: Scandinavian Institute of Comparative Vandalism, 1964.

Kaufmann, Vincent. *Poétique des groupes littéraires: Avant-gardes 1920–1970.* Paris: Presses Universitaires de France, 1997.

Lebiez, Marc. "L'illusoire et le ludique." *Les Temps modernes* 128 (November 1989).

Lewino, Walter, and Jo Schnapp. *L'imagination au pouvoir.* Paris: Losfeld, 1968.

Marcus, Greil. *Lipstick Traces: A Secret History of the Twentieth Century.* Cambridge: Harvard University Press, 1989.

Marelli, Gianfranco. *L'Amère victoire du situationnisme: Pour une histoire critique de l'Internationale situationniste (1957–1971).* Arles: Sulliver, 1998.

———. *La dernière Internationale: Les situationnistes au-delà de l'art et de la politique.* Arles: Sulliver, 2000.

Martos, Jean-François. *Histoire de l'Internationale situationniste.* Paris: Éditions Gérard Lebovici, 1989.

McDonough, Tom. ed. *Guy Debord and the Situationist International: Texts and Documents.* Cambridge: MIT Press, 2002.

Mension, Jean-Michel. *La tribu, entretiens avec Gérard Berreby et Francesco Milo.* Paris: Allia, 1998. *The Tribe.* Translated by Donald Nicholson-Smith. San Francisco: City Lights Books, 2001.

Ohrt, Roberto. *Phantom Avantgarde: Eine Geschichte der Situationistischen Internationale und der modernen Kunst.* Hamburg: Galerie van de Loo/Nautilus, 1990.

Plant, Sadie. *The Most Radical Gesture: The Situationist International in a Postmodern Age.* London: Routledge, 1992.

Raspaud, Jean-Jacques, and Jean-Pierre Voyer. *L'Internationale situationniste: Protagonistes/Chronologie/Bibliographie (avec un index des noms insultés).* Paris: Champ Libre, 1972.

Rumney, Ralph. *The Consul.* Translated by Malcolm Imrie. San Francisco: City Lights, 2002.

Sadler, Simon. *The Situationist City.* Cambridge, Mass., and London: MIT Press, 1998.

Schiffter, Frédéric. *Guy Debord l'atrabilaire.* Biarritz: Éditions Distance, 1997.

Sussman, Elizabeth, ed. *On the Passage of a Few Persons through a Rather Brief Moment in Time: The Situationist International, 1957–1972.* Cambridge, Mass., and London: MIT Press, 1989.

Viénet, René. *Enragés et situationnistes dans le mouvement des occupations.* Paris: Gallimard, [1968] 1998.

Reviews and Catalogs

Lignes, no. 31 (1997) (partially devoted to Guy Debord).

October, no. 79 (1997), special issue: "Guy Debord and the *Internationale situationniste.*"

Sub-Stance, no. 90 (1999), special issue on Guy Debord.

Sur le passage de quelques personnes à travers une assez courte unité de temps: à propos de l'Internationale situationniste, 1957–1972. Catalog of the exhibition at the Georges-Pompidou Center, Paris (February 21–April 9, 1989).

Related Texts

Beneath the Paving Stones: Situationists and the Beach, May 1968. Texts collected by Dark Star. San Francisco: AK Press/Dark Star, 2001.

Cobra. Paris: Jean-Michel Place, 1980.

Documents relatifs à la fondation de l'Internationale situationniste (1948–1957). Edited by Gérard Berreby. Paris: Allia, 1985.

Ion. Paris: Jean-Paul Rocher, 1999.

Potlatch (1954–1957). Paris: Gallimard, "Folio" collection, as *Guy Debord présente Potlatch (1954–1957),* 1996.

Les Lèvres nues (1954–58). Paris: Plasma, 1978; Paris: Allia, 1995.

Internationale situationniste (1958–69). Amsterdam: Van Gennep, 1971; Paris: Champ Libre, 1975; Paris: Fayard (expanded edition), 1997.

De la misère en milieu étudiant (by members of the Situationist International and the students of Strasbourg University), 1966. Paris: Champ Libre, 1976; reprinted as "On the Poverty of Student Life," in *Beneath the Paving Stones: Situationists and the Beach, May 1968.* Texts collected by Dark Star. Oakland, Calif.: AK Press/Dark Star, 2001.

Spur. Review published by the German section of the Situationist International, 1962.

Écrits complets (1969–1972) de la section italienne de l'Internationale situationniste. Cintre-Moule, 1988.

Débat d'orientation de l'ex-Internationale situationniste. Paris: Centre de recherche sur la question sociale, 1974.

Chronique des secrets publics. Written by members of the Centre de recherche sur la question sociale. Paris, 1975.

Allemagne, Henry-René d'. *Les saint-simoniens, 1827–1832.* Paris, 1930.

Becker-Ho, Alice. *L'essence du jargon.* Paris: Gallimard, 1994.

———. *Les princes du jargon.* Paris: Éditions Gérard Lebovici, 1990; Paris: Gallimard, 1995. *The Princes of Jargon.* Translated by John McHale. Lewiston, N.Y.: Mellen Press, 2004.

———. *D'azur au triangle vidé de sable.* Cognac: Le temps qu'il fait, 1998.

Bernstein, Michèle. *Tous les chevaux du roi.* Paris: Buchet-Chastel, 1960.

———. *La nuit.* Paris: Buchet-Chastel, 1961.

Blanchot, Maurice. *The Unavowable Community.* Translated by Pierre Joris. Barrytown, N.Y.: Station Hill Press, 2003.

Boras, Maria Luïsa. *Cravan, une stratégie du scandale.* Paris: Jean-Michel Place, 1996.

Chevalier, Louis. *The Assassination of Paris.* Translated by David P. Jordan. Paris and Chicago: University of Chicago Press, 1994.

Clark, Timothy J. *The Painting of Modern Life: Paris in the Age of Manet and His Followers.* London: Thames and Hudson, 1990.

Curtay, Jean-Paul. *La poésie lettriste.* Paris: Seghers, 1974.

Estivals, Robert. *L'avant-garde culturelle parisienne depuis 1945.* Paris: Guy Lepart, 1962.

Flomenhauf, Eleanor. *The Roots and Development of Cobra Art.* The Fine Arts Museum of Long Island (FAMLI), 1985.

Gottraux, Philippe. *Socialisme ou Barbarie: un engagement politique et intellectuel dans la France de l'après-guerre.* Paris: Payot, 1997.

Hamon, Hervé, and Patrick Rotman. *Génération.* Vol. 1, *Les années de rêve.* Paris: Seuil, 1987; vol. 2, *Les années de poudre.* Paris: Seuil, 1988; "Points Actuels" collection, 1990.

Isou, Isidore. *L'agrégation d'un nom et d'un messie.* Paris: Gallimard, 1947.

———. *Introduction à une nouvelle poésie et une nouvelle musique.* Paris: Gallimard, 1947.

———. *Traité d'économie nucléaire: le soulèvement de la jeunesse.* Paris, 1949.

———. *Contre l'Internationale situationniste.* Paris: Éditions Hors Commerce-d'art, 2001.

Jorn, Asger. *Critique de la politique économique.* Brussels, 1960.

Lebovici, Gérard. *Tout sur le personnage.* Paris: Éditions Gérard Lebovici, 1984.

Lefebvre, Henri. *La somme et le reste.* Paris: Minuit, 1958.

———. *Le temps des méprises.* Paris: Stock, 1975.

———. *Critique of Everyday Life.* Vol. 1. Translated by John Moore. New York: Verso, 1991.

———. *Introduction to Modernity: Twelve Preludes, September 1959–May 1961.* Translated by John Moore. New York: Verso, 1995.

———. *Critique of Everyday Life.* Vol. 2. Translated by John Moore. New York: Verso, 2002.

Mourre, Michel. *Malgré le blasphème.* Paris: Juilliard, 1951.

Taccussel, Patrick. *L'attraction sociale: Le dynamisme de l'imaginaire dans une société monocéphale.* Paris: Méridiens/Klincksieck, 1984.

Vaneigem, Raoul. *Le livre des plaisirs.* Encre, 1979; Brussels: Labor, 1993, 1998.

———. *Adresse aux vivants sur la mort qui les gouverne et les moyens de s'en débarasser.* Paris: Seghers, 1990.

———. *The Revolution of Everyday Life.* 2d edition. Translated by Donald Nicholson-Smith. London: Rebel Press/Seattle: Left Bank Books, 1994.

Vidler, Anthony. *The Architectural Uncanny.* Cambridge, Mass., and London: MIT Press, 1992.

Wolman, Gil Joseph. *L'Anti-concept.* Paris: Allia, 1994; reprinted in Gérard Berreby, ed., *Documents relatifs à la fondation de l'Internationale situationniste.* Paris: Allia, 1985.

———. *Défense de mourir.* Paris: Allia, 2001.

INDEX

action: avant-garde view of, 217–18, 312n.6

Action Directe, 241

Action française, 82

Adamov, Arthur, 89, 92

Adresse aux vivants sur la mort qui les gouverne et les moyens de s'en débarrasser, 313n.7, 314n.13

African independence movements, 88, 110, 112, 173–74

aging: Debord's writing about, 13

Alberts, Anton, 144, 146

alcohol: Debord's theories on use of, 46, 56–57, 92, 151–54; *dérive* poetics and necessity of, 114, 293n.9

Alechinsky, Pierre, 132

Algerian partisans: lettrists' defense of, 88, 110, 112, 215; situationist defense of, 166, 170

Allia publishers, 30–31

"All the King's Men," 175–76, 305nn.27,29

antifunctionalist movement, 131–35, 296n.12

Apostolidès, Jean-Marie, 37, 57, 286n.17, 319n.10

appearance-disappearance dialectic: in Debord's work, 23–31, 41–45, 65–66

Appel, Karel, 132

appropriation: Debord's discussion of, 34, 206–7, 310n.6; Ducasse's theory of, 313n.7; Jorn's discussion of, 133–34; situationists' technique of, 183–84

Aragon, Louis, 89, 110, 112–14, 116, 292n.6

architecture: New Babylon movement, 141–47; psychoanalysis and theories of, 119–27, 293n.2; situationism and, 133–35, 149–61, 296n.12; unitary urbanism and, 127–31

Arguments, 170, 302nn.8,12, 305n.29

Arles: Debord's exile in, 66, 217–18

art: communication through, 151–54; Debord on end of, 48–50, 91–97; of *dérive,* 101; *dérive* poetics and, 114–18; lettrist view of, 79–85, 288n.14; offensiveness as, 227–32; situationism and, 150–51, 154–61, 297n.18; sociological aspects of, 165–66; totalization of, 158–61, 300n.12; unitary urbanism and, 131–41

Artaud, Antonin, 20, 89, 153–54, 157, 159, 177, 315n.14

Association Fédérative Générale des Étudiants de Strasbourg (AFGES), 180

"Game of War" images in, 266–69;
lettrist politics and, 91; lost children
metaphor in, 3, 45, 50–55, 76–77,
214; May 1968 protests in, 64–65,
203, 213–14; Notre Dame scandal
in, 82; offensiveness in, 227, 229–30;
Papaï's image in, 60; planned "critical" edition of, 310n.6; public reception of, 316n.13; refutation of
public in, 232–38; situationism in,
197–98; Strasbourg scandal in, 182;
Venice images in, 66; war imagery
in, 210–12, 214, 233
Initiation à la haute volupté, 287n.8
Inner Experience, 126
"integral art": lettrist concept of, 85,
288n.14
International Congress of Modern
Architecture (CIAM), 296n.12
Internationale lettriste, 40–42, 281n.1,
282n.9
Internationale situationniste, 56, 282n.5;
282n.1, 284n.37; antifunctionalism
and, 134–35; constructed situation
concept discussed in, 156–57; *dérive*
poetics in, 117, 120, 149; *détournement* in, 162, 301n.16; dissolution of
SI and, 190–91, 198, 202–4, 309n.14;
early issues of, 98; Gallimard attacked in, 289n.24, 318n.2; historical interpretation of, 252–53; lettrist
movement and, 94, 287n.7, 290n.27;
May 1968 protests described in,
64–65, 285n.7; New Babylon vision
in, 141–47; poetics of revolution in,
165–78; psychoanalysis in, 122–27;
psychogeography and, 104, 107; revolutionary romanticism discussed in,
167–78, 301n.8, 302n.12; sociological
phase of, 166, 170–78, 301n.2; spectacle concept of, 159–61; Strasbourg
scandal and, 181–82; style and form
of, 183, 307n.12; unitary urbanism

in, 127–28, 135–41, 150, 295n.6,
297n.16, 298n.22
International Movement for an Imaginist Bauhaus, 132–34, 297n.13
*Introduction à une nouvelle poésie et
une nouvelle musique*, 80, 287n.8
Ion: Howls for Sade advertised in, 21–22,
25–26; images of Debord in, 10–12,
16, 18
Ionesco, Eugene, 89, 92
Isou, Isidore: avant-garde movement
and, 17–21; dadaism and, 23; Debord
and, 31, 38, 81–83, 85–91, 219; lettrist
movement and, 10–11, 39, 79–85, 89,
96–97; Prix de l'avant-garde awarded
to, 19–20; situationists influenced
by, 279n.4
Italy, situationists in, 192, 216–17, 255,
312n.4
Ivain, Gilles, 137–38
Ivrea publishers, 317n.4

Jack the Ripper, 295n.3
Jacquot, Benoît, 280n.5
Jappe, Anselm, 286n.5, 287n.7, 290n.26
Jerez, Maria, 308n.23
Jorn, Asger, 12, 32, 34–35, 46, 282n.1; on
Le Corbusier, 295n.6; lettrist move-
ment and, 131–35, 165, 296nn.10,12;
psychogeography movement and,
102, 104–5; situationism and, 93, 99,
135–36, 146–47, 192, 299n.33
Joyce, James, 92, 152

Kenya, rebellion in, 88
Khatib, Abdelhafid, 135, 162–63
Khayati, Mustapha, 146, 174–75, 180,
192, 251, 306n.4, 319n.14
Khayyám, Omar, 54, 284n.31
Kiehman, Georges, 250–51
Klossowski, Pierre, 280n.5
Korsch, Karl, 73, 303n.14
Kotanyi, Attila, 146, 169, 302n.12

VINCENT KAUFMANN is professor of French at the University for Business, Law, and Social Sciences of St. Gallen, Switzerland, where he also directs the Humanities and Social Sciences Program.

ROBERT BONONNO has translated many works of fiction and nonfiction from French. He is currently translating the work of Isabelle Eberhardt.